CAKEWALK
POWER!

Written By
Scott R. Garrigus

Y0-AGU-693

Cakewalk Power!

Copyright ©2000 Muska & Lipman Publishing

All rights reserved. No part of this book may be reproduced by any means without written permission from the publisher, except for brief passages for review purposes. Address all permission requests to the publisher.

All copyrights and trademarks used as examples or references in this book are retained by their individual owners.

Technology and the Internet are constantly changing, and by necessity of the lapse of time between the writing and distribution of this book, some aspects might be out of date. Accordingly, the author and publisher assume no responsibility for actions taken by readers based upon the contents of this book.

Library of Congress Catalog Number: 00-102901

ISBN 1-929685-02-5

5   4   3

Educational facilities, companies, and organizations interested in multiple copies of this book should contact the publisher for quantity discount information. Training manuals, CD-ROMs, electronic versions, and portions of this book are also available individually or can be tailored for specific needs.

Muska & Lipman Publishing
2645 Erie Avenue, Suite 41
Cincinnati, Ohio 45208
www.muskalipman.com
publisher@muskalipman.com

This book is composed in Melior, Columbia, Helvetica, and Courier typefaces
using QuarkXpress 4.1, Adobe PhotoShop 5.0.2, and Adobe Illustrator 8.0.
Created in Cincinnati, Ohio, in the United States of America

Credits

Publisher
Andy Shafran

Managing Editor
Hope Stephan

Development Editor
Ben Milstead

Copy Editor
Chuck Hutchinson

Technical Editors
Cakewalk
   Adam Burch
   Matthew Saunders

Proofreader
Julie MacLean

Cover Designers
Michael Williams
John Windhorst

Production Manager
Cathie Tibbetts

Production Artist
DOV Graphics
   Michelle Frey

Indexer
Kevin Broccoli

Printer
R.R. Donnelley and Sons

About the Author

Scott R. Garrigus

Scott R. Garrigus has been obsessed with music and computers since he was 12 years old. After graduating from high school, he went on to earn a B.A. in music performance with an emphasis in sound recording technology at UMass, Lowell. In 1993, he released his first instrumental album on cassette, called *Pieces Of Imagination*. In 1995, he began his professional writing career when his first article appeared in *Electronic Musician* magazine. Today, Garrigus contributes articles to a number of additional print and online publications, including *Keyboard*, CNET, and *Web Review*. He also publishes his own e-zine, called *NewTechReview*. You can contact him via the Web at **www.garrigus.com**.

Dedications

To Mom, Dad, Babci, Dzidzi, Grandma, Grandpa, and my brother, Mark. Thanks for all your love and support. Oh, and to my cat, Figaro, for keeping my feet warm during those long winter writing sessions.

Acknowledgements

This project was one of the most difficult I've ever tackled, and I couldn't have completed it without the help and support of many different people. I want to thank my friends at *Electronic Musician* magazine for giving me a chance, and for helping me begin my professional writing career.

Thanks to you, the Cakewalk users, for making Cakewalk Pro Audio such a successful and popular product. This book wouldn't exist without your dedication and support. Thanks to the people at Cakewalk for creating Pro Audio, and also for helping prepare and promote this book.

Of course, a special thanks to all my new friends at Muska & Lipman Publishing. Thanks to Andy Shafran for giving me the chance to write my first book. And thank you to Hope Stephan, Ben Milstead, Chuck Hutchinson, and Julie MacLean for their suggestions and editing expertise.

I also want to thank my friends Brad Biondo and Jim DeVault for their continued support in helping me keep *NewTechReview* afloat, especially during those very busy months of writing. And a very special thanks to my friend and neighbor Ron LaMonica, whose incessant nagging helped me to get this project completed.

Finally, thank you, God, for blessing me with all the love and success that I've experienced in my life.

Contents

Chapter 4 Working with Projects

Chapter 5 Getting Around in Pro Audio

Chapter 6 Recording and Playback

Chapter 7 Editing Basics

Chapter 8 Exploring the Editing Tools

Chapter 9 Effects: The Really Cool Stuff

Chapter 10 Mixing It Down

Chapter 11 Making Sheet Music

Chapter 12 Studio Control with StudioWare and Sysx

Chapter 13 Advanced StudioWare Techniques

Chapter 14 CAL 101

Chapter 15 Advanced CAL Techniques

Chapter 16 Taking Your Pro Audio Project to CD

Appendix A Sample Project Roadmap: From Recording to Mixdown

Appendix B Backing Up Your Project Files

Appendix C Producing for Multimedia and the Web

Appendix D Cakewalk Resources on the Web

Index

Introduction

There is only one other Cakewalk book on the market, but it is outdated and only covers the MIDI aspects of Pro Audio. You can find plenty of generic books about using computers to create and record music, though. Plus, Cakewalk provides excellent printed manuals with its products, which include a great deal of descriptive feature information and basic knowledge, such as how to connect your MIDI and audio cables. I'm not going to cover that information here, however.

Instead, I'm going to get right down to the nitty-gritty and focus specifically on how you can use Cakewalk Pro Audio to make your composing and recording sessions run more smoothly. I'll explain some of the more common features as well as some of the more obscure ones, and I'll do it in a manner you can understand and use right away. Home Studio and Guitar Studio users will be interested to know that all of the functions found in those two programs can be found in Pro Audio as well. Therefore, this book will be of use to you, too.

So why should you listen to me? Well, I've been using Pro Audio ever since it was spawned from the programming code of Cakewalk Professional. I've also written about Pro Audio and other Cakewalk products in numerous review articles for magazines such as *Electronic Musician*, *Keyboard*, and *Recording*. In addition, I've been working with the people at Cakewalk for quite some time now, learning all there is to know about Pro Audio. And the people at Cakewalk have helped me develop much of the information in this book, making sure that everything is "officially" technically accurate. How's that for a seal of approval? Suffice it to say, I know my way around the product, and now I want to share that knowledge with you.

I'm going to assume that Cakewalk Pro Audio is installed on your computer and that you know how to start the program. In addition, you should have at least skimmed through the user's guide that comes with the software and have all your external audio and MIDI gear set up already. I'm also going to assume that you know how to use your mouse for clicking, dragging, double-clicking, and right-clicking. You should also know how to work with basic Windows features such as Windows Explorer and the Windows Control Panel. And you should have access to the World Wide Web, or perhaps a friend who does. Other than that, all you need is a strong interest in learning how to get the most out of Pro Audio. Not to worry. I'll take you through it step-by-step, and I promise it'll be fun, too.

How This Book Is Organized

You'll find that while I've tried to avoid overlapping content between this book and the user's guide that comes with Cakewalk Pro Audio, in some instances, this overlap just can't be avoided. I wanted to be sure to help you understand all of the important features of the program, and that means including some basic explanations to begin with. For the most part, though, the information included in this book is more "how-to" rather than "this feature does so-and-so."

Chapter 1,"Understanding MIDI and Digital Audio," and Chapter 2, "Getting Started with Pro Audio," provide an introduction to computer music and the software. These chapters explain the importance of registration and how to find help, as well as the major features and more obscure parts of the software, and how they work together. You'll also find a brief description of the differences between Home Studio, Guitar Studio, and Pro Audio.

Chapter 3, "Customizing Pro Audio," shows you how to make Pro Audio work the way you want it to. This chapter explains file organization, workspace customization, as well as how to find the optimal settings for both MIDI and audio functionality.

In Chapter 4, "Working with Projects," you'll learn how to work with Projects. This chapter includes step-by-step instructions for opening, closing, and saving Projects. You'll also learn about predefined Projects and how to make your own Templates.

Chapter 5, "Getting Around in Pro Audio," and Chapter 6, "Recording and Playback," describe how to navigate within a Pro Audio Project and how to record and play back your Projects. You'll find instructions on how to record and play MIDI, as well as audio, and you'll learn about recording multiple tracks at once. I'll explain the importance of the Now

Time and show you how to use the Go menu, Search, Markers and Loops, as well as the Zoom features. Before you know it, you'll be able to find any place in any Project, in the blink of an eye.

In Chapter 7, "Editing Basics," and Chapter 8, "Exploring the Editing Tools," you're ready to dive into editing. First, I'll explain the basics to you, including Tracks and Clips, the Event Editor, Piano Roll, and Audio Editor. Then you can investigate the editing tools within those parts of the program (as well as others) in more detail.

Chapter 9. "Effects: The Really Cool Stuff," explores one of my favorite parts of Pro Audio: Effects. The things you can do with these tools are amazing. I'll cover both the MIDI and audio Effects, and I'll show you how to use them in offline and real-time situations. I'll even share some cool Presets I've developed, so you can use them in your own recording projects.

Chapter 10, "Mixing It Down," takes a look at mixing. I know that mixing music via software can be confusing sometimes. Nothing beats being able to just grab a fader on a hardware-based mixer, but after you read this chapter, you may find that with all the functionality that Pro Audio provides, mixing is actually easier, and you have more control when using an on-screen software mixer.

I've received many questions as to Pro Audio's capabilities in terms of music notation, so that's the topic I'll cover in Chapter 11, "Making Sheet Music." I'll explain all the tools you have at your disposal, as well as what you can and cannot do. Although Pro Audio doesn't provide full-fledged music notation features, you might be surprised at what you find here.

Chapter 12, "Studio Control with StudioWare and Sysx," Chapter 13, "Advanced StudioWare Techniques," Chapter 14, "CAL 101," and Chapter 15, "Advanced CAL Techniques," jump into some of the more complicated features that Pro Audio offers. Don't worry if you think that StudioWare and CAL are out of your reach as a beginning user. Actually, you can use these features in plenty of ways even if you decide not to explore them fully. But just in case you're interested in learning more, I'm going to show you how to develop your own Panels in StudioWare and your own scripts in CAL. By the time you finish reading, you won't know how you lived without them.

Finally, in Chapter 16, "Take Your Pro Audio Project to CD," I'll show you how to take your Pro Audio Project and burn it onto CD.

My hope is that, by reading this book, you will learn how to master Cakewalk Pro Audio. And, along the way, if you find my writing intriguing and perhaps sometimes amusing, that's all the better.

Conventions Used in This Book

As you begin to read, you'll see that most of the information in this book is solid and useful. It contains very little fluff. I won't bore you with unrelated anecdotes or repetitious data. But to help guide you through all this material, I'll use several different conventions that highlight specific types of information that you should keep an eye out for.

TIP

Tips are extra information that you should know related to the current topic being discussed, and in some cases personal experiences and/or specific techniques not covered elsewhere.

CAUTION

Cautions highlight actions or commands that can make irreversible changes to your files or potentially cause problems in the future. Read them carefully because they may contain important information that can make the difference between keeping your files, software, and hardware safe, and you from losing a huge amount of work.

NOTES

Of course, sometimes you might like to know, but don't necessarily need to know, certain points to learn about the current topic. Notes provide additional material to help you avoid problems, and they also offer related advice.

Tell Us What You Think!

The staff (at Muska & Lipman) and I have tested the information in this book. To the best of our knowledge, the information is accurate. Of course, with all projects of this size you may find that a minute amount of mistakes have crept in. If you find any errors or have suggestions for future editions, please let us know by writing to:

Cakewalk Power!, P.O. Box 5, North Salem, NH 03073

You can also send messages via e-mail: scott@garrigus.com

And to learn about updates and corrections for the book, visit:
www.garrigus.com

1

Understanding MIDI and Digital Audio

If you're anything like I am, you want to jump right in and start learning all about Pro Audio. But if you don't understand the basic concepts and terms associated with computer music, you might have a hard time working your way through this book. So, just to give you a quick overview of the most significant aspects of music technology, this chapter will do the following:

▶ Define MIDI and explain how it works

▶ Define digital audio and explain how it works

▶ Explain the difference between MIDI and digital audio

Of course, this one chapter can't replace an entire book about the subject. If you want to learn more about MIDI and digital audio, plenty of extended resources are available. Cakewalk even has a Desktop Music Handbook available for free download on its Web site. You can find it at **http://www.cakewalk.com/Tips/Desktop.htm**.

What is MIDI?

MIDI (which stands for musical instrument digital interface) is a special kind of computer language that lets electronic music instruments (such as synthesizer keyboards) "talk" to computers. It works like this: Say you use a synthesizer keyboard as your musical instrument. Every key on the keyboard of your synthesizer has a corresponding electronic switch. When you press a key, its corresponding switch is activated and sends a signal to the computer chip inside your keyboard. The chip then sends the signal to the MIDI interface in your keyboard, which translates the signal into MIDI messages and sends those messages to the MIDI interface in your computer system.

NOTE

A *MIDI interface* is a device that is plugged into your computer, enabling it to understand the MIDI language. Basically, you can think of the interface as a translator. When your electronic music instrument sends out MIDI messages to your computer, the MIDI interface takes those messages and converts them into signals that your computer can understand.

The MIDI messages contain information telling your computer that a key was pressed (called a *Note On message*), which key it was (the name of the note, represented by a number), and how hard you hit the key (called the *MIDI velocity*). For example, if you press Middle C on your keyboard, a Note On message is sent to your computer telling it that you pressed a key. Another message containing the number 60 is sent telling the computer that you pressed Middle C. And a final message is sent containing a number from 1 to 127 (1 being very soft and 127 being very loud), which tells your computer how hard you hit the key.

Different MIDI messages represent all the performance controls on your keyboard. In addition to each key, MIDI messages represent the modulation wheel, pitch bend wheel, and other features. Your computer can store all the MIDI messages that are sent to it as you play your keyboard. The timing of your performance (how long it takes you to hit one key after another and how long you hold down each key) is stored as well. Your computer can then send those MIDI messages back to your keyboard with the same timing so that it seems like you are playing the music, but without touching the keys. The basic concept goes like this: You play a piece of music on your keyboard. Your performance is stored as instructions in your computer. Then those instructions are sent back to your keyboard from the computer, and you hear the piece of music played back exactly the way that you performed it, mistakes and all.

What is Digital Audio?

Digital audio is the representation of sound as numbers. Recording sound as digital audio is similar to recording sound by using a tape recorder, but slightly different. Let's say you have a microphone connected to your computer system. When you make a sound (such as singing a tune, playing a musical instrument, or even simply clapping your hands), the microphone "hears" it and converts the sound into an electronic signal. The microphone then sends the signal to the sound card in your computer, which translates the signal into numbers. These numbers are called *samples*.

CHAPTER 1

NOTE

A *sound card* is a device that is plugged into your computer, enabling it to understand the electronic signals of any audio device. Basically, you can think of the sound card as a translator. When an audio device (such as a microphone, electronic musical instrument, CD player, or anything else that can output an audio signal) sends out signals to your computer, the sound card takes those signals and converts them into numbers that your computer can understand.

The samples contain information that tells your computer how the recorded signal sounded at certain instants in time. The more samples used to represent the signal, the better the quality of the recorded sound. For example, to make a digital audio recording that has the same quality as audio on a CD, the computer needs to receive 44,100 samples for every second of sound that's recorded. The number of samples received per second is called the *sampling rate*.

The size of each individual sample also makes a difference in the quality of the recorded sound. This size is called the *bit depth*. The more bits used to represent a sample, the better the sound quality. For example, to make a digital audio recording with the same quality as audio on a CD, each sample has to be 16 bits in size.

NOTE

Computers use binary numerals to represent numbers. These binary numerals are called *bits*, and each bit can represent one of two numbers: 1 or 0. By combining more than one bit, computers can represent larger numbers. For instance, any number from 0 to 255 can be represented with 8 bits. With 16 bits, the range becomes 0 to 65,535.

Your computer can store all the samples that are sent to it. The timing of each sample is stored as well. Your computer can then send those samples back to the sound card with the same timing so that what you hear sounds exactly the same as what was recorded. The basic concept goes like this: Your sound card records an electronic signal from an audio device (such as a microphone or CD player). The sound card converts the signal into numbers called samples, which are stored in your computer. Then those samples are sent back to the sound card, which converts them back into an electronic signal. The signal is sent to your speakers (or other audio device), and you hear the sound exactly as it was recorded.

So, What's Really the Difference?

After reading the explanations of MIDI and digital audio, you might still be wondering what the difference between them is. Both processes involve sending signals to the computer to be recorded and then the computer sending those signals back out to be played, right? Well, the point that you have to keep in mind is that when you're recording MIDI data, you're not recording actual sound. You are recording only performance instructions. This concept is similar to a musician reading sheet music, with the sheet music representing MIDI data and the musician representing a computer. The musician (or computer) reads the sheet music (or MIDI data) and then stores it in memory. The musician then plays the music back via a musical instrument. Now what if the musician uses a different instrument to play back the music? The musical performance remains the same, but the sound changes. The same thing happens with MIDI data. A synthesizer keyboard can make all kinds of different sounds, but playing the same MIDI data back with the keyboard yields the exact same performance no matter what.

When you're recording digital audio, you are recording *actual sound*. If you record a musical performance as digital audio, you cannot change the sound of that performance, as described earlier. And because of these differences, MIDI and digital audio have their advantages and disadvantages. Because MIDI is recorded as performance data and not actual sound, you can manipulate it much more easily than you can manipulate digital audio. For example, you can easily fix mistakes in your performance by simply changing the pitch of a note. And MIDI data can be translated into standard musical notation. Digital audio can't. On the other hand, MIDI can't be used to record anything that requires actual audio, such as sound effects or vocals. With digital audio, you can record any kind of sound whatsoever. And you always can be sure that your recording will sound exactly the same every time you play it back. With MIDI, you can't be sure of that, because, although the MIDI data remain the same, the playback device or sound can be changed.

I hope that this description clears up some of the confusion you might have about MIDI and digital audio. You need to be familiar with plenty of other related terms, but I will cover them in different areas of the book as I go along. For now, as long as you understand the difference between MIDI and digital audio, I can begin talking about the real reason you bought this book—how to use Pro Audio.

2

Getting Started
with Pro Audio

Now that you have a basic understanding of the technology involved in making music with computers, I think you'll find working with Pro Audio more enjoyable. Ready to get started? This chapter will do the following:

▶ Tell you how to obtain the latest product update

▶ Explain the importance of registering your software

▶ Give you a quick tour of Pro Audio's major features

▶ Explain the differences between Pro Audio and Cakewalk's other related products, Guitar Studio and Home Studio

▶ Show you how to make a number of adjustments to your computer system to improve its performance

▶ Let you know where to look for help, if problems arise

What Version of Pro Audio Do You Have?

For all intents and purposes, most of the material in this book pertains to Cakewalk Pro Audio 9. If you're using a prior version, it's really in your best interest to upgrade. This is especially true if you're using version 7 or earlier. Some significant changes and improvements that you don't want to be without have been made to the program. Trust me. If you're using version 8, then you're not quite as bad off, but you should still upgrade. One of the most important reasons for upgrading is that Cakewalk has improved the program's playback and recording performance quite a bit. Just in case you can't upgrade yet, I've included a few extra notes throughout the book for Pro Audio 8 users, to alert you to specific changes.

Of course, if you *do* have Pro Audio 9, you still might not be using the latest version. Cakewalk is constantly fixing and improving the software. Any problems that you're currently experiencing might easily be remedied with an update. To find out exactly what version you're using, start Pro Audio, and click on Help > About Cakewalk. A dialog box similar to Figure 2.1 then appears, displaying your exact version number. You should then check to see whether or not a more recent update is available.

Figure 2.1
The About Cakewalk dialog box shows the program's current version number.

Get the Latest Product Update

Although automatically receiving new product updates would be nice, most companies (except maybe Microsoft) can't afford to send out CDs to all of their users every time they create updates. That's one of the reasons the Internet has become such a wonderful tool. Sometimes the answer to your problem is just a download away. Cakewalk provides a Support area on its Web site where you can get the latest updates for all of the Cakewalk products. Just follow these steps to get the updates:

1. Log on to the Internet, start your Web browser and type the following address: **ftp://ftp.cakewalk.com/pub/Patches/**. This address takes you to Cakewalk's Patches and Updates page, as shown in Figure 2.2.

Figure 2.2
You can download updates from the Cakewalk Patches and Updates support page.

2. From the list of available updates, select the product that you're interested in. You then see a brief description of the update and one or more download links.

3. If more than one update is available, simply compare your current version with the updates listed and select the appropriate one. For instance, if you have Pro Audio 9.01, you'll want the update that upgrades version 9.01 to the current version.

4. Create a temporary folder on your Windows desktop and download the update file to that folder.

5. Run the file, and your software is upgraded. That's all there is to upgrading.

NOTE

Think you've found a bug? Just because a software product is released to the public doesn't mean it's perfect. Improvements are always being made. That's why updates become available. If you have a problem with Pro Audio on a regular basis, and you can reproduce that problem by performing the same steps each time, you may have found a bug in the software. Before you go spreading any rumors, first tell a friend about it, and see whether he or she can reproduce the problem on his or her computer system. If so, then you should drop an e-mail to Cakewalk at support@cakewalk.com, and let the people there know about the problem. The staff might already be aware of the bug and be working on a fix for it. But then again, they might not, and although your diligence won't make you famous, you'll feel good to know that you might have saved your fellow Pro Audio users from a lot of frustration. Really, you will.

Register Your Software

Do you think registering your software is important? If not, think again. First and foremost, if you don't register your software, Cakewalk won't provide you with technical support. You'll be sorry if you run into a problem that causes you to lose some of your precious work, and the only thing between you and your sanity is the people at Cakewalk. If you're a techno-wizard, and this situation doesn't worry you, that's great. But there's something else that you might not have thought about. What if your hard drive crashes, and you need to reinstall all your software applications, including Pro Audio? And at the same time, what if you can't find the jewel case that your Pro Audio CD came in? Yes, the jewel case, not the CD. Why is it significant? Because the jewel case has a little sticker with a very important number printed on it—your CD-KEY. Without that number, you can't install Pro Audio. So, now who you gonna call?

Yeah, that's right. By the way, your product serial number is important, too. Remember to send in that registration card! And just to be safe, you might want to check with Cakewalk to make sure that your information is on file. You just do the following:

1. Find your CD jewel case and look on the back to make sure that your CD-KEY is printed there.

2. Find your product serial number, either by looking on the detachable part of your registration card or by starting Pro Audio and selecting Help > About Cakewalk.

3. Call Cakewalk at 888-CAKEWALK or 617-441-7870 (USA) and make sure that you're registered. Also check to see that your correct address and phone number are in the system.

Now you can rest easy, knowing that help is just a phone call or e-mail away.

TIP

To prevent yourself from losing your CD-KEY or serial number, you might want to write them on your Pro Audio CD. Be sure to use an indelible pen, and write the numbers on the top (the side with the printed material) of the CD. Don't write on the shiny side. You also might want to write down the numbers in a second location, just in case. I like to keep track of all the serial numbers for my software applications in a simple text file. I have a list containing the names, CD-KEYs (if available), and serial numbers of all the important software installed on my computer system. I also include the current version number and company contact information for each product. Then, if I ever run into a problem, I just refer to the list. By the way, you might also want to print the text file each time you update it. If your hard drive crashes, the text file won't do you any good because you won't be able to access it.

Take a Quick Tour of Pro Audio 9

Because Pro Audio is such a powerful application, you can use it for a variety of different tasks. They include composing music, developing computer game music and sounds, producing compact discs, creating audio for the World Wide Web, and even scoring films and videos. Pro Audio provides a number of features to support all of these endeavors and more. As a matter of fact, you can use Pro Audio as the central piece of "equipment" in your studio because it enables you to control all of your music gear from your computer via on-screen control panels. However you decide to use Pro Audio, you'll find plenty of flexibility and power in the tools provided.

Projects

In Pro Audio, all of your music data for a single body of work is organized as a *Project*. A Project can be anything from a Top 40 song or a 30-second radio spot to a full-length symphonic score, such as a movie soundtrack. Along with the music data, all of Pro Audio's settings for a single work are stored in the Project as well. A Project is saved on disk as a single file with a .WRK or .BUN extension. The difference between the two file types is that a Work (WRK) file stores only MIDI data and Project settings, whereas a Bundle (BUN) file also includes any audio data within a Project. (For more information, see Chapter 4, "Working with Projects.")

Tracks, Clips, and Events

The music data within a Project is organized into units called *Tracks*, *Clips*, and *Events*. Events, which are the smallest units, consist of single pieces of data, such as one note played on a MIDI keyboard. Clips are groups of Events. They can be anything from a simple MIDI melody to an entire vocal performance recorded as audio. And Tracks are used to store Clips. For example, a pop song Project might contain seven Tracks of music data—six for the instruments and one for the vocal performance. Each Track can contain any number of Clips that might represent one long performance or different parts of a performance. The only limitation (if you can call it that) is that Pro Audio enables up to 256 Tracks per Project. You have to admit, that's a lot of data! By the way, I'll talk more about Tracks, Clips, and Events in Chapter 7, "Editing Basics."

Track View

To work with the data in a Project, you have to use the tools called Views in Pro Audio. Views are like windows that let you see and manipulate the data in a Project in a variety of ways. The most important is the Track View, shown in Figure 2.3.

Figure 2.3
The Track View is the main window used to work with a Project in Pro Audio.

In this window, you can see all the Tracks that are available in a Project. You also can view and edit all of the basic Track settings, as well as all of the Clips contained in each Track. I'll talk about the Track View extensively in a number of different chapters in the book.

Staff View

In the Staff View, you can work with the MIDI data in your Project as standard music notation. By selecting one or more MIDI Tracks in the Track View and opening the Staff View, you can see your music just as if it were notes on a printed page, like in Figure 2.4.

Figure 2.4
In the Staff View, you can see and edit your MIDI data as standard music notation.

Using the Staff View, you also can edit your music as notation by adding, changing, or deleting notes. Special notation functions such as dynamics markings, percussion parts, and guitar chord symbols are included, too. You can notate anything from a single one-staff melody to an entire 24-part musical score. I'll talk about using the Staff View in Chapter 11, "Making Sheet Music."

Piano Roll View

Although the Staff View is great for traditional music editing, it doesn't enable you to access expressive MIDI data, such as note velocity or pitch bend controller messages. For that data, you can use the Piano Roll View. This View displays notes as they might appear on a player-piano roll, as shown in Figure 2.5.

Figure 2.5
The Piano Roll View gives you access to both note and MIDI controller messages.

You can change note pitch and duration by simply dragging on the rectangular representations. But more important, you can view and edit MIDI controller messages graphically with the mouse instead of having to deal with raw numbers. For more details about the Piano Roll View, see Chapter 7, "Editing Basics."

Event List View

If you really want precise control over the data in your Project, the Event List View is the tool for the job. The Event List View shows each individual Event in a Track (or the entire Project) as special keywords and numbers in a list, like in Figure 2.6.

Figure 2.6
For really precise editing tasks, the Event List View gives you access to the individual Events in a Project.

Using this View is similar to looking at the raw MIDI data that is recorded from your MIDI keyboard or controller. You can edit the characteristics of single notes and MIDI controller messages by typing in data. You'll probably use the Piano Roll View more often, but it's nice to know that the Event List View is available if you need it. I'll talk more about the Event List View in Chapter 7, "Editing Basics."

CHAPTER 2

Audio View

Because audio data is different in nature from MIDI data, it requires its
own editing tool: the Audio View. This window displays only the data
from Tracks that contain audio. You can't edit or view MIDI data in the
Audio View. While you're working with the Audio View, you see the
sound waves from one or more of the audio Tracks in your Project, like
in Figure 2.7.

Figure 2.7
The Audio View is a
special editing tool for
audio data only.

Not only does the Audio View enable you to see the audio data in your
Project, you also can edit the data by cutting, copying, and pasting. In
addition, you can use the Audio View to add offline effects to audio
Tracks. In Chapter 7, "Editing Basics," and in Chapter 9, "Effects: The
Really Cool Stuff," I'll get into more detail about the Audio View.

Console View

When you're ready to mix all of your MIDI and audio Tracks down to a single stereo file, you can use the Console View. This tool is made to look and function like a real recording studio mixing console, as you can see in Figure 2.8.

Figure 2.8
The Console View looks and functions similarly to a real recording studio mixing console.

You can use the Console View to adjust the panning and volume for each Track in a Project. As a matter of fact, you can use the Console View in place of the Track View for adjusting Track settings and recording new Tracks. And just like on a real mixing console, you can monitor volume levels via on-screen meters and mute and solo individual or groups of Tracks. The Console View is also the tool you use to assign real-time effects to Tracks in a Project. I'll talk more about the Console View in Chapter 5, "Recording and Playback," Chapter 9, "Effects: The Really Cool Stuff," and Chapter 10, "Mixing It Down."

StudioWare and CAL

Two of the most advanced features provided by Pro Audio are StudioWare and CAL (Cakewalk Application Language). Even though these features seem complicated, they're actually quite easy to use. Sure, if you really want to dive in and master these features, they can get complex, but for the most part, they are accessible to even the most timid user. What's more, when you start using StudioWare and CAL, you won't want to stop. Separately, StudioWare enables you to design on-screen panels to manipulate MIDI data and control your MIDI gear, and CAL enables you to create macros or small programs so that you can automate the different tasks that you perform within Pro Audio. You actually can use StudioWare and CAL together to build your own editing tools within Pro Audio. You can even create programs that will make music automatically for you. These two features alone have quite a bit of power, so I'll talk a lot more about them in Chapter 12, "Studio Control with StudioWare and Sysx," Chapter 13, "Advanced StudioWare Techniques," Chapter 14, "CAL 101," and Chapter 15, "Advanced CAL Techniques."

Examine the Differences Between Pro Audio, Guitar Studio, and Home Studio

Not everyone needs the full power of a professional digital audio sequencing application like Pro Audio. You might be an intermediate user or even a complete beginner only interested in making music as a hobby. To provide for these different levels of interest, Cakewalk offers two other products in its line of sequencers: Guitar Studio and Home Studio. Essentially, Guitar Studio and Home Studio are just scaled-down versions of Pro Audio. They both contain the same basic functionality as Pro Audio but don't include some of the more advanced features.

Guitar Studio is geared toward intermediate users and (as its name implies) guitar players interested in integrating technology into their music-making process. Guitar Studio is limited compared to Pro Audio because it enables only sixteen Tracks of digital audio to be played simultaneously. You also can apply only sixteen real-time effects at once.

Home Studio is geared toward beginners who are interested in using their computers to create music as a hobby. Home Studio has the fewest number of features of the three products, but it provides plenty of power for first-time users. Like Guitar Studio, Home Studio is limited in the number of digital audio Tracks that can be played. The real-time effects are limited, too.

I've really only touched on some of the features in Guitar Studio and Home Studio as they compare to Pro Audio. For a comparison between Pro Audio and Home Studio, Cakewalk has a comprehensive list of the features online at: **http://www.cakewalk.com/Products/Version9chart.htm**.

Set Up Your System for Better Performance

Cakewalk specifies a system with a Pentium 200MHz processor and 64MB of random access memory (RAM) as the basic requirements to run Pro Audio. Of course, you also need a Windows-compatible MIDI interface and/or sound card. If your computer system lives up to (or surpasses) these specifications, simply installing Pro Audio is more than likely all you'll need to do to get up and running with the software. If you really want to get the best performance from Pro Audio, however, you can make a number of adjustments to your computer system that will enable you to squeeze as much power out of it as possible. Depending on your computer's specifications, these changes might even enable you to play back a few more simultaneous digital audio Tracks or apply more real-time effects. (See Chapter 9, "Effects: The Really Cool Stuff," for more information.)

Microprocessor

You can't do much to tweak your computer's central processing unit (CPU), aside from maybe upgrading it to a newer chip or buying a whole new computer system. Suffice it to say, the newer and faster your CPU, the better your computer system and Pro Audio will perform. The order of available chips goes something like this: Pentium, Pentium with MMX, Pentium Pro, Pentium II, and Pentium III (being the latest at the time of this writing). Of course, although having the best chip available is nice, that doesn't mean that you need it. You also can get away with using different brands such as AMD or Cyrix, but they tend to be less powerful. For instance, the AMD K6 is similar to a Pentium/MMX at the same clock speed. Also, a Cyrix chip is usually less powerful than a standard Pentium running at a speed of about two-thirds of the Cyrix. Basically, you can apply more real-time effects at once with a more powerful CPU. Pro Audio will run more smoothly, as well.

If you would like to test just how much of your CPU power is used when you perform different tasks with your computer, Windows provides a nifty utility called the *System Monitor*. Just follow these steps to use it:

1. If the System Monitor isn't installed, open the Windows Control Panel, double-click on Add/Remove Programs and select the Windows Setup tab in the Add/Remove Programs Properties dialog box. Then select Accessories from the list, click on the Details button, select System Monitor from the resulting list, and click on the OK buttons to close the dialog boxes. Windows then installs the System Monitor.

2. Open the System Monitor by clicking the Start button and then selecting Programs > Accessories > System Tools > System Monitor. The program should look similar to Figure 2.9.

Figure 2.9
The Windows System Monitor accessory monitors your CPU usage.

3. Select Edit > Add Item. In the resulting dialog box, click on Kernel in the Category list. Then click on Processor Usage in the Item list and click the OK button.

4. Depending on the current settings, you might see a line chart, bar chart, or numerical chart. You can select the different displays via the View menu.

Now, as you use your computer, the System Monitor will continuously show the changes in your CPU power usage.

System Memory (RAM)

You probably already know this point, but the more memory you have installed in your computer, the better. This is especially true for large applications such as Pro Audio. Even though Cakewalk lists 64MB in the system requirements, you would be better off with 128MB of RAM. Not only does increased memory enable your system to run more smoothly, it makes the system run faster, too. With more RAM available, Windows is less likely to have to access virtual memory.

Virtual Memory

To fool your computer into thinking it has more RAM than it really does, Windows uses part of your hard disk space as *virtual memory*. Every time you start your system, Windows creates a "swap file" called win386.swp on your hard drive. This "swap file" grows and shrinks as you perform different tasks with your computer. Whenever you try to use more RAM than is installed in your system, Windows stores the excess data in the "swap file." For example, if you have 32MB of RAM in your system, and you run four different programs at once that each take up 16MB of RAM, technically, two of those applications shouldn't be able to run. However, Windows simply uses virtual memory to handle that extra 32MB load. Because virtual memory uses your hard disk for storage, and your hard disk provides much slower access than your system's RAM, all that "swap file" processing makes your computer run more slowly. That's why your system runs faster with more RAM installed.

Hard Disk Drive

The speed of your hard drive is one of the single most important factors in determining how many audio Tracks you'll be able to use during playback with Pro Audio. In terms of performance, SCSI is better than IDE, but a good E-IDE drive can be almost as good as SCSI. A few specifications to look out for are Average Seek Time (which should be as low as possible, preferably 9 milliseconds or less), Rotation Speed (which should be as high as possible, the average being 5400 RPM), and Sustained Data Transfer Rate (which also should be as high as possible, with at least 5MB per second being a good start). One other factor to avoid is hard disk controller cards that connect via an ISA expansion slot inside your computer. A PCI-based connection is much better. By the way, using the System Monitor, you can test your hard drive performance the same way you can test CPU usage (explained earlier).

Aside from your upgrading to a new hard drive, one Windows tweak might get you a little more speed from your current drive. It's a setting for DMA access for your hard drive controller. This setting gives your hard drive direct access to your computer's memory. This way, the data doesn't have to be processed by the CPU first, and, thus, it provides a bit more speed. If your hard drive supports DMA, you can activate it like this:

1. Open the Windows Control Panel, double-click on System and click on the Device Manager tab in the System Properties dialog box.

2. Under Disk Drives in the list of devices, select your hard disk drive. It might read something like "Generic IDE Disk."

CHAPTER 2

3. Click on the Properties button and then click on the Settings tab in the hard disk drive's Properties dialog box. The dialog box should look similar to Figure 2.10.

Figure 2.10
This generic hard disk drive Properties dialog box shows the hard drive settings.

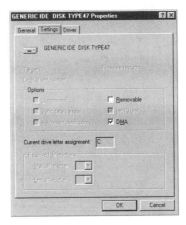

4. Select DMA in the Options section, and then click on the OK buttons to close the dialog boxes.

After Windows restarts, your hard drive will access the computer's memory directly, which might or might not provide a noticeable increase in speed.

Video Card

Believe it or not, your video card can have an effect on your computer system's performance. First, hardware video acceleration can cause problems with audio playback. If you have a PCI-based video card, and your audio is sometimes plagued with clicks, pops, or other anomalies, these sounds could mean that your hardware video acceleration is set too high. Try dragging a program window around on the screen while your computer is playing digital audio Tracks. Does this action affect the audio? If so, you can try reducing or disabling hardware video acceleration to remedy the problem. To do so, just follow these steps:

1. Open the Windows Control Panel and double-click on System.

2. In the System Properties dialog box, click on the Performance tab. Then click on the Graphics button under Advanced Settings.

3. In the Advanced Graphics Settings dialog box, drag the Hardware Acceleration slider to the left to either reduce or disable hardware video acceleration. The dialog box should look similar to Figure 2.11.

Figure 2.11
The amount of hardware video acceleration is set via the Advanced Graphics Settings dialog box.

4. You might or might not have to disable hardware video acceleration altogether. You'll have to experiment to see what works best for your system. After you set the slider, click the OK buttons to close the dialog boxes.

After Windows restarts, your new settings will take effect. If you have a newer computer system with an AGP-based graphics card, you shouldn't have to worry about hardware video acceleration problems. AGP-based cards can access the system memory directly without having to deal with the PCI bus and, thus, don't usually exhibit the problems I mentioned earlier.

Other video-related settings that can affect the performance of your system include screen savers, video resolution, and video color depth. Basically, when you're doing any processor-intensive work with your computer, you should disable your screen saver. Even when the screen saver isn't showing anything on the screen, it sits in the background monitoring your system for activity and, thus, takes up processor time. Plus, some screen savers have no regard for what your computer is currently doing, and they become active right in the middle of a recording session, ruining that great vocal Track. To turn off your screen saver, do the following:

1. Right-click anywhere on the Windows desktop and select Properties from the pop-up menu.

CHAPTER 2

2. Select the Screen Saver tab in the Display Properties dialog box. The dialog box should look similar to Figure 2.12.

Figure 2.12
In the Display Properties dialog box, you can set many different Windows parameters, including the screen saver.

3. Select None from the drop-down list in the Screen Saver settings section and then click the OK button.

Video resolution and video color depth affect how precisely your computer monitor displays graphics. A higher color depth means more colors will be displayed, and a higher resolution means a sharper image. But the higher the resolution and the higher the color depth, the harder your computer has to work. High settings can actually slow down your computer quite a bit, especially if you have an older CPU and an older video card. Your best bet is to use a resolution of 800 x 600 and a depth of 256 colors. You really don't need anything more than that, although using a higher resolution enables you to fit more MIDI/audio Tracks on the screen at once. A higher resolution is also nicer when you're working with music notation. You can experiment with higher settings to see how they affect your system. Reducing the color depth is more important than reducing the resolution, though. To change the color depth and resolution, do the following:

1. Right-click anywhere on the Windows desktop, and select Properties from the pop-up menu.

2.   Select the Settings tab in the Display Properties dialog box. The dialog box should look similar to Figure 2.13.

Figure 2.13
In the Display Properties dialog box, you can set many different Windows parameters, including the video resolution and color depth.

3.   From the drop-down list in the Colors section, select 256 Colors. Then drag the slider in the Screen Area section to the left until it reads 800 by 600 pixels. After you've set the slider, click the OK button.

After Windows restarts, your monitor will show the new resolution and color depth settings. Getting used to the new settings might take a while if you've been using higher settings all along, but don't worry, you'll live. And I think you'll like how much snappier Windows reacts.

Network Card

If you have your computer hooked up to a network, you should either use a different computer system for audio recording or temporarily disable your network card when you're using Pro Audio. Network activity is notorious for stealing CPU cycles at critical times, and this can slow down your system quite a bit. The easiest way to remove your computer from the network is simply to unplug your network cable. You can get even better performance, however, if you disable your network card like this:

1.   Open the Windows Control Panel, double-click on System and click on the Device Manager tab in the System Properties dialog box.

2.   Under Network Adapters in the list of devices, select your network card. The name will probably reflect the name of the product. An example might be "EZ-Link USB Adapter."

CHAPTER 2

3.   Click on the Properties button to open your network card's Properties dialog box. The dialog box should look similar to Figure 2.14.

Figure 2.14
This sample network card Properties dialog box shows the status of the device.

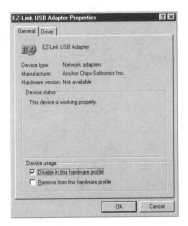

4.   Select Disable in This Hardware Profile in the Device Usage section and then click on the OK button to close the dialog box.

Windows disables your network card without your having to restart. Then you can simply close the System Properties dialog box, and you're done.

Sound Card

As far as sound cards are concerned, the only tip that I can give you here is that PCI-based sound cards perform much better than older ISA-based sound cards. The newer PCI-based cards usually include more advanced audio circuitry, which is designed to take more of the audio processing workload off your computer's CPU. It's also nice to have a card that supports the DirectSound features of Microsoft's DirectX technology. This type of card provides greater application compatibility and sometimes better performance, too.

NOTE

One of the most common questions that I get from readers is, "What sound card should I buy?" There are so many different sound cards on the market, providing so many different features, that I can't simply recommend one or the other. I can, however, tell you what features to look for so that you can make an educated choice.

I've already mentioned that you should look for a PCI-based, DirectX-compatible sound card. You also should be aware of the types of connections that sound cards supply. The typical sound card provides a number of different audio inputs and outputs, including line level, microphone level, and speaker. Line level inputs and outputs are used to transfer sound from cassette decks, radios, electronic keyboards, or any other standard audio device. Microphones generate a very small audio level by themselves, so they need a special input of their own, which is connected to an internal preamplifier on the sound card. Speakers also need their own special connector with a built-in amplifier to produce a decent amount of volume. Some high-end sound cards also offer digital inputs and outputs. These special connectors enable you to attach the sound card directly to compatible devices, such as some CD players and DAT (digital audio tape) decks. Using these connections gives you the best possible sound because audio signals stay in the digital domain and don't need to be converted into analog signals. You also should be aware that connectors come in a variety of forms. Low-cost cards usually provide the same 1/8-inch jacks used for headphones on boom boxes. For better quality, there are 1/4-inch, RCA, or XLR jacks. Connections also can be balanced or unbalanced. Balanced connections provide shielding to protect the audio signal against RFI (radio frequency interference). Unbalanced connections don't provide any type of protection.

If you want to be able to record more than one audio Track at once, you'll need a card with multiple audio connections. Most average sound cards internally mix all of their audio sources down to one stereo signal, but other higher-end (more expensive) cards enable you to record each device separately on its own discreet stereo channel. This capability is much more desirable in a music recording studio, but not everyone needs it. You'll also want to look for a card with full-duplex capabilities. This means the card can record and play back audio simultaneously. This is opposed to a half-duplex card, which can perform only one function at a time.

A good quality audio signal is something that everybody desires. During recording, the sampling rate (which I talked about in Chapter 1, "Understanding MIDI and Digital Audio") plays a big part in the quality of the audio signal. Suffice it to say, the higher the sampling rate that a sound card can handle, the better the sound quality. The sampling rate of a CD is 44.1kHz (44,100 samples per second) and all sound cards on the market support this. Professional cards can hit 48kHz or higher. Bit resolution (which I also talked about in Chapter 1) is a factor in determining digital sound quality as well. The more bits you have to represent your signal, the better it will sound. The CD standard is 16 bits, which is supported by all sound cards. Some cards (again mostly high-end) go up to 20, 22 or even 24 bits.

(continued on next page)

CHAPTER 2

NOTE (Cont.)

Two other measurements that you need to look out for are signal-to-noise ratio and frequency response. As with the other measurements mentioned previously, the higher the better. Because all electronic devices produce some amount of noise, the signal-to-noise ratio of a sound card tells you how much higher the signal strength is compared to the amount of internal noise made by the sound card. The bigger the number, the quieter the card. A good signal-to-noise measurement is about 90dB or higher. Frequency response is actually a range of numbers, which is based on the capabilities of human hearing. The frequency response of human hearing is approximately 20Hz to 20kHz. A good sound card will encompass at least that range, maybe even more.

If you want to purchase a sound card with a built-in MIDI synthesizer, there are a number of additional features that you should know about. Early sound cards sported synthesizers based on FM (frequency modulation) synthesis. Unfortunately, this method wasn't much of a step up from the basic beeps and boops of a PC speaker. Even though FM works well with organ and bell-type sounds, it fails miserably when trying to portray any other type of instrument. Fortunately, today's sound cards use a technology called *wavetable* synthesis. This process can provide some very realistic sounds. The reason for this realism lies in the fact that a wavetable synthesizer plays back pre-recorded real-life instruments and sounds. When the synthesizer receives a MIDI "note-on" message, instead of creating a sound electronically from scratch (like with FM), it plays back a small digital recording, which can be anything from the sound of a piano to the effect of ducks quacking. The only drawback to wavetable synthesis is that the samples need to be kept small because they are stored in RAM (random access memory) or ROM (read only memory). The bigger the wavetable RAM or ROM your card comes with, the better. A good number to look for is about 2MB.

You'll also want to take into account the degree of playback control over the wavetable samples that a card provides. All sound cards today support General MIDI (GM), which is a set of guidelines specifying 128 pre-set sounds that all GM-compatible synths must have, and the memory location (or MIDI program number) of those sounds. This ensures that if a sound card is told to play program number 37, it will always call up a slap electric bass sound rather than a soprano saxophone. Unlike professional synthesizers, however, GM doesn't support any kind of sound parameter programming. That's where the GS and XG formats come in. The Roland GS format expands on the GM standard by offering additional sounds along with sound-programming control over a few synthesis parameters. Yamaha's XG format goes even further by requiring three separate effects processors, more than a dozen programmable synthesis parameters (such as the brightness of a sound), and more than one hundred sets of 128 sounds each. So be sure to get a card that supports GS, XG, or both.

By following these guidelines, and taking some time to research your purchase, you should be able to find the right sound card to fit your needs. Good luck!

Set Up Your Cakewalk Hardware Profile

Of course, making many of the previously mentioned changes to your computer system every time you want to use Pro Audio and then changing them back for normal system use can be a major hassle. Luckily, Windows includes a handy feature called *Hardware Profiles*. You can think of Hardware Profiles as Windows presets, similar to synthesizer or audio effects gear presets. Using the Hardware Profiles feature, you can store a number of Windows configuration settings under a unique name and then recall those settings when you start your computer system. So, for instance, you can have a profile to set up your hardware for normal system use, another profile for computer gaming, yet another profile for audio recording, and so on. Creating Hardware Profiles is very simple, too; you just do the following:

1. Open the Windows Control Panel, double-click on System and click on the Hardware Profiles tab in the System Properties dialog box. The dialog box should look similar to Figure 2.15.

Figure 2.15
The Hardware Profiles tab of the System Properties dialog box shows the different hardware configurations.

CHAPTER 2

2. More than likely, a default profile called "Original Configuration" will be listed. This configuration holds your current system settings. Click on it to select it.

3. Click on the Copy button to make a copy of the Original Configuration profile.

4. In the Copy Profile dialog box, type a new name for the new profile—something like Cakewalk Configuration. Then click on the OK buttons to close both dialog boxes.

5. Restart your computer. At startup, your system will ask you to choose a hardware profile. Select Cakewalk Configuration.

6. Go through the list of tweaks that I described earlier, such as the hard drive DMA setting, video acceleration setting, and so on.

Now, the next time you start Windows, you can choose a system configuration to fit your needs for that computing session. The only setting from the list of tweaks that isn't saved in a Hardware Profile is the screen saver setting. You have to change it manually each time. Yeah, I know it's a bummer. Personally, I always leave the screen saver disabled. If I know I'm going to be away from the computer for more than fifteen minutes, I just turn off the monitor.

Find Help When You Need It

Cakewalk provides a number of ways for you to find help when you're having a problem with Pro Audio. The two most obvious places to look are the user's guide and the Pro Audio Help file. Actually, these two sources contain basically the same information, but with the Help file, you can perform a search to find something really specific. At the first signs of trouble, you should go through the included troubleshooting information. If you can't find an answer to your problem there, then you can pay a visit to the Cakewalk Web site.

The Support page of the Cakewalk Web site (**http://www.cakewalk.com/ Support/**) contains a ton of helpful information, including FAQs (lists of frequently asked questions and their answers) and technical documents that provide details on a number of Cakewalk-related topics. You should check them first. If you still can't find an answer to your problem, the next place to look is in the Cakewalk newsgroups (**http://www.cakewalk.com/Support/newsgroups.html**). In the newsgroups, you can trade tips, advice, and information with other Cakewalk users. And many times, you'll find that someone has had the same problem that you are having, and he or she has already found a solution. Isn't sharing great? Also, be sure to check out Appendix D, "Cakewalk Resources on the Web," for even more helpful information.

Of course, you also can contact Cakewalk Technical Support directly. You can either e-mail your questions to **support@cakewalk.com**, or you can call 617-441-7891 (USA). Currently, the hours are Monday through Friday, from 10 a.m. to 6 p.m. Eastern time. Tech Support also offers extended hours on Thursday until 10 p.m. But remember, to receive technical support, you have to be a registered user. If you call or send e-mail, you'll be asked for your serial number. As I said before, remember to send in that registration card! You'll be a much happier camper, er—Cakewalker.

3

Customizing Pro Audio

As the old Yiddish proverb goes, "Everyone is kneaded out of the same dough, but not baked in the same oven." The point I'm trying to make is that although we all might be Pro Audio users, it doesn't mean that we like to work with the product in the same exact way. I have my way of doing things, and you probably have your own way. Luckily, Pro Audio provides a number of settings so that you can make the program conform to your own way of working. In this chapter, you'll learn the following:

▶ How to organize all the different files associated with Pro Audio

▶ How to customize the program's workspace, including colors, Toolbars, Window Layouts, and Key Bindings

▶ How to set up all the MIDI parameters

▶ How to find the optimal audio settings

Organize Your Files

As you work with Pro Audio, you'll be dealing with many different types of files. They include Project files, StudioWare files, CAL files, and so on. By default, Pro Audio places all these files in the same location on your hard drive: the Program Files\Cakewalk\Cakewalk Pro Audio 9 folder. This location might be fine with you, but personally I like to have everything neatly organized in its own place on my hard drive. (A bit obsessive-compulsive perhaps, but hey, I can always find what I'm looking for, right?) My other reason for not liking this scenario is that the Cakewalk program files are in that folder, too. Everything is just mixed up in one huge folder, which makes it difficult to back up important Project files and so on. (I talk about backing up files in Appendix B, "Backing Up Your Project Files.")

CHAPTER 3

My Documents

What I like to do is keep all of my important files in the My Documents folder on my hard drive. And I'm not just talking about Cakewalk files, although that's what I'll be discussing here. By keeping them together, I can easily back up all my important files in one fell swoop by simply making a copy of the My Documents folder. In case you're wondering, the My Documents folder is set up automatically by Windows when you install it. Keeping all your important files in a single location was initially Microsoft's idea. You don't have to go along with it, but it really does work.

Create My Documents Subfolders

To make sure that all of your files aren't mixed together within the My Documents folder, you can create a number of subfolders—one for each of the different file categories. Pro Audio has ten different categories of files associated with it. The best way I've found to organize them is as follows:

1. Open the Windows Explorer. Then locate and open the My Documents folder on your hard drive.

2. Create a new subfolder by right-clicking within the My Documents folder and selecting New > Folder from the pop-up menus. Name the new folder "Cakewalk Pro Audio."

3. Open the Cakewalk Pro Audio folder and create ten new subfolders with the following names:

   ▶ Audio Files
   ▶ CAL Files
   ▶ Groove Quantize Files
   ▶ Play Lists
   ▶ Project Files
   ▶ StudioWare Panels
   ▶ Sysx Files
   ▶ Templates
   ▶ Video Files
   ▶ Window Layouts

When you're finished, the file structure should look similar to what's shown in Figure 3.1. Don't worry about all the different file types. I'll talk about them throughout the book, when appropriate.

Figure 3.1
Your Cakewalk Pro Audio subfolders should look like this within the My Documents folder.

Put Everything in Its Place

Now that you have your folders organized, you can move all of your existing files to the appropriate locations. Just follow these steps to do so:

1.   Open the Windows Explorer. Then locate and open the Program Files\Cakewalk\Cakewalk Pro Audio 9 folder on your hard drive.

2.   Take a look at Table 3.1.

Table 3.1
Pro Audio File Type Extensions and Their Assigned My Documents Folder Locations

File Extension	Folder Location
.MID	Project Files
.WRK	Project Files
.BUN	Project Files
.TPL	Templates
.CAL	CAL Files
.CWL	Window Layouts
.WAV	Audio Files
.RA	Audio Files

CHAPTER 3

File Extension	Folder Location
.ASF	Audio Files
.MP3	Audio Files
.AVI	Video Files
.MPG	Video Files
.MOV	Video Files
.SYX	Sysx Files
.SET	Play Lists
.GRV	Groove Quantize Files
.CSW	StudioWare Panels

3. Find all of the files with the extensions shown in the first column of Table 3.1 and move them to the appropriate folders shown in the second column of Table 3.1.

4. Take each row one at a time until you've gone through all of the file types. For example, start with row one and find all files with an .MID extension; then move them to the My Documents\Cakewalk Pro Audio\Project Files folder.

NOTE

Notice that although you set up folders for only ten file categories, quite a few more file types are listed in Table 3.1. More file types exist because some of Pro Audio's files come in different forms even though they belong to the same category. For instance, Project files can come in the form of MIDI (.MID) files, Work (.WRK) files, and Bundle (.BUN) files. I explain the differences in Chapter 4, "Working with Projects."

Isn't it nice to have everything neatly organized and in its proper place? Believe me, you'll appreciate it in the long run. But you're still not quite finished.

Location, Location, Location

After you've created your folders and moved all of your files, you need to let Pro Audio know about the new locations. If you don't, and you try loading one of your Project files, you might get an error message because Pro Audio won't be able to locate some of the Project's accompanying files. Here's what you need to do:

1. In Pro Audio, select Options > Global.

2. In the Global Options dialog box, select the Folders tab. You then see a list of ten folder locations, as shown in Figure 3.2.

Figure 3.2
You can set folder locations in Pro Audio's Global Options dialog box.

3. For each of the file categories, you need to type the new folder location. As an example, for the Songs category, type C:\MyDocuments\Cakewalk Pro Audio\Project Files. Be sure to substitute the letter C with the appropriate letter that represents your hard drive, if it's different.

NOTE

You might have noticed that not all of the folder locations that we created match those listed in the Global Options dialog box. Most of the names are close enough for you to know which folder each category should point to, but a few are totally different. The Song category should point to the Project Files folder; and the Wave Files category should point to the Audio Files folder.

4. Click on the OK button. From now on, Pro Audio will know where to look for each of the different file types and will automatically open the appropriate folder when you open a Project file, for instance.

CHAPTER 3

The Workspace

Not only can you change the way Pro Audio handles files, but you also can change the way Pro Audio looks and the way it responds to your commands. By customizing the Pro Audio workspace, you can increase your efficiency with the program and make it more comfortable to work with. Some of the adjustments that you can make are to the colors, Toolbars, Window Layouts, and Key Bindings.

Colors

Pro Audio enables you to change the colors of almost every element on the screen within the program. I haven't found much use for making color changes, though. The default colors that the program ships with work just fine for me. You might find a different set of colors more pleasant to work with, however, or maybe you can see some colors better than others. Changing the colors Pro Audio uses is simple; just follow these steps:

1. In Pro Audio, select Options > Colors. The Colors dialog box then appears, as shown in Figure 3.3.

Figure 3.3
In the Colors dialog box, you can change the appearance of Pro Audio to your liking.

2. On the left side of the dialog box is a list of all the screen elements that you can change. To change the color of an element, select it.

3. Select how you want that screen element to look by choosing a color from the right side of the dialog box. You can have the color of the element follow the color of some of the default Windows element colors, or you can use a specific color.

4. You also can change the background wallpaper of the Pro Audio workspace by choosing one of the options at the bottom of the Colors dialog box. If you choose this option, you can even load your own Windows bitmap (.BMP) file for display. Loading your own file is not very useful, but it can be fun.

5. When you've completed your changes, just click on the OK button.

Toolbars

To increase your productivity, Pro Audio provides a number of Toolbars for quick access to many of its major functions. So, instead of having to click through a series of menus, you can simply click on a single Toolbar button. Toolbars are available for standard file access functions, recording and playback controls, and so on.

Pro Audio enables you to change the look and position of its Toolbars, as well as whether they are visible. Why wouldn't you want to have all the Toolbars on the screen all the time? Because they can clutter up the workspace and get in the way while you're working on a Project.

Change Their Position

Just as with most Toolbars in other Windows programs, you can dock these Toolbars to the top or the bottom of the Pro Audio workspace by dragging and dropping them with the mouse. Pro Audio doesn't enable you to dock them to the sides of the workspace, though. And if you drop a Toolbar anywhere within the workspace, it becomes a little floating window, as shown in Figure 3.4.

Figure 3.4
Toolbars can be docked at the top or bottom of the Pro Audio workspace. They also can reside anywhere else within the workspace as small floating windows.

CHAPTER 3

Change Their Appearance

To change the appearance of the Toolbars, you need to access the Toolbars dialog box. Just choose View > Toolbars, and the dialog box will appear, as shown in Figure 3.5.

Figure 3.5
Using the Toolbars dialog box, you can change the appearance of Pro Audio's Toolbars.

By placing or removing the check mark next to each selection in the box, you control whether the associated Toolbar will be visible. For example, if you remove the check mark in the box next to the Standard selection, the Standard File Functions Toolbar will disappear. You also can have the buttons in the Toolbars appear either flat or similar to 3D by changing the Flat Style selection at the bottom of the Toolbars dialog box.

NOTE

The only thing that disappoints me about Pro Audio's Toolbars is that you can't customize them in any other ways. For instance, you can't change which buttons appear in each Toolbar, and you can't create your own specialized Toolbars for rapid access to the features that you use most often. Plus, no Toolbars are available for any of the editing functions within the program. Well, guess what? I found a way around this little dilemma by utilizing StudioWare. I tell you all about it in Chapter 13, "Advanced StudioWare Techniques."

Window Layouts

As you work on a Project in Pro Audio, you need to use many of the Views described in Chapter 2, "Getting Started with Pro Audio." When you want to save the Project, the size and position of the View windows are saved along with it. This capability is nice because you can pick up exactly where you left off the next time you open the Project. As you get more experienced with Pro Audio, you'll probably find that having the Views set up in certain configurations helps your recording sessions go more smoothly. For instance, you might like having the Track View positioned at the top of the workspace, with the Staff View and the Audio View positioned underneath it, as shown in Figure 3.6.

Figure 3.6
The size and position of all Views are saved along with a Project.

What if you come up with a few favorite configurations that you like to use during different stages of the same Project? Or what if you want to use those configurations on a different Project? That's where Window Layouts come in. Using Window Layouts, you can save the current size and position of the View windows as a Layout file. Then you can load the saved Layout later and apply it to any open Project. You also can update a saved Layout, delete it, or rename it. You do so by using the Window Layouts dialog box.

CHAPTER 3

Create a Layout

You create a Window Layout like this:

1. Arrange the Views in the workspace in the positions and sizes that you would like them to be saved. You also must decide whether you want certain Views to be open.

2. Select View > Layouts to open the Window Layouts dialog box, as shown in Figure 3.7.

Figure 3.7

You can create new Layouts by using the Window Layouts dialog box.

3. Click on the Add button and type a name for the new Layout in the New Global Layout dialog box that appears.

TIP

I've found that giving a descriptive name to each Layout helps me when I want to load them. For example, I include the names of each open View in the name of the Layout. If I have the Track, Staff, and Audio Views open in the Layout, I name it "Track-Staff-Audio."

4. Click on the OK button, and your new Layout is then listed in the Window Layouts dialog box.

5. From here, you can rename or delete a Layout in the list. You also can load a Layout by selecting it from the list and clicking on the Load button.

6. When you're finished, click on the Close button.

Layout Options

The Window Layouts dialog box contains two optional settings that enable you to control how Layouts are loaded. The Close Old Windows Before Loading New Ones option determines whether any Views you have currently open in the workspace will be closed when you load a new Layout. The option When Opening a File, Load its Layout determines whether Pro Audio will load the accompanying Layout when a Project is opened. I like to keep both of these options activated.

Key Bindings

One of the most useful customization features that Pro Audio provides is Key Bindings. Like Toolbars, they give you quick access to most of Pro Audio's features. Instead of having to click through a series of menus, you can simply press a key combination on your computer's keyboard. Initially, Pro Audio ships with a few default Key Bindings for opening and saving a Project, for example. These Bindings are displayed next to their assigned menu functions, as in the File menu shown in Figure 3.8.

Figure 3.8
Initially, the Key Binding for opening a Project is Ctrl+O.

CHAPTER 3

The wonderful thing about Key Bindings is that if you don't like them, you can change them. You also can create new ones for functions that don't already have them preassigned. There's only one limitation: a maximum of sixty-two Key Bindings. You can work around this limitation, however; I'll talk about that later. The sixty-two available computer keyboard combinations include the following:

▶ The Ctrl key in combination with any letter of the alphabet

▶ Any function key (F1 through F12)

▶ The Ctrl key in combination with any function key

▶ The Shift key in combination with any function key

Create Your Own Key Bindings

You can easily create your own Key Bindings and change existing ones. Here's how:

1. Select Options > Key Bindings to open the Key Bindings dialog box, as shown in Figure 3.9.

Figure 3.9

You can set key combinations in the Key Bindings dialog box.

2. In the Function list under the Bindings section of the dialog box, select the Pro Audio function that you want to bind to a key combination.

3. In the Key list, select the key combination that you want to bind to the selected function.

4. Click on the Bind button. You then see a connection created, as shown in Figure 3.10.

Figure 3.10
A connection between a function and key combination is made when you click on the Bind button.

5. As I mentioned before, you can create up to sixty-two Key Bindings. You also can remove single Key Bindings by using the Unbind button. And if you want to get rid of them all, just click on the Zap All button.

6. When you're done, click on the OK button.

CAUTION

Near the bottom of the Key Bindings dialog box is the Save Changes for Next Session option. When you select it, any Key Bindings that you create will be saved so that you can use them every time you run Pro Audio. If this option is not selected, you will lose any changes that you make when you exit the program. By default, this option is selected. I suggest that you keep it selected, unless you just need a few temporary Key Bindings during a recording session for some reason.

After you've created (or changed) some Key Bindings, you'll notice the changes in Pro Audio's menus. As I mentioned earlier, the Key Bindings are displayed next to their assigned menu functions.

MIDI Key Bindings

Remember when I mentioned that you can get around the limit of the sixty-two available Key Bindings? This is it: MIDI Key Bindings. You can assign the keys on your MIDI keyboard synthesizer or controller as Key Bindings to execute functions within Pro Audio. (Cool, huh?) For example, you can assign the File > New function in Pro Audio to the middle C key on your keyboard. Then, when you press middle C, Pro Audio opens the New Project File dialog box.

CHAPTER 3

TIP

If your studio is set up so that your computer isn't located next to your MIDI keyboard or controller, using MIDI Key Bindings is a great way to still have access to Pro Audio. For example, if you want to be able to start and stop recording of Pro Audio via your MIDI keyboard, you can just assign one MIDI Key Binding to the Realtime > Play function and another MIDI Key Binding to the Realtime > Stop function.

You create MIDI Key Bindings the same way that you create computer keyboard bindings, as discussed earlier. The only difference is that you have to select MIDI as the Type of Keys option in the Key Bindings dialog box and make sure to activate MIDI Key Bindings by selecting the Enabled option, as shown in Figure 3.11. Also, when you select a key combination in the Key list, you select musical keys rather than computer keyboard keys.

Figure 3.11
You select MIDI as the Type of Keys option to activate MIDI Key Bindings.

TIP

If you create MIDI Key Bindings, pressing those notes on your MIDI keyboard activates their assigned functions in Pro Audio. You really don't want this to happen while you're performing, so you need a quick way to turn MIDI Key Bindings on and off. Under MIDI Shift Options in the Key Bindings dialog box, you can assign a MIDI key or controller message to be a sort of "on/off switch." When it is activated, you have to press and hold down the "switch" key to tell Pro Audio that you're about to use a MIDI Key Binding.

MIDI Settings

Even though Pro Audio does a good job of setting up all its MIDI options during installation, it's still a good idea for you to go through them to make sure everything is the way you want it to be. You might be surprised at how much control you have over how Pro Audio handles MIDI data. Not only can you designate which MIDI devices the program will use, you also can determine what types of MIDI data will be recorded or not and optimize MIDI playback.

MIDI Devices

The first time you run Pro Audio, it scans your computer system to see whether or not you have a MIDI interface installed. If you have a single interface installed that has only one MIDI port on it, Pro Audio configures itself to work with that one.

> **NOTE**
>
> As explained in Chapter 1, "Understanding MIDI and Digital Audio," a *MIDI interface* is a device that is plugged into your computer, enabling it to understand the MIDI language. Every MIDI interface has at least two connections on it, called *MIDI ports*. One is the MIDI In port, which is used to receive MIDI data. The other is the MIDI Out port, which is used to send MIDI data. Some of the more sophisticated MIDI interfaces on the market have multiple pairs of MIDI ports. For instance, I use a Music Quest 8Port/SE, which has eight MIDI In and Out ports. Having all of these ports enables me to connect more than one MIDI instrument to my computer.

If you have more than one interface or a single interface with multiple MIDI ports, you might have to configure Pro Audio manually. To see what MIDI ports Pro Audio is using and to designate which ports you want to use, do the following:

1. Select Options > MIDI Devices to open the MIDI Ports dialog box. This dialog box contains lists of all the input MIDI ports and output MIDI ports that you have available. For an example, see Figure 3.12.

Figure 3.12
The MIDI Ports dialog box lists all the available input and output MIDI ports.

CHAPTER 3

2.   Simply select the input and output ports that you want to be able to access for use within Pro Audio.

3.   When you're finished, click on the OK button.

All the ports selected here will be available in the Track Properties dialog box, which I'll talk about in Chapter 4, "Working with Projects."

Global MIDI Options

Pro Audio provides a number of different MIDI options, some of which are global and others that are Project-oriented. The Project-oriented options (which I'll talk about in Chapter 4, "Working with Projects") are saved and loaded along with Project files. The global options remain the same no matter which Project is currently open.

Filter Out MIDI Messages

The global MIDI options enable you to select the types of MIDI messages that you want to record in Pro Audio. Sometimes you might not want certain MIDI data to be included in your recordings. For example, if your MIDI keyboard sends Channel Aftertouch messages or Key Aftertouch messages, you might want to filter them out. These types of messages are very resource-intensive and can sometimes bog down your synthesizer with too much data.

NOTE

There are seven types of MIDI messages, each providing different kinds of functionality within the MIDI language. These categories are Notes, Key Aftertouch, Channel Aftertouch, Controllers, Program Changes, Pitch Bend, and System Exclusive.

The Notes category pertains to MIDI Note On and MIDI Note Off messages. Whenever you press a key on your MIDI keyboard, a MIDI Note On message is sent. When you let the key go, a MIDI Note Off message is sent.

On some MIDI keyboards, in addition to hitting the keys, you can press and hold them down to apply varying degrees of pressure. This pressure is called Aftertouch. Depending on how the synthesizer is programmed, Aftertouch enables you to control how loud it is or even how it sounds. Aftertouch comes in both Key and Channel varieties. Key Aftertouch enables you to have different pressure levels for each individual key on the keyboard. Channel Aftertouch restricts you to a single pressure level over the entire range of the keyboard.

A wide range of Controller MIDI messages is available. Basically, these messages give you control over different aspects of your MIDI synthesizer or device. Some controller messages enable you to control volume, whereas others enable you to control the position of a synthesizer sound in the stereo field. Far too many are available, however, to discuss them all here.

NOTE (Cont.)

Program Changes (also called Patch Changes) enable you to select from the many different sounds available in a MIDI synthesizer. For example, a Program Change #1 MIDI message might activate a piano sound in your synthesizer, and Program Change #10 might activate a glockenspiel sound.

Pitch Bend messages enable you to temporarily alter the tuning of your MIDI instrument. Many MIDI keyboards have a lever or a wheel that enables you to control Pitch Bend. Moving this wheel makes the instrument send out Pitch Bend (also called Pitch Wheel) messages.

System Exclusive messages pertain to special MIDI data that is (as the name implies) exclusive to the instrument sending and receiving it. For instance, the manufacturer of a MIDI synthesizer might include special functions in the product that can't be controlled via standard MIDI messages. By using System Exclusive messages, the manufacturer gives you access to these special functions but still keeps the product compatible with the MIDI language.

For more in-depth information about MIDI and the different types of messages available, you should read a book dedicated specifically to the subject. One of my favorites is *MIDI for Musicians* by Craig Anderton (Music Sales Corp., ISBN 0-8256-1050-8).

By default, Pro Audio has Notes, Controllers, Program Changes, Pitch Bend, and System Exclusive messages activated, and it has Key Aftertouch and Channel Aftertouch deactivated. If you want to change these settings, though, you can do the following:

1. Select Options > Global to open the Global Options dialog box.

2. Click on the MIDI tab at the top of the dialog box.

3. Under the Record section, select the types of MIDI messages that you want to enable Pro Audio to record, as shown in Figure 3.13.

Figure 3.13

You can determine the types of MIDI messages Pro Audio will be able to record.

4. Click on the OK button when you're finished.

CHAPTER 3

Optimize MIDI Playback

To get smooth and consistent playback of MIDI data, Pro Audio uses a buffer (a temporary storage area) to hold the data before it is sent out through the MIDI interface. This buffer keeps the data from getting backed up, which can cause erratic playback or even stop playback altogether. The buffer also helps to control playback *latency*. Whenever you change a parameter in Pro Audio while a Project is playing, a slight delay always occurs from when you make the adjustment to when you hear the results. That's called *latency*.

The Global Options dialog box contains a setting that enables you to adjust the size of Pro Audio's MIDI playback buffer. If the buffer is set too low, it can cause erratic playback, and if it is set too high, it can cause noticeable latency. By default, the buffer size is set to 500 milliseconds. This setting should be fine in most cases. However, you might want to experiment to find an even better setting. The trick is to find the lowest setting without affecting playback. I've been able to get away with a setting of 100 (on a Pentium II/300 computer system), so depending on the speed of your computer system, you might want to try that. You can change the buffer size like this:

1. Select Options > Global to open the Global Options dialog box.
2. Click on the MIDI tab at the top of the dialog box.
3. Under the Playback section, type the new buffer size.
4. Click on the OK button when you're finished.

Instrument Definitions

Most MIDI instruments today provide a bank of sounds compatible with the General MIDI standard. At the same time, most instruments also provide additional sounds, as well as other features that aren't defined by General MIDI. Some older MIDI instruments don't support General MIDI at all. To enable you to work more efficiently with these instruments, Pro Audio provides Instrument Definitions.

NOTE

Sounds in a MIDI instrument are stored as a group of parameter settings called a patch, and patches are stored in groups called banks. A MIDI instrument can have up to 16,384 banks of 128 patches each. This means that a MIDI instrument can theoretically contain up to 2,097,152 different sounds, although most don't.

With such a large potential for diversity, MIDI instruments from one manufacturer usually don't provide the same functionality as instruments from another manufacturer. This point is important because MIDI data is ambiguous. The same data can be played back by using any MIDI instrument, but that doesn't mean it will sound the same. Different instruments contain different sounds, and they interpret MIDI differently as well. To remedy the problem, General MIDI was created.

General MIDI (GM) is a set of rules applied to the MIDI language that standardize the types of sounds contained in a MIDI instrument (along with their patch numbers) and how different MIDI controller messages are interpreted. Most modern MIDI instruments provide a special bank of GM sounds and a GM operating mode. When running in GM mode, different MIDI instruments respond to the same MIDI data in the same way. So, MIDI data played back on one instrument is guaranteed to sound the same when played on any other instrument.

By using Instrument Definitions, you can "tell" Pro Audio all about the features and capabilities provided by each of the MIDI instruments in your studio. This information includes the name of each patch, the range of notes supported by each patch, the MIDI controller messages that are supported, which Registered Parameter Numbers (RPNs) and Non-Registered Parameter Numbers (NRPNs) are supported, and the bank select method used. Basically, Instrument Definitions enable you to refer to the patches in your MIDI instruments by name rather than by number when you're assigning sounds to Tracks in Pro Audio. (I talk more about this subject in Chapter 4, "Working with Projects.") The same applies for musical note names and MIDI controller message names.

Set Up Your Instruments

Pro Audio includes a number of predefined Instrument Definitions so that you can simply assign them without having to go through the process of creating your own. You can assign Instrument Definitions to each of the MIDI Ports on your MIDI interface. You also can assign them to the individual MIDI Channels (1 through 16).

CHAPTER 3

NOTE

The MIDI language provides sixteen channels of performance data over a single MIDI port connection. MIDI instruments can be set to receive MIDI data on a single channel, if need be. This means that you can control up to sixteen different MIDI instruments (each with its own unique sound) even if they are all connected to the same MIDI port on your MIDI interface. In addition, most MIDI instruments are capable of playing more than one sound at a time. This means that the instrument is multitimbral. If you assign a different sound to each of the sixteen MIDI channels, a single MIDI instrument can play sixteen different sounds simultaneously.

To assign Instrument Definitions to each of the MIDI ports and channels in your setup, follow these steps:

1. Select Options > Instruments to open the Assign Instruments dialog box, as shown in Figure 3.14.

Figure 3.14
You can assign Instrument Definitions in the Assign Instruments dialog box.

2. From the list on the left, select the MIDI port(s) and/or MIDI channel(s) to which you want to assign definitions.

3. From the list on the right, select the Instrument Definition you want to use. For example, if you're going to use the MIDI instrument that's connected to the selected port in General MIDI mode, choose the General MIDI Instrument Definition.

CAUTION

Near the bottom of the Assign Instruments dialog box is the Save Changes for Next Session option. When you select it, any assignments you create will be saved so that you can use them every time you run Pro Audio. If this option is not selected, when you exit the program you will lose any changes you made. I suggest you select this option, unless for some reason you change the configuration of your studio for each new recording session.

4. Click on the OK button when you're finished.

Now Pro Audio will know the capabilities of your MIDI instrument or instruments and act appropriately when you access different features, such as editing MIDI controller messages (which I discuss in Chapter 7, "Editing Basics").

Take the Easy Way Out

If you don't see a specific Instrument Definition for your MIDI instrument listed in the Assign Instruments dialog box, Pro Audio allows you to import more of them. The program ships with a large collection of additional Instrument Definitions that cover many of the MIDI instruments on the market from manufacturers such as Alesis, E-mu, Ensoniq, General Music, Korg, Kurzweil, Roland, and Yamaha. The Instrument Definitions are stored in files with .INS extensions. For example, the Yamaha Instrument Definitions are stored in the file YAMAHA.INS. Importing these files is simple; just do the following:

1. Select Options > Instruments to open the Assign Instruments dialog box.

2. Click on the Define button to open the Define Instruments and Names dialog box, as shown in Figure 3.15.

Figure 3.15
The Define Instruments and Names dialog box enables you to import additional Instrument Definitions.

3. Click on the Import button to open the Import Instrument Definitions dialog box and select the .INS file that you want to import. For example, if your MIDI instrument is manufactured by Roland, select the ROLAND.INS file.

4. When Pro Audio displays a list of the Instrument Definitions contained in that file, select the one(s) that you want and click on the OK button. Your selections are then listed under Instruments in the Define Instruments and Names dialog box.

5. Click on the Close button and you then see your selections listed under Uses Instrument in the Assign Instruments dialog box.

6. Click on the OK button when you're finished.

CHAPTER 3

If you still can't find an Instrument Definition for your MIDI instrument from the extensive collection included with Pro Audio, you can download even more from the Internet. Cakewalk provides a download section on its Web site (**ftp://ftp.cakewalk.com/pub/InstrumentDefinitions**) where you can pick up additional Instrument Definition files. Other sites on the Web supply them, too. For more details, take a look at Appendix D, "Cakewalk Resources on the Web."

Create Your Own

More than likely, you'll find Instrument Definitions for all your MIDI equipment either included with Pro Audio or available for download from the Internet. On the off chance that you don't, though, Pro Audio enables you to create your own. Creating your own Instrument Definitions can be a bit complicated, because you must have a good knowledge of the MIDI language and you need to be able to read the MIDI Implementation Charts that come with your instruments.

NOTE

The MIDI language contains more than one hundred different messages for conveying musical information, and a MIDI instrument isn't required to be able to send or recognize all of them. A MIDI instrument needs to transmit and receive only the messages that are relevant to the features that it provides. It can ignore all the other messages. Therefore, manufacturers include MIDI Implementation Charts with all their products.

A MIDI Implementation Chart lists all the types of MIDI messages that are transmitted and recognized by its accompanying MIDI instrument. The Chart includes the note range of the instrument, what MIDI controller messages it supports, whether or not it supports System Exclusive messages, and more.

To give you an idea of how to read a simple MIDI Implementation Chart and how to create a basic Instrument Definition, let's go through the process step by step:

1.   Select Options > Instruments to open the Assign Instruments dialog box.

2.   Click on the Define button to open the Define Instruments and Names dialog box.

3.   Take a look at Table 3.2, which shows the MIDI Implementation Chart for an E-mu PROformance Plus Stereo Piano MIDI instrument.

Table 3.2
E-mu PROformance
Plus MIDI
Implementation
Chart

MIDI Command	Transmitted	Received	Comments
Note On	No	Yes	
Note Off	No	Yes	
Pitch Wheel	No	Yes	
Program Change	No	Yes	0-31
Overflow Mode	Yes	Yes	
Channel Pressure	No	No	
Poly Key Pressure	No	No	
Control Change	No	Yes	PWH, #1, #7
Sustain Footswitch	No	Yes	#64
Sostenuto Footswitch	No	Yes	#66
Soft Footswitch	No	Yes	#67
Split Footswitch	No	Yes	#70
All Notes Off	No	Yes	
Omni Mode	No	No	
Poly Mode	No	No	
Mono Mode	No	No	
System Exclusives	No	No	

4. Right-click on Instruments on the left side of the Define Instruments and Names dialog box, and select Add Instrument from the pop-up menu.

5. Type a name for the new instrument. For this example, type E-mu PROformance Plus.

CHAPTER 3

6. Open the new instrument by clicking on the + (plus) box next to it, as shown in Figure 3.16.

Figure 3.16
This dialog box shows a new Instrument Definition.

7. Take a look at what the new instrument contains. Pro Audio automatically creates the standard settings needed. Because the E-mu PROformance Plus doesn't support bank select messages, RPNs, or NRPNs, you don't need to change them. The PROformance supports the standard MIDI controllers, too, so you don't have to change them either. You do need to change the patch names, though.

8. Open the Patch Names for Banks folder in the E-mu PROformance Plus instrument by clicking on the + (plus) box next to it. You should see General MIDI listed there. Because this instrument doesn't support GM, you need to change that name.

9. To change the General MIDI patch names list, you first need to create a new patch names list specifically for the PROformance by right-clicking on the Patch Names folder on the right side of the Define Instruments and Names dialog box.

10. Select Add Patch Names List from the pop-up menu and type a name for the new list. In this case, type E-mu PROformance Plus.

11. The PROformance manual shows all the patch names for the instrument (numbers 0 to 31). To add those names to the new patch name list, right-click on the list and select Add Patch Name from the pop-up menu.

12. Type a name for the first patch (in this case, "Dark Grand") and press the Enter key on your computer keyboard. Because this is just an example, you can leave the list as is, but if you were to add all the names to the list, it would look something like Figure 3.17.

Figure 3.17
This dialog box shows
a patch name list for
the E-mu PROformance
Plus.

13. Drag and drop the E-mu PROformance Plus patch names list on to the General MIDI list in the E-mu PROformance Plus Instrument Definition. The patch names list for the instrument is then changed.

14. Click on the Close button, and then click on the OK button to finish.

This set of steps was actually a very simplified demonstration on how to create your own Instrument Definition. If the controller names needed to be changed or the instrument supported RPNs or NRPNs, you would create and edit those lists in the same way you do a patch name list. It's doubtful that you'll ever need to create your own Instrument Definitions, because Pro Audio comes with a large number of them (as well as more being available for download on the Internet), but just in case, you can find more details in the Pro Audio 9 User's Guide.

Optimal Audio Settings

When Pro Audio plays back digital audio on your computer, it puts a lot of stress on the system. Remember when I talked about digital audio in Chapter 1, "Understanding MIDI and Digital Audio"? A CD-quality digital audio recording requires 44,100 numbers (samples) to be processed every second. During playback, most of your computer's processing power is used solely for that purpose. Depending on the power of your system, this processing can make the response of some of Pro Audio's controls a bit sluggish, in particular the Console View controls. For example, if you adjust the volume of a digital audio Track in the Console View during playback, you might experience a slight delay between the time you make the adjustment and the time you hear the results. This period is called latency, and you'll want as little of it as possible occurring during your sessions.

CHAPTER 3

Pro Audio provides a number of different advanced settings that enable you to reduce latency. The first time you start the program, it attempts to make some educated guesses as to what these settings should be, and although these settings usually work just fine, you might still be able to squeeze better performance out of your computer system. Adjusting these settings can be tricky, however, and unfortunately, there are no set rules. There are, however, some general guidelines that you can follow to optimize your audio settings for the best possible performance.

The Latency Slider

The single most important adjustment that you can make is to the Latency Slider, and it's actually pretty simple to use. The lower you set it, the lower the latency; and the higher you set it, the higher the latency. It can't be that simple though, can it? No, I'm afraid not. By lowering the Latency Slider, you also run the risk of making playback unstable. If you set the Latency Slider too low, you might hear dropouts or glitches, or playback might even stop altogether. And the lower you set the Latency Slider, the fewer digital audio Tracks you can play at the same time.

To find the right setting, you have to experiment with a number of different Projects. For those Projects with only a small number of digital audio Tracks, you might be able to get away with a very low Latency Slider setting. As an example, on my Pentium II/300, I was able to play a Project with six digital audio Tracks while having the Latency Slider set as low as it could go. For Projects with a large number of digital audio Tracks, you might have to raise the Latency Slider and put up with a bit of latency while you work. To set the Latency Slider, follow these steps:

1.   Select Options > Audio to open the DirectShow Audio dialog box.

2.   Click on the General tab. The Latency Slider is located in the Mixing Latency section, as shown in Figure 3.18.

Figure 3.18
In the Audio Options dialog box, you can adjust the Latency Slider.

3. Click and drag the Latency Slider to the left to lower latency. Click
    and drag the Latency Slider to the right to raise latency. On average, I
    like to keep it set at about 150 msec (milliseconds).

4. Click on the OK button when you're finished.

Queue Buffers and Buffer Size

Two other settings that affect latency and audio performance are the
number of Buffers in the Playback Queue and the File I/O (Input/Output)
Buffer Size. Like the Latency Slider, if they are set too low, you can
experience dropouts or glitches during playback. And higher settings
mean more latency. Again, you need to experiment with the settings.
I've found that the default values of 4 for the number of Buffers in the
Playback Queue and 64 for the File I/O Buffer Size work quite well. If
you want to change them, you can do the following:

1. Select Options > Audio to open the DirectShow Audio dialog box.

2. Click on the General tab. The Buffers in Playback Queue setting is
    located in the Mixing Latency section, as shown in Figure 3.19.

Figure 3.19
In this dialog box, you
can set the Buffers in
Playback Queue setting.

3. Type the new value.

4. Click on the Advanced tab. The File I/O Buffer Size setting is located in the File System section, as shown in Figure 3.20.

Figure 3.20
In this dialog box, you can set the File I/O Buffer Size setting.

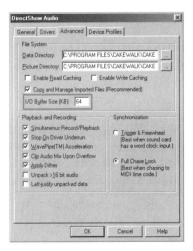

5. Type the new value.

6. Click on the OK button when you're finished.

Read and Write Caching

When your computer sets aside a part of its memory to hold recently read or written information from a disk drive, this process is known as *disk caching*. Windows uses disk caching to help speed up read and write operations to your disk drives. When data is read or written to disk as a continuous stream (as with digital audio), disk caching can actually slow things down.

Pro Audio has two options that let you either enable or disable disk caching while the program is running. By default, Pro Audio keeps disk caching disabled. If you have a large amount of memory in your computer (such as 128MB or more), disk caching might actually improve performance. If you would like to see whether enabling this option makes any difference with your computer system, follow these steps:

1. Select Options > Audio to open the DirectShow Audio dialog box.

2. Click on the Advanced tab. The Enable Read Caching and Enable Write Caching settings are located in the File System section, as shown in Figure 3.21.

Figure 3.21
In this dialog box, you can set the Enable Read Caching and Enable Write Caching settings.

3. Click on each setting to activate it.

4. Click on the OK button when you're finished.

DMA and the Wave Profiler

A device that can read your computer's memory directly without getting the CPU involved is said to support direct memory access (DMA). A sound card is such a device. Pro Audio uses the DMA settings of your sound card to ensure that MIDI and digital audio Tracks within a Project play in synchronization with one another. When you first run Pro Audio, it scans your sound card to automatically determine the DMA settings. These settings are listed in the Audio Options dialog box under the Device Profiles tab. Leave these settings alone! In all but the most extreme cases, it won't do you any good to change them. And if you're having excessive problems with MIDI and audio playback, you should contact Cakewalk Technical Support.

If you accidentally change the DMA settings (or just can't help yourself from seeing what will happen if you do), you can easily have Pro Audio scan your sound card again to bring the original settings back. Here's how to do so:

1. Select Options > Audio to open the Audio Options dialog box.

2. Click on the General tab.

3. Click on the Wave Profiler button at the bottom of the dialog box. Pro Audio then scans your sound card and resets its DMA settings.

4. Click on the OK button to close the Audio Options dialog box.

TIP

If you're still using Pro Audio 8, you should upgrade. Audio performance in Pro Audio 9 has been improved tremendously. Some of the settings have changed, too. For instance, Pro Audio 8 doesn't have a Latency Slider. And even with optimal settings, Pro Audio 8 still exhibits some latency. But just in case you don't plan to upgrade, let me give you some general guidelines for optimizing the audio settings that are available:

1. Keep both the Enable Read Caching and Enable Write Caching parameters deactivated. Unless you have an older computer system, these settings can hurt Pro Audio's performance.

2. You can leave the File I/O Buffers and I/O Buffer Size settings to their defaults of 32 and 64, respectively. These settings are directly related to the speed of your hard disk drive and have more to do with consistent playback than they do with latency. If you get hiccups during playback, you might want to increase the I/O Buffer Size settings, but more than likely the default settings will be fine.

3. Set the Wave Queue Buffers to 3. Anything less, and Pro Audio probably won't be able to commence playback. This parameter depends on the speed of your CPU, which is directly related to the latency issue. I have found 3 to be a good setting for my system. Anything more is pretty much wasting memory, but if you have a slower system, you might need to increase the setting to 4 or so.

4. The Wave Buffer Size is also directly related to latency. The higher the value, the larger the latency; the lower the value, the smaller the latency. You also have to be careful not to set the buffer too low because a smaller buffer size value also reduces the number of audio Tracks you can have playing at once, as well as the number of real-time effects that can be used simultaneously. I've found 32 to be a good setting for my system. It enables me to have 20 or so audio Tracks going at once, and the latency is very small.

5. Leave the DMA settings for your sound card at their default. If you accidentally alter them, use Pro Audio's Wave Profiler feature to have them automatically determined again.

4

Working with Projects

As I mentioned in Chapter 2, "Getting Started with Pro Audio," a Project is Pro Audio's way of representing a song or any other musical body of work. A Project holds all your music data, including MIDI and/or audio, along with a number of program settings. You can't do anything in Pro Audio without first creating a new Project or opening an existing one. So, in this chapter, I'm going to talk all about Projects, including the following topics:

▶ How to open an existing Project

▶ How to create a new Project

▶ How to create your own Templates

▶ How to save a Project

Opening Projects

Every time you start Pro Audio, it presents you with the Cakewalk Quick Start dialog box (see Figure 4.1). From here, you have the choice of opening an existing Project, opening a Project that you recently worked with, or creating a new one.

Figure 4.1
The Cakewalk Quick Start dialog box appears when you start Pro Audio.

If you choose to open an existing Project, Pro Audio displays a standard file selection dialog box so that you can select the Project that you want to load. If you've set up your My Documents folders as described in Chapter 3, "Customizing Pro Audio," the file dialog will initially display the contents of your Project Files folder. Of course, you can examine other disk locations just as you would when loading a file in any other Windows application.

By choosing the Open a Recent Project option in the Cakewalk Quick Start dialog box, you can open a Project that you've previously worked with. You simply select the Project from the drop-down list and then click on the folder button next to the list. Pro Audio keeps track of the last eight Projects that you've worked with. When you open a ninth, the Project on the bottom of the list is bumped off-not killed or deleted, just removed from the list.

You also can open an existing or recent Project by using Pro Audio's standard menu functions. To open an existing Project, just select File | Open. To open a recent Project, select the File menu and then click on the name of the Project that you want to open from the list on the bottom half of the menu (see Figure 4.2).

Figure 4.2
You can use the File menu to open an existing or recent Project.

CHAPTER 4

> **TIP**
>
> Personally, I don't like to use the Cakewalk Quick Start dialog. I find it easier to just use the standard menu functions to open a Project. To keep the dialog from popping up every time you start Pro Audio, just deactivate the Show this at Startup feature located at the bottom of the box. You can do the same thing with the Tip of the Day dialog box.

Create a New Project

To create a new Project, you can select the appropriate option in the Cakewalk Quick Start dialog box, or you can choose File > New from Pro Audio's menu. Whichever method you use, Pro Audio then displays the New Project File dialog box (see Figure 4.3).

Figure 4.3
You choose from the New Project File dialog box to start a new Project.

From here, you need to choose a Template upon which to base your new Project. After you make your selection, Pro Audio creates a new Project, complete with predefined settings that reflect the Template that you selected.

What's a Template?

A Template is a special type of file upon which new Projects are based. You can think of Templates as sort of predefined Projects. Templates contain the settings for all the parameters in a Project. Templates enable you to quickly and easily set up a new Project for a particular type of musical session. For example, if you need to record a rock song with guitar, organ, bass, and drums, you can get a head start on your Project by using Pro Audio's Rock Quartet Template. You also can use Templates to set up Pro Audio for different kinds of studio configurations or if you need to work with a particular MIDI instrument.

Pro Audio ships with more than thirty different Templates that represent a wide range of recording situations. If you want to start from scratch, you can use a Template called Normal to create a completely blank new Project. And if you don't find what you need from the Templates included with Pro Audio, you can always create your own.

Create Your Own Template

Any parameters that are saved in a Project also can be saved as a Template. To create your own Template, you simply do the following:

1. Select File > New and choose the Normal Template. Choosing this Template creates a new, blank Project for you, ready to be filled.

2. Set Pro Audio's parameters to reflect the type of Template that you want to create.

3. Select File > Save As to display the Save As dialog box (see Figure 4.4).

Figure 4.4
You can give your new Template a name in the Save As dialog box.

4. Choose Template from the Save As Type drop-down list.

5. Enter a name for your new Template in the File Name field, and click on the Save button.

The next time you want to create a new Project, your Template will be listed along with the rest in the New Project File dialog box.

TIP

If you bypass the Cakewalk Quick Start dialog-either by disabling it (as I mentioned earlier) or by clicking on its Close button, Pro Audio automatically creates an empty, new Project for you every time you start the program. This Project is based on the Normal Template, which is saved as the NORMAL.TPL file. If you want to have Pro Audio configured in a particular way every time you run the program, simply create a new Template and save it as the NORMAL.TPL file. Now Pro Audio will automatically load your special Template during startup. Be sure to make a copy of the NORMAL.TPL file, and rename it to something like BLANK.TPL, in case you ever want to create an empty new Project.

But what parameters do you need to set when you're creating a new Template? Let's go through them one at a time.

Track Configuration and Parameters

Before you start recording any MIDI or audio data in Pro Audio, you have to set up your Tracks in the Track View. You need to tell Pro Audio the types of Tracks (MIDI or audio) they are going to be, along with the accompanying parameters for each. These parameters include the Name, Source, Key Offset, Velocity Offset, Effects, Time Offset, Port, Channel, Bank, Patch, Volume, and Pan.

You can change some of these parameters directly within the Track View (see Figure 4.5), but for others you need to access the Track Properties dialog box (see Figure 4.6). Because you can change most of the parameters via the dialog box, just using that method is easiest most of the time. The few exceptions are the Name, Effects, and Time+ parameters, which you need to access within the Track View. To access the Track Properties dialog box, right-click on the Track that you want to change and select Track Properties from the pop-up menu.

CHAPTER 4

Figure 4.5
Some Track parameters can be changed within the Track View.

Figure 4.6
Most Track parameters are available within the Track Properties dialog box.

Name

To name a Track, double-click within its Name field in the Track View. Then type something and press the Enter key on your computer keyboard when you're done. That's all there is to it. A Track name can be anything from a short, simple word like *Drums* to a longer, descriptive phrase such as *Background Vocals (Left Channel).*

Source

The Source parameter performs two functions: It lets Pro Audio know the type of Track that you want (MIDI or audio) and where the data for that Track is going to be recorded from. To create an audio Track, choose one of the inputs from your sound card in the Source drop-down list in the Track Properties dialog box. For example, on my system, I could choose Left Monster Sound II Record, Right Monster Sound II Record, or Stereo Monster Sound II Record. If I pick either the left or right choices, that means the Track will record audio from either the left or right input on my sound card. If I pick the Stereo choice, the Track will record audio from both inputs at the same time, making it a stereo audio Track.

Creating a MIDI Track is a bit different. Because MIDI has sixteen channels, you can choose to record data by using any one of them. Just make sure that your MIDI instrument is set to the same channel that you choose as your Source, or your performance won't be recorded. You also can use the MIDI Omni setting. This setting enables Pro Audio to record data on all sixteen channels at the same time, so no matter what channel your MIDI instrument is set on, the data coming from it will be recorded. But if you're using multiple instruments with each set to a different channel, you're better off just setting the correct channel in each of the Tracks right from the start.

Key Offset

The Key Offset parameter (which Pro Audio displays as Key+) enables you to transpose the MIDI notes in a Track during playback. It doesn't change the data that's actually recorded into the Track, and it doesn't work on audio Tracks either. If you know that you're going to want the notes in a Track transposed after they've been recorded, though, setting up this parameter in your Template can be useful. The Key+ value can range from -127 to +127, with each number representing a semitone (or half-step). For example, a value of -12 would transpose the notes down an octave, and a value of +12 would transpose them up an octave. You can simply type the value either via the Track View or the Track Properties dialog box.

Velocity Offset

The Velocity Offset parameter (which Pro Audio displays as Vel+ or Velocity+) is similar to the Key Offset parameter, except instead of transposing MIDI notes during playback, it raises or lowers the MIDI velocity of each note in a Track by adding or subtracting a number from -127 to +127. Again, the data that's actually recorded into the Track isn't changed, and you simply can type the value either via the Track View or the Track Properties dialog box. One difference, though, is that this parameter *does* work on audio Tracks, too. It raises or lowers the volume of the audio.

Effects

Pro Audio enables you to make changes to your MIDI and audio data in a variety of ways by using Effects. A typical example of an Effect is echo. For more information about using Effects in Pro Audio, read Chapter 9, "Effects: The Really Cool Stuff." In the meantime, here's a quick way to apply Effects to a MIDI or audio Track for the purpose of creating a Template:

1. Click in the Effects field of the Track to open its Effects Bin (see Figure 4.7).

Figure 4.7
Each Track in Pro Audio has an Effects Bin for applying Effects.

2. Right-click within the Effects Bin and select the Effect you want to use from the pop-up menu. Depending on whether the Track is for MIDI or audio, the list of Effects will be different.

3. When you're finished adding Effects to the Effects Bin, click on the Done button.

Time Offset

When you record a MIDI performance in Pro Audio, the timing of your performance is recorded along with the notes and so on. Each MIDI event is "stamped" with an exact Start Time, which is measured in measures, beats, and clock ticks. The Time Offset parameter (which Pro Audio displays as Time+) is similar to Key Offset and Velocity Offset, except that it adds or subtracts an offset value to the Start Time of the events in a MIDI Track. Just like with Key Offset and Velocity Offset, the data that's actually recorded into the Track isn't changed. The offset occurs only during playback, and you can set it back to zero to hear your original performance.

The Time Offset is useful if you want to make a Track play a little faster or slower than the rest of the Tracks, in case the performance is rushed or late. To change it, just double-click on the Time+ field in the Track View, and then enter the number of the measure, beat, and clock tick where you want that Track to start playing. The Time Offset isn't available via the Track Properties dialog box.

Port

The Port parameter tells Pro Audio which MIDI port or sound card output you want it to use to play back the data in a Track. If the Track contains MIDI data, you have to select a MIDI port. If the Track contains audio data, you have to select a sound card output. You can change this parameter by making your selection via the Port drop-down list in the Track Properties dialog box.

Bank

The Bank parameter tells Pro Audio which bank of sounds you want to use in the MIDI instrument that is connected to the MIDI port assigned to a Track. You can change this parameter by making your selection via the Bank drop-down list in the Track Properties dialog box.

Patch

The Patch parameter tells Pro Audio which patch (or sound) you want to use from the bank in the MIDI instrument that is connected to the MIDI port assigned to a Track. You can select a patch via the Patch drop-down list in the Track Properties dialog box. If you've set up your Instrument Definitions as described in Chapter 3, "Customizing Pro Audio," you should see the names of the patches for your MIDI instrument in the Patch drop-down list.

Volume

The Volume parameter sets the initial loudness level of a Track. That's basically all there is to it. You can set the Volume either via the Track View or the Track Properties dialog box. The value can range from 0 (off) to 127 (maximum). Volume works on both MIDI and audio Tracks.

Pan

The Pan parameter determines where the sound of a Track will be heard in the sound field between two stereo speakers. You can make it so that the sound will play out of the left speaker, the right speaker, or anywhere in between. That is called *panning*. You can set the Pan either via the Track View or the Track Properties dialog box. The value can range from 0 (all the way left) to 127 (all the way right). A value of 64 is dead center. Pan works on both MIDI and audio Tracks.

Timebase

Just like all sequencing software, Pro Audio uses clock ticks to keep track of the timing of your MIDI performance. Most of the time, you see them as measures and beats because the program translates the clock ticks automatically. For each measure or beat, hundreds of clock ticks occur. The number of clock ticks that happen within a beat are called *pulses per quarter note* (*PPQ*) or the *Timebase*. The Timebase determines the resolution or accuracy of your MIDI timing data.

For example, if you want to use eighth-note septuplets (seven eighth notes per quarter note) in your performance, you have to use a Timebase that is divisible by 7 (such as 168 PPQ); otherwise, Pro Audio cannot record the septuplets accurately. By default, Pro Audio uses a Timebase of 120 PPQ, which means every quarter note is represented by 120 clock ticks, each eighth note by 60 ticks, and so on. The Timebase can be set anywhere from 48 to 480 PPQ. To set the Timebase, follow these steps:

1. Select Options > Project to open the Project Options dialog box (see Figure 4.8).

Figure 4.8
You can set the Timebase in the Project Options dialog box.

2.   Click on the Clock tab.

3.   Choose the Timebase you would like to use from the selections in the Ticks Per Quarter-Note section.

4.   Click on the OK button.

System Exclusive Banks

Pro Audio includes a System Exclusive (Sysx) Librarian, which enables you to store MIDI System Exclusive messages in up to 256 banks (or storage areas). All the data in the Librarian is saved along with a Project. This means that each Project can hold its own unique library of Sysx data. This capability can be very useful when you're putting together Templates for special MIDI recording situations. But because the Sysx Librarian is a significant part of Pro Audio, I'm going to talk about it in more detail in Chapter 12, "Studio Control with StudioWare and Sysx." I just wanted to be sure to mention it here so that you know that data contained in the Librarian is saved along with your Template.

File Information and Comments

Pro Audio enables you to save description information in a Project, including Title, Subtitle, Instructions, Author, Copyright, Keywords, and Comments. This information can be useful—especially when you're creating a Template—to remind yourself exactly what is contained in the file. To add information to a Project, do the following:

1.   Select File > Info to open the File Info window (see Figure 4.9).

Figure 4.9
You can use the File Info window to add description information to your Project or Template.

2. Type the appropriate information in each of the fields. By the way, the information you enter in the Title, Subtitle, Instructions, Author, and Copyright fields will appear in the Staff View and on your music notation printouts (see Chapter 11, "Making Sheet Music").

3. Close the File Info window when you're finished.

The information that you entered is then included in the Project or Template file when you save it.

TIP

If you plan to share your Project or Template files with others, and you want them to follow special instructions you've included in the File Info window (or you just want to be sure they see your copyright notice), you can have the File Info window displayed automatically when the file is opened. Just save the Project or Template while the File Info window is still open.

Tempo, Meter, and Key

Every piece of music needs to have a tempo, meter (time signature), and key, so, of course, Pro Audio enables you to set and save these parameters within a Project or Template.

Set the Tempo

You can set the tempo for your piece like this:

1. Select View > Toolbars to make sure the Tempo Toolbar is visible (see Figure 4.10).

Figure 4.10
To set the Tempo for a Project, you need to use the Tempo Toolbar.

2. Click on the Tempo display in the Tempo Toolbar. The Tempo is then highlighted.

3. Type a new value for the Tempo. The value ranges from 8.00 to 250.00. You can also use the + and − spin controls to adjust the Tempo with the mouse.

4. Press the Enter key on your computer keyboard to set the Tempo.

NOTE

For more information about changing the Tempo in an existing Project (and how that affects audio data), see Chapter 7, "Editing Basics."

Set the Meter (Time Signature) and Key (Key Signature)

Because a piece of music can have multiple time signatures and key signatures throughout, Pro Audio enables you to add multiple Meters and Keys to a Project. For the purpose of creating a Template, though, you'll more than likely just want to set the initial Meter and Key. To do so, follow these steps:

1. Select View > Meter/Key to open the Meter/Key View (see Figure 4.11).

Figure 4.11
You can add multiple time and key signatures to a Project in the Meter/Key View.

Meter/Key button

2. Select the first (and for purposes of this example, the only one that should be there) Meter/Key change in the list.

3. Click on the Change Meter/Key button to open the Meter/Key Signature dialog box (see Figure 4.12).

Figure 4.12
In the Meter/Key Signature dialog box, you can edit individual Meter/Key changes in the Meter/Key View.

4. Enter the Beats Per Measure and the Beat Value that you want to use. For example, if your song is in 6/8 time, you would change the Beats Per Measure to 6 and the Beat Value to 8.

5. Choose a Key from the Key Signature drop-down list. For example, if your song is in the key of A, choose 3 Sharps (A).

6. Click on OK, and then close the Meter/Key View.

Other Parameters

A few other parameters are saved along with Projects and Templates, including synchronization settings, MIDI echo, metronome, record mode, and punch in/out times. But you'll usually set these parameters while you're working on a Project, not beforehand. So, I'll talk more about them later in the book. For the purpose of creating a Template, you can just let them be saved at their default values.

> **TIP**
>
> A Template also can contain MIDI data. This data can be useful, for instance, if you have some favorite drum grooves or melodic phrases that you like to use frequently in your Projects. Simply store these tidbits as Clips in one of the Tracks. When you save the Template, the MIDI data is saved along with it. Then, whenever you create a new Project with that Template, the MIDI data will be ready and waiting for you to use.

CHAPTER 4

Save Your Project

When it comes time to save your Pro Audio Project, you simply do the following:

1. Select File > Save As to open the Save As dialog box.
2. Choose the type of Project file that you want to save from the Save As Type drop-down list.
3. Enter a name for the file, and click on the Save button.

The only thing you really have to decide (besides the name of the file) is the type of the file.

Project File Types

Projects can be saved as three different types of files: MIDI (.MID), Work (.WRK), and Bundle (.BUN).

MIDI Files

If you ever need to collaborate on a Project with someone who owns a sequencing application other than Pro Audio, you should save your Project as a MIDI (.MID) file. A MIDI file is a standard type of file that can be used to transfer musical data between different music software applications. Most music programs on the market today can load and save MIDI files. The problem with MIDI files, however, is that they can store only MIDI data; they can't hold audio data. And none of Pro Audio's settings are saved within a MIDI file, either. So, if you're working on a Project alone, or everyone else in your song-writing group uses Pro Audio, you don't need to deal with MIDI files. Of course, MIDI files can be useful in other circumstances, such as composing music for multimedia or sharing your music with others via the Internet.

Work Files

If you're working on a Project that contains only MIDI data and no audio data, then you should save the Project as a Work (.WRK) file. Work files store all the MIDI data in a Project, plus all the parameter settings (which you learned about earlier in this chapter) for the Project. Work files do not store audio data.

Bundle Files

For those Projects that contain both MIDI and audio data, you should save them as Bundle (.BUN) files. If you use a Bundle file, you can store all the data in a Project (MIDI data, audio data, and Project parameter settings) into a single file. Having a single file makes it very easy to keep track of all the data in a Project plus make a backup of the Project for easy recovery in case something goes wrong. I talk more about backing up your Project files in Appendix B, "Backing Up Your Project Files."

TIP

Pro Audio has an Auto Save feature that automatically saves your data to a special backup file at fixed time intervals or every time a certain number of changes have been made to the Project. Using this feature is a great way to keep your data safe in case a power outage occurs or you make a huge mistake that you can't undo. To activate Auto Save, do the following:

1. Select Options > Global to open the Global Options dialog box. Then click on the General tab.

2. For the option Auto-save Every 0 Minutes or 0 Changes, set either the number of minutes or the number of changes that need to occur between each time Pro Audio will do an automatic save of your Project.

3. If you want to disable Auto Save, set both the minute and changes values back to zero.

4. Click on the OK button.

During an automatic save, Pro Audio saves your Project in a special file with a different name. If your Project is named "myproject.wrk," for example, Pro Audio does an automatic save to a file named "auto save version of myproject.wrk." If you ever need to recover your Project, you can just open the special Auto Save file and then save it under the original filename.

5

Getting Around in Pro Audio

To record, play, and edit your music in Pro Audio, you have to know how to navigate your way through the data in your Project. As you learned in Chapter 2, "Getting Started with Pro Audio," Pro Audio includes a number of tools that enable you to examine and manipulate your data. They are the Track, Piano Roll, Staff, Audio, and Event Views. Although each of these Views provides a different way to edit your data, they all share some common means of control. In other words, even though your data appear (and are edited) differently in each View, you access the data in a similar manner no matter what View you use. A little confused? Don't worry, you'll understand exactly what I mean after I finish describing the following topics:

▶ How to use the Now Time

▶ How to use the Go menu

▶ How to set place marks in your Project

▶ How to search for specific music data in your Project

The Now Time

You learned a little about timing in Chapter 1, "Understanding MIDI and Digital Audio," and Chapter 3, "Customizing Pro Audio." Essentially, you learned that in addition to the musical data itself, the timing of your performance is stored during recording. What this means is that Pro Audio keeps track of exactly when you play each note on your MIDI keyboard during a performance, and it stores those notes along with a *timestamp* (a timing value) containing the measure, beat, and clock tick when each note occurred.

To give you access to your data in a Project, Pro Audio provides a feature known as the *Now Time*. The Now Time is essentially a pointer that indicates your current time location within a Project. For example, the beginning of a Project has a Now Time of 1:01:000 (measure, beat, tick), which is the first beat of the first measure. If you want to view the data at the second beat of the tenth measure, for example, you have to set the Now Time to 10:02:000. And, of course, you can get more precise by specifying clock ticks, such as in a Now Time of 5:03:045, which would be the forty-fifth clock tick of the third beat in the fifth measure.

The Now Time is also updated in real-time, which means that it changes constantly during recording or playback of a Project. So, for example, as you play your Project, the Now Time counts along and shows you the current measure, beat, and tick while you listen to your music.

Show Me the Now Time

You can view the Now Time in several different ways. Numerically, the Now Time is displayed in the Position Toolbar (see Figure 5.1).

Figure 5.1
You can view the Now Time in the Position Toolbar.

You also can use the Large Transport Toolbar to view the Now Time (see Figure 5.2). For more information about Toolbars, see Chapter 3, "Customizing Pro Audio."

Figure 5.2
The Now Time is displayed in the Large Transport Toolbar as well.

In either Toolbar, you'll notice that the Now Time is shown as measures, beats, and ticks. But each toolbar has an additional numeric display. This display is also the Now Time, shown as hours, minutes, seconds, and frames (known as SMPTE).

NOTE

SMPTE (which stands for the Society of Motion Picture and Television Engineers) is a special timing code used for synchronizing audio and video data, although it can be used for other purposes, too. The technology was originally developed by NASA because it needed a really accurate way to keep track of space mission data. In Pro Audio, you can use SMPTE to keep track of the timing of your Project. Pro Audio automatically converts the measures, beats, and ticks in a Project to the hours, minutes, seconds, and frames format used by SMPTE. The frames parameter comes from the fact that SMPTE is used extensively with video, film, and television. Video is created by recording a series of still picture frames very quickly. When these frames are played back, you see them as a moving picture. SMPTE can be used to time video data accurately right down to a single frame. Every second of video data usually has thirty frames, but the number depends on the format of the data. You'll learn more details about using SMPTE in Chapter 6, "Recording and Playback." For now, just know that you can view and set the Now Time of your Project either in measures, beats, and ticks or in hours, minutes, seconds, and frames.

TIP

If you're like I am, and you have some of your MIDI instruments set up in your home studio a fair distance away from your computer, you might have trouble reading the very tiny Now Time display in either of the Position or Transport Toolbars. To remedy this situation, Cakewalk has included the Big Time View in Pro Audio. Basically, it displays the Now Time as large numbers on your computer screen (see Figure 5.3). The Big Time View has its own window, so you can position it anywhere within the Cakewalk workspace. You can change the size of the Big Time View by dragging any of its corners, just like you would with any window in Windows. To toggle the time format between measures, beats, ticks, and SMPTE, just click inside the Big Time View window. You also can change the font and the color of the display by right-clicking in the window and then making your selections in the standard Windows Font dialog box.

Figure 5.3
Using the Big Time View, you can display the Now Time in varying fonts and sizes on your computer screen.

CHAPTER 5

The Now Time Cursor

In addition to being displayed numerically, the Now Time is displayed graphically within any of Pro Audio's View windows. In the Track, Piano Roll, Staff, and Audio Views, the Now Time is displayed as a vertical line cursor that extends from the top to the bottom of the View. As the Now Time changes—either from being set manually or in real-time during playback or recording—the cursor in each of the Views follows along in perfect sync and indicates graphically the place in the Project where the Now Time is currently pointing. To demonstrate what I mean, try the following:

1. Select File > Open and load one of the sample Project files that comes included with Pro Audio. For this example, choose 80's Rock.wrk (see Figure 5.4).

Figure 5.4
This screen shows the layout of the 80's Rock.wrk sample Project.

2. Select Realtime > Play or just click on the Play button in the Transport Toolbar to start playing the Project.

3. Look at the Track View. See the Now Time cursor moving across the Track display as the music plays?

4. Look at the Piano Roll View. The same thing is happening, right? Notice the row of numbers just above the place where the Now Time cursor is moving; this is the Time Ruler. Every View has one (except the Event View, which I'll talk about later). The Time Ruler displays the measure numbers in the current Project. By lining up the top of the Now Time cursor with the Time Ruler in any of the Views, you can get a quick estimate of the current Now Time.

5. Look at the Event View. It's different from all the other Views because it shows the data as one long list instead of displaying data from left to right. And instead of a vertical line, it shows the Now Time cursor as a small red box. While a Project plays, the Now Time cursor in the Event View moves down the list, and it marks the same exact place in the Project as all the other View cursors do. Everything is synchronized to the Now Time.

Set the Now Time

As you've just seen, the Now Time changes automatically as a Project is played, but you also can set the Now Time manually while a Project isn't playing. Pro Audio gives you this capability so that you can access different parts of your Project for editing, which I'll talk about in Chapter 7, "Editing Basics."

Numerically

Changing the Now Time is easy. If you want to set the Now Time to a precise numerical value, you can simply type it into the display on the Position Toolbar. Here's how:

1. If you want to set the Now Time by using measures, beats, and ticks, click on the measures, beats, and ticks display in the Position Toolbar. The display becomes highlighted (see Figure 5.5).

Figure 5.5
You can change the Now Time by clicking on the display to highlight it.

2. Type the measures, beats, and ticks value that you want to use, and press Enter on your computer keyboard.

TIP

If you want to quickly set the Now Time to a particular measure or beat, you don't have to enter all the numerical values. For example, to set the Now Time to measure two, type 2. That's it. Or to set the Now Time to measure five, beat three, type 5:3. To specify ticks, you must enter something for all the values.

CHAPTER 5

3. If you want to set the Now Time by using hours, minutes, seconds, and frames, click on the SMPTE display in the Position Toolbar. The display then becomes highlighted (see Figure 5.6).

Figure 5.6
You can change the
Now Time by specifying
SMPTE time code
values, too.

4. Type the hours, minutes, seconds, and frames value that you want to use and press Enter on your computer keyboard.

TIP

Just as with the measures, beats, and ticks, if you want to quickly set the Now Time to a particular hour, minute, or second, you don't have to enter all the numerical values. For example, to set the Now Time to two minutes, type 0:2. That's it. Or to set the Now Time to five minutes, three seconds, type 0:5:3. To specify frames, you must enter something for all the values.

Graphically

Remember when I described the Time Rulers in each of the Views in the "The Now Time Cursor" section? Well, you can quickly change the Now Time by simply clicking on any of the Time Rulers. For example, you can do the following:

1. As you did earlier, select File > Open, and load one of the sample Project files that comes with Pro Audio. For this example, choose 80's Rock.wrk.

2. Click on the Time Ruler in the Track View. See how the Now Time changes?

3. Click on the Time Ruler in the Piano Roll View. Same result, right? Depending on where you click on the Time Ruler, the Now Time changes to the appropriate value within the measure that you click.

TIP

You might notice that when you click on the Time Ruler in any of the Views, the Now Time is automatically set to the first beat of the nearest measure. This happens because of Pro Audio's Snap Grid feature. Snap Grid automatically snaps the Now Time cursor to the nearest predefined value when you try to set it via a Time Ruler. This feature makes it easy to do quick and precise settings. Without Snap Grid, setting the Now Time accurately by using a Time Ruler can be difficult.

Each View (except the Event View) in Pro Audio has its own separate Snap Grid, but the feature is set in the same manner no matter which View you're using. To activate or deactivate the Snap Grid in a View, just click on the Snap Grid button (see Figure 5.7). To set a Snap Grid interval, right-click on the Snap to Grid button to display the Snap to Grid dialog box (see Figure 5.8). Now select a Resolution by choosing a note duration from the list or typing a number of clock ticks to use. After you're finished setting the Snap Grid, click on the Time Ruler, and you'll notice that the Now Time cursor snaps to the Resolution that you've chosen.

Figure 5.7
The Snap to Grid button controls whether the Snap Grid feature is on or off.

Figure 5.8
You can set the Snap Grid via the Snap to Grid dialog box.

4. As before, the Event View works a little differently. Here, you can simply click on any Event in the list, and the Now Time changes to the exact timing value of that Event.

CHAPTER 5

The Position Slider

Another quick way to set the Now Time graphically is to use the Position Slider. The Slider is part of the Position Toolbar (see Figure 5.9). To use the Slider, just click and drag it. That's it.

Figure 5.9
You can drag the Position Slider left or right to decrease or increase the Now Time, respectively.

The Go Menu

In addition to enabling you to set the Now Time numerically and graphically, Pro Audio provides a few special functions that let you quickly change the Now Time to some musically related points in a Project. All of these functions are a part of the Go menu. To activate them, simply select the Go menu and choose the appropriate function. Following is a list of the functions along with explanations for each of them:

Go-Time

Go-Time enables you to change the Now Time numerically by entering a measure, beat, and tick value. It works in exactly the same way as the measure, beat, and tick display in the Position Toolbar. The only difference is that Go-Time opens a dialog box.

Go-From and Go-Thru

When editing data in Pro Audio, you first need to select the data that you want to work with. It's the same as in any computer program that enables you to work with data. For instance, if you want to delete some text in a word processor, you first select the data to highlight it, and then you delete it.

Well, if you have some data in your Project currently selected, you can quickly set the Now Time to the time that corresponds with the beginning (called the From Time) or the end (called the Thru Time) of the selection by using the Go-From and Go-Thru functions, respectively. You'll learn more details about selecting data in Chapter 7, "Editing Basics."

Go-Beginning and Go-End

The Go-Beginning and Go-End functions are pretty self-explanatory. Simply put, they enable you to set the Now Time to the time that corresponds with the beginning or the end of a Project.

Go-Previous Measure and Go-Next Measure

As with Go-Beginning and Go-End, Go-Previous Measure and Go-Next Measure are self-explanatory. They enable you to quickly set the Now Time to the time that corresponds to the first beat of the previous measure or the first beat of the next measure relative to the current Now Time. In other words, if the Now Time is set at 5:01:000 (beat one of measure five), selecting Go-Previous Measure changes it to 4:01:000 (beat one of measure four), and selecting Go-Next Measure changes it to 6:01:000 (beat one of measure six).

> **NOTE**
>
> If the Now Time is set to something like 5:01:050, Go-Previous Measure actually changes it to the first beat of the current measure, which in this case would be 5:01:000.

Go-Previous Marker and Go-Next Marker

The Go-Previous Marker and Go-Next Marker functions work in a similar manner as the Go-Previous Measure and Go-Next Measure functions. Go-Previous Marker and Go-Next Marker enable you to quickly set the Now Time to the time that corresponds to the closest previous Marker or next Marker relative to the current Now Time. Of course, because I haven't told you about Markers yet, you're probably wondering what I mean. So, let's talk about Markers, shall we?

Markers, Oh My!

All the methods for setting the Now Time that I've described so far have either been based on numbers or predefined musical designations such as measures, beats, or the beginning and ending of a Project. These methods are all fine when you already have the music for your Project written out so you know exactly where everything occurs ahead of time, but what if you're creating a song from scratch simply by recording the parts on the fly? In a case like that, being able to put names to certain locations within a Project would be very helpful, and that's exactly what Markers enable you to do.

With Markers, you can assign a name (in English) to any exact point in time (in either measures, beats, and ticks or SMPTE) in a Project. They're great for designating the places where the verses and choruses start and end within a song. And they make it very easy for you to jump to any point within a Project that you specify simply by name.

Make Your Mark(ers)

Creating Markers is a simple process. Essentially, you just need to set the Now Time to the measure, beat, and tick at which you want to place the Marker in the Project, activate the Marker dialog box, and type in a name. Activating the Marker dialog box is the key here, because you can do so in a number of different ways. To create a Marker, you just do the following:

1. Set the Now Time to the measure, beat, and tick or the SMPTE time at which you want to place the Marker in the Project. As you learned earlier, you can set it either numerically or graphically.

2. Select Insert > Marker to open the Marker dialog box (see Figure 5.10). You also can open the Marker dialog box by pressing F11 on your computer keyboard; holding the Ctrl key on your computer keyboard and clicking just above the Time Ruler (the Marker section) in the Track, Audio, Staff, or Piano Roll Views; right-clicking in a Time Ruler; clicking on the Insert Marker button in the Markers Toolbar; or clicking on the Insert Marker button in the Markers View. (I'll describe the Markers Toolbar and View later in this chapter.)

Figure 5.10
Using the Marker dialog box, you can create a Marker.

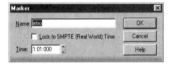

3. Type a name for the Marker.

4. If you want the Marker to be assigned to a measure, beat, tick value, you don't need to do anything more. The measure, beat, tick time of the Marker is shown at the bottom of the Marker dialog box.

5. If you want the Marker to be assigned to an SMPTE time, activate the Lock to SMPTE (Real World) Time option.

NOTE

If you use the Lock to SMPTE (Real World) Time value, your Marker is assigned an exact hour, minute, second, and frame value. It retains that value no matter what. So, even if you change the tempo of the Project, the Marker keeps the same time value, although its measure, beat, tick location might change because of the tempo. This feature is especially handy when you're putting music and sound to video, when you need to have cues that always happen at an exact moment within the Project.

By leaving a Marker assigned to a measure, beat, tick value, however, you can be sure that it always will occur at that measure, beat, and tick even if you change the tempo of the Project.

6. Click on OK.

When you're finished, your Marker (and its name) is added to the Marker section (just above the Time Ruler) in the Track, Audio, Staff, and Piano Roll Views.

> **TIP**
>
> Usually, you add Markers to a Project while no real-time activity is going on, but you also can add Markers while a Project is playing. Simply press the F11 key on your computer keyboard, and Pro Audio creates a Marker at the current Now Time. The new Marker is automatically assigned a temporary name, which you can change later.

Edit the Markers

Editing existing Markers is just as easy as creating new ones. You can change their names and times, make copies of them, and delete them.

Name Change

To change the name of a Marker, follow these steps:

1. Right-click on the Marker in the Marker section of the Time Ruler in one of the Views to open the Marker dialog box. Alternatively, select View > Markers to open the Markers View (see Figure 5.11) and double-click on the Marker in the list to open the Marker dialog box.

Figure 5.11
The Markers View displays a list of all the Markers in a Project.

2. Type a new name for the Marker.
3. Click on OK.

Time Change

Follow these steps to change the time value of a Marker numerically:

1. Right-click on the Marker in the Marker section of the Time Ruler in one of the Views to open the Marker dialog box. Alternatively, select View > Markers to open the Markers View and double-click on the Marker in the list to open the Marker dialog box.

2. Type a new measure, beat, tick value for the Marker. If you want to use an SMPTE value, activate the Lock to SMPTE (Real World) Time option, and then type a new hour, minute, second, frame value for the Marker.

3. Click on OK.

You also can change the time value of a Marker graphically by simply dragging the Marker within the Marker section of the Time Ruler in one of the Views with your mouse. Drag the Marker to the left to decrease its time value, or drag it to the right to increase its time value. Simple, no?

Make a Copy

To make a copy of a Marker, follow these steps:

1. Hold down the Ctrl key on your computer keyboard.
2. Click and drag a Marker in the Marker section of the Time Ruler in one of the Views to a new time location.
3. Release the Ctrl key and mouse button. Pro Audio displays the Marker dialog box.
4. Enter a name for the Marker. You also can change the time by typing a new value if you want. The time value is initially set to the time corresponding to the location on the Time Ruler to which you dragged the Marker.
5. Click on OK.

Delete a Marker

You can delete a Marker in one of two ways, either directly in the Track, Audio, Staff, or Piano Roll Views or via the Marker View. Here's the exact procedure:

1. If you want to use the Track, Audio, Staff, or Piano Roll Views, click and hold the left mouse button on the Marker that you want to delete.
2. If you want to use the Markers View, select View > Markers to open the Markers View. Then select the Marker that you want to delete from the list.
3. Press the Delete key on your computer keyboard.

TIP

To prevent your Markers from being edited, you can lock them into position. Just open the Markers View, select the Marker or Markers that you want to lock, and click on the Lock button (the button with the picture of a little lock on it). To unlock a Marker, the procedure is exactly the same.

Navigate with Markers

Of course, what good would creating Markers do you if you couldn't use them to navigate through the data in your Project? What's more, all you need to do is select the name of a Marker, and the Now Time is automatically set to the exact time of that Marker. You can jump to a specific Marker in a Project in two different ways: either by using the Markers View or the Markers Toolbar.

Use the Markers View

To jump to a specific Marker by using the Markers View, do the following:

1. Select View > Markers to open the Markers View.

2. Select the Marker that you want to jump to from the list. Pro Audio then sets the Now Time to the time corresponding to that Marker, and the Track, Audio, Staff, Piano Roll, and Event Views jump to that time.

Use the Markers Toolbar

To jump to a specific Marker by using the Markers Toolbar, just select the Marker from the Markers Toolbar drop-down list (see Figure 5.12).

Figure 5.12
Using the Markers Toolbar, you can quickly set the Now Time to any Marker by simply selecting a name from a list.

Pro Audio sets the Now Time to the time corresponding to that Marker, and the Track, Audio, Staff, Piano Roll, and Event Views jump to that time.

TIP

One other quick way to jump to a specific Marker in a Project is to select the Now Time in the Position Toolbar and then press the F5 key on your computer keyboard to bring up a list of all the Markers in the current Project. Select a Marker from the list and click on OK. The Now Time is then automatically set to the time corresponding to that Marker.

Where, Oh Where?

Until now, I have been describing how to navigate through the data in a Project by somehow specifying the Now Time, with the result being that you go to a specific point within the Project. Well, what happens when you don't know the exact position in a Project that you want to move to? For instance, out of all the data in all the Tracks in your Project, suppose you need to set the Now Time to the first occurrence of the note middle C? Instead of playing the Project and trying to listen for the note or looking through each and every Track manually, you can use Pro Audio's Go-Search function.

CHAPTER 5

Go-Search enables you to automatically examine all the data in your Project and find any MIDI Events that have certain attributes, which you specify. Upon finding the first Event of the specified type, Go-Search sets the Now Time to the time corresponding with that Event. This function is very useful for finding significant points within a Project and placing Markers there for precision editing tasks, which (as you've probably guessed by now) you'll learn more about later in Chapter 8, "Exploring the Editing Tools." In the meantime, you can find specific MIDI Events by using the Go-Search function like this:

1. Select Go > Beginning to set the Now Time to the beginning of the Project. If you don't take this step, Go-Search begins looking at your data by starting at the current Now Time, not the beginning of the Project. This means that if the Now Time is currently set to 10:01:000, Go-Search does not look at any of the data contained in the first nine measures.

2. Select Go > Search to open the Event Filter–Search dialog box (see Figure 5.13).

Figure 5.13
In the Event Filter–Search dialog box, you specify the criteria for your search.

3. Select the criteria for your search. Don't let all the settings in the Event Filter–Search dialog box intimidate you. They aren't very complicated to use. Basically, all you need to do is select the types of MIDI Events that you want to include in your search. For instance, if you want to look for MIDI Note and Pitch Wheel Events (but nothing else), deselect all the Event types except for Note and Wheel. By the way, whenever you open the Event Filter–Search dialog box, it automatically has all Event types selected. To quickly deselect all Event types, click on the None button. The All button does the exact opposite.

4. After you select all your Event types, you need to set the ranges for each of the parameters. For example, say you want to look for any MIDI Note Events between the pitches of C5 and G7 and with a velocity between 50 and 80. To do so, simply set the Note Key Minimum parameter to C5, the Note Key Maximum parameter to G7, the Note Velocity Minimum parameter to 50, and the Note Velocity Maximum parameter to 80. You can also specify a range of durations (note length) if you'd like. Each Event type has its own unique set of parameter ranges: Key Aftertouch has Key and Pressure parameters, Patch Change has Bank and Patch number parameters, and so on.

5. You also can set up searches that are a little more complicated by excluding ranges of parameters. If you select the Exclude option next to any of the parameter range settings, the search excludes Event types with that specific parameter range. For example, if you want to search for MIDI Note Events that do not fall within the range of C5 and G7, you set up the Minimum and Maximum parameters as in the earlier example, and you activate the Key Exclude option.

6. Using the Event Filter–Search dialog box, you can specify "Special" Events too, such as Audio, System Exclusive, Text, and Chord Events. These "Special" Events don't include any additional parameter settings, though, so Go-Search simply finds any Events of that kind within the data of your Project. And last, you can choose to set a range of MIDI Channels, beats, or ticks to search within. They are called Non-Special Events.

TIP

Because setting these search criteria every time you need to find specific data in a Project can be tedious, it would be nice if you could save the settings for future use, wouldn't it? Well, you can. Just type a name in the Preset box at the top of the Event Filter–Search dialog box and click on the Save button (the button with the little disk icon on it). All your current search criteria settings are then saved under that name. The next time you use Go-Search, you can simply select the name from the Preset box drop-down list, and all your previous settings will be loaded. You can save as many Presets as you'd like, and if you ever want to delete one, just select it from the list, and click on the Delete button (the button with the red X on it).

7. Click on OK.

Pro Audio searches through the data in your Project, finds the first Event that falls under the search parameters that you specified, and then sets the Now Time to the time that corresponds to that Event. If you want to quickly apply that same search again to find the next Event with the same criteria, select Go > Search Next. Pro Audio continues the search (beginning at the current Now Time), finds the next Event that falls under the search parameters you specified, and then sets the Now Time to the time that corresponds to that Event, and so on. Here's another fact you should be aware of: If you first select some of the data in your Project, the search is conducted only on that selected data, not all the data in the Project.

The Go-Search Challenge

So, do you think that you now have a good understanding of how the Go-Search function works? To test what you've learned, I've put together a little search challenge. First, read the challenge, and then see whether you can set up the Event Filter–Search dialog options appropriately. When you think you've got it, take a look at the answer to see how you did.

A Simple Search

Find the first MIDI Note Event in the Project that falls between the pitches of F4 and D7 and that has a velocity between 40 and 70. Also, restrict the search to MIDI Channel 2 only.

Here's the answer:

1. Select Go > Beginning to set the Now Time to the beginning of the Project.
2. Select Go > Search to open the Event Filter–Search dialog box.
3. Click on the None button to clear all settings.
4. Select the MIDI Note Event type.
5. Set the Note Key Minimum parameter to F4.
6. Set the Note Key Maximum parameter to D7.
7. Set the Note Velocity Minimum parameter to 40.
8. Set the Note Velocity Maximum parameter to 70.
9. Set the Non-Special Event Channel Minimum parameter to 2.
10. Set the Non-Special Event Channel Maximum parameter to 2.
11. Click on OK.

Did you get it right? If so, congratulations! I threw that MIDI Channel restriction in there to make it a little more confusing. Setting both the Minimum and Maximum Channel parameters to the same number restricts the search to that MIDI Channel. In this case, it was 2. If you didn't get quite the right settings, don't worry. With a little practice, you'll be able to easily master this feature.

6

Recording and Playback

In this chapter, you get to the meat and potatoes (or the beans and rice, if you're a vegetarian) portion of the product—the main ingredient in the Cakewalk Pro Audio recipe, so to speak. Being able to record and play your music with Pro Audio turns your computer into a full-fledged recording studio. Without these features, Pro Audio would be just a glorified music data editor/processor. So, if you're going to memorize one chapter in the book, this should be it. You'll probably use the recording and playback features of Pro Audio most often. Therefore, I'm going to devote separate sections of the chapter to each way that you can possibly record data in Pro Audio. The topics include the following:

► Reviewing the parameters that need to be set prior to recording
► Learning how to record and play MIDI Tracks
► Learning how to record and play audio Tracks
► Learning how to record multiple Tracks at once
► Recording new Tracks automatically by using looping
► Correcting mistakes by using Punch In and Punch Out
► Recording MIDI one note at a time
► Using importing instead of recording
► Learning what synchronization is and how to use it

Preliminary Parameters

In Chapter 4, "Working with Projects," you learned about a number of parameters that you can save to define a Project Template. Some of those parameters are related to recording, including Track Parameters, Timebase, Tempo, Meter, and Key. I'll mention these parameters throughout this chapter, but I won't go into detail on how to change them. If you need to refresh your memory, take a look at Chapter 4 again.

In addition to these parameters, you need to be aware of a few others before doing any recording in Pro Audio. I didn't describe them in Chapter 4 because you usually set these parameters while working on a Project, not beforehand, when creating a Template.

CHAPTER 6

Metronome

If you've ever taken music lessons, you know what a *metronome* is. It's a device that makes a sound for each beat in each measure of a piece of music. You simply set the tempo that you want, and the metronome sounds each beat accurately and precisely. You use this device to help play in time with the correct rhythm. In Pro Audio, the Metronome feature helps you keep the right time so that your music data is stored at the right measure and beat within the Project.

The Metronome feature in Pro Audio is electronic (of course), and it's a bit more sophisticated than what you might find in a handheld unit. First of all, the tempo for the Metronome is the same as the Tempo setting for the Project, so when you set the Project Tempo, you're also setting the Metronome Tempo. Normally, you would just have to turn the metronome on and off, but in Pro Audio, you need to set several other parameters before using the Metronome feature. You can access these parameters by selecting Options > Project to open the Project Options dialog box and then clicking on the Metronome tab (see Figure 6.1).

Figure 6.1
In the Project Options dialog box, you can access the Metronome parameters.

General

In the General section of the Project Options dialog box, you can determine whether the Metronome will sound during playback, recording, or both by activating the Playback and Recording options. The Accent First Beat option determines whether the Metronome will sound the first beat of each measure a little louder than the others. You also can select whether the Metronome will use your computer's built-in speaker or one of your MIDI instruments to make its sound by activating the Use PC Speaker or Use MIDI Note options (I'll talk more about the second one shortly). You have to activate one of them; otherwise, the Metronome won't make any sound at all.

Count-in

Using the Count-in option in the General section, you can get the feel of the tempo before Pro Audio starts recording your performance. Depending on how you set it, the Metronome will sound a number of beats or measures before recording begins. For example, if your Project is set for a 4/4 Meter, and you set the Count-in option to 1 Measure(s), the Metronome will sound four beats before Pro Audio begins recording.

MIDI Note

If you select the Use MIDI Note option in the General section of the Project Options dialog box, the settings in the MIDI Note section determine which MIDI instrument is used to make the Metronome sound and which note is used for the first beat and remaining beats of each measure. The settings are reasonably self-explanatory. Using Port and Channel, you can set the MIDI Port and Channel that your MIDI instrument uses. Duration determines how long each Metronome "beep" will sound. The duration is measured in ticks, so if you use the default Timebase of 120 ticks per quarter note, a duration of 15 would be equivalent to a thirty-second note.

You can set the pitch (Key) and loudness (Velocity) of the first beat and remaining beats in each measure by using the First Beat and Other Beats options. If you want the first beat of each measure to be accented, you should set the Velocity a little higher in the First Beat Velocity option. For example, you could set it to 127 and set the Other Beats Velocity to 110. Also, if your MIDI instrument is General MIDI-compatible, and you set the Channel option to 10, you can use a percussion instrument for the Metronome sound. I like to use a rimshot sound.

MIDI Echo

Some MIDI Instruments do not provide any way for you to play them (such as a built-in keyboard) except by sending them MIDI messages. These instruments are called modules. To play a module, you need to trigger the module's sounds by playing another instrument, such as a MIDI keyboard. By connecting the MIDI Out from the MIDI keyboard to the MIDI In of the module, you can play the sounds in the module by performing on the keyboard.

But what if you want to record your performance by using Pro Audio? In this case, you have to connect the MIDI Out from the keyboard to the MIDI In of your computer. This means you will no longer be sending MIDI messages from the keyboard to the module, so how will you hear your performance? You could connect the MIDI Out from your computer to the MIDI In of the module, but the MIDI messages from the keyboard will still go directly to the computer and not the module. To remedy this situation, Pro Audio includes a feature called MIDI Echo.

CHAPTER 6

Basically, MIDI Echo takes the MIDI messages from your computer's MIDI Input(s) and sends the messages back out to your computer's MIDI Output(s). You can control which MIDI Channels the data is echoed from and which Ports and Channels the data is echoed to. You can access these parameters by selecting Options > Project to open the Project Options dialog box and then clicking on the MIDI Input tab (see Figure 6.2).

Figure 6.2
In the Project Options dialog box, you also can access the MIDI Echo parameters.

Record and Echo MIDI Channels

In the Record and Echo MIDI Channels section of the Project Options dialog box, you can choose which MIDI Channels data will be echoed from. You usually should keep all the Channels activated, because these options also control which MIDI Channels you can record data from. For example, if you deactivate option 1, you cannot record data from MIDI Channel 1.

Echo Mode and Echo Mapping

If you don't want to use MIDI Echo, select None in the Echo Mode section of the dialog box. If you want to specify which Port and Channel the incoming data will be echoed to, select Manual, and then make your settings in the Echo Mapping section. More than likely, you'll want to leave the Echo Mode set to Auto, though. In this mode, the Port and Channel to which the currently selected Track in the Track View is set determine which Port and Channel the MIDI data is echoed to. Using Auto works out to be easier, because you might have a number of different modules in your studio. Instead of manually changing the MIDI Echo settings each time you want to work with a different module, you can have them changed automatically simply by setting up a new Track in the Track View.

NOTE

One other MIDI Echo option is rarely needed, but you should be aware of it. It's the Local On Port option. When you use one MIDI instrument (master) to play another (slave), pressing a key on the master instrument not only plays a sound on the slave, but also on the master. Most of the time, you'll want only the slave instrument to make sounds. To remedy this situation, you can turn off the sounds in the master instrument by using the Local On feature. All modern instruments have it. Pro Audio attempts to automatically set this feature every time you start it up, but sometimes it might not work (especially if you have an older instrument). If your instrument doesn't support the Local On feature, you can set the Local On Port option to block MIDI Echo for a specified MIDI Port. I doubt that you'll have to use this option, so you can just keep it set to zero, unless you run across the double note problem.

Sampling Rate and Bit Depth

You learned about the meanings of the terms *Sampling Rate* and *Bit Depth* in Chapter 1, "Understanding MIDI and Digital Audio." Pro Audio enables you to set the Sampling Rate and Bit Depth used for the audio data that you record. Depending on the sophistication of your sound card, you can set the Sampling Rate up to 96,000 Hz and the Bit Depth up to 24 bit.

So what settings should you use? Well, the higher the Sampling Rate and Bit Depth, the better the quality of your recorded audio. Higher settings also put more strain on your computer system, however, and the data takes up more memory and hard disk space. Plus, if your input signal is already bad (if you use a low-end microphone to record your vocals, for instance), higher settings won't make it sound any better.

In my opinion, if your computer has enough power, memory, and hard disk space, then you should use the highest settings your sound card will support. Using these settings ensures that you get the best quality recording. The only problem to watch out for is if you plan to put your music on CD. In that case, the audio needs to have a sampling rate of 44,100 Hz and a bit depth of 16 bit.

NOTE

To store music on a CD, the audio data is required to have a sampling rate of 44,100 Hz and a bit depth of 16 bits. These values cannot be higher or lower. They must be exact. Of course, you can start off by recording your audio with different settings. For example, if your computer has a limited amount of memory or hard disk space, you might want to use smaller values. I wouldn't recommend this, though, unless it's absolutely necessary, because lower values mean lower quality audio. You also can record by using higher values, which raises the quality of your audio data. When it comes time to put the audio on CD, however, you must convert the sampling rate and bit depth to the values just mentioned. By using Pro Audio's Change Audio Format feature, you can convert the bit depth of the audio in your Project. Just select Tools > Change Audio Format to access it. Unfortunately, the Change Audio Format feature enables you to convert only between 16 and 24 bits. For any other bit depth values (and to convert the sampling rate), you will need to use a separate digital audio editing application, such as Sonic Foundry's Sound Forge (**www.sonicfoundry.com**), Syntrillium's Cool Edit (**www.syntrillium.com**), or Steinberg's WaveLab (**www.steinberg.net**).

To access these parameters, select Options > Audio to open the DirectShow Audio dialog box, and then click on the General tab (see Figure 6.3).

Figure 6.3
In the DirectShow Audio dialog box, you can access the Sampling Rate and Bit Depth parameters.

In the Default Settings For New Projects section, you can make your selections in the Sampling Rate and File Bit Depth drop-down lists.

Duplex

After recording one audio Track, you might want to record additional Tracks. While you're recording these, you'll want to be able to hear what's going on in the Tracks that already have been recorded. Follow me so far? Well, to hear all these Tracks, you need to have a *full-duplex* sound card. Full duplex means that your sound card can record and play audio at the same time. If your card can't record *and* play, it's known as a *half-duplex* sound card. With a half-duplex sound card, you can't hear what's going on in Tracks that have already been recorded, which makes it very difficult to stay in the "groove" with the music while you're recording new Tracks.

The first time you run Pro Audio, it automatically detects whether your sound card is full duplex or not. Sometimes this detection process doesn't work, though; so even if you have a full-duplex sound card, Pro Audio might not take advantage of it. You'll find out really quickly when you try to record audio Tracks (which I'll talk about later in this chapter). If you know you have a full-duplex sound card, but it doesn't seem to be working properly, you can enable full-duplex operation in Pro Audio by activating the Simultaneous Record/Playback option. Just select Options > Audio to open the DirectShow Audio dialog box and click on the Advanced tab (see Figure 6.4).

Figure 6.4
In the DirectShow Audio dialog box, you can access the Simultaneous Record/Playback option.

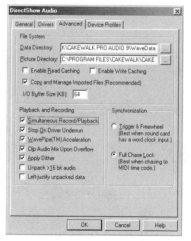

In the Playback and Recording section, activate the Simultaneous Record/Playback option. Now you should be able to record and play audio Tracks at the same time.

If you do have a half-duplex sound card, you should seriously think about getting a new card with full-duplex capabilities. Otherwise, you'll have a hard time recording audio Tracks.

CHAPTER 6

Record Mode

When you record MIDI or audio data into an empty Track, Pro Audio simply places that data into the Track within a new Clip. (In Chapter 2, "Getting Started with Pro Audio," you learned how Pro Audio stores data as Events, which are stored within Clips, which in turn are stored within Tracks.) When you record data into a Track that already contains data, what happens to that existing data?

Pro Audio provides two recording modes (actually, there are three, but I'll talk about Auto Punch later in the chapter), each of which provides a different means of dealing with existing data. The Sound on Sound mode mixes the new data with the existing data. So, for example, if you record a vocal part into a Track that already contains music, you hear both the vocal and the music when you play back that Track. The Overwrite mode replaces the existing data with the new data. So, in this example, the music is erased, and the vocal takes its place. Then, when you play the Track, you hear only the vocal.

Keep in mind that you need to deal with recording modes only when you're recording data into a Track that already contains data. More than likely, you won't be doing that very much because Pro Audio enables you to record up to 256 Tracks, and you can easily place each part of your song on a separate Track. If you do need to set the recording mode, however, just select Realtime > Record Options to open the Record Options dialog box (see Figure 6.5).

Figure 6.5
In the Record Options dialog box, you can set the recording mode.

In the Recording Mode section, select either Sound on Sound or Overwrite and click on OK.

MIDI Track Recording and Playback

Believe it or not, you now have the knowledge needed to start recording in Pro Audio. Nothing is really complicated about the process, but you should follow a number of steps to make sure that everything runs smoothly. Here and in the following sections, I'll show you step by step how to record MIDI Tracks, audio Tracks, and multiple Tracks at once. First, let's tackle MIDI Tracks. To get started, do the following:

1. Create a new Project, or open an existing one. If you use a Template to create a new Project, you might be able to skip some of the following steps, but you should probably run through them anyway, just in case.

2. Set the Meter and Key Signature for the Project. The default settings are 4/4 and the key of C Major.

3. Set the Metronome and Tempo parameters. The default Tempo for a new Project is 100 beats per minute.

4. Set the Timebase for the Project. The default setting is 120 PPQ (pulses per quarter note). More often than not, you won't have to change this setting.

5. Set the recording mode. Unless you plan to record data to a Track that already contains data, you can skip this step. The default recording mode is Sound on Sound.

6. Choose a Track to record to in the Track View and adjust the Track's properties. They include Name, Source, Port, Bank, Patch, Volume, and Pan. For more information about these properties and how to set them, refer to Chapter 4, "Working with Projects."

7. Arm the Track for recording to let Pro Audio know that you want to record data on the Track. Right after the Name parameter in the Track View, you'll see three buttons labeled M, S, and R. Click on the R button to arm the Track for recording (see Figure 6.6).

Figure 6.6
You arm a Track for recording by clicking on its associated R button in the Track View.

CHAPTER 6

8. Set the Now Time to the point in the Project where you want the recording to begin. Most of the time, it will be the very beginning of the Project, but Pro Audio provides the flexibility of enabling you to record data to a Track starting at any measure, beat, or tick within a Project.

9. Select Realtime > Record to start recording. (You also can press the R key on your computer keyboard or click on the Record button in the Transport Toolbar.) If you set a Count-in, the Metronome first counts the number of beats you entered, and then Pro Audio will begin recording.

10. Perform the material that you want to record.

11. After you finish performing, select Realtime > Stop to stop recording. (You also can press the spacebar on your computer keyboard or click on the Stop button in the Transport Toolbar.) Pro Audio creates a new Clip in the Track, containing the MIDI data that you just recorded (see Figure 6.7).

Figure 6.7
After you've finished recording, Pro Audio creates a new Clip in the Track representing the MIDI data.

12. Listen to your performance by setting the Now Time back to its original position and selecting Realtime > Play to start playback. (You also can press the spacebar on your computer keyboard or click on the Play button in the Transport Toolbar.) If you don't like the performance, you can erase it by selecting Edit > Undo Recording. Then go back to Step 8, and try recording again.

NOTE

Pro Audio provides an Undo feature that enables you to reverse any action that you take while working on a Project. You're probably familiar with this feature, because it can be found in most applications that enable you to manipulate data, such as word processing software and so on. Pro Audio goes a bit further, however, by providing an Undo History feature. This feature logs every step you take while working on a Project and enables you to undo each step all the way back to the beginning of your current session. The Undo History is not saved, though, so as soon as you close a Project, you lose the ability to undo any changes. To access the Undo History, just select Edit > History to open the Undo History dialog box (see Figure 6.8). You then see a list of all the tasks that you've done during the current session. To go back to a certain point in the session, just select a task in the list, and click on OK. Pro Audio undoes any tasks performed after the task that you selected. Pro Audio can keep track of as many as 2,147,483,647 tasks, the maximum number of which you can set in the Maximum Undo Levels parameter of the Undo History dialog box. Remember, though, the more tasks Pro Audio keeps track of, the more memory and hard disk space it needs.

Figure 6.8
You can reverse the actions that you take in the Undo History dialog box.

TIP

If you find that your performance for the most part is good except for only a few trouble spots, you might want to try fixing the mistakes by editing the MIDI notes rather than using Undo and then performing the whole thing all over again. You'll learn how to edit MIDI data in Chapter 7, "Editing Basics."

CHAPTER 6

13. After you've recorded a performance that you like, disarm the Track by clicking on its R button again. By disarming the track, you won't accidentally record over the data while you're recording any additional Tracks.

14. Go back to Step 6 and record any additional Tracks that you want to add to the Project. While you're recording the new Track(s), you will hear the previously recorded Track(s) being played back. Because you can hear these Tracks, you might want to turn off the Metronome and just follow the music of the previous Tracks as you perform the material for the new ones.

CAUTION

Be sure to save your Project after each successful Track recording. This step isn't really mandatory, but it's a good precautionary measure because you never know when your computer might decide to crash on you. Rather than lose that really great performance you just recorded, quickly select File > Save (or press Ctrl+S on your computer keyboard) so you can rest easy in knowing that your data is safe.

Audio Track Recording and Playback

Recording audio Tracks in Pro Audio is very similar to recording MIDI Tracks, but, of course, because the nature of the data is different, you need to take a few additional steps. Here's the step-by-step process for recording audio Tracks:

1. Create a new Project or open an existing one. If you use a Template to create a new Project, you might be able to skip some of the following steps, but you should probably run through them anyway, just in case.

2. Set the Meter and Key Signature for the Project. The default settings are 4/4 and the key of C Major.

3. Set the Metronome and Tempo parameters. The default Tempo for a new Project is 100 beats per minute.

4. Set the Timebase for the Project. The default setting is 120 PPQ (pulses per quarter note). More often than not, you won't have to change this setting.

5. Set the recording mode. Unless you plan to record data to a Track that already contains data, you can skip this step. The default recording mode is Sound on Sound.

6. If you have a full-duplex sound card, make sure that the Simultaneous Record/Playback option is activated.

7. Set the Sampling Rate and the Bit Depth for the Project.

8. Choose a Track to record to in the Track View and adjust the Track's properties. They include Name, Source, Port, Bank, Patch, Volume, and Pan. For more information about these properties and how to set them, refer to Chapter 4, "Working with Projects."

9. Arm the Track for recording to let Pro Audio know that you want to record data on the Track. Right after the Name parameter in the Track View, you'll see three buttons labeled M, S, and R. Click on the R button to arm the Track for recording.

10. Select View > Console to open the Console View (see Figure 6.9).

Figure 6.9
The Console View shows a graphical representation of the controls for each Track in your Project.

11. You'll see a set of controls labeled with the same name as your Track, but don't worry about them. Right now you're just concerned with the Meter that's shown with the controls. This Meter displays the level of the audio input for your sound card in decibels.

NOTE

Decibel is a very complicated term to describe, especially in a beginning to intermediate text such as this one. The most basic explanation would be that a decibel is a unit of measurement used to determine the loudness of sound. In Pro Audio, the audio Meter can range from -90dB (soft) to 0dB (loud). For now, that's really all you need to know.

CHAPTER 6

12. Set the audio input level for your sound card so that it's not too
     loud but also not too soft. To do so, you have to use the software
     mixer that came with your sound card. In the Windows Taskbar,
     you should see a small, yellow speaker icon. Double-click on the
     speaker icon to open your sound card mixer. Then select Options >
     Properties to open the sound card mixer Properties dialog box. In the
     Adjust Volume For section, select Recording, make sure all boxes
     below are checked, and click on OK to display the recording controls
     for your sound card mixer (see Figure 6.10).

Figure 6.10
Use your sound card
mixer to adjust the
input levels for your
sound card.

13. For the set of controls labeled Line-In, activate the Select option. This
     option tells your sound card that you want to record audio by using
     its line input connection. If you want to use a different connection
     (such as a microphone or internal CD player), you need to use the set
     of controls associated with that connection.

NOTE

These steps show how to use a standard Windows sound card for recording.
You might have a sound card that uses a different method for setting audio
input levels. In that case, you need to read the documentation for your sound
card to find out how to use it correctly.

14. When you have access to the input level controls for your sound
     card, begin your performance, playing at the loudest level at which
     you plan to record. As you play, the Meter for the Track in the
     Console View will light up, displaying the sound level of your
     performance. You should adjust the input level so that when you
     play the loudest part of your performance, the Meter does *not* turn
     red. If it turns red, you have overloaded the input, and if you record
     at that level, your audio signal will be distorted. If the Meter lights up
     anywhere between -6dB and -3dB when you play the loudest part of
     your performance, you have a good input level setting.

15. After you finish setting your input level, close the sound card mixer and the Console View. Next, set the Now Time to the point in the Project where you want the recording to begin. Most of the time, it will be the very beginning of the Project, but Pro Audio provides the flexibility of enabling you to record data to a Track starting at any measure, beat, or tick within a Project.

16. Select Realtime > Record to start recording. (You also can press the R key on your computer keyboard or click on the Record button in the Transport Toolbar.) If you set a Count-in, the Metronome first counts the number of beats you entered, and then Pro Audio will begin recording.

17. Perform the material that you want to record.

18. After you finish performing, select Realtime > Stop to stop recording. (You also can press the spacebar on your computer keyboard or click on the Stop button in the Transport Toolbar.) Pro Audio creates a new Clip in the Track, containing the audio data that you just recorded (see Figure 6.11).

Figure 6.11
After you finish recording, Pro Audio creates a new Clip in the Track representing the audio data.

19. Listen to your performance by setting the Now Time back to its original position and selecting Realtime > Play to start playback. (You also can press the spacebar on your computer keyboard or click on the Play button in the Transport Toolbar.) If you don't like the performance, erase it by selecting Edit > Undo Recording. Then go back to Step 8, and try recording again.

20. After you've recorded a performance that you like, disarm the Track by clicking on its R button again. By disarming the Track, you won't accidentally record over the data while you're recording any additional Tracks.

21. Go back to Step 8 and record any additional Tracks that you want to add to the Project. While you're recording the new Track(s), you will hear the previously recorded Track(s) playing back (if you have a full-duplex sound card). Therefore, you might want to turn off the Metronome and just follow the music of the previous Tracks as you perform the material for the new ones.

CHAPTER 6

TIP

If you have your home studio set up within a single room containing all of your equipment (including your computer), and you are recording audio Tracks by using a microphone, the microphone will pick up the background noise made by your electronic devices (including the fan inside your computer). To remedy this situation, you might want to set up your microphone and one of your MIDI instruments in a different room, while keeping them connected to your computer via longer cables. Then you can set up some MIDI Key Bindings (you learned about them in Chapter 3, "Customizing Pro Audio") so that you can control Pro Audio remotely. This way, when you record the audio from your microphone, it won't pick up all that background noise.

Multiple Track Recording and Playback

If you have more than one MIDI input on your MIDI Interface or more than one audio input on your sound card, you can record to multiple Tracks simultaneously. Recording multiple Tracks works well when you need to record a whole band of musicians. Instead of having each musician play individually (which can sometimes ruin the "groove"), you can record everyone's part at once (which usually makes the song flow much better).

To record multiple tracks, just follow the same instructions outlined earlier for recording MIDI and audio Tracks. The only difference is that you must set up and arm more than one Track. When you start recording, the MIDI or audio data from each musician will be recorded to separate Tracks simultaneously.

NOTE

When setting the Source property for multiple MIDI Tracks, Pro Audio doesn't enable you to select specific MIDI input ports. If you want to record more than one MIDI Track at once, you must set the Source property of each Track to a different MIDI channel. You also have to be sure that each MIDI instrument is set to send data on a specific MIDI channel. If you have more than one instrument sending data on the same channel, the data from both instruments will be recorded on the same Track.

TIP

Even if you're using a basic sound card to record audio, you can still record two different audio Tracks at once. You can do so because your sound card has a stereo input. This means that you can use the left and right audio Channels separately to record two individual Tracks. When you set up the Tracks prior to recording, just select the Source for one Track to be the left audio Channel of your sound card and the Source for the other Track to be the right audio Channel of your sound card. You also might need a special audio cable. Most basic sound cards provide only one stereo input connection at a one-eighth-inch size. The cable you will need is called a Y-Adapter Audio Cable with a Stereo 1/8" Mini Plug to Phono Plugs (or connections). You should be able to find the cable at your local Radio Shack.

Looping

If you plan to add a vocal Track or an instrumental Track (such as a guitar solo) to your Project—something that might require more than one try to get right—you might want to use *looping* instead of recording and undoing a single Track over and over again. Looping enables you to record several Tracks, one right after the other, without having to stop in between each one. Here's how it works:

1. If you want to record MIDI Tracks, follow steps 1 through 7 in the "MIDI Track Recording and Playback" section earlier in this chapter. If you want to record audio Tracks, follow steps 1 through 14 in the "Audio Track Recording and Playback" section of this chapter.

2. Set the Now Time to the point in the Project where you want looping to begin. Then select Realtime > Loop And Auto Shuttle to open the Loop/Auto Shuttle dialog box (see Figure 6.12). Press F5 on your computer keyboard to bring up the Markers dialog box. Select the Marker named <Now> from the list, and click on OK to set the Start Time where the looping will begin.

Figure 6.12
In the Loop / Auto Shuttle dialog box, you can set the looping parameters for Pro Audio.

3. Type an End Time for the loop by using measure, beat, and tick values. Then activate the Stop at the End Time and Loop Continuously options and click on OK. Setting these options tells Pro Audio that, when you start recording, it will begin at the Loop Start Time, continue to the Loop End Time, and then loop back to the Start Time to cycle through the loop over and over again, until you stop it.

CHAPTER 6

TIP
You also can use the Loop Toolbar to set the parameters for looping. Refer to Chapter 3, "Customizing Pro Audio," for more information about Toolbars.

4. Select Realtime > Record Options to open the Record Options dialog box. In the Loop Recording section, select either Store Takes in a Single Track or Store Takes in Separate Tracks. The first option stores each performance in the same Track but in different Clips stacked on top of each other. The second option stores each performance in a different Track, automatically setting the same Track parameters as the one you began with. I like to use the second option because it's more flexible, especially when I want to edit the data I just recorded. So, for this example, choose the Store Takes in Separate Tracks option. You can experiment with the other option later if you'd like.

5. Select Realtime > Record to start recording. (You also can press the R key on your computer keyboard or click on the Record button in the Transport Toolbar.) If you set a Count-in, the Metronome first counts the number of beats you entered, and then Pro Audio will begin recording.

6. Perform the material that you want to record as many times as you want (up to the limit of 256 available Tracks).

7. After you finish performing, select Realtime > Stop to stop recording. (You also can press the spacebar on your computer keyboard or click on the Stop button in the Transport Toolbar.) Pro Audio creates a new Track containing the data you just recorded for every loop you cycled through (see Figure 6.13).

Figure 6.13
For every loop you record, Pro Audio creates a new Track containing each individual performance.

8. Each Track (except for the current one) is disarmed and muted. To listen to any of your performances, turn off looping by selecting Realtime > Loop And Auto Shuttle to open the Loop/Auto Shuttle dialog box. Deactivate the Stop at the End Time option and click on OK. Set the Now Time back to its original position and select Realtime > Play to start playback. (You also can press the spacebar on your computer keyboard or click on the Play button in the Transport Toolbar.) To listen to one of the recorded Tracks, unmute it by clicking on the yellow M button next to its Name parameter in the Track View.

9. After you've found a performance that you like and want to keep, delete the others by selecting the Track (click on the appropriate Track number on the left side of the Track View) and then select Track > Kill. If you want to select more than one Track at once, just hold down the Ctrl key on your computer keyboard while you're selecting Track numbers.

> **TIP**
>
> Instead of deleting all the extra Tracks that you created during looping, you might want to keep them for use later. You can do so by using Pro Audio's Archive feature. By archiving Tracks, you store them within the current Project, but they become "invisible" to Pro Audio. This means that when you play your Project, the archived Tracks will not play. As a matter of fact, archiving Tracks helps to increase Pro Audio's performance because it doesn't process the Tracks at all when they are archived. To archive a Track, just right-click on its Track number and select Archive from the pop-up menu. You'll notice that the Track's Mute button turns into an A (Archive) button. This change in the button name shows that the Track is archived. You can still make changes to the Track (and the data in it), but Pro Audio will not play the Track.

Punching

When you make a mistake while recording MIDI data, it's usually no big deal, because you can easily make corrections (such as changing the pitch of a note) with Pro Audio's various editing tools (see Chapter 7, "Editing Basics"). But what about when you're recording audio? Sure, you can edit the data by cutting and pasting sections or processing it with effects, but you can't edit the pitch of a single note or make any other precision corrections like you can with MIDI data. So, with audio, you have to record your performance all over again. By using Pro Audio's Punching feature, however, you have to rerecord only the part of the performance that you messed up, leaving the good parts alone.

Using punching, you can set up Pro Audio to automatically start recording and stop recording at precise times during a Project. You, therefore, can record over certain parts of your performance without having to redo the whole thing. Punching is very similar to regular audio Track recording, but with a few differences. Here's the step-by-step procedure:

1. Say that you want to correct some mistakes on an audio Track you just recorded. To get started, make sure the Track is still armed for recording (its R button is red).

2. Activate Punch Recording by selecting Realtime > Record Options to open the Record Options dialog box (see Figure 6.14). In the

Recording Mode section, select Auto Punch. Then, for the Punch In Time, type the measure, beat, and tick at which you want Pro Audio to begin recording. For the Punch Out Time, type the measure, beat, and tick at which you want Pro Audio to stop recording. The section of the Track that falls between the Punch In Time and the Punch Out Time should contain the part of your performance in which you made the mistakes.

Figure 6.14
You use the Record Options dialog box to set the recording mode to Auto Punch and to set the Punch In and Punch Out Times.

3.   Set the Now Time to the point in the Project before the Punch In Time where you want playback to begin. You might want to start from the very beginning of the Project or just a few measures before the Punch In Time. However long it takes you to get into the groove of the performance is how far ahead of the Punch In Time you should set the Now Time.

4.   Select Realtime > Record to start recording. (You also can press the R key on your computer keyboard or click on the Record button in the Transport Toolbar.) If you set a Count-in, the Metronome first counts the number of beats you entered, and then Pro Audio will begin playback.

5.   Play along with the existing material, exactly as you did before when you first recorded the Track. When Pro Audio reaches the Punch In Time, it will automatically start recording the new part of your performance.

6.   When the Now Time has passed the Punch Out Time, Pro Audio will stop recording, and you can select Realtime > Stop to stop Pro Audio. (You also can press the spacebar on your computer keyboard or click on the Stop button in the Transport Toolbar.) Pro Audio replaces any existing material between the Punch In Time and the Punch Out Time with the new material that you just played. As long as you didn't make any mistakes this time, your Track will now be fixed.

7.   Listen to your performance by setting the Now Time back to its original position and selecting Realtime > Play to start playback. (You also can press the spacebar on your computer keyboard or click on the Play button in the Transport Toolbar.) If you don't like the performance, you can erase it by selecting Edit > Undo Recording. Then go back to Step 3 and try recording again.

Step Recording

Even though you might be an accomplished musician, more than likely you have one main instrument that you're good at playing. If that instrument is the keyboard, that skill puts you ahead of some other musicians because the keyboard is one of the easiest instruments to use to record a MIDI performance. You can use other MIDI instruments, such as MIDI woodwind instruments, MIDI drums, and MIDI guitars, but those instruments tend to be very expensive. And if you learn to play a wind instrument or the drums or a guitar, you probably have a real instrument of that kind, not a MIDI one. This puts you at a bit of a disadvantage when you're trying to record MIDI Tracks. However, Pro Audio provides a feature called Step Recording that enables you to record a MIDI Track one note at a time, without having to worry about the timing of your performance.

In other words, you select the type of note that you want to enter (such as a quarter note or a sixteenth note), and then you press one or more keys on your MIDI keyboard. Pro Audio then records those notes into the Track with the timing that you selected. You also can enter the measure, beat, and tick at which you want the notes to occur. Here's how the Step Recording feature works:

1. Follow steps 1 through 8 in the "MIDI Track Recording and Playback" section of this chapter.

2. Select Realtime > Step Record to open the Step Record dialog box (see Figure 6.15).

Figure 6.15
Using the Step Record dialog box, you can record MIDI data to a Track without having to worry about the timing of your performance.

CHAPTER 6

3. In the Step Size section, enter the size of the note that you want to record. For example, if you want to record a quarter note, select Quarter.

4. In the Duration section, you can set the length of the note independent of the Step Size. More often than not, though, you'll want the Duration to be the same as the Step Size. To make things easier, you can set the Duration to Follow Step Size so that both values will be the same, and you won't have to bother selecting a Duration.

5. To record the note, press a key on your MIDI instrument. For example, if you want to record a middle C to the Track, press middle C on your MIDI instrument. By the way, you also can press more than one key at a time if you want to record a chord. For example, if you want to record a C major chord, press the C, E, and G keys on your MIDI instrument at the same time.

6. Pro Audio records the data to the Track and (if the Auto Advance option is activated, which it is by default) moves the Now Time forward by the Step Size amount (which is a quarter note in this example). If the Auto Advance option isn't activated, you have to click on the Advance button to move the Now Time manually. Also, if you want to record a rest instead of a note, you have to click on the Advance button. This way, Pro Audio will move the Now Time ahead by the Step Size amount without recording anything.

7. To change the Now Time manually, just enter a new value into the field shown below the Auto Advance option. To move forward or backward by a Step, click on the arrows on the scroll bar shown next to the Now Time. Also, if you want to delete the most recent Step, click on the Delete button.

TIP

If you need to record many repeating patterns, you might want to use the Pattern option in the Step Record dialog box. In the Pattern box, you can enter a pattern of beats that Pro Audio will follow automatically so that you don't have to click on the Advance button at all, even for rests. For example, if you need to record a pattern with notes on the first two beats, a rest on the third beat, and another note on the fourth beat, you enter 12R4 in the Pattern box. Now, when you start to record the pattern, you simply press keys on your MIDI instrument for beats 1 and 2, Pro Audio advances past beat 3 because it is a rest, and then you press another key for beat 4. Then you keep repeating the same routine over and over again until you get to the point in your music where you no longer need to repeat the same rhythmic pattern. I know that this process sounds a bit complicated, but if you play with it for a while, you'll get the hang of it.

8. When you're finished recording, click on the Keep button to keep the data and have Pro Audio add it to the Track. Alternatively, you can click on the Close button to discard the data you just recorded.

9. Listen to your performance by setting the Now Time back to its original position and selecting Realtime > Play to start playback. (You also can press the spacebar on your computer keyboard or click on the Play button in the Transport Toolbar.) If you don't like the performance, you can erase it by selecting Edit > Undo Recording. Then go back to Step 2 and try recording again.

TIP

As an alternative to the Step Recording feature, you might want to try using the Staff View. With the Staff View, you can still enter your MIDI data one note at a time without worrying about performance timing. Plus, the Staff View enables you to enter and edit your data as standard music notation. I'll describe this feature in more detail in Chapter 11, "Making Sheet Music."

Importing

One other way to get MIDI and audio data into a Project is to import it rather than record it. Pro Audio enables you to import data from .WAV files (the standard Windows audio file format), MIDI files, and other Project files. Why would you want to import files? Well, you might have a great drum Track in a Project or a MIDI file that you want to use in another Project. You also might want to use sample loops for some of the material in your audio Tracks (I'll describe these loops in a moment). Importing material is actually very easy.

Importing from Project and MIDI Files

Importing data from a Project or a MIDI file into another Project is just a matter of copying and pasting, as shown in the following steps. To get started, just do the following:

1. Open the Project or MIDI file from which you want to copy data.

2. In the Track View, select the Clip(s) that you want to copy. You also can select an entire Track or a number of whole Tracks to copy.

3. Select Edit > Copy to open the Copy dialog box (see Figure 6.16). Make sure the Events in Tracks option is activated and then click on OK.

CHAPTER 6

Figure 6.16
Using the Copy dialog box, you can copy data within a Project or from one Project into another Project.

4. Open the Project to which you want to paste the data.

5. In the Track View, select the Track where you want to start pasting the data. If you copied more than one Track, the first copied Track will be pasted to the selected Track, and the other copied Tracks will be pasted to consecutive Tracks after the selected one.

6. Set the Now Time to the point in the Track to which you want the data to be pasted.

7. Select Edit > Paste to open the Paste dialog box (see Figure 6.17). You don't have to change any of the parameters here (I'll go over them in more detail in Chapter 8, "Exploring the Editing Tools"). Click on OK.

Figure 6.17
The Paste dialog box takes any previously copied data and places it where you specify.

Pro Audio copies the data you selected from the first Project or MIDI file and places a copy of the data into the second Project within the Tracks and at the Now Time you specify. In addition to reusing your own material, you can share material with a friend this way.

Importing .WAV Files

You learned about .WAV files in Chapter 3, "Customizing Pro Audio." The .WAV file format is the standard windows file format for storing audio data. This is important because at some time you might record some audio by using another program, and you might want to use that data within one of your Pro Audio Projects. Doing so is really simple; just follow these steps:

1. Select the Track to which you want to import the .WAV file.

2. Set the Now Time to the point in the Track that the file should be placed.

3. Select Insert > Wave File to open the Open dialog box.

4. Choose the .WAV file that you want to import.

5. If you want to listen to the file before you import it, click on the Play button.

6. If the .WAV file is a stereo audio file, you can have either the left and right Channels merged into one Track or split between two different Tracks (starting with the one you selected). To have the file split, activate the Stereo Split option.

7. Click on Open.

Pro Audio then imports the file and inserts it into the Track(s) you selected at the Now Time you specified.

Composing with Sample Loops

Sample loops are short audio recordings that you can piece together to create whole musical performances. Using them is a great way to add some acoustic audio Tracks to your Project without having to actually do any recording. For example, you can buy a CD full of sample loops in the .WAV format that contain nothing but acoustic drum beats. These loops are real recordings made in a professional studio. A number of companies sell these types of discs. Just open a current issue of *Electronic Musician* magazine or *Keyboard* magazine, and you'll find tons of ads for sample loop discs. Not only can you buy drum loops, but you also can buy real guitar solos, vocal chorus recordings, orchestral recordings, and so on. You can create a whole Project just by using sample loops.

Having to import these sample loops in the way I described earlier can be cumbersome, especially if you have to work with several files. That's where the Virtual Jukebox comes in. The Virtual Jukebox is a companion program included with Pro Audio. Normally, it's used to play back Project files via a playlist—you know, like a jukebox. You also can use it to work with your collection of sample loops. Here's how:

1. Select Tools > Virtual Jukebox to open the Virtual Jukebox.

2. In the Virtual Jukebox, select File > Add Files to Playlist to open the Add Files to Playlist dialog box.

3. Select the .WAV sample loop files that you want to add, and click on Add. The Virtual Jukebox then displays the name of each file in the current playlist (see Figure 6.18).

CHAPTER 6

Figure 6.18

The Virtual Jukebox doubles as a sample loop organizer.

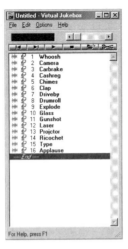

4. To audition one of the files, first select Options > Set Playback Mode > Wait for Keypress (you have to do so only once). Then simply double-click on any file to hear it play.

5. To add a file to a Track in your Project, just click and drag the file from the Virtual Jukebox to one of the Tracks in your Project. You don't need to set the Now Time. Pro Audio will place the audio file wherever you drop it within the Track.

Using the Virtual Jukebox gives you a quick and easy way to audition the files in your sample loop collection and also to piece together a Track or even a whole Project by using sample loops. Playing with audio data this way is really a lot of fun.

Synchronization

One other aspect related to recording that you should know about is *synchronization*. This subject is very complicated and a bit beyond the scope of this book, but you might need to utilize synchronization in two somewhat popular situations. So, I'll cover a few of the basics and explain how to use synchronization in those two particular situations.

Basics

All music is based on time. Without time, there is no music. To record and play music data, Pro Audio needs a timing reference. It uses this reference to determine the exact measure, beat, and tick at which an Event should be stored during recording or at which it should be played.

When you work with Pro Audio alone, it uses one of two different clock sources as its reference: either the clock built into your computer (Internal) or the clock built into your sound card (Audio). By default, Pro Audio uses the Internal clock as its timing reference. Because the Internal clock cannot be used if you have audio data in your Project, Cakewalk automatically changes the Clock to Audio when a track's Source is set to an audio input or when a Wave file is inserted into the Project. So, the built-in clock on your sound card provides the timing for all the data that you record into a Project, and it enables Pro Audio to keep all the Tracks synchronized during playback. This is internal synchronization.

Sometimes, though, you might need to synchronize Pro Audio externally with another piece of equipment. For example, if you have a drum machine (a special type of MIDI instrument that plays only drum sounds) containing some special songs that you programmed into it, you might like to have the data in your current Pro Audio Project play along with the data contained in the drum machine. You would have to synchronize Pro Audio to the drum machine. In this situation, the drum machine would be known as the *master* device, and Pro Audio would be the *slave* device. The master would send messages to the slave, telling it when to start and stop playback and what tempo to use so that they can stay in sync with one another. To accomplish this, you need to use what is called MIDI Sync.

MIDI Sync

MIDI Sync is a special set of MIDI messages that enable you to synchronize MIDI devices to one another. These messages include Start (tells a slave device to start playback at the beginning of the song), Stop (tells a slave device to stop playback), Continue (tells a slave device to continue playback from the current location in the song—the Now Time in Pro Audio), Song Position Pointer or SPP (tells a slave device to jump to a specific time position in the song—the Now Time in Pro Audio), and Clock (a steady pulse of ticks sent to the slave device, telling it the speed of the current tempo of the song).

To synchronize Pro Audio with an external MIDI device using MIDI Sync, follow these steps:

CHAPTER 6

1. Configure your drum machine (or other MIDI device you want to use as the master) to transmit MIDI Sync messages. You'll have to refer to the user's guide for your device on how to do so.

2. In Pro Audio, open the Project that you want to synchronize. Then select Options > Project to open the Project Options dialog box and click on the Clock tab (see Figure 6.19).

Figure 6.19
Using the Project Options dialog box, you can configure Pro Audio for synchronization.

3. In the Source section, click on the MIDI Sync option, and click on OK.

4. Follow the steps outlined earlier for recording or playing MIDI Tracks, but when you activate recording or playback, Pro Audio won't respond right away. Instead, it will display a message that says "Waiting for MIDI Sync."

5. After you see this message, start playback on your master device. It will then send a Start message to Pro Audio, and both the device and Pro Audio will play through the song in sync with one another. In the case of the drum machine, you will hear it play its sounds in time with the music being played by Pro Audio.

6. To stop playback, don't use the commands in Pro Audio; instead, stop playback from the master device. It will send Pro Audio a Stop message, and Pro Audio will stop at the same time automatically.

While working with Pro Audio via MIDI Sync, just remember to start, stop, and navigate through the Project by using the Master device instead of Pro Audio. Otherwise, all the other steps for recording and playback are the same.

NOTE

You cannot record or play audio Tracks in Pro Audio while using MIDI Sync. If you have some previously recorded MIDI data stored in a drum machine (or other MIDI device) that you want to use in your Pro Audio Project, first use MIDI Sync to transfer that data into Pro Audio. Then use the drum machine (or other MIDI device) as a playback device.

SMPTE/MIDI Time Code

You might need to use synchronization when you're composing music to video. Here, though, the synchronization method is different because a VCR is not a MIDI device, so MIDI Sync won't work. Instead, you have to use SMPTE/MIDI Time Code. You learned a little about SMPTE in Chapter 5, "Getting Around in Pro Audio," so you know that it is a timing reference that counts hours, minutes, seconds, and frames (as in video frames). But you didn't really learn how it works.

NOTE

In addition to video, SMPTE/MIDI Time Code is often used to synchronize a sequencer to an external multitrack tape recorder, or DAT (Digital Audio Tape) deck. The procedure for doing this (explained next) is the same.

SMPTE is a complex audio signal that is recorded onto a tape track (in the case of video, it's recorded onto one of the stereo audio tracks) by using a Time Code generator. This signal represents the absolute amount of time over the length of the tape in hours, minutes, seconds, and frames. A sequencer (such as Pro Audio) reading the code can be synchronized to any exact moment along the length of the entire tape recording. In this case, the VCR would be the master, and Pro Audio would be the slave. When you play the tape in the VCR, Pro Audio will play the current Project in sync to the exact hour, minute, second, and frame.

Reading the Time Code from tape requires an SMPTE converter, which translates the SMPTE code into MTC (MIDI Time Code). The MIDI Time Code is read by the MIDI Interface and sent to the sequencer (Pro Audio). MIDI Time Code is the equivalent of SMPTE, except that it exists as special MIDI messages rather than an audio signal. As Pro Audio receives MTC, it calculates the exact measure, beat, and tick that corresponds to the exact time reading. This means that you can start playback anywhere along the tape, and Pro Audio will begin playing or recording MIDI or audio data at precisely the right point in the current Project in perfect sync.

CHAPTER 6

Sync to SMPTE

As an example, say that you need to compose some music to video. This video might be your own or a video from a client. To synchronize Pro Audio to the video, you need to follow these steps:

1. If the video is your own, you need to add SMPTE Time Code to it by using an SMPTE generator. This process is called *striping*. I won't go into the details of doing that here. You'll need to purchase an SMPTE generator and read the instructions in the included manual on how to stripe SMPTE to tape. If the video is from a client, he or she will probably stripe the tape before sending it to you.

TIP

You also need an SMPTE converter to read the Time Code from the tape. If you have a professional MIDI Interface attached to your computer, it might provide SMPTE generating and converting capabilities. Check the user's manual to be sure. You might be able to save yourself some money. I use a Music Quest 8Port/SE MIDI Interface from Opcode (**www.opcode.com**), and it includes multiple MIDI ports as well as SMPTE capabilities.

2. In Pro Audio, open the Project that you want to synchronize. Then select Options > Project to open the Project Options dialog box, and click on the Clock tab.

3. In the SMPTE/MTC Format section, you need to select a frame rate for the Time Code. If you're composing music to your own video, just use the default selection, 30 Frame Non-Drop. If you're composing music for a client, he or she should let you know what frame rate you need to use.

NOTE

Different types of video material use different tape speeds for recording. The frame rate corresponds to how many frames per second are used to record the video to tape. For film, 24 frames per second is used. For video, several different rates are used depending on whether the video is recorded in color or black and white and so on. For more information about frame rates, you should consult the user's guide for your SMPTE generating/reading device.

4. You also might need to enter an SMPTE/MTC Offset in hours, minutes, seconds, and frames. Whether you need to enter an Offset depends on whether the video material starts at the very beginning of the Time Code stripe, which is a value of 00:00:00:00.

NOTE

When you stripe a tape with SMPTE, the Time Code always starts with a value of 00 hours, 00 minutes, 00 seconds, and 00 frames. However, the actual video material on the tape might start a bit later, say at 00 hours, 01 minutes, 20 seconds, 00 frames. If that's the case (and your client should let you know this fact), you need to enter an Offset of 00:01:20:00 into Pro Audio so that Pro Audio will begin playing the Project at that time rather than at the initial Time Code value.

5.   After you finish entering the settings, click on OK.

6.   Now you can follow the steps outlined earlier for recording or playing MIDI Tracks, but when you activate recording or playback, Pro Audio won't respond right away. Instead, it will display a message saying "Waiting for 30 Frame" (or whatever frame rate you selected).

7.   After you see this message, start playback on your master device (in this case, start the tape playing in the VCR). It will then send SMPTE code to Pro Audio, and both the device and Pro Audio will play through the song in sync with one another. In the case of the VCR, you will see it play the video in time with the music that is being played by Pro Audio.

8.   To stop playback, don't use the commands in Pro Audio; instead, stop playback from the master device.

TIP

If you would rather control playback from the Master device (the VCR) entirely without having to first start it in Pro Audio, select Realtime > Loop And Auto Shuttle to display the Loop / Auto Shuttle dialog box. Then activate the Loop Continuously option, and click on OK.

A little confused? Well, as I said, synchronization is a complicated subject. You'll find a little more information in the Pro Audio User's Guide and the Help files, but it isn't any easier to understand than the information that I've provided here. Your best bet is to experiment as much as possible with synchronization and get a good beginner's book on audio recording. Knowing how to utilize synchronization is worthwhile if a situation that requires it ever arises.

CHAPTER 6

7

Editing Basics

After you've finished recording all of your Tracks, it's time to do some editing. Actually, if you're like I am, you might end up doing some editing during the recording process. This is especially true for MIDI Tracks, because it's so easy to quickly fix the pitch or timing of a note if you happen to make a mistake or two. You'll do most of your editing after the fact, though, and Pro Audio provides a number of different tools to get the job done. I briefly described these features in Chapter 2, "Getting Started with Pro Audio," but in this chapter, I go into more detail about the following:

▶ Dealing with Tracks and Clips in the Track View

▶ Editing MIDI note and controller messages in the Piano Roll View

▶ Editing audio data in the Audio View

▶ Editing individual Events in the Event List View

▶ Changing the Tempo via the Tempo View

CAUTION

Before you do any kind of editing at all to your recently recorded material, I suggest that you make a backup of your Project file. This way, if you totally mess things up during the editing process, you'll still have your raw recorded Tracks to fall back on. Take a look at Appendix B, "Backing Up Your Project Files," for more information.

Arranging with the Track View

The first part of the editing process has to do with arranging the material in your Project. Of course, you can do any kind of editing at any time you want. You don't have to follow exactly what I say, but it's just logical to start with arranging. Basically, this step involves rearranging the Tracks and Clips in your Project so that they provide a better representation of the song you're trying to create. For example, after listening to the Project

a few times, you might find that the guitar part in the second verse
sounds better in the first verse, or you might want the vocal to come in
a little earlier during the chorus. You can accomplish these (and many
other) feats by manipulating your Tracks and Clips.

Dealing with Tracks

You already learned how to work with the Track View in terms of setting
up Track Properties, navigating within Pro Audio, and recording new
Tracks. However, I haven't talked about actually manipulating the Tracks
themselves and the data within them. Manipulating includes selecting,
sorting, inserting, and so on.

Scrolling

As you already know, the Track View consists of two areas: The Track
pane (on the left) shows the Track Properties, and the Clips pane (on the
right) shows the Track data. Both areas contain scroll bars (see Figure
7.1). These scroll bars work the same as scroll bars in any standard
Windows application. Because all of the available Track Properties can't
fit on the screen at one time, a horizontal scroll bar enables you to access
the additional parameters. You can either click on the arrows to move the
display or click and drag the scroll bar itself to move the display.

Figure 7.1
By using the scroll
bars, you can access
additional information
that doesn't fit on the
screen.

Another horizontal scroll bar enables you to display all of the data within
all the Tracks. As you scroll to the right, the measure numbers on the
Time Ruler increase. Scrolling doesn't change the Now Time, though
(as you learned in Chapter 5, "Getting Around in Pro Audio"). A vertical
scroll bar affects both the Track and Clips pane areas. As you move the
bar up or down, the different Tracks within the Project are displayed,
starting from 1 (at the top of the list) and ending at 256 (at the bottom of
the list).

In addition to the Track View, scroll bars are available in all the other Views. In the Piano Roll View, you can scroll horizontally to display the data in a Track similar to the Clips in the Track View. You also can scroll vertically to display different MIDI note ranges. In the Audio View, scrolling works almost the same as in the Track View: You can scroll horizontally to show the data in Tracks and scroll vertically to show different Tracks. The Event List View is the oddball, because it only enables you to scroll vertically to display all the Events within a Track as one long list. I'll describe the different Views later in this chapter.

Zooming

The Track View (as well as all the other Views, except the Event List View, of course) also provides Zooming functions. Using these functions, you can magnify the data in a Track in case you want to do some really precise editing. If you take a look at the bottom-right corner of the Track View (see Figure 7.2), you'll notice two sets of buttons (one along the bottom and one along the side) that have little pictures of magnifying glasses on them.

Figure 7.2
The Zoom features reside in the bottom-right corner of the View.

Using the buttons along the bottom, you can magnify the Track data horizontally. So, by clicking on the Zoom In button (the button with the magnifying glass with a + sign shown on it), the Clips grow bigger in size horizontally and give you a more detailed look at the data that they contain. Clicking on the Zoom Out button, of course, does the opposite. And the same buttons along the side of the Track View perform the same functions, except that they affect the display vertically. You'll also notice a little gauge in between each set of buttons. These gauges show you the current level of magnification being used.

TIP

Click and hold the mouse on either Zoom gauge, and up pops a Zoom meter. You can use the meter to quickly set the Zoom level by dragging your mouse (see Figure 7.3).

Figure 7.3
You also change
the Zoom level
via the Zoom
meters.

The Zoom Tool

In addition to the Zoom In and Zoom Out buttons on the right side of the View, you'll find another button with an empty magnifying glass shown on it. This button activates the Zoom tool. You can use this tool to select a range of data and just zoom in on that selection. To use it, simply do the following:

1. Click on the Zoom tool button.

2. Move your mouse pointer within the Clips pane, and it turns into a magnifying glass.

3. Click and drag anywhere within the area to select some data (see Figure 7.4).

Figure 7.4
You just click and drag
to make a selection with
the Zoom tool.

4. Release the mouse button. Pro Audio then zooms in on the selection (both horizontally and vertically, depending on how you drag the mouse), and your mouse pointer returns to normal.

You have to click on the Zoom tool button every time you want to use it.

Selecting

To manipulate your Tracks in a Project for editing, you have to be able to select them. In Chapter 6, "Recording and Playback," I mentioned how to select a single Track: You simply click on the Track number of the Track you want to select. But sometimes you might want to select more than one Track at one time. You also might need a quick way to select all the Tracks in your Project. Or after going through the trouble of selecting a number of Tracks, you might want to deselect one or two while keeping the others selected. You accomplish these tasks as follows:

▶ To select more than one Track, hold down the Ctrl key on your computer keyboard as you click on the Track numbers.

▶ To select all Tracks in a Project, select Edit > Select > All.

▶ To deselect all Tracks in a Project, select Edit > Select > None.

▶ To deselect a Track while keeping others selected, just hold down the Ctrl key on your computer keyboard as you click on the Track number.

By the way, all of these procedures also work in the other Views. The only difference is the items being selected. Just remember that to select a single item, you simply click on it. To select more than one item, you hold down the Ctrl key on your computer keyboard as you click. To select all or none of the items, you choose Edit > Select. Some special selection features are also available, but I'll talk about them later in this chapter and in Chapter 8, "Exploring the Editing Tools."

Sorting

You can change the order in which the Tracks appear in a couple of different ways. Being able to sort the Tracks can be useful if you want to keep related Tracks together in the Track list. For instance, you might want to keep all of the percussion Tracks or all of the vocal Tracks together. It's easier to work on your song when the Tracks are grouped together in this way-at least, it is for me.

Click and Drag

The easiest way to move a Track within a list is simply to drag it to a new location. Just move your mouse pointer over the Name parameter of the Track you want to move, and then click and drag it anywhere within the list. When you release your mouse button, the Track moves to the new location and takes on a new Track number.

Track Sort

You also can use the Track Sort function to sort Tracks in the list, based on the Track Properties. You use this function as follows:

1.   Select Track > Sort to open the Sort Tracks dialog box (see Figure 7.5).

Figure 7.5

By using the Sort Tracks dialog box, you can rearrange the Tracks in the Track View.

2.   In the Sort By section, select the Track property by which you want to sort the Tracks.

3.   In the Order section, select whether you want the Tracks to be sorted in ascending or descending order.

4.   Click on OK.

Pro Audio then sorts the Tracks according to the settings that you specified. And remember, the Track numbers for the Tracks are changed as well, because the Tracks have been moved to new locations within the list. Each Track maintains its parameter settings and data, though.

Inserting

If you ever need to insert a new Track in between two existing Tracks within the list, you can do the following:

1.   Right-click on the Track number of the Track above which you want to insert a new Track.

2.   From the pop-up menu, select Insert Track.

Pro Audio moves the current Track down one location in the list and inserts a new Track at the location you clicked on. For example, if you right-click on Track 2 and select Insert Track, Pro Audio moves Track 2 (and all the Tracks below it) down by one and inserts a new Track at number 2 in the list.

Cloning

If you ever need to make a copy of a Track, you can do the following:

1. Select the Track that you want to copy.

2. Select Track > Clone to open the Clone dialog box (see Figure 7.6).

Figure 7.6

You can make a copy of a Track by using the Clone dialog box.

3. You can choose to copy the Events within the Track, the Track Properties, or both. Simply activate the Events and/or Properties options.

4. In the To Track option, enter the number of the Track to which you want to copy the data.

5. Click on OK.

Pro Audio makes a copy of the Track that you selected and puts it in the Track list at the location you specified in the To Track option. For example, if you selected Track 1 and entered Track 6 in the To Track option, Pro Audio makes a copy of Track 1 and places it in Track 6.

Erasing

Getting rid of Tracks that you no longer need is very easy. Simply select the Track, and select Track > Kill. Pro Audio also provides another erasing function, however, that's a little more flexible. Instead of erasing the Track entirely, Pro Audio enables you to delete all the data from the Track while keeping the Track Properties intact. To do so, just select the Track, and then select Track > Wipe. Nothing could be easier.

Dealing with Clips

Unless you insert, copy, or erase Tracks in your Project, you're not actually doing any kind of data manipulation. If you move a Track in the Track list or sort the Tracks, that doesn't change the data within them. To make changes to the data within your Project, you have to manipulate the Clips within the Tracks.

Clip Properties

For organizational purposes, Pro Audio enables you to change the way Clips are displayed. To change the properties, you can right-click on a Clip and select Properties from the pop-up menu to open the Clip Properties dialog box (see Figure 7.7). Here, you can assign a name to the Clip (which doesn't have to be the same name as the Track in which the Clip resides) and the color of the Clip.

Figure 7.7

To change the name or color of a Clip, you use the Clip Properties dialog box.

The name and the color of a Clip don't affect the data within your Project, but you also can change the start time of the Clip in this dialog box. This is the position within the Project at which the Clip begins. If you enter a new start time for the Clip, the Clip is moved within the Track to the new time, and during playback, Pro Audio will play the Clip at the new time, as well. This move does change the data within your Project.

View Options

You also can change whether the names you assign to Clips will be displayed and whether Clips will be displayed with a graphical representation of the data that they contain. In other words, if a Clip contains audio data, it shows a drawing of what the sound wave for the audio data might look like. For MIDI data, the Clip shows a mini piano roll display.

To change these options, just right-click anywhere within the Clips pane, and select View Options from the pop-up menu to display the Track View Options dialog box (see Figure 7.8). Activate the appropriate options (Display Clip Names and Display Clip Contents) and click on OK.

Figure 7.8

By using the Track View Options dialog box, you can show or hide Clip names and contents.

By using the Track View Options dialog box, you also can specify whether right-clicking will change the Now Time (Right Click Sets Now option); whether to display vertical rule lines for the Time Ruler (Display Vertical Rules option); which Views open automatically when you double-click on a MIDI or audio Clip; and whether to use a minimum clip width (Use Minimum Clip Width option). This last one is provided just in case you have a Clip that contains only a little bit of data and doesn't show up appropriately in the Track View, meaning it might be too small to click on. In that case, you can set a minimum clip width so that all Clips have to be at least a minimum displayed size.

Selecting

You select Clips the same way you select Tracks. To select a single Clip, click on it. To select more than one Clip, hold down the Ctrl key on your computer keyboard while clicking on the Clips that you want to select. You know the rest.

There is one additional selection method that doesn't apply to Tracks— selecting only a portion of a Clip. This procedure is known as working with Partial Clips. This capability is useful when you want to split a Clip into smaller clips or combine a Clip with another Clip to make a larger Clip. I'll describe this topic in more detail later in this chapter.

To select only part of a Clip, hold down the Alt key on your computer keyboard and drag your mouse pointer across the Clip to select a part of it. You also can drag across several Clips (or even over several Tracks) to make a partial selection of multiple Clips.

NOTE

When you're making selections or moving data, the start and end times of your selections or data are affected by the Snap To Grid. You learned how to use the Snap To Grid feature in Chapter 5, "Getting Around in Pro Audio."

Splitting and Combining

Using partial selections, you can split and combine Clips into new smaller or larger Clips. To split a Clip into two new ones, just select a portion of the Clip and select Edit > Create Clips. Pro Audio then creates two new Clips from the single old one. Combining Clips is just as easy. Just select the Clips that you want to combine, right-click on one of the selected Clips, and select Combine from the pop-up menu. Pro Audio then creates one new Clip from the old, selected ones.

The Split Function

Pro Audio also enables you to split Clips in a few other ways by using its Split function. It works like this:

1. Select the Clip(s) that you want to split.

2. Right-click on the selected Clip(s) and select Split from the pop-up menu to open the Split Clips dialog box (see Figure 7.9).

Figure 7.9

By using the Split Clips dialog box, you can split Clips into new, smaller Clips in a variety of ways.

3. Choose the Split option that you want to use. The Split At Time option enables you split a Clip at a certain measure, beat, or tick. The Split Repeatedly option enables you to split a Clip into a bunch of smaller Clips instead of just two new smaller ones. Just enter at what measure you want the first split to occur and how many measures you want each consecutive split to occur after that. For example, if you have a Clip that begins at measure 2 and ends at measure 7, and you want to create three two-bar Clips out of it, enter 2 for the starting measure and 2 for the split interval. The Split Repeatedly at Each Marker Time option enables you to split Clips according to the Markers that you set up in the Track View. You learned about Markers in Chapter 5, "Getting Around in Pro Audio." Finally, the Split Repeatedly when Silent option enables you to split Clips at any place where silence occurs within them. You can set the interval of silence that Pro Audio has to look for by entering a number of measures.

4. Click on OK.

CHAPTER 7

Moving and Copying

You also can change the arrangement of your data by moving and copying Clips to new locations, either within the same Tracks or into other Tracks. One way to move a Clip is to use the Clip Properties dialog box and enter a new start time for the Clip. You also can move a Clip by simply clicking and dragging it to a new location with your mouse. As long as the Track you're dragging the Clip into doesn't contain any other existing Clips, you have nothing to worry about. Pro Audio simply moves the Clip to its new location.

If the Track does contain existing data, though, Pro Audio asks how you want the data to be handled by displaying the Drag and Drop Options dialog box (see Figure 7.10). You then have to choose one of three options: Blend Old and New, Replace Old with New, or Slide Over Old to Make Room.

Figure 7.10
If you move a Clip within a Track that contains existing material, Pro Audio displays the Drag and Drop Options dialog box.

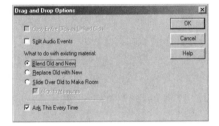

If you choose the Blend Old and New option, the Clip you're moving simply overlaps any existing Clips. This means that the Clips remain separate, but they overlap so that, during playback, the data in the overlapping sections play simultaneously. If you choose the Replace Old with New option, the overlapping portion of the Clip you are moving replaces (which means it erases and takes the place of) the portion of the Clip being overlapped. If you choose the Slide Over Old to Make Room option, the start times of any existing Clips are simply changed to make room for the new Clip. So, during playback, the new Clip plays at the time it was placed at, and the existing Clips play a little later, depending on how much their start times had to be changed.

Copy, Cut, and Paste

If you would rather copy a Clip instead of just moving it, you can use Pro Audio's Copy, Cut, and Paste functions. Actually, using the Cut function is the same as moving a Clip. If you use the Copy function, though, you can keep the original Clip in its place and put a copy of it in the new location. This procedure works as follows:

1. Select the Clip(s) that you want to copy.

2. Select Edit > Copy to open the Copy dialog box (see Figure 7.11).

Figure 7.11
To copy Clips, you use the Copy dialog box.

3. Choose the type(s) of data that you want to copy. Usually, you should choose the Events in Tracks option.

4. Click on OK.

5. Click on the Track number of the Track into which you want to copy the Clip(s).

6. Set the Now Time to the point within the Track at which you want to place the Clip(s).

7. Select Edit > Paste to open the Paste dialog box. Then click on the Advanced button to open the Advanced Paste dialog box (see Figure 7.12).

Figure 7.12
The Advanced Paste dialog box provides many different options for copying data in Pro Audio.

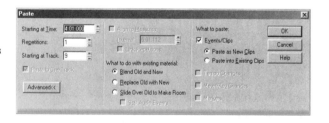

8. Choose the options that you want to use. Most of these options are self-explanatory. Setting the Starting at Time option is the same as setting the Now Time in Step 6. Setting the Starting at Track option is the same as setting the Track in Step 5. The Repetitions option simply enables you to create more than one copy of the Clip if you want. I've already talked about the What to Do with Existing Material options. The only new ones are the Paste as New Clips and Paste into Existing Clips options. The Paste as New Clips option creates a new Clip and then follows the overlapping rules that you choose with the What to Do with Existing Material options. The Paste into Existing Clips option, however, merges the Clip that you are copying with any existing Clips that it overlaps. You end up with material from both Clips merged into one.

9. Click on OK.

If some of these options sound a little confusing, just experiment with them a bit. Make an extra backup of your Project, and then use it to go wild with the copying and pasting functions. Try every possible combination, and soon you'll get the hang of using them.

Linked Clips

You might have noticed a few other options in the Copy and Paste dialog boxes—namely, the Copy Entire Clips as Linked Clips option in the Copy dialog box and the Link Repetitions option in the Paste dialog box. These options deal with a special feature in Pro Audio called Linked Clips. By using this feature, you can link copies of a Clip to one another so that any changes you make to one Clip will affect the others that are linked to it. This way, you can easily create repeating patterns and then make changes to the patterns later.

For example, you might have a cool drum pattern in a Clip that takes up one measure, and you want to repeat that pattern through the first eight measures of your song. You can simply copy the Clip (selecting the Copy Entire Clips as Linked Clips option) and then paste it (setting the Repetitions to 7 and activating the Linked Repetitions option). Pro Audio then copies your Clip and pastes seven more identical, linked copies of it. If you make any changes to one of the Clips, these changes affect them all. For instance, you can change the snare drum from sounding on beat 2 to sounding on beat 3 in one of the Clips, and the change happens in all of them. Linked Clips is a fun, cool, and time-saving feature.

Unlink

If you ever want to unlink Linked Clips, just follow these steps:

1. Select the Clips that you want to unlink. You don't have to unlink all Linked Clips in a group. For example, if you have four Linked Clips, you can select two of them to unlink, and the two that you leave unselected remain linked.

2. Right-click on one of the selected Clips and select Unlink from the pop-up menu to open the Unlink Clips dialog box.

3. Choose an unlink option. The New Linked Group option unlinks the selected Clips from the other Clips but keeps them linked to one another. The Independent, not Linked at All option totally unlinks the Clips from any others.

4. Click on OK.

Linked Clips are shown with dotted outlines in the Clips pane of the Track View. When you unlink them, they appear as normal Clips again.

Erasing

Deleting any Clips that you no longer need is an easy process; just follow these steps:

1. Select the Clips that you want to delete.

2. Select Edit > Delete to open the Delete dialog box (see Figure 7.13).

Figure 7.13
In the Delete dialog box, you can determine the type of data that you want to erase.

3. Make sure the Events in Tracks option is activated.

4. If you want to have Pro Audio remove the space that's created when you delete the Clip(s), activate the Delete Hole option. Pro Audio moves any other existing Clips in the Track backward (toward the beginning of the Project) by the amount of time opened when you delete the Clip(s). Just give it a try, and you'll see what I mean.

5. Click on OK.

Inserting

Instead of manipulating existing data, you sometimes might need to introduce silent parts into your Project. You can do so by using Pro Audio's Insert > Time/Measures feature. This feature enables you to insert blank space in the form of measures, ticks, seconds, or frames. You also can insert the space either into the whole Project or into selected Tracks. It works like this:

1. Select Edit > Select > None to clear any currently selected data in the Project.

2. If you want to insert space into the whole Project, skip to Step 3. Otherwise, select the Track(s) into which you want to insert space.

3. Set the Now Time to the point in the Track(s) or Project at which you want the space inserted.

4. Select Insert > Time/Measures to open the Insert Time/Measures dialog box (see Figure 7.14).

Figure 7.14
In the Insert Time/Measures dialog box, you can insert blank space into selected Tracks or the entire Project.

5. The At Time parameter reflects the current Now Time. Type a new time here or make adjustments if you want.

6. For the Insert parameter, type the number of units of blank space that you want to have inserted.

7. Select the type of unit that you want to have inserted. You can choose to insert measures, ticks, seconds, or frames.

8. In the Slide section, choose the types of data that will be affected by the insert process. The types of data that you select will be moved to make room for the new blank space. Of course, you'll almost always want to have the Events in Tracks option activated. When you're inserting space into selected Tracks, the Events in Tracks option is usually the only one that you want to have activated. When you're inserting space into the entire Project, on the other hand, you'll more than likely want to have all the options activated.

9. Click on OK.

Pro Audio then inserts the number of measures, ticks, seconds, or frames that you typed into the Insert parameter at the Now Time you specified. It also moves the types of data that you selected by sliding the data forward in time (toward the end of the Project). So, for instance, if you inserted a measure of blank space into the entire Project at measure 2, then all the data in all the Tracks starting at measure 2 is shifted forward by one measure. Whatever data was in measure 2 is now in measure 3, and any data that was in measure 3 is in measure 4, and so on.

Practice Arrangement

Before you move on to the next part of the chapter, I thought you might like to try out some of the arranging techniques that I just described. You can use one of the sample Projects that comes supplied with Pro Audio to practice a few of the techniques and make that Project sound a bit different by simply manipulating its Tracks and Clips. Just follow these steps:

1. Open the sample Project called Ballad #1.wrk. Because you'll be working only with the Tracks and Clips in the Project, close all of the open Views except for the Track View.

2. Save the Project under a new name by using File > Save As so that you don't ruin the original Project file. Just type something like Practice Arrangement.wrk for the filename.

3. Play through the Project once so that you can hear what it sounds like before you make any changes.

4. The first couple of changes you're going to make are to both the beginning and end of the song. I don't particularly like the ending, and I think the beginning needs a little more excitement. So, for this example, you can move the last Clips in Tracks 1, 2, 3, and 6 to the beginning of those Tracks. First, select the Clips (see Figure 7.15).

Figure 7.15
Select the last Clips in
Tracks 1, 2, 3, and 6.

5. Choose Edit > Cut to open the Cut dialog box. Make sure that the Events in Tracks option is activated. If you want to move the Marker, just keep the Markers option activated, too. Then click on OK. Pro Audio temporarily removes those Clips from the Project.

6. To add the Clips back into the Project at the beginning, set the Now Time to the beginning of the Project.

7. Choose Edit > Paste to open the Paste dialog box. If only the basic Paste dialog box is displayed, click on the Advanced button to open the Advanced Paste dialog box.

8. Make sure the Repetitions parameter is set to 1 and the Starting at Track parameter is set to 1.

9. In the What to Do with Existing Material section, activate the Slide Over Old to Make Room option. In the What to Paste section, make sure that the Events/Clips and the Paste as New Clips options are activated. Then click on OK.

    Pro Audio takes the Clips you removed from the end of the Project and inserts them into the beginning of the Project. It also moves any existing Clips in Tracks 1, 2, 3, and 6 forward in time (see Figure 7.16).

Figure 7.16
The Clips from Tracks 1, 2, 3, and 6 at the end of the Project have been moved to the beginning of the Project.

10. Try playing the Project again to see what it sounds like now. Something isn't quite right, is it? When you pasted the material at the beginning of Tracks 1, 2, 3, and 6, the existing material in those Tracks was moved forward, but the material in Tracks 4, 5, and 7 stayed in the same place. So now the music in those Tracks doesn't line up correctly with the others. You have to move that material forward by four measures so that the music sounds the way it's supposed to. First, select Edit > Select > None to remove any current Track and Clips selections.

11. Select Tracks 4, 5, and 7. Be sure to select the entire Tracks, not just the individual Clips within them.

12. Click and drag the first Clip in Track 4 four measures forward in time. This action opens the Drag and Drop Options dialog box. Be sure the Slide Over Old to Make Room and Align to Measures options are activated. Then click on OK. Pro Audio moves all the Clips in Tracks 4, 5, and 7 forward four measures, and now everything is aligned correctly.

13. One last change you need to make is at the end of Track 6. When you removed the last Clip in that Track, a very tiny Clip that was meant as an intro to that last Clip was left behind. Because you've changed the ending, though, you no longer need that intro Clip, so just delete it.

14. Set the Now Time to the beginning of the Project and start playback.

See how powerful the arranging features in Pro Audio are? With only a few simple changes, you've given this song a much nicer beginning and ending, and you didn't even have to add any new material. Of course, you could have made even more changes to make the song sound radically different, but I'll leave that to you to experiment with. Remember, you can't ruin anything, because you have the original Project file saved to disk. This one is a practice file, so you can arrange to your heart's content. You might also want to try some arranging techniques on some of the other sample files included with Pro Audio.

Using the Piano Roll View

By manipulating the Tracks and Clips in your Project, you can change the overall structure, but to fix single-note mistakes and make smaller changes, you need to do some precision editing. You do so by selecting individual or multiple Tracks or Clips in the Track View and then by using the View menu to open the data within one of the other available Views. For editing MIDI data, that would be the Piano Roll View. (You also can edit MIDI data as standard music notation in the Staff View, but I'll talk about that topic in Chapter 11, "Making Sheet Music.")

By using the Piano Roll View (see Figure 7.17), you can add, edit, and delete MIDI note and controller data within your MIDI Tracks. Looking somewhat like a player piano roll, the Piano Roll View represents notes as colored rectangles on a grid display with the pitches of the notes designated by an on-screen music keyboard.

Figure 7.17

The Piano Roll View resembles that of the old player piano rolls used in the late 1800s and early 1900s.

More precisely, the Piano Roll View consists of five major sections: the Toolbar (located at the top of the View, containing all the View's related controls); the Note pane (located in the center of the View, displaying the notes in the currently selected Track); the Keyboard pane (located on the left side of the View, displaying the pitch values of the notes shown in the Note pane); the Controller pane (located at the bottom of the View, displaying the MIDI controller data in the currently selected Track); and the Track List pane (located at the right side of the View, showing a list of all the Tracks currently being displayed-the Piano Roll View can display the data from more than one Track at one time).

You'll also notice that the Piano Roll View has scroll bars and Zoom tools just like the Track View. These tools work the same way as they do in the Track View. In addition, a Snap to Grid function is represented by the Grid button in the Toolbar. Other similarities are the Marker area and the Time Ruler, which are located just above the Note pane. Basically, you can use the Piano Roll View to edit and view the data within the MIDI Tracks of your Project in more detail.

You can open the View in three different ways:

▶ In the Track View, select the Track(s) that you want to edit and then select View > Piano Roll.

▶ In the Track View, right-click on a Track or Clip and choose Piano Roll from the pop-up menu.

▶ In the Track View, double-click on a MIDI Clip in the Clips pane.

Whichever method you choose, Pro Audio then opens the Piano Roll View and displays the data from the Track(s) that you selected.

CHAPTER 7

Working with Multiple Tracks

If you select more than one Track to be displayed at one time, the Piano Roll View shows the data from each Track by using a unique color. For example, the notes and controllers from one Track might be shown as yellow, and the data from another Track might be shown as blue.

NOTE

The one exception to the use of Track colors is that Tracks with numbers ending in the same digit (that is, 1, 11, 21, and so on) must all share the same color. There's no way around this. You can change the color used by each number group, however, by using the Colors dialog box, which you access by selecting Options > Colors. You learned how to customize Pro Audio's colors in Chapter 3, "Customizing Pro Audio."

Each Track is also listed in the Track List pane with a set of individual controls (see Figure 7.18).

Figure 7.18
The data from multiple Tracks is shown with different colors, and each Track is listed in the Track List pane.

The Track List Pane

When you open the Piano Roll View, the names and numbers of the Tracks that you selected are listed in the Track List pane. For convenience, the associated Mute, Solo, and Record buttons for each Track also are provided. Plus, you'll notice two other controls available for each Track in the List:

▶ *Mask Selection*: The white button shown next to each Track in the Track List pane is the Mask Selection button. This button determines whether the notes for its associated Track can be edited. When the button is white, the notes appear in color in the Note pane, and they can be edited. When the button is gray, the notes appear gray in the Note pane, and they cannot be edited. Clicking on the Mask Selection button toggles it on and off.

▶ *Show/Hide Track*: The button to the left of the Mask Selection button is the Show/Hide Track button. This button determines whether the notes for its associated Track will be displayed in the Note pane. When the button is in color (which is the same color as the notes for that Track), the notes are shown in the Note pane. When the button is white, the notes are not shown in the Note pane. Clicking on the Show/Hide Track button toggles it on and off.

The Track Tools

In addition to the Track List pane controls, five other Track-related controls are located in the Toolbar. They are the last five buttons in the Toolbar, at the right side of the Piano Roll View:

▶ *Invert Tracks*: The first button in the group (going from right to left) is the Invert Tracks button. Clicking on this button toggles the Show/Hide Track buttons for each of the Tracks in the Track List pane. This means that if one Track has its Show/Hide Track button on, and another Track has its button off, clicking on the Invert Tracks button turns off the first Track's Show/Hide button and turns on the second Track's Show/Hide button. It toggles the current state of each Show/Hide Track button.

▶ *No Tracks*: The next button over in the Toolbar is the No Tracks button. Clicking on this button turns off the Show/Hide Track buttons for each Track in the Track List pane. No matter what state each Show/Hide Track button is in (either on or off), the No Track button turns them all off.

▶ *All Tracks*: The next button over in the Toolbar is the All Tracks button. This button is the exact opposite of the No Tracks button. Clicking on the All Tracks button turns on the Show/Hide Track buttons for each Track in the Track List pane.

▶ *Show/Hide Track Pane*: The next button over in the Toolbar is the Show/Hide Track Pane button. Clicking on this button simply toggles between having the Track List pane open or closed.

▶ *Pick Tracks*: While you have the Piano Roll View open, you might want to add or remove some of the Tracks in the Track List pane. Instead of having to close the Piano Roll View, select other Tracks in the Track View, and then open the Piano Roll View again, you can use the Pick Tracks feature.

▶ Clicking on the Pick Tracks button (the next button over from the Show/Hide Track Pane button in the Toolbar) opens the Pick Tracks dialog box. This box displays a list of all the Tracks in your Project. You can select one or more Tracks from the list. After you click on the OK button, the Tracks that you selected are listed in the Track List pane, and the notes in those Tracks are shown in the Note pane.

TIP

If you have two or more Tracks that contain the same exact notes, those notes overlap one another in the Note pane. What determines which Track's notes are on top is the order of the Tracks in the Track List pane. For example, if Track 4 is listed above Track 2 in the Track List pane, the data from Track 4 overlaps the data from Track 2 in the Note pane. If you want to change this order (meaning that you want the data from Track 2 to overlap the data from Track 4), you can click and drag the Track listing in the Track List pane to a new position in the list.

Dealing with Notes

When you open a MIDI Track in the Piano Roll View, the notes in that Track are displayed in the Note pane. Each note is represented by a colored rectangle. The horizontal location of a note designates its start time when you line up the left side of the rectangle with the numbers in the Time Ruler, and the vertical location of a note designates its pitch when you line up the whole rectangle with the keys in the Keyboard pane. The length of the rectangle designates the duration of the note (for instance, quarter note, eighth note, and so on).

NOTE

In one instance, the notes in the Note pane and the keys in the Keyboard pane appear differently. If you open the Piano Roll View for a Track that uses a MIDI channel that has been assigned to a percussion instrument, instead of keys in the Keyboard pane, you'll see percussion instrument names. And instead of rectangles in the Note pane, you'll see small colored diamonds (see Figure 7.19). This mode is known as the Drum Mode. The colored diamonds still represent notes, but because there's no use for duration (or note length) when dealing with percussion, the diamonds all appear the same size. Also, instead of changing the pitch of a note when you move its diamond up or down in the Note pane, the actual instrument for that Note changes, according to the instrument names displayed in the Keyboard pane. Remember the description of assigning instruments and Instrument Definitions in Chapter 3, "Customizing Pro Audio."

If you need to manually activate Drum Mode in the Piano Roll View, you can right-click in the Keyboard pane to open the Note Names dialog box. Just select the Use These Note Names Instead option to change the Keyboard pane display.

Figure 7.19

In Drum Mode, you can use the Piano Roll View to edit percussion Tracks in a more intuitive manner.

You can add new notes to a Track or edit the existing ones by using the tools represented by the first five buttons in the Toolbar (from left to right on the left side of the Piano Roll View).

Selecting

The first button in the Toolbar represents the Select tool. By using this tool, you can select notes for further manipulation, such as deleting, copying, moving, and so on. Essentially, you select notes the same way in which you select Clips in the Track View. To select a single note, click on it. To select more than one note, hold down the Ctrl key on your computer keyboard while clicking on the notes that you want to select. You know the rest.

One additional selection method involves the Keyboard pane. To select all the notes of a certain pitch, you can click on one of the keys in the Keyboard pane. You also can drag your mouse pointer across several keys to select the notes of a number of different pitches.

Editing

After you've made a selection, you can copy, cut, paste, move, and delete the notes the same way you do with Clips in the Track View. You also can edit notes individually by using the Draw tool. The second button in the Toolbar represents the Draw tool. By using this tool, you can add (which I'll describe shortly) and edit the notes in the Note pane.

To change the Start Time of a note, simply drag the left edge of its rectangle left or right. This action moves it to a different horizontal location along the Time Ruler.

To change the pitch of a note, simply drag the middle of its rectangle up or down. This action moves it to a different vertical location along the Keyboard pane.

To change the duration of a note, simply drag the right edge of its rectangle left or right. This action changes the length of the rectangle and, thus, the duration of the note.

Note Properties

Of course, sometimes you might want to make more precise changes to a note. You can do so by using the Note Properties dialog box. With the Draw tool, just right-click on a note to open the Note Properties dialog box (see Figure 7.20).

Figure 7.20
In the Note Properties dialog box, you can make precise changes to a note in the Piano Roll View.

In the Note Properties dialog box, you can make precise changes to the Start Time, Pitch, Velocity, Duration, and MIDI Channel of an individual note by typing numerical values. If you're wondering about the Fret and String parameters, I'll describe them in Chapter 11, "Making Sheet Music."

Drawing (or Adding)

In addition to editing, the Draw tool enables you to add notes to a Track by actually drawing them in. To do so, just follow these steps:

1.   Select the Draw tool by clicking on its Toolbar button.

2.   Select a duration for the new note(s). If you look a little further over in the Toolbar, you'll notice a number of buttons with note values shown on them. Clicking on these buttons determines the duration for your new note(s). For example, if you click on the Quarter Note button, the duration is set to a quarter note. You'll also see two additional buttons: one representing a dotted note and another representing a triplet note. So, if you want your notes to be dotted or triplets, click on one of those buttons, as well.

3.   Click anywhere within the Note pane at the point at which you want to place the new note(s). Remember, the horizontal position of the note determines its Start Time, and the vertical position of the note determines its pitch.

Erasing

Even though you can select and delete notes (as I described earlier), the Piano Roll View includes an Erase tool for added convenience. To use it, just select the Erase tool and then click on any note(s) in the Note pane that you want to delete. You also can click and drag the Erase tool over a number of notes to erase them all at once. By the way, the Erase tool is represented by the button in the Toolbar with the picture of an eraser shown on it. It is not the next button over from the Draw tool. I'll describe that other tool later.

Scrubbing

When you're editing the data in a Track, the procedure usually involves making your edits and then playing back the Project to hear how the changes sound. Playing back very small sections can be a bit difficult, however, especially when you're working with a fast tempo. To remedy this situation, Pro Audio provides a Scrub tool.

By using the Scrub tool, you can drag your mouse pointer over the data in the Piano Roll View and hear what it sounds like. To use it, simply select the Scrub tool by clicking on its button in the Toolbar (the one with the small yellow speaker shown on it). Then click and drag your mouse pointer over the data in the Note pane. Dragging left to right plays the data forward (what would normally happen during playback), and dragging right to left enables you to hear the data played in reverse. This capability can be useful for testing very short (one or two measure) sections.

TIP

Instead of using the Scrub tool, you might want to try a more useful technique for hearing what your changes sound like. Did you know that you can edit the data in your Project as it's being played back? Of course, it's a bit difficult to edit anything while Pro Audio is scrolling the display as the Project plays. I like to work on a small section of a Project at a time. I set up a section of the Project to loop over and over, and as Pro Audio is playing the data, I make any changes I think might be needed. Because the data is being played back while I edit, I can instantly hear what the changes sound like. This procedure is much easier than having to keep going back and forth, making changes and manually starting and stopping playback. You learned about looping in Chapter 6, "Recording and Playback." By the way, you can use any of the Views to edit your data while Pro Audio is playing a Project. This tip is not just for the Piano Roll View.

Dealing with Controllers

When you open a MIDI Track in the Piano Roll view, in addition to the notes in the Note pane, Pro Audio displays the MIDI controller data for that Track in the Controller pane (see Figure 7.21). Because there are many different types of MIDI controller messages, to help you avoid confusion, the Piano Roll View displays only one type at a time. You can tell the type of MIDI controller that's being displayed by looking at the Control Type drop-down lists located in the Toolbar right next to the Scrub tool button. The first list shows the type of controller being displayed. The second list shows the number of the controller being displayed. And the third list shows the MIDI channel being used for that controller. You can change the values for any of these lists by simply clicking on them and selecting a new value from the list that pops up. Initially, MIDI Note Velocity is shown when you open the Piano Roll View.

Figure 7.21
MIDI controller data for a Track is displayed in the Controller pane when you open the Piano Roll View.

Each controller is represented by a colored line that runs from the bottom of the Controller pane to the top. The height of the line designates the value of the controller according to the ruler on the left side of the Controller pane. This ruler gives you a reference to go by for determining the value of a controller; it usually runs from 0 to 127, starting at the bottom of the Controller pane and going all the way to the top. The values can be different according to the type of controller being edited. The horizontal location of a controller designates its Start Time according to the Time Ruler at the top of the Piano Roll View.

NOTE

In one instance, the controllers in the Controller pane and the ruler values appear differently. If you select the Pitch Wheel Event type for editing, you'll notice that, instead of originating at the bottom of the Controller pane, the controllers start at the center and extend either up or down (see Figure 7.22). They do so because values for the Pitch Wheel range from -8192 to 0 to +8191, which you can see in the ruler values. Other than that, Pitch Wheel Events are handled exactly the same way as any other types.

Figure 7.22
The Pitch Wheel is the one exception to how controllers are displayed in the Controller pane.

Editing

You edit controllers exactly the same way as you do notes in terms of selecting, copying, cutting, deleting, pasting, and so on. Unfortunately, no precision editing is available as is available with the Note Properties dialog box, although you can edit the numerical values of controllers via the Event List View (which you'll learn about later in the chapter). One other exception is that you can't move controllers by simply dragging them, like you can with notes. You have to cut and paste them instead.

Erasing and Scrubbing

The Eraser and Scrub tools work with controllers exactly the same as they do with notes.

Drawing

You add controllers pretty much in the same way that you add notes, but with a couple of exceptions. When you're using the Draw tool, in addition to clicking in the pane to add a single controller, you also can click and drag within the pane to add a whole series of controllers at once.

In addition, you can use another tool, called the Draw Line tool (its button is located right next to the Draw tool button in the Toolbar), to create a smooth series of controllers starting at one value and smoothly increasing or decreasing to another value. Without this tool, it's a bit difficult to achieve the same effect by drawing freely with the Draw tool. To use the Draw Line tool, you just click anywhere within the Controller pane at the controller value you want to begin with and then drag either to the left or right within the pane to draw a line that ends at a different time and a different value. When you release the mouse button, Pro Audio adds a smooth series of controller values from the first point to the second point in the pane.

CAUTION

If you draw over existing controller values in the Controller pane, the existing values are deleted and replaced with the new values that you have added.

Inserting

Pro Audio provides one other way to add a smooth series of controller values to your Tracks: the Insert Series of Controllers function. I find using the Draw Line tool in the Piano Roll View much more intuitive, but if you need to add controllers over a very long span of time, the Insert Series of Controllers function can be useful. You use it as follows:

1. Select the Track to which you want to add the controller values. You can do so either in the Piano Roll View or the Track View.

2. Select Insert > Series of Controllers to open the Insert Series of Controllers dialog box (see Figure 7.23).

Figure 7.23
By using the Insert Series of Controllers dialog box, you can add a series of controllers that change smoothly from one value to another.

3. In the Insert section, choose the type of controller that you want to add, the number of the controller (if appropriate), and the MIDI channel you want the controller to use.

4. In the Value Range section, type numbers for the Begin and End parameters. These numbers determine the values of the controller over the range of the series. For example, if you're using a volume controller type, you can have an instrument get louder over time by typing in a small value for Begin and a larger value for End. If you want the instrument to get softer over time, type a larger value for Begin and a smaller value for End.

5   In the Time Range section, type the measure, beat, and tick values for the location in the Project where you want the series of controllers to be inserted.

TIP

You also can set the Time Range parameters before you open the Insert Series of Controllers dialog box by dragging your mouse pointer over the Time Ruler in either the Piano Roll View or the Track View. This action sets up a selection within the Project that is automatically used to set the From and Thru values of the Time Range parameters.

Bank/Patch Change

The one type of data that the Piano Roll View doesn't enable you to manipulate is the Bank/Patch Change. This type of Event is useful when you want the sound of your MIDI instrument to change automatically during playback of your Project. Pro Audio provides an Insert Bank/Patch Change function that you can use in case you need it.

Utilizing the Insert Bank/Patch Change function is very simple. You just do the following:

1. Click on the name of the Track in the Track List pane into which you want to insert the Bank/Patch Change.

2. Set the Now Time to the measure, beat, and tick at which you want the Bank/Patch Change to occur.

3. Select Insert > Bank/Patch Change to open the Bank/Patch Change dialog box.

4. Choose a Bank Select Method, Bank, and Patch from the appropriate drop-down lists.

5. Click on OK.

Pro Audio then inserts a Bank/Patch Change Event in the Track at the Now Time that you specified. By the way, you can insert (and also edit) Bank/Patch Change Events by using the Event List View, but I'll describe that task later in this chapter.

Using the Audio View

For precise editing of the audio data in your Project, you need to use the Audio View (see Figure 7.24). Using the Audio View, you can edit, process, and delete the audio data within your audio Tracks. Similar in appearance to the Track View, the Audio View displays Tracks in a vertical list, with the data in each Track running horizontally from left to right along a Time Ruler.

Figure 7.24
The Audio View resembles the Track View in appearance.

More precisely, the Audio View consists of three major sections: the Toolbar (located at the top of the View, containing all the View's related controls); the Clips pane (located in the main part of the View, displaying the audio Events in the currently selected Track); and the Track List (located at the left side of the View, showing a list of all the Tracks currently being displayed). The Audio View can display the data from more than one Track at a time. As in the Piano Roll View, this View offers a Pick Tracks button located in the Toolbar. Using this button, you can change the Tracks being displayed without having to close and reopen the Audio View.

You'll also notice that the Audio View has scroll bars and Zoom tools just like the Track View. These tools work the same way that they do in the Track View. In addition, this View contains a Snap to Grid function, which is represented by the Grid button in the Toolbar. Other similarities are the Marker area and the Time Ruler, which are located just above the Clips pane. The Time Ruler in the Audio View is a little more sophisticated, however, because in addition to showing time in measures, beats, and ticks, it also can show time as hours, minutes, seconds, and frames (SMPTE) or as digital audio sample numbers. (Remember, you learned about samples in Chapter 1, "Understanding MIDI and Digital Audio.") You can change the Time Ruler units by clicking on the appropriate buttons in the Toolbar, which are located just to the left of the Snap to Grid button.

Opening the View

You open the Audio View the same way you do the Piano Roll View, but instead of selecting a Track or Clip containing MIDI data, you must select a Track or Clip containing audio data. Whichever method you use to open the Audio View, the data from the Track(s) you selected is displayed with the Track information and controls shown in the Track List and the Clips/Events shown in the Clips pane. At this point, the Audio View starts to show its differences from the Track View.

The Track List contains Mute, Solo, and Record buttons for each Track, along with the Track number and the Amplitude Scale. By using the Amplitude Scale, you can measure the loudness of the audio data in the Track. You can set the Scale to show its measurements in decibels (dB), digital audio sample numbers, or as a percentage by right-clicking on the Scale and selecting the appropriate setting from the pop-up menu.

The Clips pane is also a bit different in the Audio View; in addition to the Clips within a Track, the individual audio Events within each Clip also are shown.

NOTE

An audio Event is similar to a MIDI Event in that it can contain a single sound just as a MIDI Event represents a single note. Audio Events are different, however, because they also can represent a recording of any length. Basically, audio Events are used to split audio Clips into smaller, more manageable pieces of data. For example, say you have a long audio Clip that contains a percussion performance—like that of a solo snare drum—and you want to process some of the snare drum hits differently. You can split the Clip into separate Events (each containing a single snare drum hit), which enables you to process the single snare sounds more easily. Notice that audio Events are indicated by a small red triangle located at the bottom of the Clip display, which is attached to a vertical blue line running across the Clip. These triangles are called *Anchors*. Also, the beginning of each Clip has an Anchor because, even if a Clip doesn't contain any individual audio Events, the Clip itself is considered to be an audio Event. Pro Audio identifies all audio data in a Project by identifying the Anchors.

Another difference between the Audio View and the Track View is that you can view the audio waveforms in much more detail.

NOTE

An *audio waveform* is a graphical representation of sound. Let me try to explain by using the cup and string analogy. Remember when you were a kid, and you set up your own intercom system between your bedroom and your tree house by using nothing but a couple of paper cups and a long piece of string? You poked a hole in the bottom of each cup and then tied one end of the string to one cup and the other end of the string to the other cup. Your friend would be in the tree house with one of the cups, and you would be in your bedroom with the other. As you talked into your cup, your friend could hear you by putting his cup to his ear and vice versa. Why did it work?

Well, when you talked into the cup, the sound of your voice vibrated the bottom of the cup, making it act like a microphone. This movement, in turn, vibrated the string up and down, and the string carried the vibrations to the other cup. This movement made the bottom of that cup vibrate so that it acted like a speaker, thus enabling your friend hear what you said. If it were possible for you to freeze the string while it was in motion and then zoom in on it so that you could see the vibrations, it would look similar to the audio waveforms shown in the Audio View (see Figure 7.25).

As you can see, a waveform shows up and down movements just like a vibrating string. A line, called the *Zero Axis*, runs horizontally through the center of the waveform. The Zero Axis represents the point in a waveform at which there are no vibrations or there is no sound, so the value of the audio data at the Zero Axis is the number zero (also known as *zero amplitude*). When a waveform moves above or below the Zero Axis, vibrations occur, and thus there is sound. The amplitude value of a waveform in these places depends on how high above or how low below the Zero Axis the waveform is at a certain point in time (shown on the Time Ruler). You can read the value of a waveform by using the Amplitude Scale.

Figure 7.25
An audio waveform is similar to that of a vibrating string if you could freeze and zoom in on it to observe the vibrations.

CHAPTER 7

Editing

As you might have guessed already, most of the editing functions in the Audio View work in the same way that they do in the Track View. For example, to select a Track, just click on the Track number in the Track List. To select a Clip or audio Event, just click on it. All other methods of selection (that I've described previously), such as selecting only part of a Clip, work here as well. You just need to be sure that the Select tool is activated by clicking on the Select tool button (same as in the Piano Roll View) in the Toolbar.

Other editing functions work the same way, too. You can copy, cut, paste, move, and delete as you learned in the Track View section of this chapter. The Audio View even provides a Scrub tool, which works exactly the same way as in the Piano Roll View. I do, however, need to explain a few differences.

Snap to Zero Crossing Function

One of these differences is that you need to make sure to edit your audio at zero crossings in the waveform to avoid noisy pops or clicks. You can do so by using the Snap to Zero Crossing function, which you access via the Toolbar. The Snap to Zero Crossing button is located between the Snap to Grid and Pick Tracks buttons.

The Snap to Zero Crossing function (when activated) makes sure that, when you make a selection, both the beginning and the end of your selection fall on zero crossings in the audio waveform.

NOTE

Remember the description of the Zero Axis? Well, any point in an audio waveform that lands on the Zero Axis is called a *zero crossing*. It's called that because, as the waveform moves up and down, it crosses over the Zero Axis.

Why is it important that your selections line up with zero crossings? Because a zero crossing is a point in the audio waveform at which no sound is being made, it provides a perfect spot at which to edit the waveform-for example, when you're cutting and pasting pieces of audio. If you edit an audio waveform at a point where it's either above or below the Zero Axis, you might introduce glitches, which can come in the form of audible pops and clicks. You get these glitches because you cut at a moment when sound is being produced. You also get them because, when you're pasting pieces of audio together, you cannot guarantee that the ends of each waveform will line up perfectly (except, of course, if they both are at zero crossings).

The Split Select Tool

Another difference about the Audio View is that it provides a tool, the Scissors tool, which you won't find in any of the other Views. You access this tool via the Scissors tool button in the Toolbar (the button with the picture of a pair of scissors shown on it).

By using the Scissors tool, you can split long audio Clips and Events into smaller ones. It's actually very simple to use. Just select the Scissors tool by clicking on the Scissors tool button in the Toolbar, and then click anywhere within a Clip or Event in the Clips pane. Pro Audio places an Anchor at the point in the waveform at which you clicked, and the Clip or Event is split into two different Events.

You also can use the Scissors tool to create an audio Event of an exact size by clicking and dragging within an existing audio Event. As you drag, a rectangle is drawn within the waveform (see Figure 7.26).

Figure 7.26

You can create a new audio Event by clicking and dragging.

When the rectangle becomes the size that you want the new audio Event to be, release your mouse button. This action splits the original audio Event into three new audio Events, with the one that you defined placed in between the other two.

The Draw Line Tool

Like the Piano Roll View, the Audio View provides a Draw Line tool. This tool works differently in the Audio View, however. Here, you use the Draw Line tool to create a fade-in or a fade-out for your audio data.

> **NOTE**
>
> A *fade-in* is a gradual and smooth increase from a low volume (loudness) to a higher volume. This increase in volume is also called a *crescendo* in musical terms. A *fade-out* is the exact opposite—a gradual and smooth decrease from a high volume to a lower volume. In musical terms, this decrease in volume is called a *decrescendo*.

To apply a fade-in or fade-out to an audio Event, follow these steps:

1. Activate the Draw Line tool by clicking on the Draw Line tool button in the Toolbar.

2. Click and hold the mouse on the waveform of the audio Event to which you want to add a fade. If you want to add a fade-in, be sure to click at a low amplitude point on the waveform. For example, to have the audio fade in from total silence, click at zero percent (the Zero Axis) on the waveform. If you want to add a fade-out, be sure to click at a high amplitude point on the waveform. For example, to have the audio fade out from the loudest amplitude, click at 100 percent on the waveform.

3. Drag either to the left or to the right (depending on what part of the audio Event you want to change). As you drag, Pro Audio draws two lines to give you a graphical representation of the fade that you are creating (see Figure 7.27).

Figure 7.27
Click and drag by using the Draw Line tool to add a fade to an audio Event.

4. If you're creating a fade-in, drag to an amplitude value that is higher than the value you initially set in Step 2. If you're creating a fade-out, drag to an amplitude value that is lower than the value you initially set in Step 2.

5. Release your mouse button.

Pro Audio then changes the audio data in the audio Event by raising or lowering the amplitude values to create either a fade-in or fade-out, depending on your actions.

Audio Event Properties

Just as the notes in the Piano Roll View have properties that you can change, so do audio Events. You change the properties of an audio Event by right-clicking on the Event and selecting Properties from the pop-up menu to open the Audio Event Properties dialog box (see Figure 7.28).

Figure 7.28
By using the Audio Event Properties dialog box, you can change the properties of an audio Event.

Time and Sample

You use the Time parameter of the Audio Event Properties dialog box to set the measure, beat, and tick at which the audio Event will be positioned within the Project. Just type a value. The Sample parameter has the same effect, but you can set the position as a number of samples from the beginning of the Project (being sample zero). Remember that you can set the Time Ruler in the Audio View to show sample numbers as the units of measurement.

Velocity

The Velocity parameter could actually be called Volume or Loudness, because it controls how loud an audio Event will sound during playback. The trick here, though, is that changing this value does not change the actual audio data in the Event. Instead, Pro Audio either amplifies or reduces the volume of the Event by scaling the audio data being played with the Velocity value that you enter. The Velocity can have a value between 0 (no sound) and 127 (the loudest). The default Velocity value is 103, which corresponds to the actual volume of the waveform. This means that if you leave the Velocity value at 103, Pro Audio will play the audio Event at the actual volume of the waveform (the volume at which it was recorded). If you enter a value that's higher than 103, Pro Audio will play the audio Event at a higher volume than the actual volume of the waveform. And if you enter a value that is lower than 103, Pro Audio will play the audio Event at a lower volume than the actual volume of the waveform.

Name

You use the Name parameter to assign a name to an audio Event. Just type something in, if you want.

Duration

The Duration parameter basically tells you the length of an audio Event in sample numbers. For obvious reasons, you can't change this parameter directly. However, you can change the length of an audio Event via editing, as you learned earlier.

Anchor Sample

The Anchor Sample parameter controls at what sample number within an audio Event its Anchor is placed. Normally, the Anchor is placed at the very beginning of an audio Event, thus having an Anchor Sample of zero. But you can change the position of the Anchor within the audio Event by typing in a different sample number.

TIP

You also can change the position of the Anchor in an audio Event by simply clicking and dragging on its red triangle with the Select tool.

Why would you want to change the position of an Anchor? Well, changing an Anchor position also changes the time at which an audio Event will be played. Basically, it gives you a quick way to move the Event to an earlier time along the Time Ruler. But even more important, it provides a different reference for your editing operations, as well. For example, if you drag and drop an Event to a new position, Pro Audio uses the Anchor as the time for the Event, even if it is not placed at the beginning of the Event. So, Pro Audio lines up other Events according to the Anchor rather than the beginning of the Event. You can use this procedure if you want to line up overlapping Events and so on. Do a little experimenting, and you'll see what I mean.

TIP

I was going to create a little audio editing practice example like I did with the practice arrangement in the Track View section of this chapter, but Cakewalk has already provided a nice tutorial on audio editing. You can find it in the Pro Audio User's Manual on pages 2-29 to 2-39. Actually, it runs a little bit longer, but these pages cover the audio editing part of the tutorial. Be sure to check it out to get some basic practice with the Audio View.

Using the Event List View

For the most precise data editing (meaning individual Events and their properties), you have to use the Event List View (see Figure 7.29). Using this View, you can add, edit, and delete any kind of Event in any Track within the entire Project. The Event List View doesn't resemble any of the other Views; instead of providing a graphical representation of your data, it provides a numerical representation, which you can edit and view. The Event List View displays Events as one long list of columns and rows (similar to that of a spreadsheet). Each row holds the data for a single Event, and the Event's different properties are separated by columns.

Figure 7.29

You can use the Event List View to edit Events numerically by using a spreadsheet-like format.

You can use the first column in the List to select Events (which I'll describe later). The second column (titled Trk) shows the Track number in which an Event is stored. The third column (titled HMSF) shows the start time of an Event as hours, minutes, seconds, and frames. The fourth column (titled MBT) also shows the start time of an Event but as measures, beats, and ticks. If an Event is a MIDI Event, the fifth column (titled Ch) shows the MIDI channel to which that Event is assigned. The sixth column (titled Kind) shows the type of data an Event holds (for example, a MIDI Note Event or an Audio Event). The seventh, eighth, and ninth columns (titled Data) hold the data values associated with each Event. For instance, for a MIDI Note Event, the seventh column holds the pitch, the eighth column holds the velocity, and the ninth column holds the duration for the note.

Because the Event List View doesn't have any graphical data to contend with, it doesn't provide any Snap to Grid, Zoom, Time Ruler, or Marker features. It does enable you to scroll the List up and down and left and right so that you can access all the Events shown. It also provides a Toolbar full of buttons (which I'll describe later). One button that you'll recognize, though, is the Pick Tracks button. Just as with the other Views, the Event List View enables you to display the data from multiple Tracks at once.

Opening the View

You open the Event List View via the Track View. You simply select one or more Tracks and then either select View > Event List or right-click on one of the selected Tracks and choose Event List from the pop-up menu. That's all there is to it.

Filtering Events

Many different types of Events are available in Pro Audio, and sometimes having to wade through them all in the Event List View can get a bit confusing, especially when you're displaying the data from multiple Tracks. To help you deal with the problem, the Event List View enables you to filter out each of the Event types from being displayed. This filtering does not affect the data at all; it just helps to unclutter the List display if that's what you need.

The first seventeen buttons in the Toolbar represent different Event types. Initially, all of these buttons are set so that all Event types are shown in the List when you open the Event List View. By clicking on a button, you can filter out its associated Event type from the List. You can click as many of the buttons as you want to filter out multiple types of Events. Clicking on a button again turns off its associated Event type filter so that the Events can be shown in the List again. To see the type of Event with which each button is associated, just hover your mouse pointer over a button until the pop-up text appears, showing the name of the Event type.

The Event Manager

If you find it easier to deal with the Event types by name rather than by using the buttons, you can use the Event Manager. Just click on the Event Manager button on the Toolbar (the one with the check mark shown on it) to open the Event Manager dialog box (see Figure 7.30).

Figure 7.30
You can use the Event Manager dialog box to filter Event types by name.

Initially, all the Event types are activated so that they will be displayed in the List. To filter out a certain type, just click on it to remove its check mark. You also can use the All/None buttons to quickly activate or deactivate groups of Event types. Click on the Close button when you're done.

TIP
You also can filter out Event types by simply right-clicking anywhere within the Event List and then selecting an Event type from the pop-up list.

Editing Events

If you've ever used a spreadsheet application, you'll be right at home with editing Events in the Event List View. To navigate through the list, you use the arrow keys on your computer keyboard. These keys move a small, rectangular cursor through the List. This cursor represents the Now Time. As you move the cursor up and down through the List, the Now Time changes to reflect the time of the Event upon which the cursor is positioned. You also can move the cursor (which I'll call the Now Time cursor from now on) left and right to access the different Event parameters.

Changing

To change an Event parameter, just position the Now Time cursor over the parameter, type a new value, and then press the Enter key on your computer keyboard to accept the new value.

CHAPTER 7

TIP

You can also change an Event parameter by double-clicking on it and then clicking on the little plus or minus buttons that appear to increase or decrease the value, respectively.

You can change the start time in the HMSF or MBT columns, the MIDI channel, the type of Event, and most or all of the values in the data columns, depending on the type of Event that you're editing. The only thing you can't change is the Track number of an Event.

The Kind Column

Changing the type of an Event via the parameter in the Kind column is a bit different from changing the values of the other parameters. Instead of typing a new value, you must either press the Enter key on your computer keyboard or double-click the parameter. This action opens the Kind of Event dialog box (see Figure 7.31). The Kind of Event dialog box displays a list of all the Event types available. Select the type of Event you want to use, and then click on OK.

Figure 7.31
You use the Kind of Event dialog box to change the type of an Event.

Selecting

If you ever need to copy, cut, or paste Events in the Event List View, you have to select them first. To select a single Event, just click in the first column of the row representing the Event. You also can select more than one Event by dragging your mouse pointer within the first column of the List. If you want to remove a selection, click or drag a second time.

Inserting

You also can add new Events to the List by using the Insert function. It works as follows:

1. Position the Now Time cursor at the point in the List at which you want to insert a new Event.

TIP

Setting the position of the Now Time cursor in the Event List View isn't very intuitive. Because the List gives you such a specific close-up look at your data, it's sometimes difficult to tell where in your Project the Now Time cursor is pointing. You might find it easier by using one of the other Views (such as the Track View or the Piano Roll View) to position the Now Time cursor. That way, you get a graphical representation of your project and a better feel for the placement of the cursor. Then you can simply switch to the Event View, and the cursor will be positioned exactly (or at least very close) to the point where you want to insert the new Event.

2. Either press the Insert key on your computer keyboard or click on the Insert Event button in the Toolbar (the one with the bright yellow star shown on it). Pro Audio creates a new Event in the List by using the same parameter values as the Event upon which the Now Time was positioned.

3. Edit the Event parameters.

TIP

When you're changing the type of Event by using the Kind parameter, the values in the Data columns change according to the type of Event that you choose. For a list of all the types of Events available, along with all of their associated parameters, look at pages 6-44 and 6-45 in your Pro Audio User's manual.

Special Events

Two types of Events in Pro Audio can be accessed only via the Event List View. You can't manipulate them in any of the other Views. The first one, called a Text Event, enables you to add notes to the data in your Project. I'm not talking about musical notes. I'm talking about text notes—you know, like those little sticky notes that you have plastered all over your studio. Text Events can act as little reminders to yourself, in case you need to keep track of some kind of special information in certain parts of your Project. I've never had a lot of use for Text Events, but it's nice to know they're available if I need them.

The other type of special Event is called the MCIcmd Event or the Windows Media Control Interface (MCI) command Event. You can use the MCIcmd Event to control the multimedia-related hardware and software in your computer system. For example, by setting the type of an Event to MCIcmd and setting the Event's Data parameter to PLAY CDAUDIO, you can make the audio CD inside your CD-ROM drive start to play. You also can use MCIcmd Events to play audio files, video files, and more. But the problem is that none of these files can be synchronized to the music in your Project, so you can't really use these Events for too many things. In addition, the subject of MCI commands can be complex, and it's well beyond the scope of this chapter. If you want to find more information, take a look at the following area on the Microsoft World Wide Web site: **http://msdn.microsoft.com/library/psdk/multimed/mci_7vvt.htm**.

Deleting

Erasing Events from the List is as easy as it gets. Just move the Now Time cursor to the row of the Event that you want to remove and then click on the Delete Event button in the Toolbar (the one with the big red X shown on it).

Multiple Events

If you want to delete more than one Event at once, select the Events that you want to remove and then select Edit > Cut to open the Cut dialog box. The parameters in this dialog box work the same way as described in the Track View section of this chapter.

Playing

If you want to quickly preview the Event that you're currently editing, you can have Pro Audio play back that single Event by holding down the Shift key on your computer keyboard and then pressing the spacebar. If you continue holding the Shift key, each press of the spacebar scrolls down through the List and plays each Event. This capability is especially useful for testing MIDI Note Events.

TIP

You can print a hard copy reference of the Event List by using your printer (if you have one connected to your computer system). While the Event List View is open, just select File > Print to print a copy of the list. You also can preview the List before printing it by choosing File > Print Preview.

Using the Tempo View

You learned how to set the initial tempo for a Project by using the Tempo Toolbar in Chapter 4, "Working with Projects." But, in addition to the initial Project tempo, you also can have the tempo change automatically during playback. To enable you to specify tempo changes within a Project, Pro Audio provides the Tempo View (see Figure 7.32). The Tempo View has some similarities to the Piano Roll View in that it displays a graphical representation of the data that you need to manipulate—in this case, tempo. The Tempo View shows the tempo as a line graph with the horizontal axis denoting time (via the Time Ruler) and the vertical axis denoting tempo value.

Figure 7.32
The Tempo View displays the tempo in a Project as a line graph.

More precisely, the Tempo View consists of three major sections: the Toolbar (located at the top of the View, containing all the View's related controls); the Tempo pane (located in the main part of the View, displaying all the tempo changes in the Project as a line graph); and the Tempo Change List pane (located at the right side of the View, showing a list of all the Tempo changes within the Project). Because tempo affects the whole Project, no Track selection tools are available here.

Because the Tempo View shows tempo changes graphically, it has scroll bars and Zoom tools just like in the Piano Roll View. And, of course, these tools work the same way here. In addition, this View provides a Snap to Grid function, which is represented by the Grid button in the Toolbar. The Tempo View also contains a Marker area and a Time Ruler located just above the Tempo pane. Along the left side of the Tempo pane are the tempo measurements, which are used to show the value of the tempo changes displayed in the line graph.

Opening the View

To open the Tempo View, simply select View > Tempo. You don't need to select a Track or Clip or anything else. For a new Project (or a Project that doesn't contain any tempo changes), the Tempo View displays a straight horizontal line located vertically on the graph at the tempo measurement value that corresponds to the current tempo setting for the Project. So, for instance, if your Project has a main tempo of 100, then the line is shown at a tempo measurement of 100 on the graph. In addition to the horizontal line, a single entry in the Tempo Change List pane shows the measure, beat, and tick at which the Tempo Event occurs, along with the tempo value itself. In this example, it is 1:01:000 for the measure, beat, and tick, and 100 for the tempo value.

Editing

Just as you can edit controller messages graphically in the Piano Roll View, you can use the Tempo View to edit tempo changes. Also, like the Piano Roll View, the Tempo View provides Select, Draw, Draw Line, and Erase tools. All of these tools work the same way as they do in the Piano Roll View. You can use the Select tool to select individual and groups of tempo changes by clicking and dragging. By using the Draw tool, you can literally draw in tempo changes on the line graph in the Tempo pane. The Draw Line tool enables you to create smooth tempo changes from one value to another by clicking and dragging. And by using the Erase tool, you can erase single and multiple tempo changes by clicking and dragging. As you draw and erase within the Tempo pane, the line graph changes its shape accordingly to display how the tempo will change over time as the Project plays. An increase in the tempo (*accelerando*, in musical terms) is shown as an incline in the line graph, and a decrease in tempo (*diminuendo*, in musical terms) is shown as a decline in the line graph.

The Tempo Change List

As I mentioned earlier, tempo changes are also listed numerically in the Tempo Change List. Luckily, you can edit them here, too. I find it easier and more accurate to add and edit tempo changes via the Tempo Change List rather than draw them in.

Inserting

To add a new tempo change to the list, do the following:

1. Set the Now Time to the measure, beat, and tick at which you want the tempo change to occur.

2. Click on the Insert Tempo button in the Toolbar (the one with the bright yellow star shown on it) to open the Tempo dialog box (see Figure 7.33).

Figure 7.33
In the Tempo dialog box, you can add and edit Tempo Events.

3. Enter a value for the Tempo parameter. You also can tap out a tempo by clicking on the Click Here to Tap Tempo button. When you click repeatedly on the button, Pro Audio measures the time between each click and calculates the tempo at which you're clicking. It then enters the value into the Tempo parameter automatically.

TIP

Instead of using your mouse to click on the Click Here to Tap Tempo button, you might find it easier (and more accurate) to use the spacebar on your computer keyboard. Click on the button with your mouse once just to highlight it, and then use your spacebar to tap out a tempo value.

4. Make sure that the Insert a New Tempo option is activated.

5. You shouldn't have to enter a value for the Starting at Time parameter because you set the Now Time earlier. However, you can change it here if you want to.

6. Either activate or deactivate the Stretch Audio option.

NOTE

When you add tempo changes to your Project, you change the speed of playback. For MIDI data, changing the speed is no problem, because Pro Audio simply sends the data out to your instruments at a different rate in time. Audio data, however, is a different story. Because audio data is actual recorded sound, the tempo at which it is recorded is the tempo that must be used to play it back. To try to get around this problem, Pro Audio provides a Stretch Audio function that processes the audio data so that it can be played back at faster or slower speeds and still remain synchronized to the MIDI data in your Project. The only problem is that making drastic tempo changes to an audio recording will introduce unpleasant sounding artifacts. So, here's my advice: If you want to include tempo changes in your Project, either use only MIDI data, or map out all the tempo changes at the beginning of the session and then record all the audio, taking into account the tempo changes as you play your performance. By the way, you also can select a button in the Toolbar to switch the Stretch Audio function on or off when you're working with the graph in the Tempo pane.

7.   Click on OK.

Pro Audio adds the new tempo change and displays it in the Tempo Change List as well as on the graph in the Tempo pane.

Deleting and Editing

You also can edit or remove a tempo change from the List by using the appropriate toolbar buttons. First, select the tempo change that you want to edit or delete by clicking on it in the List. If you want to delete the tempo change, click on the Delete Tempo button in the Toolbar (the one with the big red X shown on it). If you want to edit the tempo change, click on the Tempo Properties button in the Toolbar (the very last button at the right end of the Toolbar). This action opens the Tempo dialog box. Make any changes necessary, as per the same settings that I described for inserting a new tempo change.

Using the Tempo Commands

In addition to the Tempo View (and the Tempo Toolbar), Pro Audio provides two other tempo-related functions. The Insert Tempo Change function works the same way as adding a new tempo change in the Tempo Change List in the Tempo View. However, this function can be used from within any of the other Views. To access it, just select Insert > Tempo Change to open the Tempo dialog box (which you learned about earlier).

Inserting a Series of Tempos

Pro Audio also provides a function that enables you to insert a series of tempos so that you can have the tempo change smoothly from one value to another over time. Using it is similar to using the Draw Line tool in the Tempo View, but here you specify your values numerically. You use this function as follows:

1. Select Insert > Series of Tempos to open the Insert Series of Tempos dialog box (see Figure 7.34).

Figure 7.34

You can change the tempo smoothly from one value to another by using the Insert Series of Tempos dialog box.

2. In the Tempo Range section, enter a beginning and an ending value for the range of tempos to be inserted.

3. In the Time Range section, enter a beginning and an ending value for the range of time in your Project in which you want the tempo changes to occur.

TIP

If you make a selection by dragging your mouse pointer in the Time Ruler of the Track View, for instance, before you select Insert > Series Of Tempos, the Time Range values in the Insert Series of Tempos dialog box are set according to your selection. This shortcut makes it easier to see where in your Project the tempo changes will be inserted.

4. For the Step parameter, enter a beat and tick value denoting how often you want a tempo change to be inserted within the Time Range that you specified. For example, if you enter a value of 1.00, then the Insert Series of Tempos function will insert a new tempo change at every beat within the Time Range that you specified.

5. Set the Stretch Audio option.

6. Click on OK.

Pro Audio then inserts a smooth series of tempo changes, starting and ending with the Tempo Range values that you specified within the Time Range that you specified. Any existing tempo changes are overwritten.

8

Exploring the Editing Tools

In Chapter 7, "Editing Basics," you learned about some of the essential editing features found in Pro Audio, including all the Views (and the tools they provide), as well as how to manipulate your data via copy, cut, paste, move, delete, and so on. Although these features provide a lot of power, you might be asking yourself, "Is that all there is?" Not likely! In addition to its fundamental tools, Pro Audio provides a full arsenal of sophisticated editing features. Some can be used to process audio data, some to process MIDI data, and some to process both kinds of data. One aspect that they all have in common, however, is that they can be accessed within more than one View (similar to the copy, cut, and paste functions). Of course, as you learned previously, for MIDI data, you'll be using the Track, Piano Roll, Staff, and Event Views, and for audio data, you'll be using the Track and Audio Views.

This chapter covers the following:

▶ Advanced data selection
▶ Splitting and combining audio Events
▶ Changing the loudness of audio Events
▶ Equalization
▶ Quantization
▶ Transposition
▶ Various advanced timing features

CHAPTER 8

Advanced Data Selection

As you learned in the preceding chapter, you can select the data in your Project within each of the Views by using some basic clicking and dragging techniques. Pro Audio also provides some more sophisticated data selection features that enable you to use time as well as individual Event Properties for more precise editing.

By Time

If you ever need to select a range of data within a Project that is based on time rather than data that is neatly tucked away into individual Clips, you can select Edit > Select > By Time to do so. For example, say you need to copy the data in Track 8 that falls between the range of 4:2:010 (measure, beat, tick) and 13:3:050. But what if that data is stored in multiple Clips within that range, and the Clips don't neatly start and end at the beginning and ending times that you specified? That's the kind of situation for which this feature is useful. It works like this:

1.   Select Edit > Select > By Time to open the Select by Time dialog box (see Figure 8.1).

Figure 8.1
You can use the Select by Time dialog box to define a time range within your Project in which data will be selected for editing.

2.   Type the beginning (From) and ending (Thru) measure, beat, and tick values to define the range of time that you want to select. Then click on OK. You use this dialog box to select a range of time within your Project, but it doesn't select any actual data. For that, you need to select the Track(s) that you want to edit.

3.   In the Track View or the Audio View (the only two Views in which you can select Tracks), select the Track(s) containing the data that you want to edit.

Pro Audio selects the data within the Clips within the Tracks within the time range that you specified so that you can edit it by using copy, cut, and the other features that you'll learn about in this chapter.

> **TIP**
> You also can make time selections within any of the Views by simply clicking and dragging on the Time Ruler (you learned about this approach in Chapter 7, "Editing Basics"), but by selecting Edit > Select > By Time, you can make more precise selections because you can enter the exact numerical values for the measures, beats, and ticks that define the range.

By Filter

For really precise editing tasks, you can select Edit > Select > By Filter. Using this approach, you can refine a selection that you've already made with any of the other methods discussed previously. For instance, if you select some Clips or Tracks in the Track View, you can then select Edit > Select > By Filter to zero in (so to speak) your selection even further to the individual Events within those Clips and Tracks, based on their Event Properties.

For example, say you have a MIDI Track in which you want to change all the notes with a pitch of C4 to C5. You can easily select only those notes by selecting Edit > Select > By Filter and then change their pitch by using the Transpose feature (which you'll learn about later). All the C4 pitches are then changed to C5, but none of the other notes in the Track are affected. This feature works as follows:

1. Select the Clip(s), Track(s), or set of Events that you want to use as your initial selection. You can select Clips and Tracks in the Track View or a group of Events in the Piano Roll View, Event View, or Staff View.

2. Select Edit > Select > By Filter to open the Event Filter–Select Some dialog box (see Figure 8.2).

Figure 8.2
You can use the Event Filter–Select Some dialog box to set the criteria for the type of data that you want to have selected.

CHAPTER 8

3. Does this dialog box look familiar? The Event Filter–Select Some dialog box is the same as the Event Filter–Search dialog box, which you learned about in Chapter 5, "Getting Around in Pro Audio." The same information about how to use all the options applies here, so go ahead and set the options as you want.

> **TIP**
>
> As with the Event Filter–Search dialog box, the Event Filter–Select Some dialog box enables you to save Presets for instant access to your favorite settings. By the way, Presets are also available in many of the features that you'll learn about later in this chapter. I described how to use them in Chapter 5, "Getting Around in Pro Audio."

4. Click on OK.

Pro Audio searches through the data in your initial selection, finds the Events that fall under the filter parameters that you specified, and then selects those Events while leaving any other Events alone. If you want to refine your selection even further, just select Edit > Select > By Filter again on the previous selection results.

Advanced Audio Editing

By using the Select, Scissors, and Draw Line tools in the Audio View, you can manipulate the data in your audio Tracks in a variety of ways. The Audio View also provides a number of advanced features that you can use to adjust the volume, apply equalization, extract timing and pitch, and even reverse the data within audio Events. You access all of these features by right-clicking in the Clips pane of the Audio View. (You also can access them by selecting Edit > Audio, but right-clicking is quicker and easier.)

Splitting and Combining Audio Events

In Chapter 7, "Editing Basics," you learned how to split audio Events by using the Scissors tool, but you can accomplish the same thing by using the Split feature. Plus, Pro Audio enables you to join audio Events together via the Combine feature.

Split

What makes the Split feature different from the Scissors tool is that, instead of clicking to define a split point, you type a measure, beat, and tick value. Just select an audio Event, right-click on it, and select Split from the pop-up menu to open the Split Selected Audio Events dialog box. Then type a measure, beat, and tick value, and click on OK. Pro Audio splits that Event into two separate Events at that precise point in time.

TIP

The problem with the Split feature is that it isn't affected by the Snap to Zero Crossing feature (which you learned about in Chapter 7, "Editing Basics"). This means that you can end up splitting Events at points where the audio waveform is not at a zero crossing, thus, introducing glitches into your audio data. So, if possible, you always should use the Scissors tool when splitting audio Events.

Combine

Of course, it's only logical to assume that sometimes you might need to combine multiple audio Events into one. If that's the case, you can use the Combine feature as follows:

1. Select the Events in the Clips pane that you want to combine. You can select any number of Events, but those Events have to be within the same Track and located adjacent to one another. You can, however, combine Events in different Tracks at the same time. For example, if you select the first two audio Events in Track 1 and the first two audio Events in Track 2, using the Combine feature combines the first two audio Events in Track 1 to each other and combines the first two audio Events in Track 2 to each other. This method doesn't combine the Events in Track 1 to the Events in Track 2, though.

2. Right-click on the selected Events, and choose Combine from the pop-up menu. At this point, things can go one of two ways. If the Events that you selected don't overlap, Pro Audio simply combines the Events into one, and that's the end of the operation. If the Events do overlap, however, Pro Audio opens the Combine Audio Events dialog box (see Figure 8.3).

Figure 8.3
If your selected audio Events overlap, Pro Audio opens the Combine Audio Events dialog box.

CHAPTER 8

3. You need to choose whether the Events should be combined polyphonically or monophonically. If you choose the Polyphonic option, even though the Events are combined with one Event overlapping the other, you can still hear the data from both Events being played. When the Now Time hits the section during playback where the Events overlap, you hear a mixture of the data from both Events. If you choose the Monophonic option, the data from the Event that is covered by the data from the overlapping Event gets cut off. So, initially, you hear the data from the first Event being played, and then it gets cut off, and you hear only the data from the second Event.

    Give it a try so that you can hear the difference between the two. More often than not, you'll want to choose the Polyphonic option; that way, you don't lose any of your recorded data.

4. After you've made your selection, click on OK.

Pro Audio combines the Events into one larger Event. If the Events that you combined weren't overlapping, and they had the same Velocity settings, then the new Event will have the same Velocity setting as well. (You learned about changing the Velocity of audio Events in Chapter 7, "Editing Basics"). The new Event will play back at the same volume, too. If the Events that you combined were overlapping or had different Velocity settings, then each section of the new Event, which was previously represented by a separate Event, will keep its original volume. For example, if you combined two Events (one having a Velocity of 120 and the other having a Velocity of 80), the first part of the new Event will play loudly, and the second part of the new Event will play softly.

Adjusting Audio Event Volume

You already know that you can change the volume of an audio Event by manipulating its Velocity parameter, but changing this parameter doesn't change the actual data in the Event. Changing the Velocity only determines whether Pro Audio will increase or decrease the volume of an Event during playback. If you want to make a more permanent volume change, you can use a number of different Pro Audio features to increase or decrease the volume of the actual data in an audio Event.

3dB Louder

Using the 3dB Louder feature, you can increase the volume of audio Events by 3dB each time you apply it. So, if you want to increase the volume of an Event by 6dB, you can apply the 3dB Louder feature to it twice. To use it, simply select the audio Event(s) that you want to change, right-click on the selected Event(s), and choose 3dB Louder from the pop-up menu. Pro Audio processes the data in the Event(s), and you can see the results via the higher amplitude value(s) in the audio waveform(s).

CAUTION

Remember the description about setting your input level during the recording process in Chapter 6, "Recording and Playback"? I mentioned that you have to be careful not to set the level too high because it can overload the input and cause your audio to be distorted. Well, when you're raising the volume of the data in an audio Event, you also have to watch out not to raise it too high. Setting it too high can cause clipping. Clipping occurs when Pro Audio attempts to raise the amplitude of audio data higher than 100 percent. The top and bottom of the waveform become clipped, and when you play the audio, it sounds distorted. So, be careful when using the 3dB Louder feature. Be sure to keep an eye on the amplitude levels of your audio waveforms, and also be sure to listen to an audio Event right after you increase its volume to see if it sounds okay. If you hear distortion, then use Undo to remove the volume change.

3dB Quieter

The 3dB Quieter feature works in the same way as the 3dB Louder feature except that it decreases the volume of audio Events by 3dB.

CAUTION

You also have to be careful when using the 3dB Quieter feature—not because you might introduce distortion into the audio, but because every time you use it, it degrades the audio slightly. For instance, if you use the 3dB Quieter feature to lower the volume of an audio Event and then use the 3dB Louder feature to raise the volume, the quality of the audio will not be the same as it was originally. This difference is due to the limitations of processing digital audio signals, a subject that is a bit complex to explain. More than likely, though, you won't be able to hear the difference in quality because it really is only a slight degradation, so you don't need to worry about it too much.

Normalize

Like the 3dB Louder feature, the Normalize feature also raises the volume of audio but in a different way. Instead of just simply raising the volume, Normalize first scans the waveform of an audio Event to find its highest amplitude level. It subtracts that amplitude level from the maximum level, which is 100 percent. Normalize then takes that value and uses it to increase the volume of the audio Event. So, when all is said and done, the highest amplitude in the waveform is 100 percent, and all the other amplitude values are increased.

In other words, if an audio Event waveform has its highest amplitude value at 80 percent, Normalize subtracts that value from 100 percent to get 20 percent. It then increases the volume of the audio Event by 20 percent so that the highest amplitude value is 100 percent, and all the other amplitude values are 20 percent higher. Basically, you can use Normalize to raise the volume of an audio Event to the highest it can be without causing any clipping.

To use Normalize, simply select the audio data, right-click on it, and choose Normalize from the pop-up menu.

CAUTION

You knew this caution was coming, didn't you? When you use the Normalize feature, just like the 3dB Louder and 3dB Quieter features, you have to be careful. If you raise the volume of audio data to its maximum, you can easily introduce clipping to the signal if you process it later with some of the other editing or effects features in Pro Audio. Usually, you should use the Normalize feature only after you know that you're not going to do any more processing on that particular audio data. Then again, you probably shouldn't even use the Normalize feature at all (see the tip at the end of the "Crossfade" section).

Fade

In Chapter 7, "Editing Basics," you learned how to apply fades to audio Events by using the Draw Line tool. But they were just basic linear fades, meaning the fades could be drawn by using simple straight lines only, and the volume of the audio would increase or decrease in a uniform fashion. If you want to get a little more creative with your volume changes, you can build much more complex fades by using the Fade feature as follows:

1. Select the audio data to which you want to apply the fade. Then right-click on it and choose Fade from the pop-up menu to open the Fade/Envelope dialog box (see Figure 8.4). The dialog box displays a graph. The left side of the graph displays amplitude values, 0 to 100 percent from bottom to top. Inside the graph is a line, which represents the fade that will be applied to your selected audio data. If you look at the line from left to right, the left end of the line represents the beginning of your audio data selection, and the right end of the line represents the end of your audio data selection. When you first open the dialog box, the line runs from the bottom left to the top right of the graph. If you leave it this way, a straight linear fade-in is applied to your audio data because, as you look at the graph, the left end of the line is set at 0 percent, and the right end of the line is set at 100 percent. So, the volume of the audio data would begin at 0 percent and fade all the way up to 100 percent. See how it works?

Figure 8.4
You can use the Fade/Envelope dialog box to apply complex fades to your audio data.

2. You can change the shape of the fade line in one of two ways. You can simply select one of the six available presets from the drop-down list at the top of the dialog box. Alternatively, you can change the fade line graphically by clicking and dragging the small squares at the ends of the line. These squares are called Nodes.

3. If you want to create some really complex fades, you can add more Nodes by clicking anywhere on the fade line. The more Nodes you add, the more flexibility you have in changing the shape of the line (see Figure 8.5).

Figure 8.5
You can create some really complex fades by adding more Nodes.

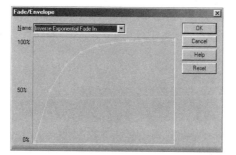

4. After you've finished setting up the graph the way you want it, click on OK.

Pro Audio changes the volume of your audio data selection according to the fade that you defined in the Fade/Envelope dialog box.

Crossfade

A *crossfade* is a special kind of fade that can be applied only to overlapping audio Events. This kind of fade can come in handy when you want to make a smooth transition from one style of music to another or from one instrument to another. It is especially useful when you're composing to video; you can smoothly change from one type of background music to another as the scene changes. Of course, it has many other types of creative uses as well.

When you apply a crossfade to two overlapping audio Events, it works like this: During playback as the Now Time reaches the point at which the two audio Events overlap, the first audio Event fades out, and the second audio Event fades in at the same time. You can apply a crossfade as follows:

1. Select the two overlapping audio Events to which you want to apply the crossfade.

TIP

The two audio Events that you select don't have to reside on the same Track; they only have to overlap in time.

2. Right-click on one of the selected Events and choose Crossfade from the pop-up menu to open the Crossfade dialog box (see Figure 8.6).

Figure 8.6

You can apply a crossfade to two overlapping audio Events by using the Crossfade dialog box.

3. Notice that the Crossfade dialog box looks almost exactly the same as the Fade/Envelope dialog box. It works almost exactly the same, too. You can choose from three preset fades, and you can manipulate the fade line with your mouse by adding, clicking, and dragging Nodes. The only difference here is that an additional line appears on the graph. The darker line represents the second selected audio Event and can't be manipulated directly. As you make changes to the lighter line, the darker line mimics it. This feature ensures that the volumes of both audio Events are synchronized and provides a perfectly smooth crossfade. So, go ahead and make your changes, as discussed earlier.

4. Click on OK.

Pro Audio applies the crossfade to the parts of the two audio Events that are overlapping. When you play back the audio, you hear the data from the first Event gradually fade out at the same time the data from the second audio Event gradually fades in.

CHAPTER 8

TIP

I use the 3dB Louder, 3dB Quieter, and Normalize features only in certain situations (some of which I'll talk about later). Instead, I like to record my audio data initially at a good amplitude level and then adjust the volume by using the Velocity parameter. This way, the adjustment doesn't affect the data permanently, and I can change the volume of the audio as many times as I want without affecting the quality. Plus, by using the Envelope feature, I can have the volume change automatically over time just like with a fade but without affecting the audio data permanently. I'll talk more about the Envelope feature in Chapter 10, "Mixing It Down."

Equalization (EQ)

You have a radio in your car, right? Maybe even a cassette or CD player, too? If so, then you've probably used equalization without even knowing it. Adjusting the bass and treble controls on your car radio is a form of equalization. Equalization (EQ) enables you to adjust the tonal characteristics of an audio signal by increasing (boosting) or decreasing (cutting) the amplitude of different frequencies in the audio spectrum.

NOTE

When a musical object (such as a string) vibrates, it emits a sound. The speed at which the object vibrates is called the *frequency*, which is measured in vibrations (or cycles) per second. This measurement is also called *Hertz* (Hz). If an object vibrates 60 times per second, the frequency would be 60Hz. The tricky point to remember here, though, is that most objects vibrate at a number of different frequencies at the same time. The combination of all these different vibrations makes up the distinct sound (or *timbre*) of a vibrating object. That's why a bell sounds like a bell, a horn sounds like a horn, and so on with all other types of sounds.

Of course, we humans can't perceive some very slow and very fast vibrations. Technically, the range of human hearing resides between the frequencies of 20Hz and 20KHz (1KHz is equal to 1000Hz). This range is known as the *audio spectrum*.

Equalization enables you to manipulate the frequencies of the audio spectrum, and because sounds contain many of these frequencies, you can change their tonal characteristics (or timbre). Of course, this explanation is very basic. If you really want to learn more about acoustics, pick up a good book about sound recording, such as *Home Recording for Musicians* by Craig Anderton (Music Sales Corp, 1996, ISBN 0-8256-1500-3).

In other words, using EQ, you can bump up the bass, add more presence, reduce rumble, and sometimes eliminate noise in your audio material. Not only that, but you also can use EQ as an effect. You know how in some of the modern dance tunes the vocals sound like they're coming out of a telephone receiver or an old radio? That's an effect done with EQ.

Pro Audio provides two different types of EQ features: Graphic EQ and Parametric EQ. (Actually, four different EQ features are available, but I'll describe the other two in Chapter 9, "Effects: The Really Cool Stuff.") Both have their strengths and weaknesses.

Graphic EQ

You already might be familiar with graphic equalizers because they are sometimes included on boom boxes and home stereo systems. Pro Audio's Graphic EQ feature simulates a hardware-based graphic equalizer. It even looks similar (see Figure 8.7).

Figure 8.7
The Graphic EQ feature resembles a real graphic equalizer.

The Graphic EQ feature provides ten different frequencies (called *bands*) that you can adjust. Each band can either be boosted or cut by 12dB. You simply drag the appropriate slider up (boost) or down (cut) to increase or decrease the amplitude of that frequency. But herein lies the weakness of Graphic EQ. Although it's very easy to use, you are limited by the frequencies that you can manipulate. You can't change any of the frequencies below, above, or in between the ones provided. Still, Graphic EQ is very useful if you want to make quick equalization changes, and the frequencies provided are the most common ones. It works like this:

1. Select the audio data that you want to change.

2. Right-click on the selected data, and choose Graphic EQ from the pop-up menu to open the Graphic EQ dialog box.

3. Adjust the sliders for the frequencies that you want to cut or boost.

CAUTION

Be careful when you're boosting frequencies, because doing so also increases the overall volume of the audio data. If you raise the volume too high, you can introduce clipping into the data.

4. Click on the Audition button to hear the first few seconds of the processed audio before you go ahead and accept the settings. That way, you can decide whether you like the way it sounds. By listening to a few seconds of the audio, you can test whether any clipping occurs. When you're done listening, click on Stop. By the way, Pro Audio includes the Audition button in many of its other features, too, and it always works in exactly the same way.

TIP

If clipping does occur, but you really want to boost some of the frequencies in your audio data, click on Cancel to exit the Graphic EQ dialog box without making any changes. Now, lower the volume of the audio data by using the 3dB Quieter feature. Then go back and try to apply the EQ again. By lowering the volume of the audio first, you can make enough room to allow more frequency boosting.

5. If you want to be able to use the same EQ settings again later without having to keep making the same slider adjustments, save them as a Preset. You learned about Presets in Chapter 5, "Getting Around in Pro Audio."

6. Click on OK.

Pro Audio processes the selected audio data, and when you play it back, it should sound the same way it did when you listened to it using the Audition feature.

TIP

By default, the Audition feature plays only the first few seconds of the selected data. You can adjust the Audition time by selecting Options > Global to open the Global Options dialog box. Under the General tab, set the Audition Commands For option to the number of seconds that you want to use for the Audition feature. I usually like to keep this set anywhere between 5 and 10 seconds.

CHAPTER 8

Parametric EQ

Parametric equalization, on the other hand, is much more powerful and flexible, but it's also a lot more complex and difficult to understand. With the Parametric EQ feature, you're not limited to specific frequencies. You can specify an exact frequency to adjust, and you can cut or boost by much larger amounts. You also can process a range of frequencies at the same time, such as cutting all frequencies above 10KHz by 20dB (which would reduce all the frequencies between 10KHz and 20KHz but leave the frequencies between 20Hz and 10KHz alone). I can explain the Parametric EQ feature a little better by showing you how it works:

1. Select the audio data that you want to change.

2. Right-click on the selected data and choose Parametric EQ from the pop-up menu to open the Parametric EQ dialog box (see Figure 8.8).

Figure 8.8
The Parametric EQ feature provides a lot more power, but it's also more difficult to use.

3. Choose one of the options in the Filter Type section: High-Pass, Low-Pass, Band-Pass (Peak), or Band-Stop (Notch). Then set the appropriate parameters in the Filter Parameters section. You can use the F1 and F2 parameters to set the frequencies that you want to adjust. They work differently depending on the type of filter that you choose (I'll talk more about this in a minute). The Cut parameter enables you to reduce the volume of the frequencies. To change this setting, just enter a negative number (such as -20) to cut by that number of decibels. The Gain parameter enables you to boost the volume of the frequencies. To change this setting, just enter a positive number (such as +20) to boost by that number of decibels. You can set the Quality parameter to determine how precise the Parameter EQ feature will be when processing your audio. If you really want to zero in on a frequency or range of frequencies, use a higher value for the Quality parameter (200 being the highest). This setting gives you a sharper (for lack of a better word) sound. A low value (such as 2) enables the Parametric EQ feature to slightly process the other frequencies not defined specifically or outside the range, which gives you a smoother sound. It's a bit difficult to describe. Experiment with it a little, and you'll be able to hear the difference.

If you select the High-Pass filter type, all the frequencies below the frequency that you set in the F1 parameter will be cut, and all the frequencies above it will be boosted, depending on how you set the Cut and Gain parameters.

If you select the Low-Pass filter type, all the frequencies above the frequency that you set in the F1 parameter will be cut, and all the frequencies below it will be boosted, depending on how you set the Cut and Gain parameters.

If you select either the Band-Pass (Peak) or Band-Stop (Notch) filter types, you have to set up a range of frequencies by using both the F1 and F2 parameters. Use the F1 parameter to mark the beginning of the range and the F2 parameter to mark the end of the range. For the Band-Pass (Peak) filter type, any frequencies outside the range are cut, and frequencies within the range are boosted, depending on how you set the Cut and Gain parameters. For the Band-Stop (Notch) filter type, any frequencies outside the range are boosted, and frequencies within the range are cut, depending on how you set the Cut and Gain parameters.

4. Click on the Audition button to hear the first few seconds of the processed audio before you go ahead and accept the settings. That way, you can decide whether you like the way it sounds. By listening to a few seconds of the audio, you can test whether any clipping occurs. When you're done listening, click on Stop.

5. If you want to be able to use the same EQ settings again later without having to keep making the same parameter adjustments, save them as a Preset.

6. Click on OK.

Pro Audio processes the selected audio data, and when you play it back, it should sound the same way it did when you listened to it using the Audition feature.

Applications

Right about now, you might be saying to yourself, "Okay, EQ sounds pretty cool, but what can I do with it?" Well, you can use EQ in many different ways to process your audio. To begin with, you might want to try some of the Presets that are included with Pro Audio. Not very many are provided for the Graphic EQ and Parametric EQ features, but you can find enough to give you a taste of what EQ can do. After that, you might want to try experimenting with some of the settings described in the following sections.

CHAPTER 8

Fullness

To make your audio sound a little fuller, try boosting the range of frequencies between 100 and 300Hz by 6dB. To do so, use the Parametric EQ feature with the Band-Pass (Peak) filter type and set the filter parameters to the following: F1 = 100, F2 = 300, Quality = 2, Cut = 0, and Gain = 6.

Punch

To add a little more punch to your audio, try boosting the range of frequencies between 800Hz and 2KHz by 6dB. To do so, use the Parametric EQ feature with the Band-Pass (Peak) filter type and set the filter parameters to the following: F1 = 800, F2 = 2000, Quality = 2, Cut = 0, and Gain = 6.

Noise Reduction

EQ also can be used as a simple means of reducing noise in your audio. This is especially true for high frequency hiss. Use the Parametric EQ feature with the Low-Pass filter type and set the filter parameters to the following: F1 = 18000, Quality = 2, Cut = -96, and Gain = 0.

To get rid of buzzing or humming noises with EQ, use the Parametric EQ feature with the Band-Stop (Notch) filter type and set the filter parameters to the following: F1 = 60, F2 = 60, Quality = 100, Cut = -96, and Gain = 0.

Specific Sounds

EQ is handy for molding specific types of sounds, such as stringed instruments like guitar and bass. For example, to give a different sound to an acoustic or electric guitar, try using the Graphic EQ feature with the following settings: 32Hz = -12, 64Hz = 0, 130Hz = +4, 260Hz = +7, 500Hz = +6, 1k = +3, 2k = 0, 4k = +4, 8.3k = +7, and 16.5k = 0.

For a bass guitar, trying using the Graphic EQ feature with the following settings: 32Hz = -12, 64Hz = 0, 130Hz = +6, 260Hz = +7, 500Hz = +5, 1k = +1, 2k = 0, 4k = +0, 8.3k = +6, and 16.5k = +12.

And So On...

I could go on and on with equalization applications, but that would fill a whole book on its own. Don't be afraid to experiment. The more you practice using the EQ features, the more skilled you will become at applying them. Keep one point in mind, though: With just the right amount of spices, a meal tastes great. Too many spices, and the taste starts taking a turn for the worse. The same goes for applying EQ to your audio. Too much EQ will make your Projects sound amateurish.

Getting Rid of Silence

When you record an audio Track in Pro Audio, even though there might be pauses in your performance (such as between musical phrases), your sound card still picks up a signal from your microphone or instrument, and that data is recorded. Although you might think that the data is just recorded silence, in actuality, it contains a very minute amount of noise that might come from your sound card itself or the microphone or instrument connected there. More often than not, you can't really hear this noise because it's masked by the other music data in your Project. And even during quiet passages, if you have only one or two audio Tracks playing, the noise is probably still inaudible. With a large number of audio Tracks, however, the noise can add up.

In addition, during playback, Pro Audio still processes those silent passages even though they don't contain any actual music. These passages take up valuable computer processing power and disk space. To remedy this problem, Pro Audio provides the Remove Silence feature. This feature automatically detects sections of silence in audio Events according to a loudness threshold that you set. Then, by first splitting long audio Events into shorter ones, it removes the resulting Events containing only silence. Thus, Pro Audio doesn't process that extra data during playback, and it doesn't save it to disk when you save your Project.

To detect silent passages in audio, the Remove Silence feature uses a digital noise gate. Depending on the parameter settings you specify, this noise gate opens up when the Remove Silence feature comes upon a section in your audio that has an amplitude level greater than the one you set. It identifies this part of the audio as acceptable sound and lets it pass through. When the level of audio dips below a certain amplitude level that you set, the noise gate identifies that part of the audio as silence, and it closes to stop it from passing through. At that point, the Remove Silence feature splits the audio Event with one new Event containing just the music and another new Event containing just the noise. This process happens over and over until the whole initial audio Event is finished being scanned.

You use this feature as follows:

1. Select the audio data that you want to scan for silence.

2. Right-click on the selected data and choose Remove Silence from the pop-up menu to open the Remove Silence dialog box (see Figure 8.9).

Figure 8.9
You can use the Remove Silence feature to clean up your audio Tracks and make them more manageable.

3. Type a value for the Open Level parameter. This parameter determines how loud the audio data has to be to make the noise gate open, thus identifying the data as acceptable sound.

4. Type a value for the Close Level parameter. This parameter determines how soft the data has to be to make the noise gate close, thus identifying the data as silence.

5. Type a value for the Attack Time parameter. This parameter determines how quickly (in milliseconds) the noise gate will open to the amplitude set in the Open Level parameter. If the beginning of your audio data starts off soft (such as with a fade in) and its amplitude is below the Open Level setting, it could get cut off by the noise gate. For example, the beginnings of the words in a vocal part might get cut. To prevent this problem, you can set the Attack Time parameter so that the noise gate takes this kind of situation into consideration.

6. Type a value for the Hold Time parameter. This parameter determines how long the noise gate will remain open even when the amplitude level of the audio dips below the Close Level. This parameter is useful when the level of your audio goes up and down very quickly, which can make the noise gate react when it's not supposed to (such as during quick percussion parts). By setting a Hold Time, you can make sure that musical passages containing quick sounds don't get cut by mistake.

7. Type a value for the Release Time parameter. This parameter is the same as the Attack Time parameter but in reverse. It determines how quickly the noise gate will close after the amplitude of the audio reaches the Close Level. This feature is useful if your audio data gradually gets softer at the end, such as with a fade out.

8. Type a value for the Granularity parameter. This parameter determines how long (in milliseconds) the amplitude of the audio must stay above the Open Level before the noise gate will open. Basically, this setting enables you to fine-tune how the noise gate determines whether the audio being scanned is acceptable sound or silence.

9. If you want Pro Audio to delete the audio Events that contain only silence, activate the Split Events option. Otherwise, the silent portions of the audio will be cut into separate audio Events, but they won't be deleted.

10. You can save your settings as a Preset, and you can use the Audition feature to hear the results of your settings if you want.

11. Click on OK.

Pro Audio scans the selected audio Event and then splits it up into pieces (and also removes the Events containing only silence) according to the settings that you specify.

TIP

Unless the musical passages and silent passages of your audio are separated pretty neatly, it can be difficult to get the right settings for the Release Time feature to perform accurately. You might find it easier and more precise if you simply split the audio Events by hand by using the Scissors tool. I do. The process is a bit more time-consuming, but hey, I like things to be perfect.

Audio to MIDI Conversion

In Chapter 1, "Understanding MIDI and Digital Audio," you learned about the differences between MIDI and audio data. MIDI data represents recorded performance instructions, and audio data represents actual sound. Because audio data is actual sound, Pro Audio doesn't really know what's being recorded in an audio Track except that it's a bunch of numbers that represent sound. It can't tell whether the sound is notes being played on an instrument, or a voice singing lyrics, or even if it's the sound of birds chirping on a sunny summer afternoon.

With recent advances in digital audio processing technology, however, under certain circumstances, audio data can be scanned for pitch and rhythmic values. This means that a program can scan audio data and determine the pitch and rhythm of the instruments being played. It can then convert that data into MIDI notes. Pro Audio provides two features that give you this capability.

CHAPTER 8

Pitch Detection

By using the Pitch Detection feature, you can have Pro Audio scan audio Events for melodic pitches and then turn that data into MIDI notes. Unfortunately, it works only in certain situations. The audio data can contain only a single-note (monophonic) melody being played by some kind of musical instrument. These are the only circumstances under which the feature will work, and even then the results aren't very good.

So why would you need this feature? You don't. The one situation in which the Pitch Detection feature might be useful would be in converting the pitches of a vocal performance into MIDI data so that it could later be printed as standard music notation. But, of course, you guessed it—the feature doesn't work well on vocal parts. If you really want to convert your acoustic instrument performances to MIDI data, you're better off just recording them a second time by using a MIDI instrument. Then you can use the MIDI data for music notation and the audio for the actual song playback. Suffice it to say, you probably won't get much (if any) use out of the Pitch Detection feature, but in case you want to try playing around with it anyway, here's how it works:

1. Select the audio data that you want to scan for pitches.

2. Right-click on the selected data and choose Pitch Detection from the pop-up menu to open the Pitch Detection dialog box (see Figure 8.10).

Figure 8.10
The Pitch Detection feature is used to detect the pitches of audio recordings.

3. Set the Pitch Range parameters. These values tell Pro Audio what range of pitches to expect when it scans the audio data. So, if the lowest note in the melody being played is an A3, and the highest note in the melody being played is a G5, you would set the first value to A3 and the second value to G5.

4. Set the Threshold parameter. This value tells Pro Audio how accurate the pitch of the note being scanned has to be in order for it to be considered a note. If you set this value low, Pro Audio will be more lenient when determining whether a pitch should be converted to a MIDI note. If you set this value high, Pro Audio will be stricter when determining whether a pitch should be converted to a MIDI note. For bass instruments, you should use a low setting, because their pitches aren't very precise. For higher pitched instruments (such as a flute), you can use a higher setting. You'll have to experiment with this setting a bit.

5. Set the Minimum Duration parameter. This value tells Pro Audio how long a detected pitch has to be in order to be converted to a MIDI note. You should set this parameter to the smallest note duration that's played in the melody being scanned.

6. Set the Bend Range parameter. In addition to detecting actual pitches, Pro Audio attempts to detect whether a pitch is bent (such as when a guitar player bends the strings on an instrument). This value tells Pro Audio the Pitch Wheel range it can use when converting bent pitches into Pitch Wheel controller messages along with the MIDI notes. The value is set in semitones, and usually a range of 2 or 3 works well.

7. Set the Bend Spacing parameter. This value also has to do with converting bent pitches to Pitch Wheel controller data. It tells Pro Audio how often it can add Pitch Wheel messages to the converted MIDI data. This value is set in ticks. The default value of 1 usually works well.

8. Set the Destination Track parameter. This value tells Pro Audio in what Track it should place the new MIDI data that it has detected from the scanned audio data.

9. Click on OK.

Pro Audio scans the selected audio data and attempts to detect the pitches of the instrumental melody. It then converts them to MIDI notes along with Pitch Wheel controller messages. It saves the new MIDI data in the Track that you specified in the Destination Track parameter. That's pretty much it.

CHAPTER 8

Extract Timing

Unlike the Pitch Detection feature, the Extract Timing feature is very useful. With this feature, Pro Audio can scan audio Events for quick percussive changes in volume and by that be able to determine the rhythm of the music. It can then convert those rhythmic values into MIDI notes and velocity messages. Although the Extract Timing feature isn't quite as limited as the Pitch Detection feature in terms of the types of musical performances it can scan, it still works best with single-note melodies and percussion performances.

You might want to use this feature in a number of different situations. One of the most obvious is in converting melodies (such as a melody played on a piano) into MIDI notes. The Extract Timing feature would pick up only the rhythm of the notes, but you could easily add the pitches by hand. To take this example one step further, you can create a new MIDI melody by scanning a percussion Track. The new melody would then play in sync with the rhythm Track, emphasizing the same notes, beats, and so on. Using this feature is a great way to sync a bass line to a percussion part. Another situation might arise in which you already have a bunch of MIDI Tracks recorded, and you have some existing percussion audio sample beats that you want to use in your Project. With the Extract Timing feature, you can convert the audio rhythm pulses into tempo changes for your song so that the MIDI Tracks play at the same tempo as the audio samples. You also can use the Extract Timing feature to create your own templates for the Groove Quantize feature (which you'll learn about later in this chapter).

Suffice it to say, you'll get a lot more use out of the Extract Timing feature than you will the Pitch Detection feature, so let me explain how it works:

1. Select the audio data that you want to scan for rhythmic values.

2. Right-click on the selected data and choose Extract Timing from the pop-up menu to open the Extract Timing dialog box (see Figure 8.11).

Figure 8.11
You can detect the rhythm of audio recordings by using the Extract Timing feature and then apply that rhythm to your MIDI data.

3. In the Pulse Analysis section, set the Trigger Level parameter. This parameter (set in decibels) tells Pro Audio how loud the audio data being scanned has to be in order to be considered a rhythmic value. For example, if you have a snare drum track, and each snare drum hit has a volume of -50dB, you have to set the Trigger Level to at least -50dB for the snare drum to be picked up. If you have audio data with many varied volume levels, you'll have to experiment with the Trigger Level to be sure all the rhythmic values are picked up.

4. Set the Minimum Length parameter. This parameter (set in milliseconds) tells Pro Audio how much time should be allowed between rhythmic values. If you set the Minimum Length parameter too low, many extraneous values (that aren't really rhythmic values) might be picked up. If you set it too high, not all the legitimate rhythmic values will be picked up. As you do with the Trigger Level parameter, you'll have to experiment with Minimum Length parameter to find the right setting for the audio material being scanned.

5. Activate or deactivate the Find A Steady Rhythm option. This option tells Pro Audio to look for a steady rhythm within the audio material being scanned. For example, if you have a snare drum Track that has even hits on each beat but also has some syncopated hits in between the beats, activating the Find A Steady Rhythm option will weed out the syncopated hits and just pick up the rhythm values that are steady.

6. Set the appropriate parameters in the Timing Synthesis section. The options and values set here depend on what you want to do with the Extract Timing feature. If you want to match the tempo of some existing MIDI Tracks to the tempo of some existing audio material, activate the Insert Tempo Changes option. Then set the Expected Pulse Duration parameter to the length of rhythmic values in your audio material. For example, if you are scanning some percussion material that has a snare drum being played as steady quarter notes, you can set the Expected Pulse Duration parameter to Quarter. If you want to convert the rhythmic values from your audio material into MIDI notes so that you can use the data in some of the situations described earlier, you can activate the Convert Each Pulse To MIDI Note option. Then enter the pitch at which you want all the MIDI notes to be set. And if you want the Velocity values of the MIDI notes to match the volume levels of the rhythmic values being scanned, under Note Velocities, activate the Vary With Pulse Level option. Otherwise, you can set all the MIDI notes to the same Velocity by activating the Set All To Same Value option and then entering a value for the Velocity that you want to use.

CHAPTER 8

7. Click on the Audition button. In this case, the button works a bit differently from any of the other editing and effects features in Pro Audio. Instead of hearing anything, you'll see some red marks placed over the audio material that you selected in the Audio View (see Figure 8.12). These marks represent the rhythmic values that will be picked up by the Extract Timing feature. You need to see if they match up to the rhythmic values in the audio material. If they do, you can move on to the next step; otherwise, you might need to adjust some of the parameters a little more to make everything line up correctly.

Figure 8.12
Before leaving the Extract Timing dialog box, you should use the Audition feature to make sure that the correct rhythmic values from the audio material are being picked up.

8. Click on OK.

Depending on the parameter settings you chose, Pro Audio scans the selected audio data and attempts to detect the rhythmic values of the material. If you activated the Insert Tempo Changes option, Pro Audio inserts tempo changes into your Project so that the MIDI Tracks will play along at the same tempo as the audio material. If you activated the Convert Each Pulse To MIDI Note option, Pro Audio temporarily stores the MIDI note data into the Clipboard. From here, you can paste the data into a Clip or Track by using the Track or Piano Roll Views and use it to create a new melody or bass line that plays along with the audio material.

Extract Timing Example

The Extract Timing feature is a bit complicated, and it can be difficult to understand why you might need it. So, let's take a look at a sample application:

1. Open the sample Project called Riff Funk Audio and MIDI Demo.bun that is included with Pro Audio.

2. Select Track 2 (the guitar Track) and then select View > Audio to open the Audio View.

3. In the Audio View, select the first audio Event in the guitar Track.

4. Right-click on the selected Event and choose Extract Timing from the pop-up menu to open the Extract Timing dialog box.

5. Set the Trigger Level parameter to -17dB.

6. Set the Minimum Length parameter to 50 milliseconds.

7. Because the audio material that you're scanning has an irregular rhythm, make sure the Find A Steady Rhythm option is deactivated.

8. Activate the Convert Each Pulse To MIDI Note option, and set the note value to G#4.

9. Under Note Velocities, activate the Vary With Pulse Level option.

10. Click on OK. Pro Audio scans the audio material, converts the rhythmic values to MIDI note and velocity data, and stores the data in the Clipboard.

11. Switch to the Track View and select Edit > Paste to open the Paste dialog box.

12. Set the Starting at Time parameter to 1:01:000 (measures, beats, ticks).

13. Set the Repetitions parameter to 8.

14. Set the Starting at Track parameter to 5.

15. Click on OK.

Pro Audio creates a new Track (Track 5) containing eight Clips, each containing the rhythmic data that was scanned from the first Clip of the guitar Track. Before you play the Project back to hear how it sounds, be sure to set the Port and Channel for Track 5. Set it so that the Track uses your General MIDI-compatible MIDI instrument and uses MIDI channel 10 (the standard channel for drums). When you play the Project, you'll hear a cowbell sound playing along in time with the rest of the Tracks. In particular, it should have close to the same rhythm as the audio material in the guitar Track. Some of the MIDI notes might be slightly off, but you can fix their timing in the Piano Roll View. In any case, this example illustrates just one of the many applications for which you can use the Extract Timing feature.

Play It Backward

Assuming you're old enough to remember vinyl recordings, did you ever take a record and play it backward to see whether your favorite band had left some satanic messages in their songs or perhaps a recipe for their favorite lentil soup? Well, guess what? You can do the same thing with your audio data. Pro Audio enables you to flip the data in an audio Event so that it plays in reverse.

CHAPTER 8

This feature doesn't have much practical use, but combined with some other processing, it can render some cool effects. To use it, simply select the audio Event that you want to change, right-click on it, and select Reverse from the pop-up menu. Now the data in that Event will play backward.

TIP

If you want to reverse the data in an entire Track, make sure to combine all of the audio Events in the Track into one big audio Event first. If you don't, the data in each separate Event will be reversed, but this is not the same as reversing the entire Track. Try it, and you'll hear what I mean.

TIP

With the combination of the audio editing features discussed so far in this chapter and the audio effects features described in Chapter 9, "Effects: The Really Cool Stuff," there's no doubt that Pro Audio packs a lot of audio data editing power. But it still can't compare to dedicated audio editing applications such as Sonic Foundry's Sound Forge **(www.sonicfoundry.com)**, Syntrillium's Cool Edit **(www.syntrillium.com)**, and Steinberg's WaveLab **(www.steinberg.net)**. Using these programs, you can edit your audio with surgical precision, and they provide many more processing features than can be found in Pro Audio. The people at Cakewalk are aware of this fact, so they included a little-known feature that enables you to access your favorite audio editing applications from within Pro Audio. I've tested the previously mentioned products, but there might be others that can use the feature as well.

To use your audio editing software from within Pro Audio, simply select the audio data that you want to edit. Then select the Tools menu. At the bottom of the menu, you should see your software listed there (Pro Audio automatically detects it during installation). Choose the program that you want to run. Your audio editing software then opens with the audio data that you selected ready to be processed. Make any changes you want, and then close the audio editing software. Before closing, the program first asks whether you want to save the changes you made. Click on Yes. The program closes, and you return to Pro Audio. Pro Audio then tells you that the audio data has changed and asks whether you want to reload it. Click on Yes. That's all there is to it. And now you have easy access to all the power of your audio editing software as well as Pro Audio. Isn't that cool?

The Edit Menu

Up until now, I've talked about editing features that pertain strictly to audio data. The remainder of Pro Audio's editing features are more diverse in their use, meaning some can be used with MIDI data, some with audio data, and some with both. The one aspect they all have in common is that they are accessed via the Edit menu. Click on the Edit menu, and you'll see them listed in the bottom half, starting with Deglitch and ending with Fit Improvisation. Because of their diversity, I'll go through each feature one by one, explaining what it does, along with how and why you would want to use it. Of course, I'll also let you know what kinds of data each feature works with.

Deglitch

Occasionally, you might find that, while you're playing your MIDI instrument, some unintended notes get recorded along with the legitimate musical material. This is especially true for people who play a MIDI guitar. The strings on a MIDI guitar can easily trigger notes when they're not supposed to. To help with this problem, Pro Audio provides the Deglitch feature. Using this feature, you can filter out any notes from your MIDI data that don't fall within the right pitch, velocity, and duration range for the music you're recording. It works like this:

1. Select the MIDI data from which you want to filter any unwanted notes.

2. Select Edit > Deglitch to open the Deglitch dialog box (see Figure 8.13).

Figure 8.13
Using the Deglitch feature, you can filter out any unintended notes from your MIDI data by specifying acceptable pitch, velocity, and duration ranges.

3. If you want to filter out notes by pitch, activate the Pitch option. Then, for the Notes Higher Than parameter, type the maximum note value allowed in your material. For example, if the highest note in your MIDI data should be C5, then you should set the Notes Higher Than parameter to C5. If the Deglitch feature finds any notes within the data that have a pitch higher than C5, it will delete them.

4. If you want to filter out notes by velocity, activate the Velocity option. Then, for the Notes Softer Than parameter, type the minimum velocity value allowed in your material. For example, if the lowest velocity in your MIDI data should be 15, then you should set the Notes Softer Than parameter to 15. If the Deglitch feature finds any notes within the data that have a velocity lower than 15, it will delete them.

5. If you want to filter out notes by duration, activate the Duration option. Then, for the Notes Shorter Than parameter, type the minimum duration value allowed in your material. Also, be sure to specify whether the duration should be measured in ticks or milliseconds by choosing either the Ticks option or Milliseconds option via the Format parameter. As an example, if the lowest duration in your MIDI data should be 20 ticks, then you should set the Notes Shorter Than parameter to 20 and the Format parameter to Ticks. If the Deglitch feature finds any notes within the data that have a duration lower than 20 ticks, it will delete them.

6. Click on OK.

Pro Audio scans the selected MIDI data and removes any notes that fall within the criteria you set. By the way, you can scan for pitch, velocity, and duration all at once by having all the options activated if you'd like.

Slide

Remember back in Chapter 7, "Editing Basics," when I described how to move Clips in the Track View by dragging and dropping them or by using the Clip Properties dialog box to change their Start Times? Well, the Slide feature performs the same function. You can use it to move Clips backward or forward within a Track. So why does Pro Audio provide the same functionality more than once? Because the Slide feature has a few differences. Instead of just working with Clips, you can use it with any kind of selected data from a group of MIDI notes to single audio Events. And instead of having to specify an exact Start Time (as in the Clips Properties dialog box), you can move data by any number of measures, ticks, seconds, or frames. In addition, the Slide feature doesn't give you the option of blending with, replacing, or sliding over existing Events in a Track. It simply moves the selected data so that it overlaps with any existing data. You use it as follows:

1. Using the appropriate View, select the MIDI data or audio Events that you want to move.

2. Select Edit > Slide to open the Slide dialog box (see Figure 8.14).

Figure 8.14

You can use the Slide feature to move any kind of data, not just Clips.

3. If you want to move Events, be sure the Events in Tracks option under the Slide parameter is activated. If you also want to move any Markers that happen to fall within the same time range as the selected data, activate the Markers option.

4. For the By parameter, type the number of units by which you want to move the selected data. If you want to move the data backward in time, enter a negative number. If you want to move the data forward in time, enter a positive number.

5. Choose the type of unit by which you want to move the selected data by activating the appropriate option. You can select Measures, Ticks, Seconds, or Frames.

6. Click on OK.

Pro Audio moves the selected data backward or forward in time by the amount you specified and the unit type that you chose.

Quantize

Even though you might be a great musician, you're bound to occasionally make mistakes when playing your instrument, especially when it comes to timing. No one I know can play in perfect time during every performance, and having to listen to a metronome while you play can sometimes be distracting. Instead of playing notes at the exact same time as the metronome sounds, you'll more than likely play some of them either a little ahead or a little behind the beat. You might even hold some notes a little longer than you're supposed to. Usually, if these timing errors are slight enough, they'll make your performance sound more "human" than anything else. But if the mistakes are large enough to stand out, they can make your performance sound sloppy. At this point, the Quantize feature can come in handy. It can help you correct some of the timing mistakes you make.

CHAPTER 8

To understand how to use the Quantize feature, you first have to know how it works. The Quantize feature scans the MIDI Events in your selected data one by one, and it changes the Start Time of each Event so that it is equal to the nearest rhythmic value that you specify. You specify this rhythmic value by using the Resolution parameter. So, if you want all the Events in your data to be moved to the nearest sixteenth note, you can set the Resolution parameter to Sixteenth. The Quantize feature uses this value to set up an imaginary (for lack of a better word) time grid over your data. In this case, the grid is divided into sixteenth notes.

During the scanning process, the Quantize feature moves an imaginary pointer along the grid one division at a time. Centered around the pointer is an imaginary window of which you can set the size by using the Window parameter. As the Quantize feature moves its pointer and window along the grid, it looks to see whether any of your Events are in the vicinity. Any Events that fall within the window have their Start Times changed so that they line up with the current position of the pointer. Any Events that fall outside the window are left alone. This procedure continues until the Quantize feature comes to the end of the data that you selected. Actually, there's a little more to the procedure than that, but I'll explain the rest as I describe how to use the feature:

1. Select the data that you want to quantize. It can be anything from all the data in your Project, a single Track or Clip, or a selected group of Events.

2. Select Edit > Quantize to open the Quantize dialog box (see Figure 8.15).

Figure 8.15
The Quantize dialog box provides a number of parameters that you can set to determine exactly how you want your data to be corrected.

3. In the Resolution section, set the Resolution parameter. This parameter determines what rhythmic value will be used to set up the imaginary grid and what will be the nearest rhythmic value to which the Events in your data will be aligned. It's best to set this parameter to the smallest note value found in your data. For instance, your data might contain quarter notes, eighth notes, and sixteenth notes. Because the smallest note value in your data is the sixteenth, you would set the Resolution parameter to Sixteenth.

4. In the Change section, activate the appropriate options for the types of Events and the Event Properties that you want to have quantized. You'll almost always want to have the Start Times option activated. Along with the Start Times of Events, you can also quantize the durations of MIDI note Events by activating the Note Durations option. You'll almost always want to have this option activated as well. If you don't, the ends of some notes can overlap the beginnings of others, which might not sound very good. If you want to create a staccato (separated notes) feel to your music, you might not want to quantize the Start Times of Events but just the durations. Activating the Only Notes, Lyrics, and Audio option causes only MIDI note, lyric, and audio Events to be quantized, leaving any other Events (such as MIDI controller Events) alone. You'll usually want to keep this option activated, too; otherwise, the Quantize feature will move controller Events to the nearest grid point, which can actually screw up their timing.

TIP

Even though the Quantize feature can change the Start Times of audio Events, don't be confused into thinking that it can correct the timing of your audio data. It can't. Remember, audio data is different from MIDI data. The Quantize feature can move an entire audio Event to the nearest rhythmic value, and it also can quantize the duration of audio Events if you activate the Stretch Audio Events option in the Change section of the Quantize dialog box. However, if you record a sloppy performance as audio data, you cannot correct it except by doing the recording over again.

You can use one trick, however, to quantize a monophonic (one note at a time) melody or percussion part that was recorded as an audio Event. If you split the Event into smaller Events, each containing one note of the melody, then each note will have its own Start Time, and you can use the Quantize feature to change the timing of each note.

5. In the Options section, set the Strength parameter. Quantizing your data so that all the Events are aligned in perfect time with the grid can make your performance sound mechanical (like it is being played by a machine). So, instead of having the Quantize feature move an Event to the exact current pointer position on the grid during the scanning process, you can have it move the Event only slightly toward the pointer, thus, taking the sloppiness out of the performance but keeping the "human" feel. You can do so by setting a percentage for the Strength parameter. A value of 100 percent means that all Events will be moved to the exact grid point. A value of 50 percent means that the Events will be moved only halfway toward the grid point. You'll have to experiment with this parameter to find the setting that sounds best.

CHAPTER 8

6. Set the Window parameter. This parameter tells Pro Audio how close to the current grid point an Event has to be in order to be quantized. If the Event falls inside the window, it is quantized. If it falls outside the window, it isn't. You set the Window parameter by using a percentage. A value of 100 percent means the window extends halfway before and halfway after the current pointer position on the grid. So, basically all Events get moved; if they don't fall inside the window at the current pointer position, they will fall inside at the next position. A value of 50 percent means the window extends only one-quarter of the way before and after the current pointer position, meaning only half of the Events in your selection will be processed.

7. Set the Offset parameter. This parameter is an extra setting thrown in to make the Quantize feature even more flexible (and complicated) than it already is. When the Quantize feature sets up its imaginary grid over your selected data, the grid is perfectly aligned to the measures and beats in your Project. So, if your data selection starts at the beginning of your Project, the grid will be set up starting at 1:01:000 (measure, beat, tick). If you enter a value for the Offset parameter (in ticks), the grid is offset by the number of ticks that you enter. For example, if you enter an Offset of +3, the grid will be set up starting at 1:01:003 instead of 1:01:000. This means that if the current Event being scanned is initially supposed to be moved to 1:01:000, it will be moved to 1:01:003 instead. Basically, you can use this parameter to offset the selected data from the other data in your Project, in case you want to create some slight timing variations, and so on. It works similarly to the Time Offset parameter in the Track View, which you learned about in Chapter 4, "Working with Projects."

8. Set the Swing parameter, which is yet another parameter that makes the Quantize feature more flexible (and more difficult to understand). You might use it to work on a song that has a "swing" feel to it, similar to that of a waltz, where the first in a pair of notes is played longer than the second. It's difficult to explain, but essentially the Swing parameter distorts the grid by making the space between the grid points uneven. If you leave the parameter set at 50 percent, it doesn't have any effect. If you set it to something like 66 percent, the space between the first two points in the grid becomes twice as much as the space between the second and third points. This pattern of long space, short space is repeated throughout the length of the grid, and your data is aligned according to the uneven grid points. You'll need to experiment with this parameter a bit to hear the effect it has on your data.

9. Click on the Audition button to hear how the quantized data will sound. Go back and make any parameter changes you think might be necessary.

10. If you want to use the same settings again later, save them as a Preset.

11. Click on OK.

Pro Audio quantizes the selected data, and when you play it back, it should sound the same way it did when you listened to it using the Audition feature.

Groove Quantize

Quantizing can be used not only to correct the timing of your performances, but also to add a bit of a creative flair. The Groove Quantize feature works in almost the same way as the Quantize feature, but it's slightly more sophisticated. Instead of using a fixed grid (meaning that you can set the grid to use only straight rhythmic values such as sixteenth notes), it uses a grid with rhythmic values that are based on an existing rhythmic pattern called a Groove Pattern. This Groove Pattern can contain any kind of musical rhythm, even one taken from an existing piece of music.

Basically, the Groove Quantize feature works by imposing the timing, duration, and velocity values of one set of Events onto another set. For example, suppose you record a melody that comes out sounding a bit too mechanical, but your friend slams out this really kickin' MIDI bass line that has the exact "feel" that you want. You can copy the bass Event data and use it as a Groove Pattern to groove quantize the melody Event data. By doing so, you impose the timing, duration, and velocity values (depending on your parameter settings) from the bass line on to the melody. Thus, the melody will have the same rhythm as the bass line but will keep its original pitches.

The preceding example is just one of the many uses for the Groove Quantize feature. Just like the Quantize feature, the Groove Quantize feature provides Strength parameters to give you control over how much influence a Groove Pattern has over the data that you're quantizing. You can define via percentages how much the timing, duration, and velocity values of the Events will be affected, so you can use this feature for all kinds of editing tasks. You can correct off-tempo tracks, add complex beat accents to each measure of a tune, synchronize rhythm and solo tracks, align tracks with bad timing to one with good timing, and steal the "feeling" from tracks, as I explained in the preceding example.

As a matter of fact, groove quantizing has become so popular that companies now sell Groove Pattern files so that you can steal the "feeling" from Tracks that have been recorded by professional keyboard, drum, and guitar players. It's almost like having Steve Vai play on your latest tune! Just look in any copy of *Electronic Musician* or *Keyboard* magazine, and you'll see advertisements for these types of products. Of course, you need to know how to use the Groove Quantize feature before you can make use of these Groove Pattern files, so let me tell you how:

1. If you want to grab the timing, duration, and velocity values from existing data, first select and copy that data so that it is placed into the Clipboard. Otherwise, you can use one of the Groove Patterns included with Pro Audio (which I'll show you how to choose later).

TIP

Earlier in this chapter, I described the Extract Timing feature. If you use this feature to first extract the rhythm from some audio data, you can use that rhythm as a Groove Pattern. Just use the Extract Timing feature to first process your audio data and place the rhythmic values into the Clipboard. Then move on to Step 2.

2. Select the data that you want to groove quantize.

3. Select Edit > Groove Quantize to open the Groove Quantize dialog box (see Figure 8.16).

Figure 8.16
The Groove Quantize dialog box provides a number of parameters that you can set to determine exactly how you want your data to be groove quantized.

4. Set the Groove File parameter. If you're grabbing the values from existing data, as explained previously, then select Clipboard from the drop-down list and skip to Step 6. Otherwise, choose an existing Groove File. Cakewalk ships with only one Groove File (Cakewalk DNA Grooves.grv), so unless you've created your own Groove Files, you can leave this parameter as it is. If you have other Groove Files available, you can load them by clicking on the small button to the right of the Groove File parameter to bring up the Open Groove File dialog box. Just select a file and then click on Open.

5. Set the Groove Pattern parameter. Each Groove File can contain any number of Groove Patterns. The Groove File that comes with Pro Audio contains twelve different Groove Patterns. Choose the Groove Pattern you want to use.

6. The rest of the parameters for the Groove Quantize feature are the same as for the Quantize feature. You need to set the Resolution parameter; the Only Notes, Lyrics, and Audio and Stretch Audio options; and the Window parameters. The Window Sensitivity parameter is the same as the Window parameter for the Quantize feature, but one additional Window parameter is available here. You can choose the If Outside Window parameter to have Groove Quantize change Events even if they fall outside the window. If you select Do Not Change, then Events outside the window are left alone (just as with the Quantize feature). If you select Quantize To Resolution, any Events outside the window are moved to the nearest grid point, as specified by the Resolution parameter. If you select Move To Nearest, then the Window Sensitivity parameter is ignored, and all Events outside the window are moved to the nearest grid point, as defined by the Groove Pattern. If you select Scale Time, Pro Audio looks at the Events located right before and after the current Event being scanned (as long as they are within the window), and it sets their relative timing so that they're the same. The Scale Time parameter is very difficult to explain, so you should try it out to hear what kind of effect it has on your music.

7. You also need to set the Strength parameters. They work the same as with the Quantize feature, but instead of just having one parameter that affects the timing of Events, three Strength parameters are provided to give you control over how the Groove Quantize feature will affect the Time, Duration, and Velocity of each Event. If you want the Events to have the exact same timing, duration, and velocity of their counterparts in the Groove Pattern, then set all these parameters to 100 percent. Otherwise, you can make it so the Events take on only some of the "feel" of the Events in the Groove Pattern by adjusting the percentages of these parameters.

8. Click on the Audition button to hear how the quantized data will
    sound. Go back and make any parameter changes you think might be
    necessary.

9. If you want to use the same settings again later, save them as a Preset.

10. Click on OK.

Pro Audio quantizes the selected data so that (depending on your
parameter settings) the timing, duration, and velocity of the Events sound
exactly or somewhat like those in the Groove Pattern you used. By the
way, if the Groove Pattern is shorter than the material you are quantizing,
the Groove Quantize feature will loop through the Groove Pattern as
many times as necessary to get to the end of your selected data. For
example, if you use a Groove Pattern that is only one measure long, but
your selected data is three measures, then the timing, duration, and
velocity values of the Groove Pattern will be repeated over each of those
three measures.

Saving Groove Patterns

If you create your own Groove Pattern by grabbing the timing, duration,
and velocity values from existing data, you can save it for later use as
follows:

1. After you've gone through steps 1 through 4 in the preceding
    example on how to use the Groove Quantize feature, and you've set
    the Groove File parameter to Clipboard, click on the Define button at
    the bottom of the Groove Quantize dialog box to open the Define
    Groove dialog box (see Figure 8.17).

Figure 8.17
Using the Define
Groove dialog box, you
can save your own
Groove Patterns and
Groove Files.

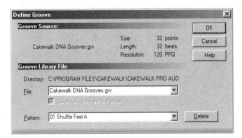

2. In the Groove Library File section, select an existing Groove File via
    the File parameter. You also can type a new name to create your own
    new Groove File.

NOTE

Pro Audio supports two types of Groove Files. One type is the DNA Groove Files, which contain only timing data but are compatible with other sequencing software. The Groove Files being sold by other companies are usually in this file format. Pro Audio also has its own proprietary Groove File format that stores timing, duration, and velocity data. Unless you really need to share your Groove Files with others who don't own Pro Audio, I suggest you save your files in the Pro Audio format because it provides more flexibility. To do so, be sure to activate the Cakewalk Groove File Format option in the Define Groove dialog box.

3. If you want to replace an existing Groove Pattern in the current Groove File, just select one from the list via the Pattern parameter. If you want to save your Groove Pattern under a new name, type the name via the Pattern parameter.

TIP

You also can delete existing Groove Patterns in the current Groove File. Just select the Groove Pattern that you want to delete via the Pattern parameter and click on the Delete button. Pro Audio then asks you to confirm the deletion process.

4. Click on OK. If you're replacing an existing Groove Pattern, Pro Audio will ask you to confirm the replacement process.

Pro Audio saves your new Groove Pattern inside the Groove File that you selected (or created) under the name that you specified.

TIP

For examples of some cool applications for the Groove Quantize feature, look at pages 6-26 and 6-27 of the Pro Audio User's Guide.

Interpolate

Throughout the text of this book, I've mentioned the name Pro Audio quite a few times. What if I want to change all those instances of the phrase to Pro Audio 9 instead? Luckily, I'm using a word processing program on my computer, so all I would have to do is use the search and replace feature to have the program automatically make the changes for me. I mention this point because the Interpolate feature is similar to the search and replace feature you find in most word processing programs. The difference is that the Interpolate feature works with Event Properties, and in addition to simply searching and replacing, it can scale whole ranges of Event Properties from one set of values to another set of values. This means that you can easily transpose notes, change key signatures, convert one type of controller message into another type of controller message, and so on. It works like this:

1. Select the data that you want to change.

2. Select Edit > Interpolate to open the Event Filter–Search dialog box. You learned about this dialog box and its parameters in Chapter 5, "Getting Around in Pro Audio."

3. Set all the available parameters so that Pro Audio can select the exact Events that you want to process.

4. Click on OK to open the Event Filter–Replace dialog box (see Figure 8.18). This dialog box is also almost the same as the Event Filter–Search dialog box. It has the same settings, except that some of the settings are not available, because here you need to enter only the values for which you want to change the original selected data. So, enter the replacement values in the appropriate parameters.

Figure 8.18
In the Event Filter–Replace dialog box, you can enter the replacement values for only the data you're trying to change.

5. Click on OK.

Pro Audio selects all the Events in your initial selection according to the parameters that you set the in Event Filter–Search dialog box. It then changes the values of those Events according to the parameters that you set in the Event Filter–Replace dialog box.

Interpolation Applications

You didn't think I was going to leave you high and dry trying to figure out such a complicated feature, did you? Actually, when you get the hang of it, using the Interpolate feature isn't too difficult, especially if you're just trying to make straight replacements of data. Anyway, the following sections describe some of the changes that you can make with this feature.

Straight Replacement

If all you want to do is replace one value with another, setting up the parameters in both dialog boxes is fairly easy. Say you want to change all the notes having a pitch of C#2 with notes having a pitch of D#7. To do so, set up the Event Filter–Search dialog box so that only the Note option is activated in the Include section. Then type C#2 for both the Key Min and Key Max parameters, and click on OK. In the Event Filter–Replace dialog box, type D#7 for the Key Min and Key Max parameters, and click on OK. All the C#2 notes are then changed to D#7 notes. Pretty easy, no? And you can use this approach with any of the data. Earlier, I mentioned changing one type of controller message to another. Just use the Control option along with the Number Min and Number Max parameters like you did with the Note option and the Key Min and Key Max parameters.

> **TIP**
>
> You also can use wild cards when designating an octave number for the pitch of a note. In regards to the example, say you want to change all the C# notes to D notes, not just the ones in octave 2 to octave 7. Instead of using C#2, you can use C#?, and instead of using D#7, you can use D#?. The ? is the wild card, which stands for any octave.

Scaling Values

When you're working with ranges of values, you can use the Interpolate feature to scale them from one range to another. This capability is useful in limiting certain values to keep them within a set of boundaries. For example, some of the note velocities in one of your MIDI Tracks might be a bit high, and you want to quiet them down a bit. Usually, quieting them means having to use the Piano Roll View to change them all one by one. With the Interpolate feature, you can compress their range down in a couple of easy steps. To do so, set up the Event Filter–Search dialog box so that only the Note option is activated in the Include section. Then type 0 for the Velocity Min and 127 for the Velocity Max, and click on OK. In the Event Filter–Replace dialog box, type 0 for the Velocity Min and 100 for the Velocity Max, and click on OK. All the note velocities are then scaled down from a range of 0 to 127 to a range of 0 to 100. See how it works? You can use this approach with any of the other value ranges, too.

Inverting Values

You also can invert any of the value ranges by reversing the Min and Max parameters. For example, what if you want to make all the loud volume controller messages soft and the soft volume controller messages loud? To do so, set up the Event Filter–Search dialog box so that only the Control option is activated in the Include section. Then type 7 (the number for volume controller messages) for both the Number Min and Number Max parameters. Also, type 0 for Value Min and 127 for Value Max, and click on OK. In the Event Filter–Replace dialog box, type 7 for both the Number Min and Number Max parameters. Also, type 127 for Value Min and 0 for Value Max, and click on OK. All the loud sections of your selected data then become soft and vice versa. Again, you can use this technique for any of the other value ranges.

As a matter of fact, you can change a whole bunch of different parameters at once (even mix straight replacement, scaling, and inverting) by activating the appropriate parameters in the Event Filter–Search dialog box. For instance, you can easily set up all three of the preceding examples so that you will have to use the Interpolate feature only one time to process the same data. This feature is very powerful. You should experiment with it as much as possible because, in the long run, it can save you a lot of editing time.

TIP
You also can find some other Interpolate application ideas on pages 6-34 and 6-35 of the Pro Audio User's Guide. Check them out.

Length

The Length feature is one of the very simple but also very useful features provided in Pro Audio. Using it, you can change the size of a Clip, audio Event, or group of selected data by specifying a percentage. It works like this:

1. Select the data that you want to change.

2. Select Edit > Length to open the Length dialog box (see Figure 8.19).

Figure 8.19
You can change the size of Clips, audio Events, or selected groups of Events by using the Length feature.

3. Activate the Start Times, Durations, and/or Stretch Audio options. Activating the Start Times option makes the Length feature change the Start Times of the selected Events so that the entire selection will change in size. Activating the Durations option makes the Length feature change the durations of the selected Events. If you activate the Durations option without the Start Times option, the Length feature will change only the size of the durations of the selected Events. This feature can be useful if you want to create a staccato effect for your notes. And, of course, if you want your audio data to be stretched, you can activate the Stretch Audio option, which you learned about earlier.

4. Enter a value for the By Percent parameter. A value of 100 percent doesn't make any changes at all. A value of 50 percent changes the selection to half of its original length. And a value of 200 percent changes the selection to twice its original length.

5. Click on OK.

Pro Audio changes the size of the Clip(s), audio Event(s), or entire selection of Events according to your parameter specifications.

TIP

For a more intuitive way to change the length of your data (meaning you can enter a length by using an actual time value instead of a percentage), use the Fit to Time feature, which you'll learn about later in this chapter.

NOTE

The Run CAL feature (which is the next feature listed in the Edit menu) is related to Pro Audio's Cakewalk Application Language (CAL). This is a very in-depth subject, so I've devoted two whole chapters to it. You can find more information in Chapter 14, "CAL 101," and Chapter 15, "Advanced CAL Techniques."

Retrograde

The Retrograde feature works similarly to the Reverse feature that you learned about earlier in this chapter. Instead of reversing the data in audio Events, however, the Retrograde feature reverses MIDI data. This means that you can have your MIDI data play backward if you apply this feature. Just select the data you want to reverse, and then select Edit > Retrograde. Pro Audio then reverses the order of the selected Events. In other words, if you were looking at the data via the Event View, the data is changed so that, essentially, the list is flipped upside down. That's about it.

Transpose

Transposition is a common occurrence when you're composing music, and Pro Audio's Transpose feature enables you to transpose quickly and easily. It works like this:

1. Select the data that you want to transpose.

2. Select Edit > Transpose to open the Transpose dialog box (see Figure 8.20).

Figure 8.20

By entering a number of steps, you can transpose the pitches of note Events up or down using the Transpose feature.

3. You can use the Transpose feature to transpose the pitches of your note Events either chromatically so that they can be changed by half steps or diatonically so that they remain in the current key signature of your Project. If you want to transpose chromatically, leave the Diatonic Math option deactivated. If you want to transpose diatonically, activate the Diatonic Math option.

4. If you have selected any audio data, you can opt to have its pitch changed as well. To do so, activate the Transpose Audio option. Pro Audio can change the pitch of audio data by an octave above or below its current pitch, but if you change it any more than a couple of half steps, it won't sound very good. The audio pitch shifting technology in Pro Audio is still in the early stages. You'll learn more about it in Chapter 9, "Effects: The Really Cool Stuff."

5. Enter a value for the Amount parameter. A positive value transposes up, and a negative value transposes down. If you are transposing chromatically, this value corresponds to half steps. If you are transposing diatonically, the Transpose feature changes the pitches of your notes according the major scale of the current key signature. So, for example, if you enter a value of +1, and the key signature is D major, a D becomes an E, an E becomes an F#, and so on.

6. Click on OK.

Pro Audio transposes the pitches of the notes (or audio) in the selected data according to your parameter settings.

Scale Velocity

You learned about scaling the velocity values of Events earlier in the description of the Interpolate feature. Using the Scale Velocity feature, you can do the same thing, but this feature has one extra option that enables you to scale the velocities by a percentage rather than enter exact values or a range of values. It works like this:

1. Select the data that you want to change.

2. Select Edit > Scale Velocity to open the Scale Velocity dialog box (see Figure 8.21).

Figure 8.21
You can scale the velocities of note Events by percentages if you use the Scale Velocity feature.

3. If you want to scale the velocities by percentages, activate the Percentages option. Otherwise, the values that you enter will be exact velocity values.

4. Enter values for the Begin and End parameters. For example, you can use the Scale Velocity feature to create crescendos and decrescendos. To create a crescendo, enter a small value (such as 0 or 50 percent) for the Begin parameter and a larger value (such as 127 or 150 percent) for the End parameter. Do the opposite for a decrescendo.

5. Click on OK.

Pro Audio scales the velocity values of the note Events within the selected data according your parameter settings.

TIP

You can create crescendos and decrescendos with more precise control by drawing them in with the Draw Line tool in the Controller pane of the Piano Roll View. You learned how to use this tool in Chapter 7, "Editing Basics."

CHAPTER 8

Fit to Time

As I mentioned earlier, the Fit to Time feature works similarly to the Length feature: Using it, you can change the size of Clips, audio Events, and selected groups of data. But instead of having to use a percentage, you can specify an actual time (according to the Time Ruler) at which the data will end. For example, if you have a Clip that begins at 1:01:000 and ends at 4:02:000, the Start Time of the Clip remains the same, but you can change the End Time of the Clip so that it stops playing at the exact moment that you specify. This feature is great when you need to compose music to a precise length, such as for a radio commercial or a video. It works like this:

1.   Select the data that you want to change.

2.   Select Edit > Fit to Time to open the Fit to Time dialog box (see Figure 8.22).

Figure 8.22

You can specify the exact length of Clips, audio Events, or selected groups of Events by using the Fit to Time feature.

3.   The Original Time Span section shows the beginning and end times for the selected data. In the Adjust to End at New Time section, enter a new end time for the selected data. You can enter either hours, minutes, seconds, and frames or measures, beats, and ticks. To change the format, click on the Format button.

4.   In the Modify by Changing section, activate either the Tempo Map option or the Event Times option. If you want the actual data to be changed (meaning the Start Times of every Event in the selection will be adjusted to accommodate the new end time), activate the Event Times option. If you would rather leave the data as it is and just have Pro Audio insert tempo changes into the Project to accommodate the new end time, activate the Tempo Map option. The key difference here is that using the Tempo Map option affects the entire Project, and all the data in all the Tracks during the selected time will play at a different rate. If you want the data in only one Track to be affected, you must use the Event Times option.

5.   If you want to change the length of audio Events, you have to activate the Stretch Audio option.

6.   Click on OK.

Pro Audio either changes the length of the selected data or inserts tempo changes into the Project (depending on your parameter settings) to accommodate the new end time that you specify.

TIP

For an example on using the Fit to Time feature, check out Tutorial 3 in the Pro Audio User's Guide, pages 2-29 to 2-39.

Fit Improvisation

Having to play along with a metronome while recording in Pro Audio can be a nuisance sometimes. Depending on the type of music you are performing, using the metronome might not be conducive to your mood during the performance, which means you might end up with a less than acceptable recording. Some people just can't stand using a metronome. The problem is that if you don't use the metronome while recording in Pro Audio, your data will not line up correctly to the measure, beat, and tick values along the Time Ruler. Therefore, editing your music can be a lot more difficult.

If you are one of those people who hate metronomes, then you're in luck. Pro Audio enables you to record your MIDI Tracks without using the metronome but still line up your data correctly after the fact by using the Fit Improvisation feature. This feature works by adding tempo changes to your Project according to an additional reference Track that you must record. This reference Track gives Pro Audio an idea of the tempo at which you were playing when you were recording your MIDI Track without the metronome. The following is a more detailed version of how this feature works:

1. Record a MIDI Track without using the metronome. For the most accurate results, try to play by using as steady a tempo as possible.

2. Select Options > Global to open the Global Options dialog box. Click on the MIDI tab. Be sure only the Notes option in the Record section is activated. It filters out any extraneous Events when you're recording your reference Track so that they don't mess up the timing. The more accurate your reference Track, the better. After you're done recording it, you can go back to the Global Options dialog box and change the options back to the way they were.

3. Record a reference MIDI Track. To do so, simply tap out the tempo of your initial MIDI recording by hitting a key on your MIDI instrument for every beat. So, if you recorded a Track in 4/4 time, you have to hit the key four times for every measure of music you recorded. Also, be sure that the first note in your reference Track has a Start Time of 1:01:000 so that it starts at the very beginning of the Project. You can adjust it manually by using the Event View or Piano Roll View if you have to.

4. Select the reference Track.

5. Select Edit > Fit Improvisation.

Pro Audio scans your reference Track, analyzing where the beats fall, and adds tempo changes to your Project so that the data in your recorded Track lines up with the measure, beat, and tick values on the Time Ruler. Now you can edit your data just as you would any other data that was recorded along with the metronome.

9

Effects: The Really Cool Stuff

Just as adding spices to a recipe makes it taste better, adding effects to your music data makes it sound better. Effects can make the difference between a dull, lifeless recording and a recording that really rocks. For example, you can apply echoes and background ambiance to give the illusion that your song was recorded in a particular environment, like a concert hall. You also can use effects to make your vocals sound rich and full. And the list goes on. Pro Audio provides a number of different Effects features that you can use to spice up both your MIDI and audio Tracks. Although applying these Effects to your data isn't overly complicated, understanding what they do and how to use them can sometimes be confusing. So, this chapter covers the following topics:

▶ Plug-ins

▶ Offline and real-time processing

▶ Audio Effects: Chorus, Equalization, Reverb, Delay, Flanging, Pitch shifting, Time and pitch stretching

▶ MIDI Effects: Quantization, Delay, Filtering, Arpeggio, Chord analyzing, Transposition, and Velocity

▶ The Session Drummer

Offline or Real-Time?

Pro Audio's Effects features are very similar to its editing features (which you learned about in Chapter 8, "Exploring the Editing Tools"), but they do have a couple of differences. One difference is that, although the Effects features are included with Pro Audio, they are not actually a part of the main application. Instead, they come in the form of plug-ins.

CHAPTER 9

NOTE

In basic terms, a *plug-in* is a small computer program that by itself does nothing, but when used together with a larger application provides added functionality to the larger program. You, therefore, can use plug-ins to easily add new features to a program. In Pro Audio's case, plug-ins provide you with additional ways to process your MIDI and audio data. As a matter of fact, Cakewalk offers additional plug-in products for sale (Audio FX 1, Audio FX 2, and Audio FX 3) so that you can add even more power to your copy of Pro Audio.

What's more, Cakewalk isn't the only vendor that can sell plug-ins for Pro Audio. You can use plug-ins from a number of different third-party vendors because many plug-ins are programmed using standard computer code. Pro Audio enables you to use any audio plug-ins that are DirectX-compatible. DirectX is special computer code built into Windows that controls all its multimedia functions, such as playing audio and video. So, if you are looking for new audio plug-ins to add to Pro Audio, just make sure they are DirectX-compatible (it will say so on the package), and you can be sure they will work.

Unfortunately, no standard computer code is available for MIDI plug-ins yet. However, Cakewalk has been kind enough to share its code with other vendors, so you can purchase additional MIDI plug-ins, too. Actually, Pro Audio includes a demonstration MIDI plug-in from another vendor: Style Enhancer Micro 1.28 Lite.

Because the Effects features are plug-ins, this means that they add not only functionality to Pro Audio, but also more flexibility. Unlike the editing features, the Effects features can be used to process your data in two different ways: offline and real-time.

Offline Processing

You already know what offline processing is, because you've performed it while using Pro Audio's editing features. With offline processing, the MIDI and audio data in your Clips and Tracks are permanently changed. Therefore, offline processing is also called *destructive processing,* because it "destroys" the original data by modifying (or overwriting) it according to any processing that you apply.

NOTE

As you know, you can remove any offline processing done to your data by using Pro Audio's Undo feature. You also can load a saved copy of your Project containing the original data. But neither of these restoration methods is as convenient as using real-time processing, which I'll explain shortly.

The basic procedure for using Effects in offline mode is essentially the same as when using any of Pro Audio's editing features. You just follow these steps:

1. Select the data that you want to change.

2. Choose the MIDI or audio Effect feature that you want to use by selecting either Edit > Audio Effects or Edit > MIDI Effects.

3. Make the appropriate parameter adjustments in the dialog box that appears.

4. Click on the Audition button to test the current parameter settings. Make further adjustments if necessary.

5. If you're using an audio Effect, click on the Mixing tab (see Figure 9.1). These parameters determine how your data will be processed. If you select the Process In-Place, Mono Result option, Pro Audio takes your originally selected data, processes it with the chosen Effect, and then replaces it with the processed data. This means your original data is overwritten. If your original data was in stereo, it is converted into *mono* (or *monophonic*, meaning only one channel, whereas stereo has two channels, left and right). If you select the Process In-Place, Stereo Result option, Pro Audio takes your originally selected data, processes it with the chosen Effect, and then replaces it with the processed data. Again, this means your original data is overwritten. Also, if your original data was in mono, it is converted into stereo. If you select the Create a Send Submix option, Pro Audio takes your selected data, mixes it all together into a stereo signal, processes it with the chosen Effect, and then places it into a new stereo Track, which you designate by setting the Return Track parameter. In addition, if you activate the Keep Original Data option, your original data is left untouched. If you deactivate the Keep Original Data option, your original data is deleted.

Figure 9.1
The Mixing parameters are available only when you're using an audio Effect in offline mode.

6. Click on OK to close the dialog box.

Pro Audio processes the data by applying the Effect according to the parameter settings you specify. It's very simple. Don't worry; I'll go over each individual Effect feature and its corresponding parameters later in the chapter.

Real-Time Processing

On the other hand, real-time processing doesn't change the actual data in your Clips and Tracks. Instead, the Effects features are applied only during playback, letting you hear the results while leaving your original data intact. Therefore, real-time processing is also called *non-destructive,* because it doesn't apply any permanent changes to your data. By simply turning off the Effects features, you can listen to your data as it was originally recorded.

The basic procedure for using Effects in real-time mode isn't any more difficult than using them in offline mode, just a little different, as you can see here:

1. In the Track View, click in the Effects field of the Track to which you want to add an Effect. The Effects Bin for that Track then opens.

NOTE

You also can apply Effects in real-time by using the Console View, but I'll talk about that approach in Chapter 10, "Mixing It Down."

2. Right-click within the Effects Bin and select the Effect that you want to use from the pop-up menu. Depending on whether the Track is for MIDI or audio, the list of Effects is different. The Effect you choose is added to the list in the Effects Bin.

3. In the Effects Bin, double-click on the name of the Effect to open its corresponding window.

NOTE

In real-time mode, the parameters of an Effect are displayed in a window instead of a dialog box. You, therefore, can access any of the other features in Pro Audio while still having access to the Effect parameters. You also can use more than one Effect at the same time, which I'll talk about in a moment.

4. Make the appropriate parameter adjustments.

5. Start playback of the Project. You immediately hear the results of the Effect being applied to the data in the Track. While the Project plays, you can make further parameter adjustments, if necessary.

TIP

If you want to make a quick comparison between how the original data sound and how the data sound with the Effect applied, use the Bypass button. This button (located within the Effect window) is available only when you're applying Effects to audio Tracks. When you activate the button, it bypasses (or turns off) the Effect so that you can hear how the original data sound. When you deactivate the button, you can hear how the data sound with the Effect being applied.

NOTE

Notice that no Audition button is shown in the Effect window. It isn't needed, because in real-time mode you can hear the results as the Project plays. Also notice that no Mixing tab is shown. In real-time mode, all mixing is handled via the Console View, which I'll talk about in Chapter 10, "Mixing It Down." In addition, Effects used in real-time mode don't provide a Cancel button. Instead, they provide a Reset and Cancel button, which still applies the Effect to the Track but with the default parameter settings. Any parameter settings that you changed are removed.

6. If you want to add another Effect to the same Track (or add some Effects to different Tracks), go back to Step 1. You either can leave the Effects windows open or you can close them. It doesn't matter. You also can let the Project continue to play as you add new Effects. As soon as you add an Effect to the Effects Bin, you hear the results according to the current parameter settings.

7. If you want to remove an Effect, click in the Effects field of the Track from which you want to remove the Effect. The Effects Bin for that Track then opens. Right-click on the Effect that you want to remove and select Delete from the pop-up menu.

TIP

If you apply more than one Effect to a Track, the order in which the Effects appear in the Effects Bin determines the order they are applied to the data in the Track. For example, if you have the Chorus and Reverb Effects added to the Effects Bin (in that order) of an audio Track, Pro Audio first applies the Chorus Effect to the data. It then takes the result of that application and applies the Reverb Effect to it. This means that the order in which you apply Effects to a Track matters. If you apply Effects in a different order, you get different results. This makes for some interesting experimentation. To change the order of the Effects listed in the Effects Bin, simply drag and drop the name of an Effect up or down within the list.

CHAPTER 9

You can simply go on using Pro Audio with the real-time Effects in place. Remember that you will be aware of the results only during playback. The original data look the same even if you examine them in the various Views. Also, doing any editing to your original data doesn't change how the Effects are applied. For example, if you have a Track set up with some Effects applied and you transpose the pitch of one of the Clips within that Track, during playback Pro Audio still applies the Effects to the Track in the same way. When the Now Time reaches the point in the Track containing the transposed Clip, you simply hear the Effect applied to the transposed data. This is one of the features that makes real-time Effects so flexible.

Advantages and Disadvantages

You might be asking yourself, "Why don't I just use real-time processing all the time because it's so much more flexible?" Well, applying Effects in real-time is very flexible, but in a couple of instances, you need to apply them offline. The first has to do with your computer's processing power. Most of Pro Audio's Effects need to perform complex mathematical calculations to achieve their results. Applying Effects in real-time means that not only does your computer have to deal with these calculations, but it also has to deal with Pro Audio playing back your MIDI and audio data. All these things going on at once can put a lot of strain on your computer's CPU. So, if you use too many Effects in real-time at once, your computer might not be able to keep up; you might hear skips in playback or Pro Audio might stop playing altogether. If this ever happens, you need to apply some of the Effects offline and just keep only a few of them going in real-time. You lose a bit of flexibility in terms of being able to make changes to your data, but there's no limit to the number of Effects that you can apply to your data offline.

TIP

One thing that you can do to make applying Effects offline a little more flexible is to select the Create a Send Submix option and activate the Keep Original Data option under the Mixing tab when you're applying an Effect. This way, you can keep your original data intact and place only the output from the Effect in another Track. Although this approach doesn't enable you to change how the Effect is applied, you can adjust how much of the Effect you want to hear by adjusting the volumes of the two Tracks. If you want to hear more of the original data, raise the volume on the original data Track and lower the volume on the Track that contains the processed data-and vice versa if you want to hear more of the processed data.

Applying Effects offline also comes in handy when you want to process some specifically selected data. For example, if you want to process a short segment of data within a Track or within a Clip, you have to do it offline. In real-time, you can apply Effects only to whole Tracks.

Audio Effects

Pro Audio provides two different sets of audio Effects: CFX Effects and Cakewalk FX Effects. If you select either Edit > Audio Effects > Cakewalk or Edit > Audio Effects > CFX, you'll notice that both sets of Effects contain the same types of plug-ins (although a few more Cakewalk FX plug-ins are available). Why would Cakewalk include two sets of Effects that accomplish the same tasks?

Well, the Cakewalk FX Effects are actually a newer set of plug-ins that provide superior quality and more parameter settings, making them more flexible. The Cakewalk FX Effects were also designed to work specifically with stereo audio. They include parameters for both the left and right stereo channels. The CFX Effects are left over from an older version of Pro Audio. Their processing quality isn't as good as the Cakewalk FX Effects, and they include fewer parameter settings; hence, they are less flexible. They are also more suited for processing monophonic audio. But using the CFX Effects does present one advantage. They don't take up as much computer processing power as the Cakewalk FX Effects. This means that you can apply a lot more of the CFX Effects to your Tracks at once in real-time.

You also might have noticed that some of the Effects mimic some of Pro Audio's editing features (as is the case with EQ). They mimic these Effects so that you can process your data with these features in real-time. Pro Audio's editing features can't be used in real-time because they aren't plug-ins. The Effects features, however, come with their own sets of parameters, so I'll go over them here for you step by step.

NOTE

Because I've already covered how to apply Effects offline and in real-time, I'm just going to include the basic offline steps (along with parameter descriptions) in each of the following explanations. For detailed step-by-step procedures for applying Effects offline and in real-time, refer to the previous sections in this chapter.

CHAPTER 9

Equalization

I talked about the how, what, and why of equalization back in Chapter 8, "Exploring the Editing Tools." In addition to the two EQ editing features, Pro Audio provides two EQ Effects for you to use. Both are similar to the Parametric EQ editing feature.

CFX 2-Band EQ

As a matter of fact, the CFX EQ Effect has the same exact available parameters as the Parametric EQ editing feature, but instead of one set of parameters, it has two. With these two parameters, you can apply two different types of equalization to your data at once. You use it as follows:

1. Select the audio data that you want to process.

2. Select Edit > Audio Effects > CFX > 2-Band EQ to open the 2-band EQ dialog box (see Figure 9.2).

Figure 9.2
You can use the CFX 2-Band EQ Effect to apply two different types of equalization to your data at once.

3. Under the Settings tab, activate one or both of the Active options to turn on each type of EQ.

4. Set the F1, F2, Gain, and Cut parameters. I explained these parameters in the Equalization section of Chapter 8, "Exploring the Editing Tools."

NOTE
You've probably noticed that one parameter setting is missing: the Q (or Quality) parameter. It isn't here because the CFX 2-Band EQ Effect has a permanent Q parameter setting of 2. This is one of the factors that keeps this Effect from taking up too much computer processing power. If you need more flexibility, use the Cakewalk FX EQ Effect.

5. Click on the Audition button to test the current parameter settings. Make further adjustments, if necessary.

6. Set the appropriate options under the Mixing tab.

7. If you want to use the current settings at a later time, save them as a Preset.

8. Click on OK.

Pro Audio processes the data by applying the Effect according to the parameter settings you specified.

Cakewalk FX EQ

Even though the Cakewalk FX EQ Effect also provides parametric equalization, its parameters are a bit different from those previously mentioned. You use it like this:

1. Select the audio data that you want to process.

2. Select Edit > Audio Effects > Cakewalk > FX EQ to open the FX EQ dialog box (see Figure 9.3).

Figure 9.3
The FX EQ Effect also provides parametric equalization but with slightly different parameter settings.

3. In the Band section under the Transfer function tab, select the number of the EQ band that you want to modify. Like the 2-Band EQ Effect, the FX EQ Effect enables you to set up more than one equalization type at once. In this case, you can have up to four different equalization types set up to process your data at the same time. This way, you can do some very complex equalization processing.

4. You'll notice a couple of familiar parameters in the Band Data section: Gain and Q. They work just as they do in all the other EQ features. You can set the Gain from -24 to +24dB, and you can set the Q from 0.1 to 30. The Center Freq (short for frequency) parameter works a bit differently depending on what type of equalization you choose in the Band Type section. Essentially, it determines the frequency below which other frequencies will be cut or boosted, above which other frequencies will be cut or boosted, or exactly where boosting or cutting will occur. You can set the Center Freq from 16 to 22050Hz. Choose the settings for these parameters that you want to use.

5. In the Band Type section, choose the type of equalization that you want to use. If you choose the Low shelf option, any frequencies below the Center Freq are either boosted or cut depending on how you set the Gain parameter. If you choose the High shelf option, any frequencies above the Center Freq are either boosted or cut depending on how you set the Gain parameter. If you choose the Peak option, the exact frequency designated by the Center Freq parameter is the frequency that is boosted or cut, depending on how you set the Gain parameter.

TIP

You've probably noticed that in addition to the parameter settings, the FX EQ dialog box contains a graph display. This graph shows all of the current equalization settings for all four types (bands). Along the left, it shows the amplitudes (gain), and along the bottom, it shows the frequencies. The shape of the line drawn on the graph shows you which frequencies in the audio spectrum are either boosted or cut, but that's not all. Four colored points on the graph represent each EQ band. Red is for band 1, blue for band 2, green for band 3, and purple for band 4. By clicking and dragging on these points, you can graphically change the Gain and Center Freq settings for each of the EQ types (bands), essentially "drawing" the EQ settings. You still have to manually set the Band Type and Q settings, though.

6. If you want to set up more than one equalization type, go through steps 3 through 5 again.

7. Click on the Audition button to test the current parameter settings. Make further adjustments if necessary.

8. Set the appropriate options under the Mixing tab.

9. If you want to use the current settings at a later time, save them as a Preset.

10. Click on OK.

Pro Audio processes the data by applying the Effect according to the parameter settings you specified.

TIP

Because equalization is such an essential tool in sculpting the sound of audio data, you'll probably find yourself using Pro Audio's EQ Effects more often than any of the others. To make setting up real-time EQ Effects a little easier, Pro Audio provides an option that automatically adds an EQ Effect plug-in to every audio Track in your Project when you open it. To turn this option on or off, select Options > Global to open the Global Options dialog box. Under the General tab, click on the Patch EQ to Audio Tracks option to activate or deactivate it.

Delay

You know what an echo is, right? It's a repeating sound that mimics an initial sound. For example, if you yell the word *hello* in a large enclosed area (like a concert hall or a canyon), you hear that word repeated (or echoed) back over and over until it fades away. This effect is exactly what delay enables you to do to your audio data. You can create echoes that vary in the number of repeats and the time between each repeat. Pro Audio includes two delay Effects: CFX Delay/Echo and Cakewalk FX Delay.

CFX Delay/Echo

The CFX Delay/Echo Effect is pretty straightforward in terms of operation. It works like this:

1. Select the audio data that you want to process.

2. Select Edit > Audio Effects > CFX > Delay/Echo to open the Delay/Echo dialog box (see Figure 9.4).

Figure 9.4
Using the CFX Delay/Echo Effect, you can add echoes to your audio data.

3. Under the Settings tab, set the Delay Time parameter. This parameter determines how much time (in milliseconds) occurs between each echo. You can set the Delay Time from 0.02 to 5000 milliseconds (which is equal to 5 seconds).

TIP

Many professional musicians use delay to synchronize the echoes with the music. For instance, you can have the echoes play in time with each quarter note, eighth note, sixteenth note, and so on. All that's required for this cool trick is a little simple math.

Begin by figuring the Delay Time needed to synchronize the echoes to each quarter note. To do so, just divide 60,000 (the number of milliseconds in one minute) by the current Tempo (measured in beats per minute) of your Project. So, for a Tempo of 120 bpm, you get 500 milliseconds. If you set the Delay Time to 500, the resulting echoes sound at the same time as each quarter note.

To figure out the Delay Time for other note values, you just need to divide or multiply. Because an eighth note is half the value of a quarter note, you simply divide 500 by 2 to get 250 milliseconds. A sixteenth note is half the value of an eighth note, so 250 divided by 2 is 125. See how it works? If you want to find out larger note values, just multiply by 2. Because a half note is twice as long as a quarter note, you multiply 500 by 2 to get 1000 milliseconds, and so on.

4. Set the Dry Mix and Wet Mix parameters. When you apply an Effect to your original data, you can determine how much of the Effect and how much of the original data ends up in the final sound. This way, you can add a certain amount of Effect without drowning out the entire original data. The Dry Mix parameter determines how much of the original data you will hear in the final signal, and the Wet Mix parameter determines how much of the Effect you will hear in the final signal. You can set both of these parameters anywhere from 0 to 100 percent.

5. Set the Feedback Mix parameter. With some Effects, you can take their resulting signals and send them back through to have the Effect applied again multiple times. That's what the Feedback Mix parameter does. The resulting sound can be different depending on the Effect. For delay Effects, the Feedback Mix controls how many echoes occur. You can set it anywhere from 0 to 100 percent. The lower the value, the fewer the number of echoes. The higher the value, the more echoes. Unfortunately, there's no way to determine exactly how many echoes will occur according to the percentage. You'll have to experiment with this one.

6. Set the Mod Rate and Mod Depth parameters. These parameters are a bit difficult to describe. They enable you to add a "warble" type of Effect to your audio data along with the echoes. The sound is also similar to that of the tremolo you hear on an electronic organ. To hear what I mean, check out the Fast Tremolo Delay Preset. The Mod Rate determines the speed (in Hz or cycles per second) of the "warble," and the Mod Depth determines how much your audio data will be affected by it. This is just another one of those features that you have to experiment with to understand.

7. Click on the Audition button to test the current parameter settings. Make further adjustments, if necessary.

8. Set the appropriate options under the Mixing tab.

9. If you want to use the current settings at a later time, save them as a Preset.

10. Click on OK.

Pro Audio processes the data by applying the Effect according to the parameter settings you specified.

Cakewalk FX Delay

Very similar to CFX Delay/Echo, the Cakewalk FX Delay Effect has most of the same parameters. Because it works with stereo audio, however, there are two sets, plus a few extras. It works like this:

1. Select the audio data that you want to process.

2. Select Edit > Audio Effects > Cakewalk > FX Delay to open the FX Delay dialog box (see Figure 9.5).

Figure 9.5
The Cakewalk FX Delay Effect has a few additional parameters because it is designed to work with stereo audio.

CHAPTER 9

3. Set the Left Delay and Right Delay parameters. These parameters work the same way as the Delay Time parameter in the CFX Delay/ Echo Effect. In this case, separate controls are available for the left and right stereo channels. A Link option is also available. Activating this option links the Left Delay and Right Delay parameters together so that if you change the value of one, the other is set to the exact same value. Most of the time, you should keep the Link option activated so that both stereo channels have the same amount of delay. However, setting different values for each channel can sometimes yield interesting results. Don't be afraid to experiment.

4. Set the Dry Mix and Wet Mix parameters. These parameters work the same way as the parameters of the same names in the CFX Delay/ Echo Effect. Separate controls are not available for each stereo channel in this case, but a Link option is available. Activating this option links the Dry Mix and Wet Mix parameters together, so if you increase the value of the Wet Mix, the value of the Dry Mix decreases and vice versa. This feature enables you to achieve a perfect balance between the original data and the Effect.

5. Set the Left Feedback and Right Feedback parameters. These parameters work the same way as the Feedback Mix parameter in the CFX Delay/Echo Effect. In this case, separate controls are available for the left and right stereo channels. A Cross Feedback parameter also is available. Using this parameter, you can take the resulting signal from the left channel and send it back through the right channel,and the resulting signal from the right channel and send it back through the left channel. Essentially, this means that this parameter also provides control over the number of echoes that will occur, and at the same time, it helps to make the stereo field sound "fuller."

6. Set the LFO Depth and LFO Rate parameters. These parameters work the same way as the Mod Depth and Mod Rate parameters in the CFX Delay/Echo Effect. In addition, two other options called Triangular and Sinusoidal are available. They determine the type of "warble" to be applied. The Triangular option creates a "coarse" or "sharp" sound, and the Sinusoidal option creates a "smooth" or "flowing" sound. You'll have to try them out to hear what I mean.

7. Click on the Audition button to test the current parameter settings. Make further adjustments, if necessary.

8. Set the appropriate options under the Mixing tab.

9. If you want to use the current settings at a later time, save them as a Preset.

10. Click on OK.

Pro Audio processes the data by applying the Effect according to the parameter settings you specified.

Chorus

Believe it or not, Pro Audio's CFX Chorus and Cakewalk FX Chorus Effects have the exact same parameters as the CFX Delay/Echo and Cakewalk FX Delay Effects. Why? Because technically, chorus is a form of delay. Chorus uses delay and detuning to achieve its results. You don't hear echoes when using chorus, though, because the delay is extremely short. Instead, chorus makes your audio data sound "fatter" or "fuller." The name *chorus* comes from the fact that people singing in a chorus produce a full sound because each person sings slightly out of tune and out of time—not enough to make the music sound bad, but actually better. You can use Pro Audio's chorus Effects to achieve similar results with your audio data. The following sections describe how to use them.

CFX Chorus

To apply the CFX Chorus Effect, you do the following:

1. Select the audio data that you want to process.

2. Select Edit > Audio Effects > CFX > Chorus to open the Chorus dialog box (see Figure 9.6).

Figure 9.6
The CFX Chorus Effect has the same exact parameters as the CFX Delay/Echo Effect, although they produce different results.

3. Under the Settings tab, set the Delay Time parameter. The only difference between this Delay Time parameter and the same parameter in the CFX Delay/Echo Effect is that this one has a range of only 20 to 80 milliseconds. If you set this parameter high enough, you can actually get some quick repeating echoes out of it. For adding chorus to your audio, though, you should keep it set somewhere between 20 and 35.

CHAPTER 9

4. Set the Dry Mix and Wet Mix parameters. I explained these parameters earlier.

5. Set the Feedback Mix parameter. Instead of setting the number of echoes to occur (as in the CFX Delay/Echo Effect), this parameter determines the "thickness" of the chorus. The higher the value, the "thicker" the chorus.

6. Set the Mod Rate and Mod Depth parameters. Instead of adding a "warble" to your audio (as in the CFX Delay/Echo Effect), these parameters determine how detuning is added to the chorus. The Mod Rate determines how quickly the detuning occurs, and the Mod Depth determines the amount of detuning. A high Mod Depth setting makes your audio sound really out of tune (which isn't usually desirable), but a lower setting produces a nice chorusing.

7. Click on the Audition button to test the current parameter settings. Make further adjustments, if necessary.

8. Set the appropriate options under the Mixing tab.

9. If you want to use the current settings at a later time, save them as a Preset.

10. Click on OK.

Pro Audio processes the data by applying the Effect according to the parameter settings you specified.

Cakewalk FX Chorus

To apply the Cakewalk FX Chorus Effect, you do the following:

1. Select the audio data that you want to process.

2. Select Edit > Audio Effects > Cakewalk > FX Chorus to open the FX Chorus dialog box (see Figure 9.7).

Figure 9.7
The Cakewalk FX Chorus Effect has the same exact parameters as the Cakewalk FX Delay Effect, although they produce different results.

3. Set the Left Delay and Right Delay parameters. They provide the same chorusing results as the Delay Time parameter in the CFX Chorus Effect but, of course, for the separate left and right stereo channels. You also can link these parameters together by activating the Link option.

4. Set the Dry Mix and Wet Mix parameters. I explained these parameters earlier.

5. Set the Left Feedback and Right Feedback parameters. They provide the same chorusing results as the Feedback Mix parameter in the CFX Chorus Effect but, of course, for the separate left and right stereo channels. Also, just as the Cross Feedback parameter in the Cakewalk FX Delay Effect enhances the delay, this Cross Feedback parameter enhances the chorus.

6. Set the LFO Depth and LFO Rate parameters. They provide the same results as the Mod Depth and Mod Rate parameters in the CFX Chorus Effect. And I explained the Triangular and Sinusoidal parameters earlier in the "Cakewalk FX Delay" section.

7. Click on the Audition button to test the current parameter settings. Make further adjustments, if necessary.

8. Set the appropriate options under the Mixing tab.

9. If you want to use the current settings at a later time, save them as a Preset.

10. Click on OK.

Pro Audio processes the data by applying the Effect according to the parameter settings you specified.

Flanging

Guess what? Pro Audio's CFX Flanger and Cakewalk FX Flanger Effects have the exact same parameters as the CFX Delay/Echo and Cakewalk FX Delay Effects, too, because (yep, that's right) flanging is also a form of delay. Flanging produces a kind of "spacey" or "whooshy" type of sound. It does so by mixing a slightly delayed version of the original data with itself. As with chorus, you don't hear echoes because the delay occurs so quickly. It's difficult to describe what flanging sounds like, so you'll have to hear it for yourself. You can apply Pro Audio's flanging Effects, as described in the following sections.

CHAPTER 9

CFX Flanger

To apply the CFX Flanger Effect, you do the following:

1.   Select the audio data that you want to process.

2.   Select Edit > Audio Effects > CFX > Flanger to open the Flanger dialog box (see Figure 9.8).

Figure 9.8
The CFX Flanger Effect also has the same exact parameters as the CFX Delay/Echo Effect, although they produce different results.

3.   Under the Settings tab, set the Delay Time parameter. The only difference between this Delay Time parameter and the same parameter in the CFX Delay/Echo Effect is that this one has a range of only 1 to 20 milliseconds. If you set this parameter high enough, you can actually get some chorusing out of it. To add flanging to your audio, though, you should keep it set somewhere between 1 and 11.

4.   Set the Dry Mix and Wet Mix parameters. I explained these parameters earlier.

5.   Set the Feedback Mix parameter. Instead of setting the number of echoes to occur (as in the CFX Delay/Echo Effect), this parameter determines the "thickness" of the flanging. The higher the value, the "thicker" the flanger.

6.   Set the Mod Rate and Mod Depth parameters. Instead of adding a "warble" to your audio (as in the CFX Delay/Echo Effect), these parameters determine the speed and amount of the flanging. The Mod Rate determines how quickly the flanging occurs, and the Mod Depth determines the amount of flanging. Check out some of the included Presets to get an idea of what values to use for these parameters.

7.   Click on the Audition button to test the current parameter settings. Make further adjustments, if necessary.

8. Set the appropriate options under the Mixing tab.

9. If you want to use the current settings at a later time, save them as a Preset.

10. Click on OK.

Pro Audio processes the data by applying the Effect according to the parameter settings you specified.

Cakewalk FX Flanger

To apply the Cakewalk FX Flanger Effect, you do the following:

1. Select the audio data that you want to process.

2. Select Edit > Audio Effects > Cakewalk > FX Flanger to open the FX Flanger dialog box (see Figure 9.9).

Figure 9.9
The Cakewalk FX Flanger Effect also has the same exact parameters as the Cakewalk FX Delay Effect, although they produce different results.

3. Set the Left Delay and Right Delay parameters. They provide the same flanging results as the Delay Time parameter in the CFX Flanger Effect but, of course, for the separate left and right stereo channels. You also can link these parameters together by activating the Link option.

4. Set the Dry Mix and Wet Mix parameters. I explained these parameters earlier.

5. Set the Left Feedback and Right Feedback parameters. They provide the same flanging results as the Feedback Mix parameter in the CFX Flanger Effect but, of course, for the separate left and right stereo channels. Also, just as the Cross Feedback parameter in the Cakewalk FX Delay Effect enhances the delay, this Cross Feedback parameter enhances the flanging.

6. Set the LFO Depth and LFO Rate parameters. They provide the same results as the Mod Depth and Mod Rate parameters in the CFX Flanger Effect. And I explained the Triangular and Sinusoidal parameters earlier in the "Cakewalk FX Delay" section.

CHAPTER 9

7. Click on the Audition button to test the current parameter settings. Make further adjustments, if necessary.

8. Set the appropriate options under the Mixing tab.

9. If you want to use the current settings at a later time, save them as a Preset.

10. Click on OK.

Pro Audio processes the data by applying the Effect according to the parameter settings you specified.

Reverberation

Reverb (short for reverberation) is also a form of delay, but it's special because, instead of distinct echoes, reverb adds a complex series of very small echoes that simulate artificial ambiance. In other words, reverb produces a dense collection of echoes that are so close together that they create a wash of sound, making the original audio data sound like it's being played in another environment, such as a large concert hall. Using Pro Audio's reverb Effects, you can make your music sound like it's being played in all kinds of different places, such as in an arena, a club, or even on a live stage. Pro Audio includes two reverb Effects: CFX Reverb and Cakewalk FX Reverb.

CFX Reverb

To apply the CFX Reverb Effect to your data, you do the following:

1. Select the audio data that you want to process.

2. Select Edit > Audio Effects > CFX > Reverb to open the Reverb dialog box (see Figure 9.10).

Figure 9.10
Using the CFX Reverb Effect, you can add reverberation to your audio data.

3. Under the Settings tab, set the Decay Time parameter. When you're applying reverb to your data, you should imagine what type of environment you want to create. Doing so will help you set the Effect parameters. Technically, the Decay Time determines how long it takes for the reverberation to fade away, but you can think of it as controlling how big the artificial environment will be. The lower the Decay Time, the smaller the environment. The higher the Decay Time, the larger the environment. You can set the Decay Time from 0.20 to 5 seconds. So, if you want to make your music sound like it's playing in a small room, a good Decay Time might be about 0.25. If you want to make your music sound like it's being played on a live stage, a good Decay Time might be about 1.50. Be sure to check out some of the included presets for more sample parameter settings.

4. Set the Dry Mix and Wet Mix parameters. I explained these parameters earlier in the chapter. One point you should note, however, is that in the case of reverb, the Dry Mix and Wet Mix parameters also make a difference on how the Effect sounds. If you set the Dry Mix high and the Wet Mix low, your audio data will sound like it's positioned closer to the "front" of the imaginary environment. If you set the Dry Mix low and the Wet Mix high, your audio data will sound like it's positioned farther away. For example, if you want to simulate what it sounds like to be seated in the very back row of a music concert, you can set the Dry Mix low and the Wet Mix high. You need to experiment to get the exact parameter settings.

5. In the Early Reflections section, choose one of the following options: None, Dense, or Sparse. When you make a sound in any enclosed environment, some very quick echoes always occur because of the reflective surfaces (such as walls) that you are standing next to. These echoes are known as *early reflections*. To make your reverb simulations sound more authentic, Pro Audio provides this parameter so that you can control the density of the early reflections. If you select None, no early reflections are added to the Effect. The Sparse option makes the reflections sound more like distinct echoes, and the Dense option makes the reverb Effect sound "thicker." Early reflections are more prevalent in larger spaces, so if you want to simulate a really large space, you'll probably want to use the Sparse option. If you want to simulate a moderately sized space, you'll probably want to use the Dense option. And if you want to simulate a small space (such as a room), you should use the None option.

6. In the Frequency Cutoff section, set the High Pass and Low Pass parameters. If you think these parameters look like equalization settings, you're right. Using these parameters also helps to create more authentic environment simulations because smaller, closed

environments tend to stifle some frequencies of the audio spectrum, and larger environments usually sound brighter, meaning they promote more of the frequencies.

The High Pass and Low Pass parameters work just like the EQ parameters I described earlier in the chapter. If you activate the High Pass parameter and set its frequency (in Hz), any frequencies above that frequency are allowed to pass and are included in the Effect, and any frequencies below that frequency are cut. If you activate the Low Pass parameter and set its frequency, any frequencies below that frequency are allowed to pass, and any frequencies above that frequency are cut. So, if you want to simulate a small room, you can leave the High Pass parameter deactivated, activate the Low Pass parameter, and set its frequency to around 8000 Hz. This setting would cut out any really high frequencies, making the room sound small and enclosed. For more examples on how to set these parameters, be sure to take a look at some of the included Presets.

7. Click on the Audition button to test the current parameter settings. Make further adjustments, if necessary.

8. Set the appropriate options under the Mixing tab.

9. If you want to use the current settings at a later time, save them as a Preset.

10. Click on OK.

Pro Audio processes the data by applying the Effect according to the parameter settings you specified.

Cakewalk FX Reverb

To apply the Cakewalk FX Reverb Effect to your data, you do the following:

1. Select the audio data that you want to process.

2. Select Edit > Audio Effects > Cakewalk > FX Reverb to open the FX Reverb dialog box (see Figure 9.11).

Figure 9.11
The Cakewalk FX Reverb Effect parameters are exactly the same as the CFX Reverb Effect except that they control both the left and right channels of the signal if your audio is in stereo.

3. Under the Settings tab, set the Decay(s) parameter. It is exactly the same as the Decay Time parameter in the CFX Reverb Effect except that it controls both the left and right channels of the signal if your audio is in stereo.

4. Set the Dry Mix and Wet Mix parameters. They are exactly the same as the Dry Mix and Wet Mix parameters in the CFX Reverb Effect except that they control both the left and right channels of the signal if your audio is in stereo. A Link option is also available, which I explained previously.

5. Choose an early reflections option. The No Echo, Dense Echo, and Sparse Echo options are exactly the same as the None, Dense, and Sparse options in the CFX Reverb Effect, respectively.

6. Activate and set the frequency cutoff parameters. The LP Filter and HP Filter parameters are exactly the same as the Low Pass and High Pass filters in the CFX Reverb Effect, respectively.

7. Click on the Audition button to test the current parameter settings. Make further adjustments, if necessary.

8. Set the appropriate options under the Mixing tab.

9. If you want to use the current settings at a later time, save them as a Preset.

10. Click on OK.

Pro Audio processes the data by applying the Effect according to the parameter settings you specified.

Changing Time and Pitch

In addition to the Length and Transpose editing features, Pro Audio provides the Cakewalk FX Pitch Shifter and Cakewalk FX Time/Pitch Stretch Effects, which you also can use to change the length and pitch of your audio data. The Effects, however, are more powerful and flexible. This is especially true of the Cakewalk FX Time/Pitch Stretch Effect.

You'll notice (when you get into how these Effects work) that the Cakewalk FX Pitch Shifter Effect is actually a CFX Effect. Somehow it got grouped in with the newer Cakewalk FX Effects. In addition, the Cakewalk FX Pitch Shifter Effect really is not as useful and the quality isn't nearly as good as the Cakewalk FX Time/Pitch Stretch Effect.

CHAPTER 9

Cakewalk FX Pitch Shifter

In case you want to try out the Cakewalk FX Pitch Shifter, here's how it works:

1. Select the audio data that you want to process.

2. Select Edit > Audio Effects > Cakewalk > FX Pitch Shifter to open the FX Pitch Shifter dialog box (see Figure 9.12).

Figure 9.12
The Cakewalk FX Pitch Shifter.

3. Under the Settings tab, set the Pitch Shift parameter. It is exactly the same as the Amount parameter in the Transpose editing function. You can use it to transpose the pitch of your audio data from -12 to +12 semitones (a whole octave down or up).

> **TIP**
>
> Normally, when you change the pitch of audio data, the length is altered, too. Raise the pitch and the data get shorter, lower the pitch and the data get longer. When this happens, though, the processed audio no longer plays in sync with the other data in your Project. Luckily, you can use Pro Audio's pitch shifting Effects to change pitch without changing the length of the audio data. The only problem to be wary of is that pitch shifting can produce unwanted artifacts if you use too large an interval. The famous Alvin & the Chipmunks were a product of this problem. It's best to stay within an interval of a major third (four semitones) up or down if possible. The Cakewalk FX Time/Pitch Stretch Effect is the more effective feature, however.

4. Set the Dry Mix and Wet Mix parameters. I explained these parameters earlier in the chapter, but in reference to pitch shifting, you almost always should keep the Dry Mix set to 0 percent and the Wet Mix set to 100 percent.

5. As far as the Feedback Mix, Delay Time, and Mod Depth parameters are concerned, they don't seem to have anything to do with the Cakewalk FX Pitch Shifter Effect. As far as I can tell, changing these parameters only introduces unwanted artifacts into the sound. My

advice is to simply leave them set at their default values: Feedback Mix = 0, Delay Time = 0, and Mod Depth = 35.

6. Click on the Audition button to test the current parameter settings. Make further adjustments, if necessary.

7. Set the appropriate options under the Mixing tab.

8. If you want to use the current settings at a later time, save them as a Preset.

9. Click on OK.

Pro Audio processes the data by applying the Effect according to the parameter settings you specified.

Cakewalk FX Time/Pitch Stretch

The Cakewalk FX Time/Pitch Stretch Effect is much more advanced, flexible, and provides much better quality than the Cakewalk FX Pitch Shifter Effect, but that doesn't mean it's difficult to use. Some of the more advanced parameters can be a bit confusing, but I'll go over them one at a time. The Effect works like this:

1. Select the audio data that you want to process.

2. Select Edit > Audio Effects > Cakewalk > FX Time/Pitch Stretch to open the FX Time/Pitch Stretch dialog box (see Figure 9.13).

Figure 9.13
The Cakewalk FX Time/Pitch Stretch Effect provides advanced time stretching and pitch shifting capabilities.

3. Under the Settings tab, set the Source Material parameter. One of the reasons the Cakewalk FX Time/Pitch Stretch Effect provides better quality than the Cakewalk FX Pitch Shifter Effect is that it takes the type of audio data you are processing into account. You should select the appropriate value for the Source Material parameter according to the type of data you want to process. For instance, if you are processing percussion data, you should set the Source Material parameter to Drums. If you can't find an appropriate setting in the supplied list, just set the Source Material parameter to Generic. This setting usually still provides good results.

CHAPTER 9

4. Set the Time parameter. Using the Time parameter, you can change the length of your audio data as a percentage. If you want to make the data shorter, set the Time parameter to a percentage smaller than 100. For example, to make the data half of its original length, use a setting of 50 percent. If you want to make the data longer, set the Time parameter to a percentage larger than 100. For example, if you want to make data the twice its original length, use a setting of 200 percent. To change the Time parameter, just type a value or use the horizontal slider.

TIP

I mentioned earlier that, when you're transposing audio, it's best to stay within a major third (four semitones) up or down if possible because audio doesn't react very well to higher values. The same concept applies when you're changing the length of audio data. You should try to stay within 10 percent longer or shorter if possible; otherwise, the results might not sound very good. This is another feature that you have to experiment with.

5. Set the Pitch parameter. Using the Pitch parameter, you can transpose your audio data up or down one octave (in semitones). To change the Pitch parameter, just type a value or use the vertical slider.

TIP

Notice that a graph is shown in the FX Time/Pitch Stretch dialog box. Using this graph, you can change the Time and Pitch parameters by dragging the small blue square. Drag the square up or down to change the Pitch parameter. Drag the square left or right to change the Time parameter. Also, if you hold down the Shift key on your computer keyboard at the same time, the square automatically snaps to the exact grid points on the graph.

6. Under the Advanced tab, you'll see three parameters called Block Rate, Overlap Ratio, and Crossfade Ratio. These very advanced settings are used by the Cakewalk FX Time/Pitch Stretch Effect to determine how your data will be processed. Luckily, you don't have to deal with them because they are automatically set to the appropriate values according to the setting you use for the Source Material parameter. So, basically, don't worry about them.

7. You'll also notice two other parameters under the Advanced tab: Accuracy and Algorithm. You do need to deal with these parameters. The Accuracy parameter determines the quality of the Effect processing. If you set the Accuracy parameter to High, you'll get better quality out of the Effect, but it also will take longer to process your data. The Algorithm parameter is strictly for use when you're processing audio data containing vocals. If you're processing any other kind of material, you should leave the Algorithm parameter set

to Normal. In the case of vocal material, though, setting the Algorithm parameter to Formant Preserving tells the Effect to preserve the original vocal characteristics when transposing the pitch up or down. Without the Algorithm parameter set to Formant Preserving, transposing your vocal material up can make it sound like Alvin & The Chipmunks, and transposing it down can make it sound like Fat Albert.

8. Click on the Audition button to test the current parameter settings. Make further adjustments, if necessary.

9. Set the appropriate options under the Mixing tab.

10. If you want to use the current settings at a later time, save them as a Preset.

11. Click on OK.

Pro Audio processes the data by applying the Effect according to the parameter settings you specified.

Amplifier Simulation

For all you electric guitar players out there, Pro Audio provides the Cakewalk FX2 Amp Sim Lite Effect. Using this Effect, you can simulate the sound of real-life guitar amplifiers, making your recorded guitar audio data sound like it's being played through different kinds of amps. To achieve this sound, the Effect uses technology called *Physical Modeling*. In this technology, the characteristics of a real instrument or device are converted into a mathematical algorithm (called a *model*). The model can then be used to apply those same characteristics to your audio data to achieve more authentic sounding recordings. This explanation of the process is simplified, of course, but that's the basic gist of it.

The Cakewalk FX2 Amp Sim Lite Effect is actually one of the plug-ins that comes in Cakewalk's separate Audio FX 2 product. Unfortunately, it is the Lite version, which means it doesn't include as many different kinds of amplifier models, and some of the parameters from the full version are not available here. But this Lite version is still useful, so I'll go over the parameters that you do have access to. It works like this:

1. Select the audio data that you want to process.

TIP

Even though the Cakewalk FX2 Amp Sim Lite Effect was designed for guitar amplifiers, that doesn't mean you can't use it on other types of data. The distorted sounds that the Effect produces also work well on vocals, especially if you're looking for that hard rock sound. Check out some of the music by Kid Rock to hear what I mean.

CHAPTER 9

2. Select Edit > Audio Effects > Cakewalk > FX2 Amp Sim Lite to open the FX2 Amp Sim Lite dialog box (see Figure 9.14).

Figure 9.14
Using the Cakewalk FX2 Amp Sim Lite Effect, you can simulate your music being played through different kinds of guitar amplifiers.

3. Under the Settings tab in the Amp Model section, select the type of guitar amplifier that you want to simulate. In this version of the Effect, you have two options: American Lead and British Overdrive. An additional parameter called Bright also is available in this section. It is similar to the Brightness switch found on many guitar amplifiers. It makes the Effect sound brighter by boosting the high frequencies (everything above 500 Hz) of the audio spectrum.

4. In the Cabinet Enclosure section, select the type of cabinet that you want to use for your virtual guitar amplifier. By setting this parameter, you can simulate different types of speaker enclosures. In this version of the Effect, you have two options: No Speaker and 4x12. If you select the No Speaker option, the Effect sounds as though you plugged your guitar directly into the output of the amplifier and recorded the sound without using a microphone or the amplifier speakers. If you select the 4x12 option, the Effect sounds as though you played your guitar through an amplifier that is 4 inches by 12 inches in size and recorded the sound with a microphone in front of the amplifier speaker. Also, when you select the 4x12 option, two other parameters become available: Open Back and Off-Axis. Activating the Open Back parameter makes the Effect simulate a guitar amplifier that has a cabinet enclosure with an open (rather than a closed) back. Activating the Off-Axis parameter makes the Effect sound as though you placed the virtual microphone (mentioned earlier) off to the side of the amplifier speaker rather than directly in front of it.

5. Normally, you can set the parameters in the Tremolo section to add a "warble" type of sound to the Effect, but you don't have to worry about these parameters because they are not available in this version of the Effect.

6. Set the Bass, Mid, and Treb parameters in the EQ section. These parameters act similarly to the parameters in Pro Audio's Graphic EQ editing feature (which I discussed in Chapter 8). Each parameter enables you to cut or boost a specific frequency by -10 or +10dB. The Bass parameter is set to 60 Hz, the Mid parameter is set to 600 KHz, and the Treb parameter is set to 6000 KHz.

7. Set the Drive parameter. This parameter basically controls how much distortion is added to the audio data being processed.

8. Set the Presence parameter. This parameter acts like a high-pass EQ with a permanent frequency of 750 Hz. You can use it to boost some of the higher frequencies of the Effect, giving it more "presence."

9. Set the Volume parameter. This parameter controls the overall volume of the Effect. No Dry Mix or Wet Mix parameters are available for this Effect, so you hear only the totally processed signal through this one.

10. Click on the Audition button to test the current parameter settings. Make further adjustments, if necessary.

11. Set the appropriate options under the Mixing tab.

12. If you want to use the current settings at a later time, save them as a Preset.

13. Click on OK.

Pro Audio processes the data by applying the Effect according to the parameter settings you specified.

An Effects Exercise

Before I begin talking about Pro Audio's MIDI Effects, I thought it might be nice to work through a simple exercise on applying some of the audio Effects to one of the sample Projects included with Pro Audio. This way, you get a chance to hear some of the Effects in action. Just follow these steps:

1. Select File > Open, choose the Don't Matter Audio and MIDI Demo.bun file, and click on Open to open that sample Project.

2. Close the File Info window, the Staff View, and the Audio View. You don't need them right now.

3. In the Track View, select Tracks 1, 8, and 9. Then select Track > Kill to delete those Tracks. They are MIDI Tracks, and you don't need them for this exercise.

CHAPTER 9

4. Add a little echo to the end of the horn Tracks so that it trails off after the rest of the music stops playing. To do so, select the last Clip in Track 6 (Horns Left) and the last Clip in Track 7 (Horns Right). Then select Edit > Audio Effects > Cakewalk > FX Delay. Choose the Preset called 98bpm Delay to automatically set the parameters for the Effect. Under the Mixing tab, be sure the Process In-Place, Mono Result option is activated. Click on OK.

5. To make the horn Tracks a little fuller, select Edit > Select > None to get rid of the current data selection. Then select Tracks 6 and 7 entirely so that you can process all the data in the Tracks. Select Edit > Audio Effects > Cakewalk > FX Chorus. Choose the Preset called Chorus Gtr to automatically set the parameters for the Effect. Under the Mixing tab, be sure the Process In-Place, Mono Result option is activated. Click on OK.

6. The guitar Track might sound nice with a bit of amp simulation applied to it, so select Track 5 (Guitar), and then select Edit > Audio Effects > Cakewalk > FX2 Amp Sim Lite. Choose the Preset called American Lead to automatically set the parameters for the Effect. Click on OK.

7. The drum and bass Tracks sound fine, but you can simulate the entire Project being played in another environment by selecting all the Tracks (2 through 7). Then select Edit > Audio Effects > Cakewalk > FX Reverb. Choose the Preset called Vocal Med. Room. Under the Mixing tab, be sure the Process In-Place, Mono Result option is activated. Click on OK.

8. Play the Project to hear what it sounds like.

The result is quite a bit different from the original, isn't it? Personally, I think the amp simulation Effect on the guitar is too harsh, but that can be changed easily. As a matter of fact, you can do anything you want. Don't be afraid to experiment to see what the different Effects sound like. With judicious application of Effects, you can make your music sound more professional. Just remember not to go overboard. As with everything else in life, the more you practice, the better you become.

MIDI Effects

Pro Audio provides one set of eight MIDI Effects, a couple of which (Chord Analyzer and Session Drummer) are not really Effects—but I'll get into that later. It also provides a demonstration third-party plug-in called Style Enhancer Micro 1.28 Lite from NTONYX Ltd. You can buy the full version and other MIDI plug-ins from this vendor, too. As far as I know, NTONYX (**www.ntonyx.com**) is currently the only other company creating MIDI plug-ins for Pro Audio at the time of this writing.

Like the audio Effects, some of the MIDI Effects mimic some of Pro Audio's editing features. Again, they have this capability so that you can process your data with these features in real-time. You cannot use Pro Audio's editing features in real-time because they aren't plug-ins. In addition, the Effects provide more power and flexibility, and they include additional parameters not found in the editing features, so I'll go over them here for you step by step.

NOTE

As I mentioned earlier, because I've already covered how to apply Effects offline and in real-time, I'm going to include just the basic offline steps (along with parameter descriptions) in each of the following explanations. For detailed step-by-step procedures for applying Effects offline and in real-time, refer to the previous sections in this chapter.

Automatic Arpeggios

In music, you can play the notes of a chord in a number of different ways. Most often, the notes are played all at once. You also can play them one at a time in sequence; this is called an arpeggio. Pro Audio's Cakewalk FX Arpeggiator Effect automatically creates arpeggios for each note or chord in your selected MIDI data. Depending on how you set the parameters, however, you can achieve some very strange and interesting "melodies." This feature works as follows:

1. Select the MIDI data that you want to process.
2. Select Edit > MIDI Effects > Cakewalk FX > Arpeggiator to open the Arpeggiator dialog box (see Figure 9.15).

Figure 9.15
The Cakewalk FX Arpeggiator Effect automatically converts your selected MIDI data into arpeggios.

3. Set the Swing parameter. This parameter works the same way as the Swing parameter in the Quantize editing feature (which I talked about in Chapter 8). The only difference is that of 50 percent being the normal setting (meaning no "swing" is applied); in this case, 0 percent is the normal setting. And you can set this Swing parameter from -100 to +100 percent. More often than not, you want to keep it set to 0 percent.

4. Set the Rate and Units parameters. These two parameters work together. The Rate parameter determines the amount of time between each note in the arpeggio. The Units parameter determines what units you want to use to set the Rate parameter. You can set the Rate parameter in Notes, Ticks, or Milliseconds. By setting the Units parameter to Notes, you can easily synchronize the notes in the arpeggio to a certain note value so that you know they will play in sync with the rest of the music in your Project.

5. Set the Legato parameter. This parameter determines the duration of the notes in the arpeggio. If you set the Legato parameter to 1 percent (the lowest value), the notes in the arpeggio are played with a very short duration (as in a staccato fashion in which the note is played and let go very quickly). If you set the Legato parameter to 99 percent (the highest value), the notes in the arpeggio are played with a very long duration. To be exact, each note plays until the start of the next note in the arpeggio.

6. Set the Path parameter. This parameter determines the direction in which the notes in the arpeggio will be played. If you select Up, Up, the notes in the arpeggio consecutively go up in pitch. If you select Up, Down, the notes in the arpeggio first go up in pitch and then come back down. If you select Down, Down, the notes in the arpeggio consecutively go down in pitch. If you select Down, Up, the notes in the arpeggio first go down in pitch and then come back up.

7. Set the Play Thru option. If you activate the Play Thru option, your original remains intact and plays along with the new arpeggio data. If you deactivate the Play Thru option, only the arpeggio data remains, and your original data is removed.

8. Set the Specify Output Range option, along with the Lowest Note and Span (Notes) parameters. If you activate the Specify Output Range option, additional notes are added so that the arpeggio will play smoothly over each octave in the range you specify. Otherwise, only your original is used to create the arpeggio. The Lowest Note parameter determines the lowest note that will be included in the arpeggio. The Span (Notes) parameter determines the number of half-steps in the range (from 12 to 127).

9. Set the Use Chord Control option, along with the Lowest Note and Span (Notes) parameters. If you activate the Use Chord Control option, the Cakewalk FX Arpeggiator Effect first analyzes the original data that falls in the range you specify, and it guesses at what chord is being played. If you use the Effect in real-time mode, the name of the chord that is guessed is shown in the Chord Recognized field. The Effect uses the recognized chord to create the notes for the arpeggio (meaning the notes in the arpeggio are based on the recognized chord).

10. Click on the Audition button to test the current parameter settings. Make further adjustments, if necessary.

11. If you want to use the current settings at a later time, save them as a Preset.

12. Click on OK.

Pro Audio processes the data by applying the Effect according to the parameter settings you specified.

Arpeggio Example

I know the parameter settings for the Cakewalk FX Arpeggiator Effect can be a bit confusing. Sometimes it's difficult to tell what the results will be after you apply the Effect. Basically, they'll be different depending on the data that you process. You'll have to experiment. But just to give you a quick idea of what you can do with the Effect, try the following example:

1. Select File > Open, select the file called Ballad #1.wrk, and click on Open to open that sample Project.

2. Change the Vel+ parameter for Track 3 (piano) to 100. This setting makes it a bit louder so that you can hear the changes being made to it above the other instruments in the Project.

3. Play the Project to see what the original data in Track 3 sounds like.

4. Select Track 3.

5. Select Edit > MIDI Effects > Cakewalk FX > Arpeggiator.

6. Choose the Preset called Bouncing.

7. Click on OK.

8. Play the Project again.

Sounds cool, huh? Pro Audio has taken the original data in Track 3 and turned it into an arpeggio. By the way, this Effect usually works best on this type of slow, chord-based data. Of course, you can try it out on faster, different kinds of data. Like I said, be sure to experiment with it.

CHAPTER 9

Chord Analysis

Earlier, I mentioned that a couple of the MIDI Effects aren't really Effects at all. The Cakewalk FX Chord Analyzer is one of them. This Effect doesn't really do anything to your data, meaning it doesn't make any changes to the data. The Cakewalk FX Chord Analyzer simply analyzes your data and guesses what kind of chord is being played. This Effect is useful as a learning tool, because it displays the chords being played on a piano keyboard and as music notation. Plus, it lists (in the Chord Recognized section) some possible alternatives that you might want to try in place of the chord currently being used.

Here's how the Effect works:

> **NOTE**
> Although you can use the Cakewalk FX Chord Analyzer Effect offline, it works best in real-time as your Project is playing. Therefore, I'll go through the real-time procedure here instead of the offline procedure.

1. In the Track View, click in the Effects field of the Track to which you want to add an Effect. The Effects Bin for that Track opens.

2. Right-click in the Effects Bin and select Cakewalk FX > Chord Analyzer to add the Chord Analyzer to the list.

3. Double-click on Chord Analyzer in the list to open the Cakewalk FX Chord Analyzer window (see Figure 9.16).

Figure 9.16
The Cakewalk FX Chord Analyzer is best used in real-time.

4. Set the Examine Every parameter. Using this parameter, you can control how often the Cakewalk FX Chord Analyzer Effect analyzes your data. The lower the number, the more accurate it is at guessing the names of the chords being played. This feature also requires more processing power from your computer, but I've never had any problems keeping this parameter set at 1 (the lowest setting). So, unless you have trouble with playback, I recommend that you just leave this setting at its default value.

5. Start Playback of the Project. As the Project plays, the Effect analyzes your data and displays the name of the chord it thinks is being played, along with how the chord looks in music notation and on a piano keyboard.

Echo Delay

Just as the CFX Delay/Echo and Cakewalk FX Delay Effects enable you to add echoes to your audio data, the Cakewalk FX Echo Delay Effects enables you to add echoes to your MIDI data. But because this Effect works on MIDI data, some of the parameters are different, and some additional parameters are available, as well. This feature works as follows:

1. Select the MIDI data that you want to process.

2. Select Edit > MIDI Effects > Cakewalk FX > Echo Delay to open the Echo Delay dialog box (see Figure 9.17).

Figure 9.17
You can use the Cakewalk FX Echo Delay Effect to add echoes to your MIDI data.

3. Set the Delay and Delay Units parameters. These two parameters work together. The Delay parameter determines the amount of time between each echo. The Delay Units parameter determines what units you want to use to set the Delay parameter. You can set the Delay parameter in Notes, Ticks, and Milliseconds. By setting the Delay Units parameter to Notes, you can easily synchronize the echoes to a certain note value so that you know they will play in sync with the rest of the music in your Project.

TIP

You also can set the Delay parameter by clicking on the Tap button in the Echo Delay dialog box. Clicking on the button at a certain tempo sets the Delay parameter to that tempo.

4. Set the Decay parameter. This parameter determines whether the echoes get softer or louder (and by how much). If you set the Decay parameter to a value below 100 percent, the echoes get softer. If you set the Decay to a value above 100 percent, the echoes get louder.

CHAPTER 9

5. Set the Echoes parameter. This parameter determines how many echoes you will have.

6. Set the Swing parameter. This parameter works the same way as the Swing parameter in the Quantize editing feature (which I talked about in Chapter 8). The only difference is that of 50 percent being the normal setting (meaning no "swing" is applied); 0 percent is the normal setting. And you can set this Swing parameter from -100 to +100 percent. More often than not, you'll want to keep it set to 0 percent.

7. Set the Transpose (Steps) parameter. If you want, you can have each echo transposed to a different pitch value. This way, you can create some interesting sounds. You can set the Transpose (Steps) parameter from -12 to +12 steps. You determine the types of steps by choosing either the Diatonic (the pitches follow the diatonic musical scale) or the Chromatic (the pitches follow the chromatic musical scale) options.

8. Click on the Audition button to test the current parameter settings. Make further adjustments, if necessary.

9. If you want to use the current settings at a later time, save them as a Preset.

10. Click on OK.

Pro Audio processes the data by applying the Effect according to the parameter settings you specified.

Echo Delay Example

The Cakewalk FX Echo Delay Effect is fairly easy to use, but just to give you a quick idea of what you can do with the Effect, try the following example:

1. Select File > Open, select the file called Ballad #1.wrk and click on Open to open that sample Project.

2. Change the Vel+ parameter for Track 3 (piano) to 100. This setting just makes it a bit louder so that you can hear the changes being made to it above the other instruments in the Project.

3. Play the Project to see what the original data in Track 3 sounds like.

4. Select Track 3.

5. Select Edit > MIDI Effects > Cakewalk FX > Echo Delay.

6. Choose the Preset called Going Up.

7. Click on OK.

8. Play the Project again.

Sounds sort of like an arpeggio, doesn't it? That's because of the Transpose parameter settings. You can achieve some pretty cool sounds by using this Effect. As always, don't be afraid to experiment.

MIDI Event Filter

The Cakewalk FX MIDI Event Filter Effect works almost exactly the same as the Select By Filter editing feature (which I talked about in Chapter 8). The only difference is that, instead of simply selecting the specified Events, it deletes them. This feature gives you a quick way to remove specific kinds of MIDI data from your Clips or Tracks. It works like this:

1. Select the MIDI data that you want to process.

2. Select Edit > MIDI Effects > Cakewalk FX > MIDI Event Filter to open the MIDI Event Filter dialog box (see Figure 9.18).

Figure 9.18
Using the Cakewalk FX MIDI Event Filter Effect, you can easily remove specific kinds of MIDI data from your Clips and Tracks.

3. Set the appropriate parameters for the types of MIDI data that you want to remove. These settings are exactly the same as the settings for the Event Filter–Select Some dialog box (which I explained in Chapter 8).

4. Click on the Audition button to test the current parameter settings. Make further adjustments, if necessary.

5. If you want to use the current settings at a later time, save them as a Preset.

6. Click on OK.

Pro Audio processes the selected data and removes the types of MIDI data you specified via the Effect parameter settings.

Quantize

The Cakewalk FX Quantize Effect works almost exactly the same as the Quantize editing feature (which I talked about in Chapter 8). The only difference is that the Effect provides a couple of additional parameters. It works like this:

1. Select the MIDI data that you want to process.

2. Select Edit > MIDI Effects > Cakewalk FX > Quantize to open the Cakewalk FX Quantize dialog box (see Figure 9.19).

Figure 9.19
The Cakewalk FX Quantize Effect works almost exactly the same way as the Quantize editing feature.

3. Set the Quantize parameter by activating/deactivating the Start Times and Note Durations options. These settings simply tell Pro Audio whether you want to quantize the start times and/or durations of each selected MIDI Event.

4. Set the Resolution parameter. This parameter works in exactly the same way as the Resolution parameter in the Quantize editing feature (which I talked about in Chapter 8).

5. Set the Tuplet option. Using this option, you can further define the Resolution parameter. For example, if you want to quantize your data according to an odd note value, activate the Tuplet option and set its related parameters to 5 and 4 (which would mean that you want to quantize your data to the value of 5 notes occurring in the time of 4 notes).

6. Set the Strength, Swing, Window, and Offset parameters. These parameters work in exactly the same way as the Strength, Swing, Window, and Offset parameters in the Quantize editing feature (which I talked about in Chapter 8).

7. Set the Randomize By option. If you activate this option, a random time offset is applied to the timing of each quantized Event. You can use this option to achieve some very strange sounds. Do a little experimenting to hear what I mean.

8. Click on the Audition button to test the current parameter settings. Make further adjustments, if necessary.

9. If you want to use the current settings at a later time, save them as a Preset.

10. Click on OK.

Pro Audio processes the data by applying the Effect according to the parameter settings you specified.

Transpose

Like the Transpose editing feature, the Cakewalk FX Transpose Effect enables you to transpose your MIDI note data up or down by a number of half steps either chromatically or diatonically. However, the Cakewalk FX Transpose Effect also provides some more advanced transposition methods. It works like this:

1. Select the MIDI data that you want to process.

2. Select Edit > MIDI Effects > Cakewalk FX > Transpose to open the Transpose dialog box (see Figure 9.20).

Figure 9.20
Using the Cakewalk FX Transpose Effect, you can transpose your MIDI note data in a number of different ways.

3. If you want to transpose your data by a simple musical interval, choose the Interval option for the Transposition Method parameter. Then enter the number of half steps (-127 to +127) into the Offset parameter by which you want to transpose the data.

4. If you want to transpose your data diatonically so that the notes are changed according to degrees of a certain musical scale, choose the Diatonic option for the Transposition Method parameter. Then enter the number of scale degrees (-24 to +24) into the Offset parameter by which you want to transpose the data. Also, choose the musical scale that you want to use by setting the Key parameter.

CHAPTER 9

TIP

If you want any of the notes in your data that don't fit within the chosen musical scale to be transposed so that they will fit, activate the Constrain to Scale option. This feature works well for pop music. For something like jazz, though, in which many different non-scale notes are used in the music, it's best to keep this option deactivated. This option works for both the Diatonic and Key/Scale Transposition Methods.

5. If you want to transpose your data from one musical key and scale to another, choose the Key/Scale option for the Transposition Method parameter. In the From and To parameters, choose the musical keys and scales by which you want to transpose your data. You also can transpose the data up or down by a number of octaves at the same time by setting the Offset parameter.

6. To specify exactly how each note in the musical scale will be transposed, choose the Custom Map option for the Transposition Method parameter. Using this option, you can define your own Transposition Map. This means that you can set what note each note in the musical scale will be transposed to. To change the transposition value of a note in the musical scale, select the note in the From column of the Transposition Map. Then click on the plus or minus buttons to transpose that note up or down. This option is pretty tedious, but it gives you precise control over every musical note.

TIP

You can view notes in the Transposition Map either by note name or by MIDI note number. Simply select the appropriate option (Pitch or Note Number) located above the Transposition Map in the Transpose dialog box.

7. Click on the Audition button to test the current parameter settings. Make further adjustments, if necessary.

8. If you want to use the current settings at a later time, save them as a Preset.

9. Click on OK.

Pro Audio processes the data by applying the Effect according to the parameter settings you specified.

Velocity

I'm tempted to compare the Cakewalk FX Velocity Effect to the Scale Velocity editing feature (which I talked about in Chapter 8), but the Effect enables you to not only scale MIDI velocity data, but also to change it in many more advanced ways. As a matter of fact, you'll probably stop using the Scale Velocity editing feature when you get the hang of the Cakewalk FX Velocity Effect, because you can use this Effect as an editing tool as well. It works like this:

1. Select the MIDI data that you want to process.

2. Select Edit > MIDI Effects > Cakewalk FX > Velocity to open the Velocity dialog box (see Figure 9.21).

Figure 9.21
Using the Cakewalk FX Velocity Effect, you can change your MIDI velocity data in many more ways than you can by using the Scale Velocity editing feature.

3. To change all MIDI velocity values to an exact number, choose the Set All Velocities To parameter, and type the value (1 to 127) that you want to use.

4. To add or subtract a certain amount from each MIDI velocity in your selected data, choose the Change Velocities By option, and type the value (-127 to +127) that you want to use.

5. To scale all MIDI velocity values by a certain percentage, choose the Scale Velocities To option, and type the value (1 to 900 percent) that you want to use.

6. The next two options also enable you to scale MIDI velocities, but from one value to another. If you choose the first Change Gradually From option, you can scale MIDI velocities by exact values (1 to 127). If you choose the second Change Gradually From option, you can scale MIDI velocities by a percentage (1 to 900 percent).

7. If you choose the Limit Range From option, all the MIDI velocities in your selected data are changed to fit within the range of velocity values (1 to 127) that you specify.

CHAPTER 9

8. In addition to choosing one of the previous options, you can choose the Cakewalk FX Velocity Effect's Randomize By option, which works in tandem with the others. By activating this option, you can add or subtract a random offset to each MIDI velocity in your selected data. You can enter a maximum value (1 to 127) to be used, and you can give priority over whether the random offset will be lower or higher (-10 to +10) than the maximum value that you specify.

9. Click on the Audition button to test the current parameter settings. Make further adjustments, if necessary.

10. If you want to use the current settings at a later time, save them as a Preset.

11. Click on OK.

Pro Audio processes the data by applying the Effect according to the parameter settings you specified.

Session Drummer

Even though the Session Drummer is listed along with all the other MIDI Effects, technically it is not an Effect because it doesn't process existing data. Instead, it actually generates new MIDI data. You can think of the Session Drummer like a drum machine, a programmable MIDI instrument used to create drum parts. With the Session Drummer, you can compose your own MIDI drum Tracks by combining existing rhythmic patterns into songs. You even can create your own patterns for use with the Session Drummer.

Using the Session Drummer consists of a number of multi-step processes, so I'll provide you with step-by-step procedures for each part of the process.

Opening and Setting Up

The best way to use the Session Drummer is in real-time because you can use it to compose a drum Track while listening to the existing Tracks in your Project. You can get started by following these steps:

1. Create a new Project, or open an existing one.

2. In the Track View, create a new MIDI Track by right-clicking on the number of an empty track and selecting Properties from the pop-up menu.

3. In the Track Properties dialog box, set the Port and Channel for the new Track. The Channel should probably be set to 10 because that is the standard channel for General MIDI drums on most sound cards and synthesizers. Click on OK.

4. Add the Cakewalk FX Session Drummer Effect to the Effects Bin of the new Track by clicking in the Effects field, right-clicking in the Effects Bin, and selecting Cakewalk FX > Session Drummer.

5. Double-click on the Session Drummer listing in the Effects Bin to open the Session Drummer window (see Figure 9.22).

Figure 9.22
The Session Drummer window enables you to compose your own MIDI drum Tracks by combining existing rhythmic patterns.

6. You'll see three different sections within the window: Style, Pattern, and Song. Just below the Style section is a row of buttons. These buttons control the different Session Drummer features. Click on the Plugin Settings button (the one with the picture of the yellow sprocket shown on it), to open the Settings dialog box (see Figure 9.23). Don't worry; I'll go over all the other Session Drummer features shortly.

Figure 9.23
In the Settings dialog box, you can set the Session Drummer's Drum Map, Output Port, MIDI Channel, and Content Folder parameters.

7. All the drum patterns and styles included with Pro Audio are programmed to work with General MIDI. So, if you're using a General MIDI compatible synthesizer, you should be all set. If not, you can change the Drum Map parameter so that each drum instrument is mapped to a different MIDI pitch. To do so, click on the name of the drum instrument that you want to change in the From column of the Drum Map. Then, to raise or lower the pitch for that instrument, press the plus or minus keys on the numeric keypad of your computer's keyboard, respectively.

8. Set the Output Port and MIDI Channel parameters to the same settings that you used for the Track Port and Channel parameters you entered earlier.

9. All the drum styles and patterns included with Pro Audio are contained in special MIDI files. These files are initially located in the C:\Program Files\Cakewalk\Cakewalk Pro Audio 9\Drum Styles folder on your hard drive. If you want to change the location of the files, enter a new location in the Content Folder parameter. Be sure to remember to move any existing files from the old folder to the new folder.

10. Click on OK to close the Settings dialog box.

TIP

If you want to use these same settings again in the future, you can save them as a Preset. The Presets parameter in the Session Drummer window saves only the parameter values from the Settings dialog box. Saving your Session Drummer songs requires a different procedure, which I'll talk about later.

Creating a Song

As I mentioned earlier, the Session Drummer window is divided into three sections: Style, Pattern, and Song. The Style section lists all the available drum style files currently in the Content Folder. Each file contains a number of different drum patterns. When you select a style from the list in the Style section, all the patterns contained in that style are listed in the Pattern section. By selecting patterns from the Pattern section, you can piece together a song. A song is an entire percussion performance that spans a certain number of measures, depending on how many patterns it contains and the length of each pattern used. The basic procedure for creating a song is as follows (I'm assuming you've already gone through the setup procedure, and the Session Drummer window is open and waiting to be used):

1. Select a style from the Style section.

2. In the Pattern section, you'll see all the patterns within the selected style. The name of each pattern and its length in measures is shown. To hear what a pattern sounds like, click on it to select it, and then start your Project playing. You can keep the Project playing while you select different patterns. After you find a pattern you like, double-click on it (or click on the Add Pattern To Song button, the one with the picture of a plus sign shown on it) to add the pattern to the Song section.

3. In the Song section, the name, length, and the time (in measures, beats, ticks) of when the pattern will be played within the Project is shown. You'll also see a Loop Count parameter for the pattern. It tells the Session Drummer how many times to play that pattern before moving on to the next pattern in the song. Set the Loop Count by double-clicking on it and typing a number.

4. Go back to Step 2 to add more patterns to the song.

5. If you want to remove a pattern from the song, select the pattern from the list in the Song section, and click on the Remove Pattern From Song button (the one with the picture of a minus sign shown on it). You also can remove all the patterns from the song by clicking on the Clear Song button (the one with the picture of a red X shown on it).

6. If you want to change the order of a pattern within the song, select the pattern. Then click on the Move Down button (the one with the picture of a downward-pointing arrow shown on it) to move the pattern toward the end of the song. Alternatively, click on the Move Up button (the one with the picture of an upward-pointing arrow shown on it) to move the pattern toward the beginning of the song.

7. To listen to the song, select the first pattern in the list and then start your Project playing.

Saving and Loading Song Files

After you've finished creating your song, you can save it as a special Session Drummer Song file. This file type has an .SFX extension, and the files are stored in the same disk location as the styles. To save your song, follow these steps:

1. Click on the Save Song To File button (the one with the picture of a floppy disk shown on it) to open the Save As dialog box.

2. Type a name for the file, using an .SFX extension.

3. Click on Save.

CHAPTER 9

To load your song for use in Session Drummer at a later date, do the following:

1. Click on the Load Song From File button (the one with the picture of a yellow folder shown on it) to open the Open dialog box.

2. Select the file that you want to load.

3. Click on Open.

CAUTION
If you don't save your song, you'll lose it when you close the current Project.

Applying the Song to Your Project

When you save a song, only the information that makes up the song is saved. In other words, only the names of each pattern, their locations in the song, and their number of loops are saved. The actual MIDI data is not saved. To save the MIDI data that generated from a song into a Track (I'm assuming you've already gone through the setup procedure, you've created a song, and the Session Drummer window is still open), follow these steps:

1. Go to the Track View and select the Track that you set up previously.

2. Open the Console View by selecting View > Console.

3. At the top of the Console View, click on the Apply MIDI Effects button (the one with the letters *FX* shown on it).

4. When the Apply MIDI Effect dialog box appears, make sure the Delete the Effects from the Track Inserts option is activated. This setting removes the Session Drummer Effect from the Effects Bin of the Track because, after the song data is saved into the Track, you no longer need the Session Drummer.

5. Click on OK.

Pro Audio places the song data into the selected Track. No matter where the Now Time is currently set, the song data is always placed at the beginning of the Project.

Creating Your Own Session Drummer Styles

Styles are stored as standard MIDI files. Therefore, you can easily create your own styles for use in Session Drummer. If you open one of the existing style files as a Project in Pro Audio (see Figure 9.24), you'll notice that a style is made up of nothing more than a single Track, containing MIDI data composed specifically to be played by General MIDI drum sounds. The Track is separated into sections with markers. Each marker designates a different drum pattern. The name of the style file is what shows up in the Style section of the Session Drummer, and the names of the markers are what show up in the Pattern section.

Figure 9.24

You can create your own Session Drummer Styles by recording your own drum patterns and placing them together as a single Track.

After you've recorded your own drum patterns, you can easily create your own Session Drummer style by following these steps:

1. Open the Project that contains the existing drum patterns that you recorded.

2. Create a new Project and set a Tempo for the Project.

3. In the Track View of the original Project, copy one of the drum patterns by using Edit > Copy.

4. In the Track View of the new Project, paste the drum pattern at the very beginning of Track 10. Track 10 is the standard Track used for MIDI drum parts.

5. Set the Now Time to the beginning of the Project.

6. Select Insert > Marker to open the Marker dialog box. Type a name. This is the name of the pattern, and it will appear in the Pattern section of the Session Drummer. Click on OK.

7. If you want to add more patterns, be sure to paste each new pattern at the end of the previous one. Each pattern should start at the beginning of a measure and should be at least one measure long.

8. Save the Project as a style by selecting File > Save As to open the Save As dialog box. Type a name for the file. This is the name that will appear in the Style section of the Session Drummer. Also, be sure to choose MIDI Format 0 for the Save as Type parameter. And be sure to save the file to the same directory that you set in the Content Folder parameter of the Session Drummer Settings. Click on Save.

CHAPTER 9

The next time you open the Session Drummer, your new style should be listed in the Style section.

Session Drummer Song Example

To give you a quick idea of the results that you can get from the Session Drummer, I've put together this short demonstration:

1. Select File > Open, select the file called 2-Part Invention #13 in A minor.wrk, and click on Open to open the sample Project.

2. Close the File Info window, along with the Staff and Big Time Views. You don't need them.

3. In the Track View, right-click on Track 3 and select Track Properties from the pop-up menu to open the Track Properties dialog box.

4. Set the Port and Channel parameters. You should probably set the Channel to 10. Click on OK.

5. Add the Cakewalk FX Session Drummer Effect to the Effects Bin of Track 3 by clicking in the Effects field, right-clicking in the Effects Bin, and selecting Cakewalk FX > Session Drummer.

6. Double-click on the Session Drummer listing in the Effects Bin to open the Session Drummer window.

7. Select the style named Alternative 080–Straight 16ths.

8. Add the following patterns to the song in the order listed:

    —Crash/Kick/SN/Hat/Tamb–1 Loop

    —SN/Tom fill1–2 Loops

    —var1/Crash/Kick/SN/Hat/Tamb–1 Loop

    —SN/Tom fill2–2 Loops

    —Crash/Kick/SN/Hat–1 Loop

    —SN/Tom fill3–2 Loops

    —var1/Crash/Kick/SN/Hat-1 Loop

    —SN fill1–2 Loops

    —var2/Crash/Kick/SN/Hat–1 Loop

    —SN fill3–2 Loops

9. At this point, you can save the song and apply it to the Track if you want, but because this is just a demonstration, it's up to you.

10. Before you play the Project, change the Tempo to 100. The original Tempo sounds too slow.

11. Play the Project.

Sounds like one of those rearranged classical recordings like the ones on the CD called "BachBusters" by Don Dorsey, doesn't it? Have fun!

10

Mixing It Down

After you've recorded, edited, and added Effects to your MIDI and audio data, it's time to mix down your Project. It is called the *mixdown process* because you are taking all the MIDI and audio Tracks in your Project and mixing them together into a single stereo audio Track (or a stereo pair of audio Tracks). From there, you can put your music on CD, distribute it over the Internet, or record it onto tape. Pro Audio provides a number of different features that make the mixdown process as simple and intuitive as possible. Here's what I cover in this chapter:

▶ Using the Console View
▶ Using the Module Manager
▶ Taking a Snapshot
▶ Recording and editing automation
▶ Grouping
▶ Working with audio Envelopes

The Console View

For mixing down the MIDI and audio Tracks in your Project, you need to use the Console View. The Console View enables you to adjust the main parameters for each Track in your Project via on-screen buttons, knobs, sliders, and faders (vertical sliders). Similar in appearance to a hardware-based mixing board found in most recording studios, the Console View displays Tracks as a collection of Modules, each with its own set of adjustable controls.

More precisely, the Console View consists of four major sections: the Toolbar (located at the top of the View, containing some of the View's related controls); the MIDI and audio Track Modules (located in the main part of the View; displaying the controls for each MIDI and audio Track in the Project); the Aux Busses (located to the right of the MIDI and audio Track Modules, containing additional mixing controls, which I'll explain later); and the Mains (located to the right of the Aux Busses, also containing additional mixing controls, which I'll explain later).

Opening the Console View

To open the Console View, simply select View > Console. The Console View then opens, displaying Modules for every Track in the current Project. To see how it works, follow these steps:

1. Select File > Open. In the Open dialog box that appears, select the file named Riff Funk Audio and MIDI Demo.bun and click on Open to open that sample Project file.

2. Select View > Console to open the Console View.

The Console View should look similar to the one shown in Figure 10.1.

Figure 10.1
When you open the Console View, it automatically displays a Module for every Track in the current Project.

You'll also notice that one of the modules has a dotted outline around it. This dotted line indicates that the cursor in the Track list pane of the Track View is currently located on that Track.

The MIDI Track Modules

Each MIDI Track Module contains a number of different controls that enable you to manipulate many of its corresponding Track parameters (see Figure 10.2).

Figure 10.2
A MIDI Track Module
contains controls
for adjusting the
parameters of its
corresponding Track.

As matter of fact, almost all the controls are the equivalent of the Track
parameters shown in the Track list pane of the Track View (all of which I
have described in previous chapters). This means that if you change the
value of a control in the Console View, the equivalent Track parameter
also is changed in the Track View. From top to bottom, the controls in a
MIDI Track Module correspond to the controls described in the following
sections:

Name

The Name control displays the name of the Track represented by the
MIDI Track Module. It is the equivalent of the Name parameter in the
Track View. You can change the Name by clicking on the control, typing
some new text, and pressing the Enter key on your computer keyboard.

Effects Bin

You can use the Effects Bin control to assign Effects to the Track
represented by the MIDI Track Module. These Effects are applied only in
real-time. This control works in exactly the same way as the Effects Bin
in the Track View (which I described in Chapter 9, "Effects: The Really
Cool Stuff").

Port

Using the Port control, you can set the MIDI port of the Track represented
by the MIDI Track Module. It is the equivalent of the Port parameter in
the Track View. You can change the Port by clicking on the control and
selecting a new MIDI port from the pop-up menu.

Channel

The Channel control enables you to set the MIDI channel of the Track represented by the MIDI Track Module. It is the equivalent of the Channel parameter in the Track View. You can change the Channel by clicking on the control and selecting a new MIDI channel from the pop-up menu.

Bank

You can use the Bank control to set the MIDI patch bank of the Track represented by the MIDI Track Module. It is the equivalent of the Bank parameter in the Track View. You can change the Bank by clicking on the control and selecting a new MIDI patch bank from the pop-up menu.

Patch

You can use the Patch control to set the MIDI patch of the Track represented by the MIDI Track Module. It is the equivalent of the Patch parameter in the Track View. You can change the Patch by clicking on the control and selecting a new MIDI patch from the pop-up menu.

Chorus and Reverb

Some MIDI instruments have built-in chorus and reverb effects. Some special MIDI controller messages even enable you to change the settings for these effects. Using the Chorus and Reverb controls, you can adjust the appropriate MIDI controller messages so that you can apply the chorus and reverb effects to your MIDI instrument. To adjust either control, simply click and drag the corresponding slider left or right. As you drag the slider, the Value parameter in the Toolbar at the top of the Console View displays the current value of the control that you are adjusting. If you drag the slider left, the value gets lower. If you drag the slider right, the value gets higher. Both the Chorus and Reverb controls can be adjusted from 0 to 127. They are the only two controls for which there are no equivalents in the Track View.

TIP

When you're adjusting sliders, knobs, or faders in the Console View, a quick way to return them to their original positions is to double-click on them. When you do, the control snaps back to its default value. You also can change the default value for a control. To do so, set the control to the value that you want to use as its default. Then right-click on the control, and select Set Snap-To = Current from the pop-up menu.

Mute, Solo, and Arm

The Mute, Solo, and Arm controls enable you to turn the Mute, Solo, and Arm (for recording) options on or off for the Track represented by the MIDI Track Module. They are the equivalents of the Mute, Solo, and Arm options in the Track View (which I described in Chapter 6, "Recording and Playback"). You can toggle these options on and off by clicking on them.

> **TIP**
>
> The Arm (for recording) option is available in the Console View because you can actually use the View during recording instead of the Track View, if you'd like. You can even create new Tracks in the Console View. To do so, simply right-click in any blank space (like just below the Aux Busses), and select Add Track > Audio or Add Track > MIDI from the pop-up menu. A new MIDI or audio Track Module is added, representing the new Track. You'll notice that the new Track is added to the Track View, as well.

Pan

You can use the Pan control to set the MIDI panning of the Track represented by the MIDI Track Module. It is the equivalent of the Pan parameter in the Track View. You can change the Pan by clicking and dragging the slider left or right. As you drag the slider, the Value parameter in the Toolbar at the top of the Console View displays the current value of the control. The value can range from 0 (all the way left) to 127 (all the way right). A value of 64 is dead center.

Volume

Using the Volume control, you can set the MIDI volume of the Track represented by the MIDI Track Module. It is the equivalent of the Volume parameter in the Track View. You can change the Volume by clicking and dragging the fader (vertical slider) up or down. As you drag the fader, the Value parameter in the Toolbar at the top of the Console View displays the current value of the control. The value can range from 0 (lowest volume level) to 127 (highest volume level).

Source

The Source control enables you to set the MIDI source of the Track represented by the MIDI Track Module. It is the equivalent of the Source parameter in the Track View. You can change the Source by clicking on the control and selecting a new source from the pop-up menu.

The Audio Track Modules

Like the MIDI Track Modules, the audio Track Modules contain a number of different controls that you can use to manipulate many of its corresponding Track parameters (see Figure 10.3).

Figure 10.3
The audio Track Modules are very similar to the MIDI Track Modules in terms of the controls that they provide.

As a matter of fact, almost all the controls are the same as those on the MIDI Track Modules. Included are the Name, Effects Bin, Mute, Solo, Arm, Pan, Volume, and Source controls. They all work in exactly the same manner as they do on the MIDI Track Modules, except, of course, they are controlling audio data instead of MIDI data. The one difference is with the Volume control. Instead of displaying its value as a MIDI volume controller number, its value is shown as decibels (dB).

Other than that, only two completely different types of controls are available on the audio Track Modules: Output and Aux Sends.

Output

The Output control (located directly below the Volume control and directly above the Source control) enables you to route the data from the Track represented by the audio Track Module to one of the Mains (which I'll explain later). This control is the equivalent of the Port parameter in the Track View. You can change the Output by clicking on the control and selecting a new Main from the pop-up menu.

Aux Sends

The Aux Send controls (located directly below the Effects Bin) enable you to route (send) the audio data from the Track represented by the audio Track Module to one of the Aux Busses (which I'll explain later). You can have up to sixteen Aux Sends for each audio Track Module, although, by default, there are only two (I'll show you how to change this number later). Each Aux Send has a number (1 to 16), which corresponds to the number of the Aux Bus to which its data will be sent. Each Aux Send also has two controls within it: an on/off button and a Send Level slider. The on/off buttons are located in the bottom-right corner of each Aux Send. To toggle an Aux Send on or off, just click on its on/off button. The Send Level slider controls the volume (or level) of the audio data that will be sent to the Aux Bus. To adjust the slider, simply drag it left or right. As you drag the slider, the Value parameter in the Toolbar at the top of the Console View displays the current value of the Send Level. If you drag the slider left, the value gets lower. If you drag the slider right, the value gets higher. The Send Level can be adjusted from -INF (infinity, the lowest level setting) to 0dB (the highest level setting).

The Aux Busses

The Aux Busses provide additional mixing control of your audio signals. Like the audio Track Modules, each Aux Bus contains Name, Effects Bin, and Output controls (see Figure 10.4).

Figure 10.4
The Aux Busses provide some of the same controls as the audio Track Modules.

In addition, five other controls are provided: Send Level, Send Balance, Return Level, Return Balance, and Pre Fader Enable.

Send Level

Although the name might be misleading, the Send Level control enables you to set the input level of the audio data coming into the Aux Bus. You can change the Send Level by clicking and holding down on the knob and then dragging up or down. As you drag your mouse, the Value parameter in the Toolbar at the top of the Console View displays the current value of the control. If you drag up, the value gets higher. If you drag down, the value gets lower. The value can range from -INF to 0dB.

Send Balance

Each Aux Bus works in stereo, so they provide balance controls. Using the Send Balance controls, you can set the panning of the audio data coming into the Aux Bus. You can change the Send Balance by clicking and dragging the slider left or right. As you drag the slider, the Value parameter in the Toolbar at the top of the Console View displays the current value of the control. The value can range from 0 (all the way left) to 127 (all the way right). A value of 64 is dead center.

Return Level

The Return Level control works just like the Send Level control except that it enables you to adjust the output level of the audio data going out of the Aux Bus. You can change the Return Level by clicking and holding down on the knob and then dragging up or down. As you drag your mouse, the Value parameter in the Toolbar at the top of the Console View displays the current value of the control. If you drag up, the value gets higher. If you drag down, the value gets lower. The value can range from -INF to 0dB.

Return Balance

The Return Balance control works just like the Send Balance control except that it enables you to adjust the panning of the audio data going out of the Aux Bus. You can change the Return Balance by clicking and dragging the slider left or right. As you drag the slider, the Value parameter in the Toolbar at the top of the Console View displays the current value of the control. The value can range from 0 (all the way left) to 127 (all the way right). A value of 64 is dead center.

Pre Fader Enable

The Pre Fader Enable control determines from what point in the audio Track Module the audio data will be taken and sent to the Aux Bus. You can toggle the Pre Fader Enable control on or off by clicking on it. When on, the button changes its name to Post and its color turns blue. When off, the name of the button shows as Pre and its color is black.

NOTE

As Pro Audio plays a Project, it reads the data for each audio Track from your hard drive. It then routes the data through the appropriate sections of the Console View, until it is finally sent to your sound card and then to your speakers so you can hear it. The routing works as follows: The data for an audio Track is read from your hard drive and routed through the corresponding audio Track Module. Within the Module, the data first passes through the Effects Bin (where any assigned Effects are applied). The data is then sent through the Volume control (where its level can be adjusted), then the Pan control, and finally to the Output control. From here, it is sent out of the Module and into the assigned Main (which I'll talk about shortly). During this routing process, the data can be sent to an Aux Send either before or after it reaches the Volume control. If the Pre Fader Enable control is off (set to Pre), the data is routed to the Aux Bus after it goes through the Effects Bin but before it reaches the Volume control. This means that the Volume control will have no effect on the level of the signal being sent to the Aux Bus. If the Pre Fader Enable control is on (set to Post), the data is routed to the Aux Bus after it goes through the Volume control. This means that the Volume control does affect the level of the signal being sent to the Aux Bus.

What's it Good for?

One good use for the Aux Busses is to add the same Effects to a number of different Tracks. For example, say you have four audio Tracks (1, 2, 3, and 4), containing the background vocals for your Project, and you want to add some nice chorus to them. Without using an Aux Bus, you would have to set up a Cakewalk FX Chorus Effect (each with identical parameter settings) in the Effects Bins of each of the audio Track Modules for Tracks 1, 2, 3, and 4. Not only is this approach cumbersome and tedious, it also puts extra strain on your computer because it has to process each of the four Effects at the same time.

Using an Aux Bus, however, the process becomes much more streamlined. You can use Aux Bus 1 for this example. First, you activate Aux Send 1 in each of the four audio Track Modules (1, 2, 3, and 4). Then you set the Send Levels for each of the Aux Sends. In the Effects Bin of Aux Bus 1, you set up the Cakewalk FX Chorus Effect. Only one Effect needs to be set up because all four Tracks are being sent to the Aux Bus. You then set the Send Level and Send Balance controls, along with the Return Level and Return Balance controls. Finally, you set the Pre Fader Enable control to Pre or Post. If you set the control to Pre, the data in each audio Track Module is sent to the Aux Bus before it's routed through each Volume control. This means that you can control the level of the Effect (with the Send Level), and the level of the original data (with the Volume control) independently. If you set the Pre Fader Enable control to Post, the level of the Effect goes up and down with the level of the original data via the Volume control.

The Mains

For every individual output on your sound card, a Main is displayed in the Console View (see Figure 10.5).

Figure 10.5
A Main looks very similar to an audio Track Module.

So, if your sound card has only one output, only one Main is displayed, and all the audio data from the audio Track Modules is sent to it. If your sound card has more than one output, more than one Main is shown, and you can choose to which Main the data from each audio Track Module and Aux Bus is sent.

A Main provides four different controls. From top to bottom, the Name control displays the name of the sound card output assigned to the Main. You can't change it. Next is the Effects Bin. Because the outputs from all the Modules and Busses are routed through the Main, adding Effects to its Effects Bin applies those Effects to your entire final stereo signal. A good use for this control is to apply reverb to your entire mix. After the Effects Bin comes the Main Meter, which shows the output level of your final stereo signal as Pro Audio plays the Project. Levels are shown in decibels. Last are the Volume controls (one for the left channel of the stereo signal and one for the right). Using them, you can adjust the output level of your final stereo signal, which is sent to your sound card output.

NOTE

If your sound card output is not stereo, select Options > Audio to open the DirectShow Audio dialog box. Click on the General tab, and then activate the Mono option. Now the Mains in the Console View will display only one Volume control.

Configuring the Console View

Earlier, I mentioned that you can change the number of Aux Busses shown in the Console View. Along with these changes, you can customize how the Console View looks and works in many other ways. These methods are described in the following sections.

General Options

Select Options > Audio to open the DirectShow Audio dialog box, and click on the General tab (see Figure 10.6).

Figure 10.6
You can adjust a number of Console View-related features in the DirectShow Audio dialog box.

From here, you can adjust the parameters described in the following sections.

Number of Aux Busses

To designate the number of Aux Busses you want displayed in the Console View, just type a number in the Number of Aux Busses parameter. Up to sixteen Aux Busses can be displayed.

> **TIP**
>
> If you know that you won't need any Aux Busses during mixdown, you can enter a value of 0 in the Number of Aux Busses parameter. This setting helps keeps the Console View neat and compact.

MIDI Volume Mapping

To control the volume of the audio Tracks in Pro Audio, you can use both MIDI Volume and Velocity values. The process is a complicated one, so I won't go into the details here. Basically, here's what you need to know: If you choose the Linear Scale option for the MIDI Volume Mapping parameter, the volume control of your audio Tracks will be a bit coarse at lower levels. If you choose the Quadratic Taper option, Pro Audio does some fancy quadratic mathematical manipulating so that you get finer control over the volume of your audio Tracks at lower levels. Test each option to see which one sounds best to you.

CHAPTER 10

MIDI Pan Mapping

Pro Audio can control the panning of your audio Tracks in two different ways. If you choose the Balance Control option for the MIDI Pan Mapping parameter, a constant level of audio is not maintained in the left and right stereo channels as you adjust the Pan control of an audio Track Module. In other words, if you move the Pan control left, the volume of the right stereo channel is gradually reduced, while the volume of the left stereo channel stays the same.

If you choose the Constant Power option for the MIDI Pan Mapping parameter, a constant level of audio is maintained. In other words, if you move the Pan control of an audio Track Module to the left, both the left and right stereo channels are adjusted so that their combined output level is always the same. Again, you should test each option to see which one sounds best to you.

The Module Manager

If you click on the Module Manager button in the Toolbar at the top of Console View (it's the first button from the left, after the Value parameter), the Module Manager opens (see Figure 10.7). Using the Module Manager, you can hide Modules, Aux Busses, and Mains in the Console View.

Figure 10.7
You can hide different parts of the Console View by using the Module Manager.

The Module Manager works as follows:

1. To hide an individual component, click to remove the check mark next to that component in the list. Then click on OK.

2. To hide a group of components (such as all the MIDI Track Modules, all the audio Track Modules, all the Aux Buses, or all the Mains), click on the appropriate button—Toggle Audio, Toggle MIDI, Toggle Aux Busses, Toggle Mains—to select the appropriate group. Then press the spacebar on your computer keyboard to remove the check marks. Finally, click on OK.

Of course, you also can make the components appear again by doing the opposite of the preceding procedures. These changes to the Console View are in appearance only. They don't affect what you hear during playback. For example, if you hide an audio Track Module that outputs data during playback, you still hear that data even if you hide the Module. Hiding components of the Console View can come in handy when you want to work only on a certain group of Tracks at time and you don't want to be distracted or overwhelmed by the number of controls being displayed.

Changing the Meters

You also can change how the meters in the Console View behave. If you use the Console View while recording your audio Tracks, you'll notice that a meter appears on the Tracks that have their Arm controls activated. These meters show the input level for the Tracks (which I described in Chapter 6, "Recording and Playback"). To toggle these meters on or off, simply click on the Record Meters button in the Toolbar at the top of Console View (the second button from the left). You can do the same thing with the Main Meters by clicking on the Playback Meters button (the third button from the left). And by clicking on the Peaks Only button (the fourth button from the left), you can control whether the Main Meters will show the entire output level or just if the output level peaks (meaning it hits 0dB).

You might want to turn off these meters, because they can sometimes take up quite a bit of your computer's processing power. If you ever need to lighten the load on your computer during recording or playback, you might want to try turning off some or all of the meters.

Taking Snapshots

Pro Audio provides two different methods of mixdown, one of which is called Snapshots. Using Snapshots, you can take a "picture" of all the current control values in the Console View and then store those values in your Project at a specified Now Time. For example, if your Project is a pop song with a number of different sections (such as the intro, verse, chorus, and so on), you might want to change the mix each time a new section is reached by the Now Time during playback. You can easily do so by creating a different Snapshot at the beginning of each section of the song. During playback, as the Now Time passes a point in the Project where a Snapshot is stored, the values for all the controls in the Console View are automatically changed to reflect the Snapshot. You can create Snapshots in two different ways; these methods are described next.

Recording Snapshots Manually

To create a Snapshot while your Project is not playing, just follow these steps:

1. Set the Now Time to the point in the Project where you want the Snapshot to be stored.

2. Adjust the controls in the Console View to values at which you want them to be set during that part of the Project.

3. Click on the Snapshot button (the one with the picture of a camera shown on it) in the Toolbar at the top of the Console View.

4. Repeat steps 1 through 3 until you've created all the Snapshots that you need for your Project.

Snapshot control values for each of the MIDI and audio Track Modules are stored as controller messages in the individual Tracks represented by those Modules. Snapshot control values for the Aux Busses and the Mains are stored in a special Track called Console Automation Data. When you create a Snapshot, this Track is automatically created in the Track View. It doesn't appear in the Console View, though.

Recording Snapshots During Playback

You also can record Snapshots on the fly while a Project is playing. You just do the following:

1. Turn off the Console View Update feature by making sure that the Update button (the button with the picture of a fader shown on it, located just to the right of the Snapshot button) in the Toolbar is not pressed.

NOTE

When activated, the Console View Update feature makes the on-screen controls in the Console View move according to the Snapshot data (and Automation Data, which I'll talk about later) saved in the Project. In other words, if you've created some Snapshots in your Project, during playback when the Now Time comes upon a Snapshot, not only do the values of the Console View controls change, but the actual buttons, knobs, sliders, and faders move, too. It's cool to watch the faders move up and down as your music plays. When you're creating Snapshots, though, you don't want your settings to change as the Project plays, so that's why you have to turn off the Update feature.

2. Set the Now Time to just before the point in the Project where you want to create the Snapshot.

3. Adjust the controls in the Console View to values at which you want them to be set during that part of the Project.

4.   Start the Project playing.

5.   When the Now Time gets to the point in the Project where you want to create the Snapshot, click on the Snapshot button.

6.   Stop playback of the Project.

7.   Repeat steps 2 through 6 until you've created all the Snapshots that you need for your Project.

As before, Snapshot control values for each of the MIDI and audio Track Modules are stored as controller messages in the individual Tracks represented by those Modules. Snapshot control values for the Aux Busses and the Mains are stored in a special Track called Console Automation Data.

Automating the Mix

Snapshots are great if you need quick control value changing at certain points in your Project, but most of the time you'll want the controls to change smoothly over time as the Project plays. To achieve this effect, you need to use Pro Audio's Record Automation feature. Using Record Automation, you can record the movements of any of the controls in the Console View. You do so in real-time as your Project plays.

Recording Automation

You can record the values of the controls in the Console View into your Project by activating the Record Automation feature and manipulating the controls with your mouse as the Project plays. This feature works like this:

1.   Turn on the Record Automation feature by making sure the Record Automation button (the button with the big red dot shown on it, located just to the left of the Snapshot button) in the Toolbar is pressed.

2.   Set the Now Time to just before the point in the Project where you want to start recording control changes.

3.   Start the Project playing.

4.   When the Now Time gets to the point in the Project where you want to begin recording control changes, adjust the controls in the Console View with your mouse.

5.   When you're finished, stop playback of the Project.

6.   Because you're manipulating on-screen controls with your mouse, you can make only one change at a time. What if you want to have two different controls change at the same time? For every control that you want to have change in the same timeframe, you must repeat steps 2 through 5.

TIP

Instead of starting and stopping playback each time you want to record additional control changes, try setting up a loop so that Pro Audio will just play the Project (or section of the Project) over and over again. I described looping in Chapter 6, "Recording and Playback."

7. After you've finished recording all the control changes that you need for your mix, be sure to turn off the Record Automation feature.

Just like with Snapshots, the control values for each of the MIDI and audio Track Modules are stored as controller messages in the individual Tracks represented by those Modules. The control values for the Aux Busses and the Mains are stored in a special Track called Console Automation Data.

Editing Automation

To delete or edit the Snapshot or automation data for a Track, right-click on the Volume control of the appropriate Module, and select Edit Automation Data from the pop-up menu. Pro Audio opens the data in the Controller pane of the Piano Roll View so that you can edit it graphically. I described editing data with the Piano Roll View in Chapter 7, "Editing Basics."

To delete or edit the Snapshot or automation data for the Aux Busses and Mains, either follow the procedure just described or simply go to the Track View and open the Track called Console Automation Data into the Piano Roll View.

Grouping

As I mentioned earlier, to change more than one control at a time while you're recording automation data, you have to play through your Project several times. To make things even easier, however, you can connect a number of controls together so that, if you move one, the others will move with it. You do so by using Pro Audio's Grouping feature. With the Grouping feature, you can create groups of buttons, knobs, sliders, and faders whose movements are linked to one another. Knobs, sliders, and faders can be grouped together, but buttons can be grouped only with other buttons.

Creating Groups

You can create up to twelve different groups, each of which is designated by a letter of the alphabet (A through L) and a color. The number of controls that can belong to a group is unlimited. To create a group, follow these steps:

1. Right-click on a control and select Group > A-L. Depending on the letter you choose, that control takes on the associated color.

2. Right-click on another control and select Group > A-L. This time, choose the same letter as you did for the first control. This other control then takes on the same color.

3. Continue to add as many other controls to the group as you want. You even can create other groups. The same control, however, cannot belong to more than one group.

Now if you move the first control, the second control will move, too, and vice versa. The values of both of these controls also are recorded if you have them grouped while recording automation data.

Ungrouping

To remove a control from a group, right-click on the control and then select Ungroup from the pop-up menu. The color of the control turns back to normal.

Group Properties

In addition to simple groups, in which you link different controls together so that they move identically, you can create some advanced control groups by manipulating the properties of a group. To change the properties of a group, right-click on one of the controls in the group and select Group Properties from the pop-up menu to open the Group Properties dialog box (see Figure 10.8).

Figure 10.8
You can use the Group Properties dialog box to change the properties of a group.

By changing the properties of a group, you can change the way the controls in the group are related to one another in terms of the way they move. Controls in groups can be related absolutely, relatively, or via a custom definition.

Absolute

To make it so that the controls in a group are related absolutely, select the Absolute option (which is the default setting when you create a new group) in the Group Properties dialog box and click on OK. Controls in a group that are related absolutely have the same range of motion. This means that if you move one control in the group, the others move by the same amount. This is true even if one control starts at one value and another control starts at a different value. For example, suppose you have two Volume controls on two different MIDI Track Modules linked together, and one of the Volume controls has a value of 10, and the other has a value of 20. If you move the first control up by 10, the other control moves up by 10, too. Now the first control has a value of 20, and the second control has a value of 30.

Relative

To make it so that the controls in a group are related relatively, select the Relative option in the Group Properties dialog box and click on OK. Controls in a group that are related relatively do not have the same range of motion. This means that if you move one control in the group, the others can move by different amounts. For example, suppose you have two Pan controls linked together, and one has a value of 0 (all the way left), and the other has a value of 64 (centered in the middle). If you move the first control so that it has a value of 64 (centered in the middle), the other moves so that it has a value of 127 (all the way right). Now if you move the first control to a value of 127 (all the way right), the second control remains at 127 (all the way right). The second control remains in this position because it can't go any higher, so it stays at that value while the first control continues to be raised in value. I know this concept is a bit confusing, but if you fool with it awhile, you'll begin to understand it.

Custom

To make it so that the controls in a group are related according to your own custom definition, select the Custom option in the Group Properties dialog box. All the controls in the group are listed in the dialog box (see Figure 10.9).

Figure 10.9

You can create complex relationships between controls in a group by using the Custom option.

Along with the names of each control, the Start and End Values also are listed. By changing the Start and End Values of each control, you can define some complex ranges of motion. For example, one good use of the Custom option is to create a "crossfade" motion between two Volume controls. Suppose you have one Volume control in a group with a Start Value of 0 and an End Value of 127, and you have another Volume control in the same group with a Start Value of 127 and an End Value of 0. As you move the first control up in value, the second control comes down, and vice versa. Of course, you also can set up more complex relationships simply by assigning different Start and End Values to each control in a group.

To change the Start or End Value of a control in the list in the Group Properties dialog box, select the control and then type a value for either the Start Value or End Value parameters located at the bottom of the box. If you want to exchange the current Start and End Values, click on the Swap button. After you've finished creating your custom definition, click on OK.

TIP

You also can change the Start and End Values of a control without having to open the Group Properties dialog box. Just set the control to the value that you want to set as the Start or End, and then right-click on the control and select either Set Start = Current or Set End = Current.

Remote Control

Even with Grouping, you still might find it cumbersome having to adjust on-screen controls with your mouse. To remedy this situation, Pro Audio provides a Remote Control feature. With the Remote Control feature, you can use an external MIDI device to control the movements of the on-screen controls in the Console View. For example, if you have a MIDI keyboard, you can use a key on the keyboard to manipulate one of the button controls. Or if you have a Pitch Bend Wheel on your keyboard, you can use it to manipulate one of the knob, slider, or fader controls.

By assigning different types of MIDI controller messages to the controls in the Console View, you'll no longer have to use your mouse to change the value of the controls. You can use the actual buttons and keys or levers and sliders on your MIDI instrument or device. To activate the Remote Control feature for a control in the Console View, just do the following:

1. Right-click on the control, and select Remote Control from the pop-up menu to open the Remote Control dialog box (see Figure 10.10).

Figure 10.10
You can use the Remote Control dialog box to assign MIDI controller messages to controls in the Console View so that they can be changed via an external MIDI device.

2. If you want to turn off Remote Control for this control, select the None option.

3. If you want to use a key on your MIDI keyboard to manipulate this control, select either the Note On option or the Note On/Off option. Then enter the pitch of the key that you want to use. If you choose Note On, the value of the control is toggled on or off (for a button control) or to minimum value or maximum value (for knobs and sliders) each time you press the key. If you select the Note On/Off option, the value of the control is toggled on when you press the key and off when you let go of the key.

4. If you want to use a lever or slider on your MIDI keyboard to manipulate this control, select the Controller option. Then enter the value of the MIDI controller that you want to use. You can use this option to manipulate only knob, slider, and fader controls.

5. If you want to use the Pitch Bend Wheel on your MIDI keyboard to manipulate this control, select the Wheel option.

6. If you want to use the special Registered Parameter Number or Non-Registered Parameter Number MIDI messages to manipulate this control, choose either the RPN or NRPN option. Then enter the number of the parameter that you want to use.

7. Set the MIDI Channel that your MIDI keyboard or device is using.

8. Click on OK.

Now you can manipulate the control from your MIDI keyboard or device. By the way, Cakewalk sells a MIDI device called StudioMix. Its sole purpose is to provide hardware-based knobs, buttons, and sliders so that you can manipulate the controls in the Console View remotely. I haven't tried it, but you might want to look into it if you're really fed up with using your mouse for mixing.

Audio Envelopes

In addition to all the previously mentioned ways for adjusting the controls in the Console View, Pro Audio provides yet one more. Unfortunately, it works only with audio data, and it enables you to change only the Volume and Pan. Still, it can be very useful. I'm talking about the Envelope feature. Using this feature, you can "draw" Volume and Pan changes into individual audio Events by using the Audio View. These changes are non-destructive, meaning they don't change the actual data, just the way it sounds during playback. This works like this:

1. Select an audio Track in the Track View and select View > Audio to open that Track in the Audio View.

2. In the Audio View, right-click on one of the audio Events in the Clips pane and select either Envelope > Create Volume or Envelope > Create Pan to add a volume or pan Envelope to the Event. Initially, the Envelope is shown as a straight line that runs right across the center of the Event horizontally (see Figure 10.11).

Figure 10.11
When you first add an Envelope to an audio Event, it looks like a straight horizontal line.

TIP

If you don't see the Envelope, make sure the Show Volume Envelopes and Show Pan Envelopes buttons (the last two buttons in the Audio View Toolbar from left to right) are pressed.

3. At the beginning of the Envelope is a small square (called a *Node*). To change the value of the Envelope, click and drag the Node up or down. If it's a volume Envelope, dragging the Node up increases the volume of the audio Event, and dragging the Node down decreases the audio Event. If it's a pan Envelope, dragging the Node up pans the data in the audio Event to the left, and dragging the Node down pans the data in the audio Event to the right.

4. To make things more interesting, you can add more Nodes to the Envelope either by double-clicking anywhere on the Envelope or by right-clicking on the Envelope and selecting Add Node from the pop-up menu. You can add as many Nodes as you need, which enables you to create some very complex volume and pan changes. Unlike the Node at the beginning of the Envelope, the added Nodes can be dragged up, down, left, and right, so you can create any Envelope shape that you want (see Figure 10.12). You also can change the time and value of a Node more precisely by right-clicking on it and selecting Properties from the pop-up menu. Then you can simply type the new values into the Node Properties dialog box.

Figure 10.12
You can create complex Envelopes by adding more Nodes.

5. To make things even more interesting, you can change the shape of the line segments between two Nodes. Right-click on a line segment and select one of the following options from the pop-up menu: Jump, Linear, Fast Curve, or Slow Curve. If you want abrupt changes in the volume or pan values of your audio data, select Jump. For straight changes in the values, select Linear. For fast but smooth changes in the values, select Fast Curve. For slow and smooth changes in the values, select Slow Curve. Depending on the option that you choose, the shape of the line segment will change respectively.

6. If you need to delete a Node, right-click on it and select Delete Node from the pop-up menu. And to delete all Nodes, just right-click on the Envelope and select Clear All from the pop-up menu.

7. If you need to reset a Node to its original position, right-click on it and select Reset Node from the pop-up menu.

8. If you want to delete an entire Envelope, right-click on it and select Delete Envelope from the pop-up menu.

Now, when you play your Project, the volume and/or pan values for the audio Events that you edited will follow the shape of the Envelopes. Using Envelopes is the equivalent of mixing your audio Tracks by "drawing" in the changes. Experiment and have fun with this feature.

A Mixdown Exercise

Of course, what would a chapter on mixing be without a sample mixdown session, right? Follow along as I show you how to use some of the features I described earlier in the chapter by mixing one of the sample Projects included with Pro Audio:

1. Select File > Open, choose the Don't Matter Audio and MIDI Demo.bun file, and click on Open to open that sample Project.

2. Close the File Info window, the Staff View, and the Audio View. You don't need them right now.

3. In the Track View, select Tracks 1, 8, and 9. Then select Track > Kill to delete those Tracks. They are MIDI Tracks, and you don't need them for this exercise.

4. Select View > Console to open the Console View.

5. Because Tracks 2 and 3 and Tracks 6 and 7 are stereo pairs, their Volume controls should be grouped together so that the drums and horns volume can be adjusted easily. Go ahead and group Tracks 2 and 3 together by using Group A; then group Tracks 6 and 7 together by using Group B.

6. Set up a flanging Effect on the guitar by adding the Cakewalk FX Flanger to the Effects Bin in Track 5. Open the Effect and choose the Preset called Classic Flange; then change the Wet Mix parameter to 40 percent. The original setting adds a bit too much of the Effect to the guitar. Remember, subtlety is the key to applying good-sounding Effects.

7. Set up a delay Effect on the horns by activating the Aux Send 1 controls on Tracks 6 and 7. Then set both Send Levels to 0dB. In the Effects Bin of Aux Bus 1, add the Cakewalk FX Delay. Open the Effect and choose the Preset called 120bpm Delay. On Aux Bus 1, set the Send Level to 0dB, the Return Level to -3dB, both the Send and Return Balances to 64, and the Pre Fader Enable to Pre. Now adjust the Volume controls for Tracks 6 and 7 to -3dB.

8. Set up a reverb Effect for the entire mix by activating the Aux Send 2 controls on all the Tracks except Track 4 (reverb isn't usually applied to bass instruments). Then set the Send Levels for the drums (Tracks 2 and 3) to -8dB, for the guitar (Track 5) to -8dB, and for the horns (Tracks 6 and 7) to -10dB.

9. In the Effects Bin of Aux Bus 2, add the Cakewalk FX Reverb. Open the Effect and choose the Preset called Jazz Club. On Aux Bus 2, set the Send Level to 0dB, the Return Level to 0dB, both the Send and Return Balances to 64, and the Pre Fader Enable to Pre. Now adjust the Volume controls for the drums to -4dB, for the guitar to -3dB, and leave the bass at 0dB. Your Console View should now look similar to the one shown in Figure 10.13.

Figure 10.13
The initial settings for the mixdown exercise should look something like the Console View shown here.

TIP

You can use the Effects Bin in the Main to apply reverb to all the Tracks, but then you don't have the flexibility of leaving the Effect off the bass and also having varying degrees of the Effect on the other instruments via the Send Levels. Using the Aux Bus provides you with more choices in creating the mix.

10. Play the Project. Sounds pretty good, no? But I think it could be a little more interesting. Set the Pan controls for the drums to 64. Set the Now Time to 1:01:000 (the beginning of the Project). Now take a Snapshot of all the initial mix settings. Set the Now Time to 1:04:000. Set the Pan controls to 0 for Track 2 (Drums Left) and 127 for Track 3 (Drums Right). Take another Snapshot. Right in the beginning of the song, the drums play in the very center of the stereo field. Then a few beats in, they quickly spread to the far left and right. This arrangement gives the mix a really powerful introduction.

11. Add a bit of movement to the guitar by first setting the Now Time to 1:01:000 (the beginning of the Project). Then activate the Record Automation feature and deactivate the Update feature. Play the Project. As the music plays, move the Pan control for the guitar slowly back and forth between the values 30 and 98. Don't worry if you go a little past one of the values; just try to move the control slowly so that the position of the guitar doesn't change too quickly. When the Project stops playing, deactivate Record Automation and activate the Update feature. During playback, the guitar moves subtly from left to right and vice versa through the stereo field.

12. Play the Project again from the beginning. Isn't that cool?

Feel free to add more changes or expand upon the mix a bit by applying other Effects or maybe an Envelope or two. Mixing music is an art form, but with a little practice, you'll find it's really not all that difficult. As always, don't be afraid to try new things. Just play with the mix, and if you like what you hear, great! If not, change it.

The Next Steps

After you've finished mixing all the data in your Tracks together at just the right settings, it's time to create a final stereo Track, which you can use to burn your Project on to CD or get it ready for distribution in a multimedia project or on the Internet. Instead of including the information on how to do that here in this chapter, I've decided to break things up a bit. The next few chapters deal with some other important features found in Pro Audio, such as music notation and using StudioWare and CAL. If you would prefer to read these chapters later, you can skip to Chapter 16, "Taking Your Pro Audio Project to CD," to learn how to finish the mixing process and burn your music to a compact disc. For information on converting your Project to a compatible format for multimedia or the Internet, read Appendix C, "Producing for Multimedia and the Web."

11

Making Sheet Music

In Chapter 7, "Editing Basics," I described how you can edit the data in your MIDI Tracks graphically by using the Piano Roll View. Pro Audio also provides tools so that you can edit your MIDI data as standard music notation and guitar tablature. As a matter of fact, you can compose new music while working with notation by graphically adding, editing, and deleting notes. You also can add many of the symbols used in music notation, such as chord symbols, expression markings, and lyrics. And when you're ready, you can print your music as sheet music, complete with title, copyright notice, page numbers, and more by using the printer attached to your computer. To give you an idea of how to use all these wonderful features, in this chapter, I'll cover the following:

▶ Using the Staff View

▶ Editing music as notes and tablature

▶ Applying musical symbols

▶ Handling percussion

▶ Using the Lyrics View

▶ Printing your music

The Staff View

Pro Audio provides three different tools for editing MIDI data: the Event View, the Piano Roll View, and the Staff View. For really precise numerical editing, the Event View can't be beaten. For precise graphical editing of both MIDI note and controller data, the Piano Roll View is the tool you'll want to use. (I described the Event and Piano Roll Views in Chapter 7, "Editing Basics.") Many musicians, however, are used to composing and editing in standard music notation. The Staff View comes into play at this point.

Using the Staff View (see Figure 11.1), you can add, edit, and delete MIDI note data within your MIDI Tracks. Looking similar to sheet music on a piece of paper, the Staff View represents notes as standard music notation and guitar tablature on musical staves with clefs, key signatures, time signatures, and many of the other symbols you might expect to see on a sheet of music.

Figure 11.1
Working in the Staff View is just like composing music on paper, but a lot easier.

More precisely, the Staff View consists of three major sections: the Toolbars (located at the top of the View, containing all the View's related controls); the Staff pane (located in the center of the View, displaying the notes in the currently selected Track[s]); and the Fretboard pane (located at the bottom of the View, displaying the notes currently being played as they would appear on a six-string guitar neck that uses standard tuning).

You'll also notice that the Staff View has scroll bars. They work just as they do in the other Views. In addition, this View has a Snap to Grid function, which is represented by the Grid button in the first Toolbar. Other similarities are the Marker area and the Time Ruler, which are located just above the Staff pane. The Staff View also has zoom tools, but they are located in the first Toolbar rather than in the lower-right corner of the View. The reason for this placement is that, when you're zooming in the Staff View, it makes the notation grow larger both horizontally and vertically in equal proportions, so you don't need multiple zoom tools.

You can open the Staff View in two different ways:

▶ In the Track View, select the MIDI Track(s) that you want to edit, and then select View > Staff.

▶ In the Track View, right-click on a Track or Clip and choose Staff from the pop-up menu.

Whatever method you choose, Pro Audio then opens the Staff View and displays the data from the Track(s) that you selected.

Changing the Layout

If you select more than one Track to be displayed at once, the Staff View shows the data from each Track on a separate stave.

TIP

Just like the other Views, the Staff View provides a Pick Tracks button in the first Toolbar. You can use it to change the Tracks being displayed.

Pro Audio picks the clef (treble or bass) for each stave automatically by looking at the range of notes contained in the data. If a Track has notes that fall into both clefs, it shows the data on two connected staves, one with a treble clef and one with a bass clef.

NOTE

Up to twenty-four staves of notation can be displayed in the Staff View at once. This does not necessarily mean twenty-four Tracks can be displayed, though. If the data from each Track is shown on a single stave, then twenty-four Tracks can be displayed at once. If, however, the data from each Track is shown on a pair of staves (as previously mentioned), only twelve Tracks can be displayed at once. Of course, you also can have some Tracks shown with one stave and some shown with two, so the number of Tracks will vary.

You can override these automatic stave settings though, if you want, by adjusting the Staff View Layout parameters. To adjust the way the data from your MIDI Tracks is displayed in the Staff View, just do the following:

1. Right-click anywhere within the Staff pane and select Layout from the pop-up menu to open the Staff View Layout dialog box (see Figure 11.2).

Figure 11.2
You can use the Staff View Layout dialog box to change the way your data is displayed in the Staff View.

2. From the list, select the name of the Track that you want to change.
3. In the Staff Properties section, set the Clef parameter to the type of clef you want to use for that Track. If you choose the Treble/Bass option, the Track is displayed on two staves. To determine which notes will be shown on which stave, enter a note value for the split parameter. Notes that are at or above the pitch that you enter are shown on the treble clef staff, and notes below are shown on the bass clef staff.
4. Click on Close.

The Track is now shown with the stave settings that you specified.

Percussion Tracks

If you open a MIDI Track in the Staff View that has its Channel parameter set to 10, and you had previously set up your sound card ports to use the General MIDI Instrument Definitions (which you learned about in Chapter 3, "Customizing Pro Audio"), the Staff View automatically displays that Track as percussion notation in a percussion staff. It displays the Track this way because, when you're using General MIDI, it is standard practice to put all percussion instruments on MIDI channel 10. If you want to override this automatic setting, you can do so, as explained previously.

You also can change a number of other settings to customize the way your percussion staves appear. If you select your percussion Track in the Staff View Layout dialog box, a new button (called Percussion Settings) becomes active. If you click on this button, the Percussion Notation Key dialog box appears (see Figure 11.3).

Figure 11.3
You can use the Percussion Notation Key dialog box to further adjust how your percussion Tracks appear.

By manipulating the parameters in this dialog box, you can change the noteheads and articulation symbols used to display your percussion notes. You also can change which percussion sounds correspond to the different positions on the percussion staff. You do so as follows:

1. In the MIDI Note section, select the name of the instrument that you want to change.

2. If you want to change the position on the percussion staff where that instrument will be shown, select the appropriate pitch in the Display As section. Then click on the Bind button to assign that staff position to the selected instrument.

3. If you don't want an instrument to have a specific staff position assignment, select the instrument and click on either the Unbind button or the Default note button. To remove all instrument assignments, click on the Zap All button.

NOTE
Any instruments that don't have a specific assigned staff position automatically use the default position, shown at the bottom of the Display As section. This means that those instruments are shown at that pitch position on the percussion staff. You can change the default position by typing in a new pitch value.

4. After you've bound an instrument to a position on the staff, you can designate the Notehead Type and Articulation Symbol it will use. Just select the appropriate options in those sections of the dialog box. When setting the Notehead Type, you also can opt to have the notehead circled or not by setting the Notehead circled parameter.

5. If you want to use these settings again later, save them as a Preset.

6. Click on OK to close the Percussion Notation Key dialog box.

7. Click on Close to close the Staff View Layout dialog box.

Now the data in your percussion Tracks is shown, using the settings you specified.

TIP

Pro Audio displays ghost strokes (percussion notes played very softly for ornamentation) by using the standard method of parentheses around the percussion notehead. It determines ghost strokes by testing to see whether the note velocity is lower than 32. This number is a fixed value that can't be changed. You can, however, change the note velocities of your data and then use the Vel+ Track parameter to trick Pro Audio into using a different determining value. For example, to stop notes from being shown as ghost notes, simply raise their velocity values. Then, so that the sound of the data isn't changed, set the Vel+ parameter so that it lowers the velocities to their original values during playback. Do the opposite to have notes shown as ghost notes.

Showing Pedal Events and Chord Grids

You also can control whether or not the Staff View will display pedal Events or guitar chord grids (I'll talk more about both of these symbols later). To do so, in the Display section of the Staff View Layout dialog box, set the Show Pedal Events and Show Chord Grids options.

Changing Text Fonts

You also can change how the text used in your data will be displayed. For example, you can change Track names, measure numbers, lyric text, expression text, chord text, triplet numbers, and tablature fret numbers. To do so, just follow these steps:

1. Right-click anywhere within the Staff pane and select Layout from the pop-up menu to open the Staff View Layout dialog box.

2. In the Display section, choose the type of text that you want to change by picking its designation from the Set Font drop-down list. For example, if you want to change how the Track names look in your sheet music, select Track names from the list.

3. Click on the Set Font button to open the Font dialog box (see Figure 11.4).

Figure 11.4
Using the Font dialog box, you can set how you want the text in your sheet music to appear.

4. In the Font section, choose the font that you want to use.

5. In the Font style section, choose a style for your text, such as Bold or Italic.

6. In the Size section, choose the size of the text that you want to use.

> **NOTE**
>
> As you are changing these parameters, you can see a preview of how the text will look, as shown in the Sample section.

7. Click on OK to close the Font dialog box.

8. Click on Close to close the Staff View Layout dialog box.

Your text is now displayed according to the settings that you specified.

Rhythmic Appearance

When converting your MIDI data into music notation, Pro Audio has to make some educated guesses about how to display the rhythmic values of the notes. It does so because, when you record your musical performance in real-time, instead of playing notes with perfect timing, you probably will play some of them a little ahead or a little behind the beat. You also might hold some notes a little longer than they should be held. Most often, these slight timing "errors" are desirable because they give your music a more "human" feel.

Pro Audio doesn't understand these slight rhythmic variations, however; it knows only exact note timing and durations. So, when it displays your data in the Staff View, the data might not always look like it's supposed to. That's why Pro Audio provides a number of parameters that you can adjust to give it a better idea about how the music should be displayed.

CHAPTER 11

Beaming Rests

When you're notating music with very complex rhythms, it's standard practice to lengthen the beams on beamed groups of notes to also include rests. Lengthening the beams makes it much easier for the person reading the music to pick out the right rhythms. For rhythmically simple music, however, it's usually best not to beam rests. In case you need this feature, though, you can turn it on and off by opening the Staff View Layout dialog box and setting the Beam Rests option in the Display section.

Setting the Display Resolution

For Pro Audio to make an educated guess as to how the rhythms in your music should be displayed, you have to give it a point of reference, which is called the Display Resolution. By setting this parameter, you are telling Pro Audio what is the smallest rhythmic note value used in your music. For example, if the smallest rhythmic value that can be found in your music is a sixteenth note, then you would set a sixteenth note value to be used for the Display Resolution. Pro Audio then rounds any start times and note durations to the nearest sixteenth note so that your music looks more like it should. This setting changes only the appearance of the music, not how it sounds. To set the Display Resolution, select a rhythmic value from the Display Resolution drop-down list located in the first Toolbar (see Figure 11.5).

Figure 11.5
You can set the Display Resolution so that Pro Audio can make a better guess as to how your data should be displayed.

Filling and Trimming Durations

In addition to the Display Resolution parameter, Pro Audio provides two other options you can set to help it better understand how to display your music. The Fill Durations option rounds note durations up to the next beat or note (whichever comes first). For example, instead of showing two quarter notes tied together in the same measure, Pro Audio simply shows a single half note.

The Trim Durations option rounds note durations down so that they do not overlap with one another. For example, if you have a note with a duration that extends past the start of the next note, the first note's duration is shortened so that you don't end up with something like a half note tied to a quarter note with an eighth note sitting in between the two.

Neither of these options changes the music in any way, just how it's displayed. The results vary depending on the music you are trying to display as notation, so you'll have to try either or both of these options to see whether they help "clean up" the rhythmic notation values. To turn the options on or off, just click on the Fill Durations and Trim Durations buttons (located in the first Toolbar to the immediate left of the Display Resolution parameter).

Dealing with Notes

As you know, when you open a MIDI Track in the Staff View, the notes in that Track are displayed in the Staff pane as standard music notation. In addition to simply displaying the notes, the Staff View also enables you to edit and delete them, as well as add new ones.

You can add new notes to a Track or edit the existing ones by using the tools represented by the first four buttons in the first Toolbar (going from left to right on the left side of the Staff View).

Selecting

The first button in the Toolbar represents the Select tool. Using this tool, you can select the notes for further manipulation, such as deleting, copying, moving, and so on. Essentially, you select notes the same way you would in the Piano Roll View. To select a single note, click on it. To select more than one note, hold down the Ctrl key on your computer keyboard while clicking on the notes that you want to select. You know the rest. For more information, check out Chapter 7, "Editing Basics."

NOTE

When you select a note that is tied to another note, both notes are selected automatically because they are essentially the same MIDI note with its duration shown as two tied notes rather than one note with a larger rhythmic value.

Editing

After you've made a selection, you can copy, cut, paste, move, and delete the notes the same way you would in the Piano Roll View. You also can edit notes individually by using the Draw tool. The second button in the Toolbar represents the Draw tool. Using this tool, you can add (which I'll talk about shortly) and edit the notes in the Staff pane.

To move a note to a different location within a staff, simply click on its note head and drag it left or right. This action moves the note to a different horizontal location within the staff and along the Time Ruler.

NOTE

If you have the Snap to Grid featured activated, the note snaps to the nearest note value set in the Snap to Grid dialog box.

To change the pitch of a note, simply click on its note head and drag it up or down within the same staff or into another staff. As you move the note, Pro Audio plays the different pitches so that you can hear what they sound like.

TIP

By default, Pro Audio uses note pitches that match the current diatonic key signature of the music. This means that as you drag a note to a new pitch, it automatically remains in the correct musical key. If you don't want the note to stay within the key, however, click the right mouse button after you've begun to drag the note to a new pitch. This way, you can change the pitch of the note chromatically in half steps. When you want to return to diatonic pitch values, click the right mouse button again.

Note Properties

Of course, you sometimes might want to make more precise changes to a note or change its duration. You can do so by using the Note Properties dialog box. With the Draw tool, just right-click on a note to open the Note Properties dialog box (see Figure 11.6).

Figure 11.6
Using the Note Properties dialog box, you can make precise changes to a note in the Staff View.

In the Note Properties dialog box, you can make precise changes to the Start Time, Pitch, Velocity, Duration, and MIDI Channel of an individual note by typing in numerical values. You also can specify the fret and string upon which the note will be played in the Fretboard pane (which I'll talk about later).

Drawing (or Adding)

In addition to editing, the Draw tool enables you to add notes to a staff by literally drawing them in. To do so, follow these steps:

1. Select the Draw tool by clicking on its Toolbar button.

2. Select a duration for the new note(s). If you look at the second Toolbar (just below the first one), you'll notice a number of buttons with note values shown on them. Clicking on these buttons determines the duration for your new note(s). For example, if you click on the Quarter Note button, the duration is set to a quarter note. This Toolbar also contains two additional buttons: one representing a dotted note and another representing a triplet. If you want your notes to be dotted or part of a triplet, click on one of these buttons as well.

NOTE

When you create a triplet, Pro Audio places all three notes on the staff with the same pitch. Triplets have to be created with a full set of three notes without rests or ties. After you add the triplet, you can change the pitches of the notes to whatever you desire.

3. Click anywhere on a staff in the Staff pane to place the new note(s) at the start time(s) and pitch(es) that you want.

TIP

It's a good idea to turn off the Fill Durations and Trim Durations options when you're entering new notes in the Staff pane. While you add notes, Pro Audio tries to change the way they are displayed, so you might find this confusing when you're trying to read the music.

Erasing

Even though you can select and delete notes (as described earlier), the Staff View includes an Erase tool for added convenience. To use it, just select the Erase tool and then click on any note(s) in the Staff pane that you want to delete. You also can click and drag the Erase tool over a number of notes to erase them all at once. By the way, the Erase tool is represented by the button in the Toolbar with the picture of an eraser shown on it, located right next to the Draw tool.

Scrub and Step Play

When you're editing the data in a Track, the procedure usually involves making your edits and then playing back the Project to hear how the changes sound. But playing back very small sections can be a bit difficult, especially when you're working with a fast tempo. To remedy this situation, you can use the Scrub tool and the Step Play feature in the Staff View.

Scrub

Using the Scrub tool, you can drag over the notes in the Staff View to hear what they sound like. To use it, simply select the Scrub tool by clicking on its button in the first Toolbar (the one with the small yellow speaker shown it, located right next to the Erase tool). Then click and drag over the notes in the Staff pane. Dragging left to right plays the data forward (what would normally happen during playback), and dragging right to left enables you to hear the data played in reverse. This feature can be useful for testing very short (one or two measure) sections.

Step Play

The Step Play feature enables you to step through (play) the notes in the Staff View note by note. To use it, just follow these steps:

1. Set the Now Time to the point in the music where you want to begin stepping through the notes. You can do so by simply clicking in the Time Ruler.

2. To step forward through the notes, click on the Play Next button in the first Toolbar (the third-to-last button, going from left to right). You also can press Ctrl plus the right-arrow keys on your computer keyboard.

3. To step backward through the notes, click on the Play Previous button in the first Toolbar (the fourth-to-last button, going from left to right). You also can press Ctrl plus the left-arrow keys on your computer keyboard.

Pro Audio then moves the Now Time cursor one set of notes at a time, either to the right or left and plays the notes it lands on.

> **TIP**
>
> Instead of using the Scrub tool or the Step Play feature, you might want to try another useful technique for hearing what your changes sound like. Did you know that you can edit the data in your Project as it's being played back? Of course, it's a bit difficult to edit anything while Pro Audio is scrolling the display as the Project plays. What I like to do is work on a small section of a Project at a time. I set up a section of the Project to loop over and over, and as Pro Audio is playing the data, I make any changes I think might be needed. Because the data is being played back while I edit, I can instantly hear what the changes sound like. Using this approach is much easier than having to keep going back and forth, making changes, and manually starting and stopping playback. I described looping in Chapter 6, "Recording and Playback."

Dealing with Symbols and Lyrics

In addition to notes, Pro Audio enables you to add other markings to your notated music, including chord symbols, guitar chord grids, expression marks, and pedal marks. These markings, however, are only ornamental in nature; they have nothing to do with the data in your MIDI Tracks. With one exception, they also do not affect your music in any way. I'll explain the exception later.

Essentially, Pro Audio provides these features so that you can create sheet music with a more professional look, but you have to enter the marks manually. The procedures are basically the same as when you're working with notes. You use the Draw tool to add the markings, and you can also select, copy, cut, paste, delete, and move them. To give you an idea on how to utilize them, I'll go through them one at a time.

Chord Symbols and Grids

Most sheet music sold to the public includes chord symbols either with just simple chord names or with both names and guitar grids. Pro Audio gives you the flexibility to enter one or both.

Adding and Editing

To add a chord symbol to your music, do the following:

1. Select the Draw tool.

2. Select the Chord tool by clicking on the Chord button in the second Toolbar (the one with the letter *C* shown on it).

3. Position your mouse pointer above the staff to which you want to add the symbol.

NOTE

You can add chord symbols only in certain positions within your music. If a Track is displayed as a single staff, you can place symbols above that staff. If a Track is shown using a pair of staves (treble and bass clefs), you can place symbols above the top (treble clef) staff only.

Also, chord symbols in music are usually lined up with the notes in the staff. Pro Audio enables you to place chord symbols in the same horizontal location above a note along the staff only (although there is an exception, which I'll explain later). As you move your mouse pointer along the top of the staff, the pointer changes to look like a pencil when you find a "legal" position to place a chord symbol.

4. Left-click to place the symbol above the staff. Pro Audio adds a copy of the most recently added chord (the default is C).

5. To change the name of the chord symbol, right-click on it to open the Chord Properties dialog box (see Figure 11.7).

Figure 11.7
You can change the name (and other assets) of a chord symbol by using the Chord Properties dialog box.

6. Select the types of chords that you want to choose from by selecting a group from the Group parameter drop-down list. Pro Audio includes only a single group of chords, called Guitar. You can, however, create your own groups and chord symbols, which I'll talk about shortly.

7. For the Name parameter, select a new name from the drop-down list. You'll notice that multiple chords in the list have the same name. They're named the same because some chords have guitar chord grids associated with them and some don't. If a chord includes a grid, the grid is shown in the Grid section of the dialog box. You'll also find multiple chords with grids having the same name. This is to accommodate the different fingerings that can be used to play each chord on a guitar.

CHAPTER 11

TIP

The list of chords is very long, and sometimes it can be tedious trying to scroll through them all just to find the one that you want. For a quicker way to navigate through the list, type the name of the chord that you want to find in the Name parameter. Then click on the up- or down-arrow keys (depending on which way you want to move through the list) on your computer keyboard.

8. Earlier, I mentioned that Pro Audio enables you to place chords only at certain horizontal locations along the top of a staff. Although this is true when you are initially adding a chord, you can change the position of the chord by changing its start time. Just enter a new time (measures, beats, ticks) in the Time parameter of the Chord Properties dialog box. This way, chord symbols can be placed anywhere along the top of a staff. They don't have to line up with the notes.

9. Click on OK.

Pro Audio changes the name and position of the chord symbol and adds a grid to it according the new properties that you specified.

The Chord Library

Pro Audio includes a large number of predefined chord symbols, which it stores as a Chord Library in a file named CHORDS.LIW. (This file is located on your hard drive in the folder named C:\Program Files\ Cakewalk\Cakewalk Pro Audio 9). You can edit these chords or even add your own by using the Chord Properties dialog box.

To add a chord into a new or existing group, do the following:

1. Right-click on a chord symbol to open the Chord Properties dialog box.

2. To add a chord to an existing group, select the group from the Group parameter drop-down list. To add a chord to a new group, type the name of the new group in the Group parameter.

3. Type the name of the new chord in the Name parameter.

4. To add a grid to the new chord, click on the New Grid button. An empty grid is displayed in the Grid area (see Figure 11.8).

Figure 11.8
You can add a grid to a chord symbol by clicking on the New Grid button.

5. To place a dot on the grid, first choose a finger number from the Finger options, and then click on the appropriate string and fret location on the grid. To assign an open string, select O for the finger number. To assign a muted string, select X for the finger number.

6. To insert a fret designation for the grid, click just to the right of the grid in the Grid section to open the Chord Fret Number dialog box. Then type a fret number and click on OK.

7. To hear what the chord sounds like, click on the Play button.

8. When you're satisfied with the new chord, click on the Save button to save it to the Chord Library.

9. Click on OK.

To edit a chord or group in the Chord Library, follow these steps:

1. Right-click on a chord symbol to open the Chord Properties dialog box.

2. To delete a group, select the group in the Group parameter drop-down list and click on the Delete button.

3. To edit a chord in an existing group, select the group from the Group parameter drop-down list.

4. To delete a chord, select the chord from the Name parameter drop-down list and click on the Delete button.

5. To edit a chord, select the chord from the Name parameter drop-down list and then type a new name.

6. If the chord has an accompanying chord grid, you can either delete it or edit it. To delete it, click on the Remove Grid button.

7. To edit the grid, change the finger assignment for a dot by clicking on the dot repeatedly to cycle through the Finger options.

8. To hear what the chord sounds like, click on the Play button.

9. When you're satisfied with the edited chord, click on the Save button to save it to the Chord Library.

10. Click on OK.

> **TIP**
>
> You also can import new chord definitions into the Chord Library by clicking on the Import button and selecting an .LIW file.

Expression Marks

Expression marks in music designate any kind of text that provides instructions on how the music should be played during different passages. These marks include tempo designations (such as *Allegro*), musical characteristics (such as *Play with feeling*), and dynamics instructions (such as *cresc.*, *ppp*, or *fff*). Essentially, expression marks are just simple text added to the sheet music.

Adding an Expression Mark

To add an expression mark to your music, do the following:

1. Select the Draw tool.

2. Select the Expression tool by clicking on the Expression button in the second Toolbar (the one with the letter *f* shown on it).

3. Position your mouse pointer below the staff to which you want to add the mark.

> **NOTE**
>
> As with chord symbols, you can place expression marks only in certain positions within your music. If a Track is displayed as a single staff, you can place the marks below that staff. If a Track is shown using a pair of staves (treble and bass clefs), you can place marks below the top (treble clef) staff only.
>
> Also, as with chord symbols, marks are initially lined up with the notes in the staff (although you can change the way they're lined up by editing the marks and altering their start times). As you move your mouse pointer below the staff, the pointer changes to look like a pencil when you find a "legal" position to place a mark.

4. Left-click to place the mark below the staff. Pro Audio opens an insertion box.

5. Type the text that you want to use for the mark (see Figure 11.9).

Figure 11.9
Expression marks are just simple text that you type into the Staff pane.

TIP

To leave a dangling hyphen at the end of an expression mark, type a space and a single hyphen after the text in the insertion box. Dangling hyphens often are used with expression marks in sheet music to show that the expression should be continued over a range of notes or measures until the next expression mark appears.

6. Press the Enter key on your computer keyboard.

TIP

You also can press the Tab or Shift+Tab keys on your computer keyboard to move to the next or previous expression mark location, respectively.

Pro Audio then adds the expression mark to your music.

Editing an Expression Mark

To edit an expression mark, do the following:

1. Right-click on the expression mark to open the Expression Text Properties dialog box (see Figure 11.10).

Figure 11.10
Using the Expression Text Properties dialog box, you can edit expression marks.

2. To change the position of the expression mark, enter a new start time (measures, beats, ticks) in the Time parameter.

3. To change the text of the expression mark, enter the new text in the Text parameter.

4. Click on OK.

The expression mark is then displayed in the new position, showing the new text according to your settings.

> **TIP**
> You also can edit the text of an expression mark by clicking on it with the Draw tool to reopen the insertion box.

Hairpin Symbols

In addition to showing crescendos and decrescendos as text via expression marks, they also can be shown graphically via hairpin symbols. These symbols look like large greater than and less than signs (see Figure 11.11).

Figure 11.11
Crescendos and decrescendos also can be designated via hairpin symbols.

Adding a Hairpin Symbol

To add a hairpin symbol to your music, follow these steps:

1. Select the Draw tool.

2. Select the Hairpin tool by clicking on the Hairpin button in the second Toolbar (the one with the less than sign shown on it).

3. Position your mouse pointer below the staff to which you want to add the symbol.

NOTE

As with expression marks, if a Track is displayed as a single staff, you can place the symbol below that staff. If a Track is shown using a pair of staves (treble and bass clefs), you can place the symbol below the top (treble clef) staff only.

4.   Click to place the symbol below the staff.

Pro Audio then adds a copy of the most recently added hairpin symbol. To change the symbol, you can edit it by using the Hairpin Properties dialog box.

Editing a Hairpin Symbol

To edit a hairpin symbol, do the following:

1.   Right-click on the hairpin symbol to open the Hairpin Properties dialog box (see Figure 11.12).

Figure 11.12
Using the Hairpin Properties dialog box, you can edit hairpin symbols.

2.   To change the position of the hairpin symbol, enter a new start time (measures, beats, ticks) in the Time parameter.

TIP

You also can change the position of the hairpin symbol by dragging it.

3.   To change the type of the hairpin symbol, choose either the Crescendo option or the Diminuendo (same as decrescendo) option.

4.   To change the length of the hairpin symbol, enter a new value (beats, ticks) in the Duration parameter.

5.   Click on OK.

The hairpin symbol is displayed in the new position, with the new type and duration according to your settings.

Pedal Marks

Earlier, I mentioned that there was one exception to the fact that markings do not affect the data in your MIDI Tracks. That exception is pedal marks. On a sheet of music, pedal marks usually designate when the performer is supposed to press and let go of the sustain pedal on a piano. In Pro Audio, they mean essentially the same thing, but they refer to the sustain pedal attached to your MIDI keyboard (if it has one). More precisely, pedal marks in the Staff View designate MIDI controller number 64 (Pedal-sustain) messages in your MIDI Tracks (which also can be edited in the Controller pane of the Piano Roll View). So, whenever you add or edit pedal marks in the Staff View, you also are editing the MIDI controller number 64 messages in that Track.

Adding a Pedal Mark

To add a pedal mark to your music, follow these steps:

1. Select the Draw tool.

2. Select the Pedal tool by clicking on the Pedal button in the second Toolbar (the one with the letter *P* shown on it).

3. Position your mouse pointer below the staff to which you want to add the mark.

> **NOTE**
>
> Similar to expression marks, if a Track is displayed as a single staff, you can place the symbol below that staff. If, however, a Track is shown using a pair of staves (treble and bass clefs), you can place the symbol below the bottom (bass clef) staff only.

4. Click to place the mark below the staff.

Pro Audio adds a pair of pedal marks (pedal down, which looks like an asterisk, and pedal up, which looks like a *P*) to your music. To edit the marks, you can use the Pedal Properties dialog box.

Editing a Pedal Mark

To edit a pedal mark, do the following:

1. Right-click on the pedal mark (either a pedal down mark or a pedal up mark; you can't edit them both at once) to open the Pedal Properties dialog box (see Figure 11.13).

Figure 11.13
You can use the Pedal Properties dialog box to edit pedal marks.

2. To change the position of the pedal mark, enter a new start time (measures, beats, ticks) in the Time parameter.

> **TIP**
> You also can change the position of the pedal mark by dragging it.

3. To change the MIDI channel for the pedal mark, type a new channel number in the Channel parameter.

4. To change the type of the pedal mark, enter a new number in the Value parameter. Enter 0 to make it a pedal up mark. Enter 127 to make it a pedal down mark. Entering any numbers in between that range doesn't have any effect.

5. Click on OK.

The pedal mark is displayed in the new position, with the new type and MIDI channel according to your settings.

Lyrics

Just like any good notation software, Pro Audio enables you to add lyrics to your sheet music. Lyrics (like expression marks) are represented by simple text displayed below a staff. You can add lyrics to a Track by using the Lyrics tool or the Lyrics View.

The Lyrics Tool

Follow these steps to add lyrics to your music with the Lyrics tool:

1. In the Staff View, select the Draw tool.

2. Select the Lyrics tool by clicking on the Lyrics button in the second Toolbar (the one with the letter *L* shown on it).

3. Position your mouse pointer below the staff, underneath the first note to which you want to add lyrics.

> **NOTE**
> If a Track is displayed as a single staff, you can place the lyrics below that staff. If a Track is shown using a pair of staves (treble and bass clefs), you can place marks below the top (treble clef) staff only.
>
> Also, each word or syllable in the lyrics must be aligned with a note. Pro Audio automatically aligns the lyrics to the notes in the staff.

4. Click to place the lyric below the staff. Pro Audio opens an insertion box (just like when you add expression marks).

5. Type a word or syllable to be aligned with the current note.

6. To move forward and add a lyric to the next note, enter a space, type a hyphen, or press the Tab key on your computer keyboard. The insertion box moves to the next note waiting for you to enter text.

7. To skip over a note, don't type any text into the insertion box. Either enter a space or type a hyphen.

8. To move back to the previous note, press the Shift+Tab keys on your computer keyboard.

9. When you're finished entering lyrics, press the Enter key on your computer keyboard.

To edit lyrics by using the Lyrics tool, do the following:

1. Select the Draw tool.

2. Select the Lyrics tool.

3. Click on the word that you want to change.

4. Edit the word.

5. Press the Enter key on your computer keyboard.

The Lyrics View

After you've entered some lyrics in the Staff View, you can display them in a separate window called the Lyrics View. This View is useful for providing a cue for performers while recording vocal Tracks because you can make the lyrics appear in any size font that you want (see Figure 11.14).

Figure 11.14
The Lyrics View is useful as a cue for vocal performers.

To open the Lyrics View, select a Track in the Track View, and then select View > Lyric. To change the size of the text, click on the fa or fb buttons. They provide two different preset font sizes. You also can use more specific font settings by clicking on the Font button to open the Font dialog box (which I described earlier). In this dialog box, you can change the font, style, and size of the text. The Lyrics View also has a Pick Tracks button that works just as in the other Views.

CHAPTER 11

Of course, you also can add and edit Lyrics in the Lyrics View, but I don't recommend doing so. The process is not very intuitive, because you can't see what notes the words and syllables are being aligned with. If you want to use the Lyrics View for adding and editing, you can do so just like you would enter and edit text in the Windows Notepad. Each word that you type is automatically aligned to a note in the current Track, and you can split words into syllables by entering hyphens either manually or automatically by pressing the Hyphenate button. That's all there is to it.

TIP

In addition to typing and editing lyrics in the Lyrics View, you also can select, cut, copy, paste, and delete text. Again, this procedure works just as in the Windows Notepad. What's nice about the Lyrics View is that if you already have some text saved in a text file, you can copy and paste it into this View to quickly add lyrics to a Track. When you look at the lyrics in the Staff View, the words are automatically aligned to the notes in the staff. And if you want all or some of the words to be hyphenated automatically, just select all or some of the text in the Lyrics View and then click on the Hyphenate button. It's very quick and simple.

The Fretboard and Tablature

For all the guitar players out there, Pro Audio provides a couple of nice notation-related features just for you. The first one I'll describe is the Fretboard pane.

The Fretboard Pane

The Fretboard pane, located at the bottom of the Staff View, is both a visual aid and an editing tool. During playback, the Fretboard displays the notes at the current Now Time in a selected Track, as they would be played on a six-string guitar using standard tuning. This makes the Fretboard a cool learning tool when you're trying to learn to play a new piece of music. It also displays notes when you use the Scrub tool or Step Play feature, which makes it even easier to pick out the fingerings. The color of the notes matches the color of the Clip (from the Track View) in which they are stored.

Fretboard Properties

You can configure certain aspects of the Fretboard, such as its background style and the orientation of the strings. You also can turn it on or off.

To toggle the Fretboard on and off, click on the Fret View button located in the first Toolbar. It's the second-to-last button, going from left to right.

To change the background style, right-click on the Fretboard and choose one of the following from the pop-up list: Rosewood Hi, Rosewood Lo, Ebony Hi, Ebony Lo, Maple Hi, or Maple Lo. The Hi and Lo designations have to do with the screen resolution that you are using on your computer monitor. If you're using a high-screen resolution, use one of the styles marked Hi. If you're using a low-screen resolution, use one of the styles marked Lo. To be honest, the resolution you choose really doesn't make that much of a difference.

To change the orientation of the strings, right-click on the Fretboard and select Mirror Fretboard from the pop-up menu to invert the Fretboard so that the highest-sounding string appears at the bottom. To change it back, just select Mirror Fretboard again.

Adding Notes

In addition to using the Fretboard to display notes, you can add new notes to a Track (staff) by clicking on the Fretboard. Just follow these steps:

1. Set the Now Time so that the cursor rests at the point in the staff where you want to add the note(s). You can do so quickly by clicking in the Time Ruler.

2. Select the Draw tool.

3. Select a note duration by clicking one of the appropriate buttons in the second Toolbar.

4. Click on the guitar strings in the Fretboard to enter notes on the staff. You can enter up to six notes (one per string).

5. Make the Now Time cursor move forward by the same amount as the current note duration setting by pressing the Shift and right-arrow keys on your computer keyboard.

6. Repeat steps 3 through 5 to continue adding more notes.

Editing Notes

You also can edit existing notes in a Track (staff) by using the Fretboard. You can change only the pitch of the notes, though. To do so, just follow these steps:

1. Set the Now Time so that the cursor rests on top of the note(s) that you want to edit. You can do so quickly by clicking in the Time Ruler. You also can use the Step Play feature.

2. Select the Draw tool.

3. Drag the note(s) along the string(s) to a new fret (thus changing the pitch).

After you let go of the mouse button, Pro Audio changes the pitch of the note(s) in the staff.

CHAPTER 11

Tablature

As a guitar or bass player, you might be more comfortable reading and working with tablature rather than standard notation. If that's the case, then you're in luck, because Pro Audio includes a number of features that enable you to display and edit your music as tablature.

Displaying Tablature

To display tablature for a Track (staff), follow these steps:

1. Right-click in the Staff pane and select Layout from the pop-up menu to open the Staff View Layout dialog box.

2. Select the name of the Track from the list for which you want to display tablature.

3. In the Tablature section, activate the Display Tablature option.

4. Select a tablature style from the Preset drop-down list.

5. Click on Close.

Pro Audio displays a tablature staff below the current staff, complete with tablature for each note in the Track (see Figure 11.15).

Figure 11.15
Adding tablature to
a Track in the Staff
View is very easy with
Pro Audio.

NOTE

Pro Audio also offers another feature called QuickTab that enables you to quickly generate tablature for a Track, but it works only when you're displaying a single Track in the Staff View. So, I recommend you simply use the previously mentioned method.

Defining a Tablature Style

While you're setting up a Track to display tablature, you might not find a preset style that fits your needs. If that's the case, you can always create your own by doing the following:

1. Right-click in the Staff pane and select Layout from the pop-up menu to open the Staff View Layout dialog box.

2. Select the name of the Track from the list for which you want to display tablature.

3. In the Tablature section, activate the Display Tablature option.

4. Click on the Define button to open the Tablature Settings dialog box (see Figure 11.16).

Figure 11.16

You can create your own tablature styles by using the Tablature Settings dialog box.

5. Under the Tablature tab, set the Method parameter. This parameter determines how the tablature will be displayed. If you select Floating, the notes can be shown anywhere on the Fretboard. If you select Fixed, notes are limited to a specific area on the neck of the guitar. To determine the size and position of that area, you must set the Finger Span parameter and the Lowest Fret parameter. The Finger Span parameter sets the size of the area in a number of frets. The Lowest Fret parameter sets the position of the area on the neck of the guitar by specifying the first fret upon which the area is based. The last tablature method (MIDI Channel) is useful if you record your guitar parts by using a MIDI guitar and you use MONO mode so that each string is recorded by using its own MIDI Channel. If this is your situation, then select the MIDI Channel method and set the 1st Channel parameter to the lowest number channel used by your MIDI guitar.

6. In the Number of Frets parameter, enter the number of frets that the tablature should be based on.

7. In the String Tuning section, choose an instrument/tuning upon which to base the tablature.

8. Set the Number of Strings parameter to the number of strings that the instrument provides.

9. The pitches of each string for the instrument appear in the parameters below the Number of Strings parameter. You can either leave them as is or you can customize the pitches to your liking.

10. Save your settings as a Preset.

11. Click on OK to close the Tablature Settings dialog box.

Your new tablature style should now appear in the Preset drop-down list in the Tablature section of the Staff View Layout dialog box.

Regenerating Tablature

You can use different tablature styles for different sections of the same tablature staff by following these steps:

1. In the Staff pane, select the notes or tablature numbers for which you want to use a different tablature style.

2. Right-click anywhere in the Staff pane and select Regenerate Tablature from the pop-up menu to open the Regenerate Tablature dialog box (see Figure 11.17).

Figure 11.17
You can define different tablature styles for selected notes by using the Regenerate Tablature feature.

3. Set the Method, Finger Span, Lowest Fret, and 1st Channel parameters, if applicable. These parameters work the same way as described previously.

4. Click on OK.

Pro Audio changes the tablature style of the selected notes, based on your parameter settings.

Adding Notes via Tablature

In addition to just displaying tablature, you can use a tablature staff to add notes to a Track by doing the following:

1. Select the Draw tool.

2. Choose a note duration by clicking on the appropriate note duration button in the second Toolbar.

3. Move the mouse pointer over the tablature staff. It changes its shape to a crosshair.

4. Position the crosshair within any measure and over a line in the tablature staff.

5. Click and hold the left mouse button. Now drag your mouse pointer up and down to select a fret number.

6. Release the mouse button to enter the note.

Editing Notes via Tablature

You also can edit notes via a tablature staff. To do so, just follow these steps:

1. Select the Draw tool.

2. To change the fret number of a note, right-click on it and select a new number from the pop-up menu.

3. To move a note to a different string (line) on the tablature staff, click and drag the note while pressing the Alt key on your computer keyboard. Drag the note up or down to move it. If the note is not supposed to play on a certain string, it will not be allowed to move there.

Exporting Tablature to a Text File

One last tablature feature that you might find useful is being able to save the tablature as a text file either for printing or distributing over the Internet. By saving the tablature this way, you can share your tablature with other guitarists even if they don't own Pro Audio. You use this feature as follows:

1. Select a MIDI Track in the Track View.

2. In the Staff View, right-click anywhere in the Staff pane, and select Export to ASCII TAB. The Save As dialog box opens.

3. Type a name for the file.

4. Click on Save.

CHAPTER 11

Pro Audio saves the data in the MIDI Track as tablature in a text file.

TIP
You might want to try quantizing the Track before you save it as tablature. Doing so usually produces more accurate results.

Printing Your Music

After all is notated and done, you can print your music to paper if you have a printer connected to your computer. Pro Audio automatically sets up your music on separate pages, including the song title, composer, and other information, along with the notation. You can print your musical score like this:

1. Select File > Info to open the File Info window, and fill out all the information you want to have included on your sheet music. You can use the Title, Subtitle, Instructions, Author, and Copyright parameters. For more information about the File Info window, see Chapter 4, "Working with Projects."

2. With the Staff View open, select File > Print Preview. Pro Audio goes into Print Preview mode (see Figure 11.18) and displays your music on virtual pages, enabling you to see how it will look before you print it.

Figure 11.18
You can see how your music will look on paper before you print it by using the Print Preview mode.

3. To zoom the display in or out, click on the Zoom In or Zoom Out buttons.

4. Depending on the length of your song, Pro Audio usually shows two pages at once on the screen. If you would rather view only one page at a time, click on the One Page button.

5. If your song takes up more than two pages, you can navigate through them by using the Next Page and Prev Page buttons.

6. Before you print your music, you need to select a size for your score. To do so, click on the Configure button to open the Staff View Print Configure dialog box.

7. From the single drop-down list, choose the size you want to use. Pro Audio provides nine different sizes to choose from. They are standard music-engraving sizes used by professional music publishers. Each size is used for a different purpose. Size 0 (Commercial or Public) is usually used for wire-bound manuscripts. Size 1 (Giant or English) is usually used for school band music books or instructional books. Sizes 2 or 3 (Regular, Common, or Ordinary) are usually used for printing classical music. Size 4 (Peter) is usually used for folios or organ music. Size 5 (Large Middle) is usually used for ensemble music. Size 6 (Small Middle) is usually used for condensed sheet music. Size 7 (Cadenza) is usually used for pocket music editions. And Size 8 (Pearl) is usually used for thematic advertisement.

8. Click on OK. The music is redrawn, using the new size.

9. Click on the Print button.

When the standard Windows Print dialog box opens, you can set up your printer and print your music.

TIP

Here's one final tip. If you like to compose your music from scratch by using the Staff View, you can use one of the included templates listed in the New Project File dialog box when creating your new Project. For example, if you want to compose for a string quartet, select the Classical String Quartet template.

The templates come with all the Track parameters preset, but you might need to change a few of them to match your studio setup. After that, select all the Tracks in the Track View, and then select View > Staff to open them in the Staff View.

Everything is set up with the proper clefs, staff names, and more. The only settings you might need to adjust are the meter and key. Other than that, you have a blank slate ready and waiting to be filled with the music notation for your latest masterpiece.

CHAPTER 11

12

Studio Control with StudioWare and Sysx

Most of today's modern appliances are computer controlled. Need to cook a meal? Push a few buttons on the stove, and it automatically sets the right time and temperature for your recipe. Need to wash your clothes? Yada, yada, yada… It's the same thing with modern recording studio gear—most everything is computer controlled, and it supports MIDI, too. I'm not just talking about MIDI instruments (such as synthesizer keyboards), but audio processing equipment and mixing boards as well.

Why would these products include support for MIDI? Because, like MIDI instruments, they have internal parameters that can be changed and stored. Because these products provide support for MIDI, these parameters become accessible to other MIDI devices, such as your computer. This means it is now possible to control just about every piece of equipment in your studio via your computer, provided the equipment supports MIDI and you have the right software. Lucky for you, you don't need to buy any additional software, because Pro Audio has some built-in features for controlling and storing the parameters for any outboard MIDI gear. All you have to do is connect your MIDI devices to your computer (just as you would any MIDI instrument), and they can "talk" to each other, which brings me to the topics I'm going to discuss in this chapter. They include the following:

▶ Working with System Exclusive data

▶ Learning how to use the Sysx View

▶ Introducing StudioWare

▶ Taking Snapshots with StudioWare

▶ Recording control movements in StudioWare

CHAPTER 12

System Exclusive

MIDI devices (other than MIDI instruments) don't usually provide standard musical functions, so their internal parameters are not compatible with standard MIDI messages, such as Note On messages, for instance. Instead, they have to communicate using special MIDI messages called *System Exclusive*. I talked a little about System Exclusive messages in Chapter 3, "Customizing Pro Audio." System Exclusive messages give you access to any special functions that a manufacturer includes in a MIDI instrument or device.

Not only do you have access to these functions, but by utilizing System Exclusive messages, you can send all the data from the MIDI instruments and devices in your studio to Pro Audio to be stored in your Projects. Why is this capability important? Because you can set up all your equipment with specific settings for a Project, store the data in the Project, and then send the data back to the devices at the beginning of your next recording session. This means that the next time you open the Project, you can have all the equipment in your studio set up automatically, without your having to touch a single knob. Cool, no?

The Sysx View

Pro Audio gives you access to System Exclusive data via the Sysx View (see Figure 12.1). Using the Sysx View, you can store up to 8,191 banks, each of which can contain any number of System Exclusive messages (limited only by the amount of memory in your computer system). So, for example, you could dedicate a different bank to store the data for each separate piece of equipment in your studio. You could also store different sets of Patch data for a single MIDI instrument in separate banks. Then, during different times in your Project, you could send specific Patch data to change the sounds in the instrument for that part of the song (you'll learn more about this topic later).

Figure 12.1
The Sysx View lets you store System Exclusive data within the current Project.

Receiving System Exclusive Data

To store System Exclusive data in a bank in the Sysx View, you need to do a *data dump*. Essentially, the MIDI device from which you want to grab data dumps (or sends) it to your computer to be stored in one of the Sysx View banks.

NOTE

Be sure to check Pro Audio's Global MIDI Options to see whether the Record System Exclusive data setting is activated. To do so, select Options > Global to open the Global Options dialog box. Then select the MIDI tab. In the Record section, click on System Exclusive to place a check mark next to it. If this setting isn't turned on, Pro Audio will block all incoming System Exclusive data.

To do a data dump, follow these steps:

1. Select View > Sysx to open the Sysx View and then click on a bank to highlight it for incoming System Exclusive data.

2. Click on the Receive Bank button (the one with the downward-pointing red arrow) to open the Receive System Exclusive dialog box (see Figure 12.2).

Figure 12.2

You use the Receive System Exclusive dialog box to request a data dump from your MIDI device.

3. Choose a DRM (Dump Request Macro) from the list. If you don't see your MIDI device listed, select the very first option: <You start dump on instrument > . Click on OK. Then start the data dump using the Control Panel on your device. (See the device's user's guide for more information on how to use the Control Panel.)

CHAPTER 12

NOTE

Dump Request Macros (DRMs) are special System Exclusive messages. Some MIDI devices support them and some don't. If you have a MIDI device that supports DRMs, Pro Audio can send a DRM to the device, asking it to send back its parameter data. If you have a MIDI device that doesn't support DRMs, you have to initiate the data dump manually from the Control Panel on the device.

TIP

Just because your MIDI device isn't listed in the Receive System Exclusive dialog box doesn't mean the device doesn't support DRMs. You'll need to look in the device's user's guide to see whether it has DRMs available. If so, you can set them up to be used within Pro Audio. To do so, open the file C:\Program Files\Cakewalk\Cakewalk Pro Audio 9\cakewalk.ini using the Windows Notepad. Inside that file, you'll find instructions on how to add new DRMs to the list in the Receive System Exclusive dialog box.

4. If you do see your device listed, select the appropriate DRM and click on OK. The DRM may ask you for additional information. For instance, if the DRM requests that the device send the data for a single sound patch, you'll need to input the patch number you want it to send. This process is pretty straightforward; you can just follow the prompts.

5. Whichever method you use to initiate the data dump, Pro Audio ultimately displays the Sysx Receive dialog box when it's ready to receive the data (see Figure 12.3). The dialog box shows the number of bytes of data being received as the dump takes place.

Figure 12.3
The Sysx Receive dialog box displays a count of the System Exclusive data.

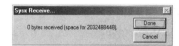

6. When the count stops, click on Done.

NOTE

If the number of bytes stays at zero for more than a few seconds, then most likely something is wrong. Your MIDI device might not be hooked up properly or you could have given the wrong answers for the additional DRM questions. Those answers differ depending on the MIDI device, so you'll need to consult its user's guide. In any event, if you have this problem, click on Cancel. Then check your connections and try the procedure again.

After the dump is complete, the Sysx View shows the bank you selected with a new name and length (in bytes).

Name Change

If you want to change the name of a bank, follow these steps:

1. Select the bank.

2. Click on the Name button (the one with the lowercase *abc* shown on it) to open the Bank Name dialog box (see Figure 12.4).

Figure 12.4
In the Bank Name dialog box, you can change the name of a bank.

3. Type a new name.

4. Click on OK.

TIP

You can also record System Exclusive data directly to a Track, just like you would any other MIDI data. To do so, just set up your Track parameters, start Pro Audio recording and then manually initiate a data dump from your MIDI device. You should be aware of some limitations, though. When you're recording directly to a Track, Pro Audio stores the data in Sysx Data Events instead of banks. Each Sysx Data Event can hold a single System Exclusive message of only 255 bytes in length. This means that if your MIDI device sends a message longer than 255 bytes, the message will get cut off and it won't work when you try to send the data back. Plus, you won't get any warning that this has happened. It just won't work. So, essentially, you're better off using the Sysx View and banks to handle System Exclusive data. It's much easier, more efficient, and you can still send data back to a device during playback (I'll talk more about that in the next section).

CHAPTER 12

Sending System Exclusive Data

After you set up your banks in a Project, you can send the data back to your MIDI devices. Before you do, though, you should be sure that each bank being sent is first set to the appropriate MIDI Port. Just like each Track in the Track View can be set to send data to a particular MIDI Port on your MIDI interface, each bank in the Sysx View can be set to a specific Port as well. To do so, follow these steps:

1. Select the bank.

2. Click on the Port button (the one with the picture of a MIDI connection shown on it) to open the Bank Port dialog box (see Figure 12.5).

Figure 12.5

In the Bank Port dialog box, you can change the MIDI Port assigned to a bank.

3. Type a new Port number. Remember that the data in this bank will be sent only to this MIDI Port, so be sure the number is the same as the Port number your device is connected to.

4. Click on OK.

After you assign the right Port numbers to each of your banks, you can easily transmit the data to the appropriate MIDI devices in three different ways.

Manually

To send the data in a bank manually, just select the bank and click on the Send Bank button (the one with the single, green upward-pointing arrow shown on it). That's all there is to it. No muss, no fuss. You can also send all the data in every bank at once. You don't need to make any selections; just click on the Send All Banks button (the one with the three green, upward-pointing arrows shown on it).

Automatically

Each bank in the Sysx View has an option called Auto. If you activate this option for a bank, that bank will be sent automatically every time you open the Project. For example, if you store all the parameter data from all your MIDI devices in a number of banks using the Sysx View and you set the Auto option on each of those banks, the next time you open your Project, Pro Audio will send the System Exclusive data to your MIDI devices automatically. Your studio will then be ready to go with all the correct settings for your Project, without your having to do anything manually. To set the Auto option on a bank, just select the bank, and click on the Auto Send Bank button (the one with the green, upward-pointing arrow and yellow plus sign shown on it).

During Playback

Although using the Auto option is a very convenient way to send System Exclusive data, sometimes you might want to send a bank at a specific time during the playback of your Project. For this purpose, Pro Audio provides a special Sysx Bank Event that you can place in any MIDI Track in your Project. Whenever Pro Audio encounters a Sysx Bank Event, it looks up the Event's associated bank number in the Sysx View and then sends that bank.

To add a Sysx Bank Event to a MIDI Track, you have to do so manually by using the Event View. Here's how:

1. Right-click on a MIDI Track in your Project, and select Event List from the pop-up menu to open the Event List View for that Track (see Figure 12.6).

Figure 12.6
Using the Event List View, you can add Sysx Bank Events to your MIDI Tracks.

2. Move the Now Time cursor to the point within the list where you want to insert the new Sysx Bank Event.

3. Click on the Insert Event button (the one with the yellow star shown on it) to insert a new Event. Initially, the Event will take on the characteristics of the Event at which the Now Time cursor was placed.

4. To change the Event to a Sysx Bank Event, move the Now Time cursor over to the Kind column and press the Enter key on your computer keyboard to open the Kind Of Event dialog box (see Figure 12.7).

Figure 12.7
In the Kind of Event dialog box, you can change the type of the current Event.

5. Select the Sysx Bank option in the Special section and click on OK.

6. Move the Now Time cursor over to the Data column and press the Enter key on your computer keyboard. The number in the Data column becomes highlighted. Here, you enter the number of the bank you want to be sent.

7. Type a bank number and press the Enter key on your computer keyboard.

Now, during playback when Pro Audio encounters that Sysx Bank Event, it will send the appropriate System Exclusive data to your MIDI device.

CAUTION

MIDI is meant to transmit only one piece of data at a time. Of course, it transmits the data so fast that it sounds like all the data in the Tracks is playing simultaneously. But MIDI does have its limits, and if you try to transmit huge amounts of data in a short amount of time, playback will be interrupted. This happens quite often with System Exclusive data. So, if you're going to send banks of data during playback, try to send only one bank at a time throughout your Project and also try to keep each bank short in length. You'll have to do a little experimenting, but if you keep each bank between 100 and 255 bytes, you shouldn't have any problems.

Editing Bank Data

The Sysx View provides a feature that allows you to edit the data in a bank. To edit this data, select a bank and click on the Edit Data button (the one with a hand pointing to a piece of paper shown on it). Clicking on this button opens the Edit System Exclusive Bytes dialog box (see Figure 12.8).

Figure 12.8
In the Edit System Exclusive Bytes dialog box, you can edit the data in a bank.

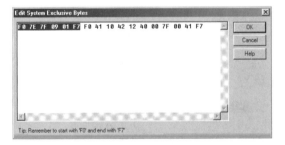

In the dialog box, you'll see a list of numbers. Each number represents one byte of System Exclusive data in hexadecimal format. You can change the numbers just like you would with text in a word processor. If the bank contains more than one System Exclusive message, the beginning of each message is designated by the number F0 and the end of each message is designated by the number F7. This way, System Exclusive data stays compatible with standard data in the MIDI language.

Whenever a MIDI device sees the number F0, it automatically knows that this number designates the beginning of a System Exclusive message. But that's as far as it goes in terms of identifying the data. All the bytes in a System Exclusive message that fall between the F0 and F7 are different, depending on which MIDI device they are associated with, so there's really not much else I can explain about this feature. If you want to learn more about the System Exclusive messages your MIDI device supports, consult the user's manual for that device.

Deleting

If you ever want to delete a bank in the Sysx View, just select the bank and click on the Clear Bank button (the one with the big red X on it). Pro Audio will ask whether you really want to delete. Be careful, because you cannot undo this procedure. When a bank is deleted, you cannot get it back without doing a data dump all over again.

Sharing with Friends

Even though all the data in the banks of the Sysx View is stored along with the data in your current Project, you can also load and save banks individually in a special System Exclusive data file format. This file format is the same one used by the public-domain System Exclusive data dump software utility called MIDIEX. MIDIEX is such a popular program that its file format became a standard for storing System Exclusive data on disk. What's great about the file format is that Pro Audio and many other sequencers support it, so you can easily share your System Exclusive data with your friends. Of course, being able to share won't matter much if you don't own the same MIDI devices, but if you do, you can easily share sound patch data for your MIDI instruments, and so on.

Saving

To save the data in a bank, follow these steps:

1. Select the bank.
2. Click on the Save Bank To File button (the one with the floppy disk shown on it) to open the Save As dialog box.
3. Type a name for the file. The file should have an .SYX extension; Pro Audio should append this extension to the name automatically.
4. Click on Save.

Loading

To load data into a bank, follow these steps:

1. Select a bank.
2. Click on the Load Bank From File button (the one with the yellow folder shown on it).

CHAPTER 12

3. If the bank you selected already has some data in it, Pro Audio will ask whether you want to append the data from the file to the existing data. Click on Yes to append the data, or click on No to replace the data. Pro Audio then displays the Open dialog box.

4. Select an .SYX file to load, and click on Open.

The data from the file is loaded into the bank you selected, and the bank is named after the file. You can change the name of the bank as you learned earlier.

TIP

There's no easy method for copying a bank either within the same Project or from one Project to another, but you can copy using the Save Bank and Load Bank features. Just save a bank to an .SYX file from the current Project. If you want to have a copy of that bank in the current Project, just load it into another bank. If you want to have a copy of that bank in another Project, open the other Project and then load the bank into the Sysx View of that Project.

Intro to StudioWare

Being able to store all the parameter settings for your MIDI gear within a Project is great. You can have your whole studio set up in a matter of seconds. To set those parameters initially, you still have to fiddle with the knobs and controls on the MIDI gear itself. Because some MIDI devices have a limited number of controls, the only way to change their parameters is to wade through an endless maze of menus on a small (and sometimes cryptic) LCD screen. Pro Audio provides a feature, called StudioWare, that lets you adjust all the parameters in your MIDI devices without ever having to leave your computer. And more importantly, it lets you access those less-than-accessible parameters in a very intuitive and easy manner.

Using StudioWare, you can create on-screen Control Panels that let you adjust the parameters in any of your MIDI devices remotely from your computer. Basically, you can have virtual buttons, knobs, and faders on your computer screen that represent each of the adjustable parameters in your MIDI devices. When you move a knob or fader on your computer screen, it changes the value of an assigned parameter in a MIDI device. So now, not only can you store MIDI device parameters, but you also can adjust them. Using the Sysx View and StudioWare, you may never have to touch your MIDI gear again (except maybe to turn it on). Plus, the adjustments you make to any on-screen controls can be recorded and then played back in real-time, which means you can automate parameter changes for a MIDI device as well.

The StudioWare View

Creating your own StudioWare Panels may sound like a complicated task-and, yes, it can be. You need to have a good understanding of MIDI and System Exclusive data, but that doesn't mean you can't get any use out of StudioWare. Besides, some basic Panels are easy enough for anyone to put together, but I'll discuss that topic in Chapter 13, "Advanced StudioWare Techniques."

Getting started with StudioWare is actually very easy. As a matter of fact, for a really quick demonstration, you can have Pro Audio automatically create a Panel for you from the Track setup in your Project. To see what I mean, do the following:

1. Select File > Open and load one of the sample Projects that is included with Pro Audio. For this example, use the Don't Matter Audio and Midi Demo.bun Project.

2. After the file loads, take a look at the Track View (see Figure 12.9). Notice that Tracks 2, 3, 4, 5, 6, and 7 are audio Tracks, and Tracks 8 and 9 are MIDI Tracks. Highlight all of them. (Forget about Track 1. It's blank.)

Figure 12.9
The Track View for Don't Matter Audio and Midi Demo.bun shows both audio and MIDI Tracks.

3. Select View > StudioWare to open the StudioWare View (see Figure 12.10).

Figure 12.10
The StudioWare View houses the virtual on-screen Control Panels.

CHAPTER 12

As you can see in Figure 12.10, StudioWare has created a Control Panel representing all the Tracks you selected in the Track View. Each Track has its own set of controls and, yes, they really work. If you don't believe me, go ahead and start playing the Project. Then try changing one of the volume faders (by clicking and dragging it)—say, for the guitar Track. See? Of course, you might be saying to yourself, "This View looks similar to the Console View, so why would I need it?" You're absolutely right. It mimics the same controls that are in the Console View, and you really don't need it. It's just a cool demonstration trick. StudioWare's real power lies in mimicking the Control Panels of your external MIDI devices.

Unfortunately, there's no quick trick for creating those types of Panels, but Pro Audio does include a number of predesigned Panels that you can use within your own Projects. If you can't find a Panel for your MIDI device, Cakewalk also provides a nice library of additional StudioWare Panels on its Web site; you can download these Panels for free. And you can even find other places on the Internet where you can download free Panels written by other users (see Appendix D, "Cakewalk Resources on the Web").

Opening a StudioWare Panel

A StudioWare Panel is either stored as part of a Project file or as a separate StudioWare file with the extension .CakewalkStudioWare. If a Project file contains a Panel, the Panel is automatically opened when you open the Project. To open a StudioWare file, just do the following:

1. Select File > Open to display the Open dialog box.
2. Select StudioWare from the Files Of Type drop-down list to display only StudioWare files.
3. Choose a file.
4. Click on Open.

Pro Audio then displays the StudioWare View containing the Panel from the file you just opened. Because all Panels are different, I can't really explain how each one works. Usually, a Panel mimics the controls of a MIDI device, so if you own the corresponding MIDI device, you shouldn't have any trouble figuring out how to use its StudioWare counterpart.

After you've opened a Panel, you can adjust the controls, take a Snapshot, or record your control movements, and so on. Adjusting the controls is straightforward. The buttons, knobs, and faders in a StudioWare Panel work the same way they do in the Console View (which you learned about in Chapter 10, "Mixing It Down").

Taking a Snapshot

The Snapshot function works almost exactly the same way as with the Console View too, but there's one little difference. Instead of recording the control data in separate Tracks, the control data from a StudioWare Panel is recorded into a single Track. Most StudioWare Panels include a knob control that allows you to set which Track the control data will be recorded into. As an example, take a look at the General MIDI.CakewalkStudioWare Panel. You'll see a knob labeled Track. Adjusting that knob changes the Track number for the Panel. If you open some of the other sample Panels, you'll notice the same type of Track control. It might look a little different, but it functions in the same way. By the way, if a Panel doesn't have a Track control knob, either the Panel wasn't designed to record data to a Track (some of them don't) or the Panel will automatically record its data to Track 1. So, when you're working with this kind of Panel, it's a good idea to leave Track 1 dedicated to recording control data.

Recording Control Movements

Recording the movements of the controls on a StudioWare Panel is also similar to the same procedure in the Console View, but as with taking a Snapshot, there are a few differences. The first difference is the Track number procedure I described in the preceding section.

The second difference is in grouping controls together. Just as you can do in the Console View, you can group multiple controls together in a StudioWare Panel so that you can easily change more than one control simultaneously. The differences here are in how controls are grouped and in how single controls in a group are adjusted.

For grouping controls, instead of right-clicking on a control and assigning it to a colored group, you simply select an initial control, hold down the Ctrl key on your computer keyboard, and click on one or more additional controls in the Panel. Those controls are then grouped. Grouping controls in a StudioWare Panel is much less sophisticated. They don't have any grouping properties like there are in the Console View either.

For adjusting a single control that belongs to a group, just hold down the Shift key on your computer keyboard and then adjust the control. In the Console View, the procedure is the same, except that you hold down the Ctrl key.

All these techniques work with any StudioWare Panel, even the ones you design yourself, which you'll learn about in Chapter 13, "Advanced StudioWare Techniques."

CHAPTER 12

13

Advanced StudioWare Techniques

Chapter 12, "Studio Control with StudioWare and Sysx," ended with an introduction to StudioWare—what it is, what it does, and how you can use it to control your outboard MIDI devices from your computer with on-screen Panels. That chapter also briefly touched on the topic of creating your own StudioWare Panels. Initially, you might think that StudioWare should be left to the real techno-oriented musicians among us, but that's not true. Anyone can get some good use out of Pro Audio's StudioWare features. This chapter further describes StudioWare, covering the following topics:

▶ The basics of designing your own Panels

▶ Widgets

▶ Widget properties and how to use them

▶ A step-by-step Panel: Custom Pro Audio Toolbars

Designing Basics

Designing your own StudioWare Panels can get very involved, so Cakewalk has tried to make the process as intuitive as possible. Instead of making you wade through all kinds of complex computer programming code, Pro Audio lets you essentially drag and drop your way to creating a Panel.

If you take a look at the StudioWare View (see Figure 13.1), you'll notice a button labeled Design at the top of the window.

Figure 13.1
The Design button
puts StudioWare into
Design mode.

Clicking on that button puts StudioWare into Design mode and, at the
same time, reveals ten new buttons along the top of the window (see
Figure 13.2).

Figure 13.2
In Design mode, ten
new buttons become
available in the
StudioWare View.

The first new button (the one with the grid shown on it) controls the
Snap to Grid feature. It is similar to the Snap to Grid feature found in
other areas of Pro Audio; you learned about Snap to Grid in Chapter 5,
"Getting Around in Pro Audio." Instead of musical intervals, though, the
grid is based on the pixels (dots) that make up your computer screen
display. Clicking on the Snap to Grid button toggles that feature on or off.
And if you click on the button while holding down the Shift key on your
computer keyboard, the Snap to Grid dialog box is displayed. In this
dialog, you can set the size of the grid.

Clicking on the second button (the one with the mouse arrow shown on it) activates the Select tool. This tool allows you to select, move, and set the size of the Widgets. The other eight buttons represent the Widgets—the elements that make up a StudioWare Panel. (I'll describe the Widgets in more detail later in the chapter.) Clicking on any of these buttons activates their associated Widgets, allowing you to visually design a Panel by placing objects (Widgets) within the StudioWare View.

In other words, you can create a StudioWare Panel by selecting different Widgets and placing them within the StudioWare View with your mouse; for example, you can use the Button Widget to add buttons to your Panel. Then you can assign functions to each Widget, making them perform different tasks. After you've finished your design, you can save the Panel and then later use it within any of your Projects. Using Widgets isn't really very complicated, although assigning functions to Widgets can get a bit confusing. I'll go over that topic later.

Creating a New Panel

The basic procedure for designing a new StudioWare Panel is as follows:

1. Either create a new Project or open an existing one. StudioWare Panels can be designed or used only while a Project is open.

2. Select View > StudioWare to open the StudioWare View (see Figure 13.3). You can also open the StudioWare View by selecting File > New and choosing StudioWare Panel from the New Project File dialog box.

Figure 13.3
This new StudioWare Panel contains the default set of controls.

3. Click on the Design button to put StudioWare into Design mode.

4. As you can see in Figure 13.3, whenever you create a new Panel, Pro Audio automatically adds a set of controls for each Track that's currently selected in the Track View. If no Tracks are selected, just one set of controls is added for Track 1. But because you want to create your own Panel from scratch, you should remove those default controls. To do so, click on each of the controls (Widgets) one by one and press the Delete key on your computer keyboard.

TIP

You also can get rid of all the Widgets simultaneously by clicking at the top of the set of controls, where you see the Track number—for example, Track 1. Clicking here selects the Cluster Widget (I'll explain this term in a moment), which contains all the other Widgets. Then just press the Delete key on your computer keyboard to remove everything.

5. The StudioWare View should now look like the View shown in Figure 13.4. That gray rectangle is the blank slate that serves as the initial building block for your Panel. This blank Panel is actually a permanent Cluster Widget. You can't erase it. It will hold any other Widgets you plan to add to the Panel. Click on the Cluster Widget to select it and then drag the sides or corners with your mouse to change its size, thus setting the size of your Panel.

Figure 13.4
The permanent Cluster Widget holds all the other Widgets in your Panel.

6. Add new Widgets to your Panel by clicking on one of the eight Widget buttons at the top of the window to select it. Then click somewhere within the permanent Cluster Widget to place the new Widget on your Panel (see Figure 13.5). You can add as many Widgets as you need (limited only by the amount of memory in your computer).

Figure 13.5
You just point and
click to add a Widget to
your Panel.

7. To change the position of a Widget, just select it and drag it to a new
    location within the Panel. To change the size of a Widget, just select
    it and drag the highlighted sides or corners, just like you would a
    window. You can also copy, cut, and paste Widgets just like you
    would with anything else by using Pro Audio's Edit > Copy, Edit >
    Cut, and Edit > Paste menu commands.

8. Assign properties to each of the Widgets in your Panel. To do so,
    double-click on a Widget to open the Widget Properties dialog box
    (see Figure 13.6). Adjust the relevant parameters and click on OK.
    (I'll explain Widget properties in the next section of this chapter.)

Figure 13.6
Using the Widget
Properties dialog box,
you can assign functions
to each of the Widgets
in your Panel.

9. After you finish making additions or changes to your new Panel, you should save it. You either can save it along with the current Project (you learned how to save Projects in Chapter 4, "Working with Projects") or as a separate .CakewalkStudioWare file. To save it as a file, click on the Save button (the one with the floppy disk shown on it) to open the Save StudioWare dialog box (see Figure 13.7). There, type a name for the Panel and click on OK.

Figure 13.7
You can save your new Panel by using the Save StudioWare dialog box.

TIP

If you want to share your Panel with friends, but you don't want them to be able to make any design changes to it, type a password in addition to a name in the Save StudioWare dialog box. The next time you open the StudioWare Panel and click on the Design button, you will first be asked to enter the password. Don't forget your password, because you cannot make changes to your Panel without it!

If you're sometimes forgetful—like Yours Truly—try encoding the password into the name of the Panel. For example, you could use every other letter in the name of the Panel as your password. So, for a Panel named Special Proteus Panel, the password would be seil poes pnl. It's doubtful that anyone will ever guess it, but you'll still have a quick and easy way to remember it.

Widgets and Their Properties

Graphically designing a StudioWare Panel is one thing, but assigning properties to the Widgets to make the Panel work like you want it to is quite another. The basics are relatively easy to understand, and if you know the MIDI language well enough, you should get the hang of creating Panels fairly quickly. Teaching how to create StudioWare Panels could easily take up a whole book on its own, so instead I'll just get you started by providing some basic information about each of the Widgets—what they are, how to change their properties, and how to use them.

Cluster Widget

The Cluster Widget is a special Widget that has but one purpose: to hold other Widgets. Using it, you can design different sections of controls in your Panel, just like what can be found in many real Control Panels on MIDI devices. For example, you could use one Cluster Widget to hold all the pitch-related controls for your device and another Cluster Widget to hold all the volume-related controls. You can also put Cluster Widgets inside each other so that you can divide your Panel into additional subsections.

Name Change

Because a Cluster Widget doesn't provide any function other than acting as a "container" for other Widgets, its only alterable property is its name. To change the name of a Cluster Widget, do the following:

1. Double-click on the Cluster Widget to open the Widget Properties dialog box.
2. In the field marked Label, type a name for the Cluster Widget.
3. Make sure the Show Label option is activated.
4. Click on OK.

By the way, you can change the name of other Widgets in your Panel using this same procedure.

Hidden Panel Sections

A Cluster Widget is good for one more thing: creating hidden sections of a Panel. Why would you want to hide a part of your Panel? Well, perhaps part of the Panel should be accessible to the user only when certain conditions are met within another part of the Panel. For example, you may have a very sophisticated MIDI device with a large number of alterable parameters—too many to fit nicely within the visible area of your Panel. So, to keep things tidy, you could simply create a number of master buttons that, when clicked, would reveal their associated set of controls. Or you might just want to add a cool informational window containing author and copyright information about your Panel. You do so as follows:

1. Click on the Cluster Widget button (the one with the dual faders shown on it) and then click anywhere within the Panel to add a new Cluster Widget to the Panel.
2. Resize the Cluster Widget so that it can fit the text of your name and perhaps a copyright notice.
3. Click on the Text/Numeric Widget button (the one with the lowercase *ab* shown on it) and then click inside the new Cluster Widget to add a new Text/Numeric Widget.

4. Double-click on the Text/Numeric Widget to open the Widget Properties dialog box. Then, in the Label field, type Created by Insert Your Name Here and click on OK. You might have to resize the Text/Numeric Widget so that your text will show correctly. At this point, your Panel should look similar to Figure 13.8.

Figure 13.8
Creating a hidden Cluster Widget is a fairly easy task, although it does involve quite a few steps.

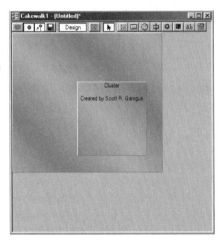

5. Add another Text/Numeric Widget and label it Copyright 2000 All Rights Reserved.

6. Change the name of the Cluster Widget to About this Panel..., but don't close the Widget Properties dialog box just yet. In the field named Alias, type HideAbout to assign a variable to the Cluster Widget.

NOTE

An *Alias* is a variable that allows you to assign a numeric value to a Widget. In other words, an Alias lets a Widget hold a number that can vary according to input from other Widgets in the Panel or from a user adjusting the Widget's on-screen control. This programmable nature allows for some very sophisticated and complex Panels.

In the case of a Cluster Widget, the value of its Alias determines whether it will be visible. As soon as the Alias surpasses a minimum value (that you set), the Cluster Widget becomes visible. As long as the Alias remains less than the minimum value, however, the Cluster Widget stays invisible.

7. Under the Range section of the Widget Properties dialog box, type a Minimum value of 126 and an Initial value of 126. Also, make sure the Maximum value is 127.

8. Click on OK. The Cluster Widget will disappear. Don't worry; it's still there. You just can't see it.

9. To control the appearance of the Cluster Widget, you need to add a button to the Panel. Click on the Button Widget button (yeah, the one with a button shown on it), and then click inside the Panel (preferably somewhere other than where the Cluster Widget is located).

10. Double-click on the Button Widget and in the Widget Properties dialog box, type HideAbout in the Alias field. Then make sure the Maximum value in the Range section is set to 127. Next, click on OK. (You can also give a name to the button, but I'll talk more about Button Widgets later.)

11. Remember to click on the Design button to exit Design mode.

Now try clicking on the button in your Panel. The first time you click on the button, the About this Panel... Cluster Widget should appear. You see this Panel because, when you click on the button, it changes the value of the "HideAbout" Alias to 127 (which is higher than the Minimum value). This makes the Cluster Widget become visible. Click on the button again, and the Cluster should disappear. This time, the button changes the value of the "HideAbout" Alias back to 0 (which is lower than the Minimum value), thus making the Cluster invisible again. What a neat trick, huh?

Text/Numeric Widget

The Text/Numeric Widget is similar to the Cluster Widget in that it has a very simple nature; it enables you to add text to your Panels. That's pretty much it. Text is useful for providing simple instructions on how to use the Panel or for identification purposes, as I mentioned earlier. To change the text content of a Text/Numeric Widget, just type some text in the Label field of the Widget Properties dialog box.

Show the Widget Value

The Text/Numeric Widget *does* have one advanced use, though. You can use it to display the numerical values of other Widgets in the Panel. You simply assign the same Alias to the Text/Numeric Widget as another Widget, such as a Button, Knob, or Slider. Then, when the value of the Alias is changed by clicking on the Button or moving the Knob or Slider, for example, the Text/Numeric Widget will display the numerical value of the Alias. You can set up a working example as follows:

1. If you don't already have a Project open, do so now, and set up a blank Panel in the StudioWare View.

2. Click on the Slider Widget button (the one with the single vertical fader shown on it) and then click somewhere inside the blank Panel to add the Slider Widget to it.

3. Double-click on the Slider Widget to open the Widget Properties dialog box.

4. Type SlideValue as the Alias and click on OK. Don't worry about any of the other properties. The default values are fine.

5. Click on the Text/Numeric Widget button (the one with the lowercase *ab* shown on it) and then click somewhere inside the Panel to add the Text/Numeric Widget to it.

6. Double-click on the Text/Numeric Widget to open the Widget Properties dialog box.

7. Type SlideValue as the Alias and type The Slider Value Is %d as the Label.

TIP

In addition to the Alias, StudioWare provides some special default variables that allow you to display the value of an Alias via the Text/Numeric Widget. By placing %d in the Label property of a Text/Numeric Widget, you can show the value of that Widget's Alias as a decimal number. You can also display the value of an Alias in hexadecimal form by using %x instead of %d. In addition, you can even specify the number of decimal digits that you want to see displayed by using the special variable %04d. In this case, if the Alias were equal to 42, it would be displayed with four decimal places like this: 0042.

8. Click on OK and turn off Design mode by clicking on the Design button. Your finished Panel should look something like the one shown in Figure 13.9.

Figure 13.9
You can use the Text/Numeric Widget like this to display the value of its Alias.

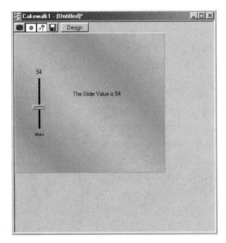

Now try dragging the slider control up and down. See how the text changes to reflect the value of the slider? When you move the slider up and down, it changes the value of its Alias property (in this case "SlideValue"). Because the Text/Numeric Widget also has "SlideValue" as an Alias, it is linked to the Slider Widget. Plus, the special %d variable allows the value of the Alias to be displayed in the Label property of the Text/Numeric Widget.

Image Widget and Widget Appearance

To improve the look of your Panels, you can use StudioWare to assign images to any of the Widgets or place graphics directly in a Panel using the Image Widget. Actually, because StudioWare enables you to assign images to any of the other Widgets, you probably won't use the Image Widget very much. Perhaps if you want to add a logo to your Panel, you might use the Image Widget, but then you could also do so by simply assigning an image to a Cluster Widget. To see what you can do with images, take a look at some of the sample Panels included with Pro Audio—in particular, the Line 6 POD.CakewalkStudioWare and the Roland JV-2080 Patch.CakewalkStudioWare files. They use images extensively to make the Panels look very cool. By the way, these samples also use the hidden Cluster Widget technique I described earlier. Try clicking on some of the buttons and you'll see what I mean.

Adding an Image Widget

If you ever need to use the Image Widget, you can just follow these steps:

1. If you don't already have a Project open, do so now, and set up a blank Panel in the StudioWare View.

2. Click on the Image Widget button (the one with the picture shown on it) and then click somewhere inside the blank Panel to add the Image Widget to it.

3. Right-click on the Image Widget and select Foreground Bitmap from the pop-up menu to open the Widget Bitmap file selector.

TIP

When you select Foreground Bitmap, the image you choose will be stretched to fill the Image Widget. If you want to add a tiled background instead (the same thing you can do to the Windows Desktop), select Background Bitmap from the pop-menu.

4. Select a file and then click on Open. The image file has to be in the Windows Bitmap (.BMP) image file format, or you won't be able to open it.

TIP

If you want to put the Image Widget back to its original state (just a blank gray box), click on either the Default or the None buttons in the Widget Bitmap file selector.

Your new Image Widget is then filled with the image you selected. If the image is bigger than the default Image Widget size, the Image Widget will expand to fit the entire image. As an example, take a look at Figure 13.10.

Figure 13.10
This Image Widget is filled with a picture of Yours Truly.

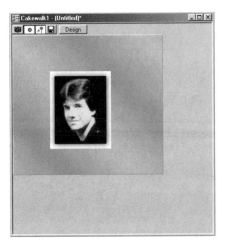

Changing Widget Appearance

Earlier, I mentioned that you can also simply assign an image to any of the Widgets instead of having to use the Image Widget. You do so in the same way you add an image to an Image Widget, but with one small difference: The Foreground Bitmap and Background Bitmap options fill different parts of the Widget with their images. For example, if you assign a Background Bitmap to a Meter Widget, the image fills the dark part of the meter display. If you assign a Foreground Bitmap, the image fills the lit part of the meter display. The Background and Foreground options work differently with each Widget. To find out how, either do a little experimenting or simply refer to the table on page 11-30 of the Pro Audio User's Guide.

NOTE

You must consider two exceptions when assigning images to Widgets. First, the feature doesn't work at all with Text/Numeric Widgets for obvious reasons. Second, a Cluster Widget can accept only a Background Bitmap and the image always fills the entire Widget.

Color

Instead of assigning an image to a Widget, you can change its color. The procedure is the same as when you assign an image, except that you select either Foreground Color or Background Color from the pop-up menu and choose a color from the standard Windows Color Chooser dialog box.

Indicator Widgets

In addition to the Text/Numeric Widget, two other Widgets provide feedback on Alias values. They are the LED and Meter Widgets. Instead of textual or numeric feedback, though, the LED and Meter Widgets provide graphical indications of Alias values.

The LED Widget

The LED Widget works similarly to the Cluster Widget in that it reacts whenever its Alias becomes greater than the specified Minimum value. Instead of appearing or disappearing, however, the LED Widget turns its "virtual light" on and off. You can use this Widget for many different purposes; for example, you can use it to indicate when a button is pressed or not. Here's an example:

1. If you don't already have a Project open, do so now, and set up a blank Panel in the StudioWare View.

2. Click on the Button Widget button (the one with the button shown on it) and then click somewhere inside the blank Panel to add the Button Widget to it.

3. Double-click on the Button Widget to open the Widget Properties dialog box.

4. Type LEDTest as an Alias and click on OK.

5. Click on the LED Widget button (the one with the red "light" shown on it) and then click somewhere inside the Panel to add the LED Widget to it.

6. Double-click on the LED Widget to open the Widget Properties dialog box.

7. Type LEDTest as an Alias and enter 126 for the Minimum and Initial values in the Range section. Then click on OK.

8. Turn off Design mode by clicking on the Design button. Your finished Panel should look something like the one shown in Figure 13.11.

Figure 13.11
This Panel example shows how to use an LED Widget.

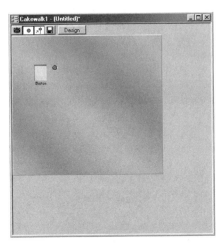

Now try clicking on the button in your Panel. The first time you click on the button, the LED should light up (with the color red). It lights up because, when you click on the button, it changes the value of the "LEDtest" Alias to 127 (which is higher than the Minimum value). This makes the LED Widget light up. Click on the button again and the LED should turn off. This time, the button changes the value of the "LEDtest" Alias back to 0 (which is lower than the Minimum value), thus turning off the LED.

The Meter Widget

Instead of just a simple on/off indication, the Meter Widget can display a whole range of values. This Widget works well for graphically showing the value of the Knob or Slider Widgets (which I'll talk about in a moment). Essentially, it works the same way as a Text/Numeric Widget in that, if you assign the same Alias to a Knob or Slider Widget and the Meter Widget, they are linked together, and the Meter Widget provides a graphical representation of the value of the Alias. As an example, try the following steps:

1. If you don't already have a Project open, do so now, and set up a blank Panel in the StudioWare View.

2. Click on the Slider Widget button (the one with the single vertical fader shown on it) and then click somewhere inside the blank Panel to add the Slider Widget to it.

3. Double-click on the Slider Widget to open the Widget Properties dialog box.

4. Type SlideValue as the Alias and click on OK. Don't worry about any of the other properties. The default values are fine.

5. Click on the Meter Widget button (the one with the double bar meter shown on it) and then click somewhere inside the Panel to add the Meter Widget to it.

6. Double-click on the Meter Widget to open the Widget Properties dialog box.

7. Type SlideValue as the Alias.

8. Click on OK and turn off Design mode by clicking on the Design button. Your finished Panel should look something like the one shown in Figure 13.12.

Figure 13.12
This example shows how to use the Meter Widget to graphically display the value of its Alias.

Now try dragging the slider control up and down. See how the meter changes to reflect the value of the slider? When you move the slider up and down, it changes the value of its Alias property (in this case "SlideValue"). Because the Meter Widget also has "SlideValue" as an Alias, it is linked to the Slider Widget. So, when you move the slider up and down, the meter moves along with it.

Button Widget

As I've already demonstrated in a few of the previous examples, you can use the Button Widget to make Cluster Widgets appear or disappear and to turn LED Widgets on or off. You also can use it to send MIDI data (either to be recorded into a Track or directly out to a MIDI Port), run CAL Programs (see Chapter 14, "CAL 101," and Chapter 15, "Advanced CAL Techniques," for more information about CAL), and even activate functions within Pro Audio. You do so by using the other property settings in the Widget Properties dialog box.

More Widget Properties

If you open the Widget Properties dialog box (see Figure 13.13), you'll notice a number of other properties that you can apply to the Widgets. These properties, which provide additional functionality to the Button, Knob, and Slider Widgets, are the real power behind StudioWare Panels.

Figure 13.13
The additional property settings in the Widget Properties dialog box really give StudioWare Panels their power.

Automate in Track and Direct to Port Properties

As you learned in Chapter 12, "Studio Control with StudioWare and Sysx," the movements of the controls on a Panel can either be recorded to a Track or sent directly out a MIDI Port to be received by a MIDI device. What determines whether a Widget's movements will be recorded or sent to a MIDI Port are the Automate in Track and the Direct to Port properties.

Setting these properties is actually very simple. If you want the movements of a Widget to be recorded to a Track, you activate the Automate in Track property and select a Track number from its drop-down list. If you want the movements of a Widget to be sent directly out a MIDI Port, you activate the Direct to Port property and select a Port number from its drop-down list.

TIP

You can also use Aliases with the Automate In Track and Direct To Port properties. This capability is useful if you want to be able to change the Track or Port number via another Widget on the Panel. For example, you can set up a Knob Widget to act as a Track number control. To do so, just assign the Knob Widget an Alias and then assign the same Alias to the Automate in Track property of another Widget. While you're using the panel, any adjustments you make to the Knob affect which Track is used to record the data from the other Widget. Take a look at the sample Panel called General MIDI.Cakewalk-StudioWare for a working demonstration. The Track Knob in that Panel affects which Track the data from all the other controls in the Panel will be recorded on.

Primary Action Property

Of course, a Widget also needs to be told what kind of data it's supposed to send, and that's where the Primary Action property comes in. The Primary Action property determines a Widget's main function. Its function can be sending MIDI data (note, controller, patch change, pitch wheel, Aftertouch, System Exclusive, and so on), running CAL programs, activating Pro Audio functions, or controlling Track parameters, for example.

To set the Primary Action for a Widget, you simply select the type of Action from the Primary Action Kind drop-down list. For each Action, you must set additional associated parameters. For example, if you select Note from the list, you can set the MIDI Channel, pitch, and velocity that the note will be played with when the Widget is manipulated. I'm not going to go over all the Primary Actions available. If you know your MIDI, then most of the Actions are self-explanatory. The Pro Audio User's Guide provides some basic reference information about Actions on pages 11-22 to 11-28, but as I mentioned earlier, it would take a whole book to show you how to really delve into StudioWare Panel creation. Of course, I won't leave you without anything to ponder. To set up a Button Widget to send a Sysx Bank from the Sysx View, follow these steps:

1. Click on the Button Widget button and then click somewhere inside your Panel to add the Button Widget to it.
2. Double-click on the Button Widget to open the Widget Properties dialog box.
3. Select Sysx Bank from the Primary Action Kind drop-down list.
4. Type the number of the Sysx Bank you want to send in the Bank parameter box that appears.
5. Click on OK and then click on the Design button to exit Design mode.

Now, when you click on the button, the Sysx Bank that you specified is sent. See how easy that is?

Return Action Property

Another property you should know about is the Return Action property. It is the same as the Primary Action property in that you can set it to execute the same types of Actions. Instead of carrying out its function when a Widget is first activated, however, it carries out the function in a secondary manner. In other words, if you set up a Return Action for the preceding button example, when you first click on the button, the Primary Action is initiated. When you click on the button a second time (to return it to its original up position), the Return Action is initiated. To see what I mean, assign a Return Action to the button example I just talked about and then test it.

CHAPTER 13

Adjustable Widgets

Like Button Widgets, the Knob and Slider Widgets can be used to send MIDI data, manipulate Track parameters, and so on. But instead of just a single value, the Knob and Slider Widgets can send a whole range of values. Being able to send several values is great for sending MIDI controller data such as pitch change messages.

You can assign Primary and Return Actions to Knob and Slider Widgets in the same way you would with a Button Widget, but to ensure the value of the Widget is used when sending a range of data, you need to use an Alias. You simply assign an Alias to the Knob or Slider; then you type that same Alias name into any of the Primary Action Kind parameters. For example, to set up a Knob Widget that sends MIDI volume controller data, you can do the following:

1. Click on the Knob Widget button (the one with the little knob shown on it) and then click somewhere inside your Panel to add the Knob Widget to it.

2. Double-click on the Knob Widget to open the Widget Properties dialog box.

3. Type VolumeKnob as an Alias.

4. Select Controller from the Primary Action Kind drop-down list.

5. For Channel, type the MIDI channel you want to use (1 to 16).

6. Select 7—Volume from the Number drop-down list.

7. Type the name of the Alias (VolumeKnob) into the Value parameter.

8. Click on OK and then click on the Design button to exit Design mode.

Now, when you move the knob, it sends MIDI volume controller data to the MIDI Channel you assigned.

Other Properties

Several other Widget properties can come in handy when you're designing your Panels. They include overlapping and precise sizing and positioning.

Widget Overlapping

When you place Widgets on your Panels, you can put them on top of one another. The last Widget that you place will overlap any others that are underneath it. If you ever get into a situation in which you want a Widget that's underneath to be on top instead, just right-click on it and select Bring to Top from the pop-up menu. Selecting this option brings that Widget to the foreground on top of any of the other Widgets. There is also a function for the opposite (Send to Bottom), which you access in the same manner.

Precise Sizing and Positioning

In the Widget Properties dialog box, you'll find a section called Placement. In that section, you can choose properties to specify the exact size and position of a Widget right down to the pixel. This capability can be useful if you're trying to make things look really nice on your Panel and you want to make sure all the Button Widgets are the same size and so on.

The X and Y parameters specify the location of the top-left corner of the Widget. Using these parameters, you can place the Widget at any precise location within your Panel. The Width and Height parameters do exactly what you would expect: They specify the exact width and height of the Widget in pixels.

Custom Toolbars

If you invest enough time in learning how to use StudioWare, I guarantee you'll find that it makes many tasks a whole lot easier to deal with. The possibilities are numerous, so I really can't show them all to you. Of course, I couldn't end the chapter without at least giving you one nice example to try out.

Remember back in Chapter 3, "Customizing Pro Audio," when I mentioned that Pro Audio doesn't include any way for you to create your own custom Toolbars? Well, I wasn't exactly telling the whole truth, because, by utilizing StudioWare, you can create Panels that will function like your very own custom Toolbars. And creating these kinds of Panels is very easy, too. One of my personal favorites is a custom Toolbar for Pro Audio's audio editing functions (which you can find by choosing Edit > Audio). You create it as follows:

1. If you don't already have a Project open, do so now and set up a blank Panel in the StudioWare View. Double-click on the blank panel to open the Widget Properties dialog box. Type Edit > Audio for the Label and activate the Show Label option. Then click on OK.

2. Click on the Button Widget button and then click somewhere inside the blank Panel to add the Button Widget to it.

3. Double-click on the Button Widget to open the Widget Properties dialog box.

4. Type Combine for the Label.

5. Select Binding from the Primary Action drop-down list.

6. Select Edit > Audio > Combine from the Verb drop-down list.

TIP

If you want to have a button activate your own custom editing functions that you created with CAL (see Chapter 14, "CAL 101," and Chapter 15, "Advanced CAL Techniques"), select CAL Program as the Primary Action. Then, in the Program field, type (do(include "ProgramName.CAL")), where ProgramName.CAL is the name of the program you want to run.

7. Activate the Spring-loaded option in the Range section and click on OK.

NOTE

The Spring-loaded option in the Widget Properties dialog box makes the Widget automatically snap back to its initial value after you move it. This capability is especially handy for creating single-click buttons. Normally, when you click on a button, it stays pressed until you click on it again to bring it back up to its original position. With the Spring-loaded option activated, the button "springs" back up, ready to be pressed again.

8. Repeat steps 2 through 7 until you have created buttons for all the Edit > Audio commands available.

9. Click on the Design button to exit Design mode and then save your new Panel (or custom Toolbar) as EditAudioToolbar.CakewalkStudioWare.

Now you can open the Panel and use it within any Project as a custom Toolbar. To make things even easier, you might want to save the Panel again, but this time save it inside your Project so that it will be loaded automatically every time you open the Project.

You're Not Alone

If you're still a little fuzzy about some of the information described in this chapter, don't worry. In time, you'll learn to master the full potential of StudioWare. And if you need some help along the way, you might turn to some of the other users out there who are still learning the software, just like you. There are plenty of places on the Internet where you can get in touch with your fellow users. Check out Appendix D, "Cakewalk Resources on the Web." You may even find that you're satisfied with simply downloading existing Panels that others have created. Either way, StudioWare will make your recording sessions easier and more productive.

14

CAL 101

One advantage that Pro Audio has over any other music sequencing product I've worked with is that it enables you to extend its functionality. If you find yourself in a situation in which you need to edit your MIDI or audio data in some way that is not possible with any of the current Pro Audio features—not a common occurrence, but it can happen—you can create a new editing function to take care of the task by using CAL. What is CAL, and how do you use it? Well, that's exactly what you'll learn in this chapter. This chapter covers the following:

▶ The definition of CAL
▶ How to run an existing CAL Program
▶ Prewritten CAL Programs
▶ What the CAL View is
▶ How to use the CAL View

What Is CAL?

CAL, which stands for Cakewalk Application Language, is a computer programming language that exists within the Pro Audio environment. You can use it to extend the functionality of Pro Audio by creating your own custom MIDI and audio data editing commands via CAL *Programs* (also called *Scripts*). A CAL Program is a set of instructions written in the Cakewalk Application Language that tells Pro Audio how to perform a certain task. For example, if you want to change the volume of every other MIDI note in Track 1 to a certain value automatically, you can write a CAL Program to do just that. And for future use, you can save CAL Programs to disk as files with a .CAL extension.

CHAPTER 14

NOTE

A *programming language* is a set of commands, symbols, and rules that are used to "teach" a computer how to perform tasks. By combining these language elements in different ways, you can "teach" a computer to perform any number of tasks, such as record and play music. The combination of elements for a certain task or set of tasks is called a computer *program*. For example, Pro Audio is a computer program, albeit a very complex one.

A number of different kinds of programming languages are in use, including BASIC, FORTRAN, C, LISP, and more. Each has its own unique characteristics. If you are familiar with C and LISP, you'll feel right at home with CAL; CAL derives many of its characteristics from these two languages.

You might be saying to yourself, "Um, well, that's nice, but I know nothing about computer programming, so what good is CAL going to do me?" Not to worry. Yes, CAL is a very complex feature of Pro Audio. If you really want to take full advantage of it, you have to learn how to use the language—but that doesn't mean CAL isn't accessible if you're a beginning user.

Included with Pro Audio are a number of prewritten CAL Programs that you can use within your own Projects. Cakewalk also provides a nice library of additional CAL Programs on its Web site that you can download for free. And you can even find other places on the Internet where you can download free CAL Programs that have been written by other users (see Appendix D, "Cakewalk Resources on the Web"). Additionally, Pro Audio provides a simple way for you to create your own CAL Programs by recording your actions as you use the software, but I'll leave that topic for Chapter 15, "Advanced CAL Techniques." Right now, let's talk about how you can use the existing CAL Programs included with Pro Audio and any others that you might download from the Internet.

Running a CAL Program

Because all CAL Programs are different, I can't explain how to use them in one all-encompassing way. When you run a CAL Program, it usually asks you for some kind of input, depending on what the Program is supposed to do and how it is supposed to manipulate your music data. But you can still follow this basic procedure to run a CAL Program:

1.   Select the Track or Tracks (or data within the Tracks) in the Track View that you want to be edited by the CAL Program. This first step is not always necessary. It depends on the task that the CAL Program is supposed to perform. It also depends on whether the CAL Program was written to process only selected data in a Project or all the Tracks in a Project. The only way to determine the function of a CAL Program is to use the CAL View, which you'll learn about later in this chapter.

2. Select Edit > Run CAL to display the File Open dialog box.

3. Choose the CAL Program that you want to run and click Open.

That's all there is to it. Some CAL Programs immediately carry out their tasks, whereas others first display additional dialog boxes if you need to input any values. The best way to begin using CAL (and to see how it works) is to try out some of the sample Programs included with Pro Audio.

> **TIP**
>
> You can run CAL Programs while a Project is being played back. This means you can hear the results of the editing that the CAL Program applies to your data at the same time your music is being played. If you don't like what the CAL Program does, just choose Edit > Undo to remove any changes that the Program makes to your data. If you then decide that you actually like the changes, instead of running the CAL Program again, just select Edit > Redo to put the changes back in place.

The CAL Files

To give you a better understanding of how CAL works and how you can benefit from it, I'll describe the prewritten CAL Programs included with Pro Audio in the following sections. I'll give you a brief description of what each Program does and how to use it.

Dominant 7th Chord.CAL

The Dominant 7th Chord.CAL Program builds dominant seventh chords by adding three notes with the same time, velocity, and duration to each selected MIDI note in a Track. In other words, if you select a note within a Track and you run Dominant 7th Chord.CAL, the Program treats the selected note as the root of a dominant seventh chord and adds a minor third, a perfect fifth, and a minor seventh on top of it, thus, creating a dominant seventh chord automatically.

Of course, if you know how to compose music, you probably won't get much use out of this CAL Program. However, you might find it useful while working in the Staff View. While you're editing a MIDI data Track in the Staff View, try highlighting a note and then running Dominant 7th Chord.CAL. It's cool to see those additional notes just appear as if by magic. This Program can save you some time while you're inputting notes by hand, too.

Other Chord.CAL Programs

Pro Audio includes a number of other chord-building CAL Programs that work the same way as Dominant 7th Chord.CAL, except that they build different kinds of chords.

Major 7th Chord.CAL

The Major 7th Chord.CAL Program builds major seventh chords by adding the major third, perfect fifth, and major seventh intervals to the selected root note or notes.

Major Chord.CAL

The Major Chord.CAL Program builds major chords by adding the major third and perfect fifth intervals to the selected root note or notes.

Minor 7th Chord.CAL

The Minor 7th Chord.CAL Program builds minor seventh chords by adding the minor third, perfect fifth, and minor seventh intervals to the selected root note or notes.

Minor Chord.CAL

The Minor Chord.CAL Program builds minor chords by adding the minor third and perfect fifth intervals to the selected root note or notes.

Random Time.CAL

If you overindulge yourself while using Pro Audio's quantizing features (see Chapter 8, "Exploring the Editing Tools"), your music can sometimes come out sounding like computer music with a robotic or machine-like feel to it. In some cases, this sound can be desirable, but when you're working on a jazz or rhythm and blues piece, you don't want the drums (or any of the other instruments for that matter) to sound like a robot played them. In that case, Random Time.CAL might be of some help.

This CAL Program takes the start times of each selected Event in a Track and adds a random number of ticks to them. To give you some control over this randomization, the Program first asks you for a number of ticks to base its changes on. The Program then adds a random number to each Event time that is between plus or minus one-half the number of ticks that you input. For instance, if you tell the Program to use six ticks, each Event time will have one of the following numbers-that has been chosen at random-added to it: -3, -2, -1, 0, 1, 2, or 3. Using this Program is a great way to add a little bit of a "human" feel back into those robotic-sounding Tracks. To use Random Time.CAL, just follow these steps:

1. Select the Track or Tracks in the Track View that you want to process. You also can just select a single Clip within a Track, or you can select a specific range of Events within one of the other Views, like the Piano Roll View or the Staff View.

2. Choose Edit > Run CAL to display the File Open dialog box.

3. Choose the Random Time.CAL file and click Open. The Random Time.CAL Program then displays a CAL dialog box (see Figure 14.1).

Figure 14.1
The Random Time.CAL Program asks for number of ticks upon which to base its Event time processing.

4. Enter the number of ticks that you want to use and click OK.

You'll probably need to experiment a little with the number of ticks that you use, because too large a number can make your music sound "sloppy" or too far off the beat.

RoughMix.CAL

RoughMix.CAL is a simple CAL Program that nulls the initial volume and pan values for each selected Track. The Program isn't very useful if you're working with only a small number of Tracks. If you have a large number of Tracks in your Project, however, and you want to start mixing their volume and panning levels from scratch (because the current mix doesn't sound so hot), RoughMix.CAL can save you a lot of time. Without it, you would have to reset all the values for each Track by hand. To use RoughMix.CAL, simply select the Track or Tracks that you want to process and run the Program.

Scale Velocity.CAL

The Scale Velocity.CAL Program is included with Pro Audio just to serve as a programming example because, other than that, you don't really need it. Pro Audio already includes a Scale Velocity editing function, which provides even more features than Scale Velocity.CAL. For more information about Scale Velocity, see Chapter 8, "Exploring the Editing Tools."

Split Channel to Tracks.CAL

If you ever need to share your music data with someone who owns a sequencing program other than Pro Audio, you can save your Project as a Standard MIDI File (SMF). Standard MIDI Files are supported by most computer music software products on the market; thus, they enable musicians to work together on the same song without having to own the same software. But not all Standard MIDI Files are created equal. Actually, several types of files are available; one in particular is called Type 0. A Type 0 MIDI file stores all of its data—which is all the MIDI

CHAPTER 14

data from all 16 MIDI Channels—on one Track. Type 0 files are sometimes used for video game composing, but hardly ever when composing for any other medium. Still, you might run across a Type 0 MIDI file, and if you open it in Pro Audio, all the data shows up on one Track in the Track View. Editing the data is, therefore, kind of difficult, so Split Channel to Tracks.CAL is a useful tool in this situation.

Split Channel to Tracks.CAL takes the selected Track and separates the data from it by MIDI Channel into sixteen new Tracks. For example, if the Track contains data on MIDI Channels 1, 4, 5, and 6, Split Channel to Tracks.CAL creates sixteen new Tracks (from the initial Track) with the first Track containing data from Channel 1, the fourth Track containing data from Channel 4, and so on. The remaining Tracks that don't have corresponding Channel data are just blank. You use it like this:

1.   Select a Track in the Track View.

2.   If you want to split only a portion of the Track, set the From and Thru markers to the appropriate time values.

3.   Choose Edit > Run CAL to open the File Open dialog box.

4.   Choose the Split Channel to Tracks.CAL file and click Open. The Split Channel to Tracks.CAL Program then displays a CAL dialog box (see Figure 14.2).

Figure 14.2
The Split Channel to Tracks.CAL Program asks for the number of the Track to start with when creating the new Tracks.

5.   Enter the number of the first Track that you want Split Channel to Tracks.CAL to use when it creates the new Tracks, and click OK.

CAUTION
Be sure you have enough blank Tracks (sixteen) below the one you select because Split Channel to Tracks.CAL overwrites any existing data within the Tracks that it uses.

After it's finished processing the original Track, Split Channel to Tracks.CAL creates sixteen new Tracks, starting with the Track number that you selected, each containing data from the sixteen corresponding MIDI Channels. Now you can access and edit the music data more easily.

Split Note to Tracks.CAL

The Split Note to Tracks.CAL Program is similar to Split Channel to Tracks.CAL, except that, instead of separating the MIDI data from a selected Track by Channel, it separates the data by note. For example, if you select a Track that contains notes with values of C4, A2, and G3, Split Note to Tracks.CAL separates that Track into three new Tracks, each containing all notes with only one of the available note values. So, in this example, a new Track containing only notes with a value of C4 would be created, another new Track containing only A2 notes would be created, and another new Track containing only G3 notes would be created.

This Program can be useful if you're working with a single drum track that contains the data for a number of different drum instruments. In MIDI, different drum instruments are represented by different note values, because drums can't play melodies. So, if you want to edit a single drum instrument at a time, having each instrument on its own Track would be easier. In that case, Split Note to Tracks.CAL can be put to good use. To apply Split Note to Tracks.CAL to your music data, follow these steps:

1. Choose Edit > Run to open the File Open dialog box.

2. Choose the Split Note to Tracks.CAL file and click Open.

3. The Split Note to Tracks.CAL Program asks for the number of your Source Track (see Figure 14.3). It is the Track that you want to split into new Tracks. Enter a number from 1 to 256 and click OK.

NOTE

You'll notice that this Program is different from the other CAL Programs in which you had to first select a Track in the Track View. It's different because the person who wrote this CAL Program did it differently from the rest. Why? I have no idea.

Figure 14.3
Here, you can enter the Source Track for the Split Note to Tracks.CAL Program.

CHAPTER 14

4. The Program then asks you for the number of the First Destination Track (see Figure 14.4). It is the number of the first new Track that will be created. Enter a number from 1 to 256 and click OK.

Figure 14.4
Here, you can enter the First Destination Track for the Split Note to Tracks.CAL Program.

5. The Program then asks you for the number of the Destination Channel (see Figure 14.5). It is the MIDI Channel that you want all the new Tracks to be set to. Unless you want to change the channel, you should simply select the same Channel that the Source Track is using. Enter a number from 0 to 16 and click OK.

Figure 14.5
Here, you can enter the Destination Channel for the Split Note to Tracks.CAL Program.

6. The Program finally asks you for the number of the Destination Port (see Figure 14.6). It is the MIDI Port that you want all the new Tracks to be set to. Again, you should simply select the same Port that the Source Track is using. Enter a number from 1 to 16 and click OK.

Figure 14.6
Here, you can enter the Destination Port for the Split Note to Tracks.CAL Program.

After you answer the last question, Split Note to Tracks.CAL processes the original Track and creates a number of new Tracks (depending on how many different note values are present in the original Track), each containing all the notes for each corresponding note value.

Thin Controller Data.CAL

You use MIDI controller data to add expressive qualities to your MIDI music Tracks. For example, you can make a certain passage of music get gradually louder or softer (crescendo or decrescendo) by adding MIDI Controller number 7 (Volume) to your MIDI Tracks. Sometimes, though, an overabundance of MIDI data can overload your MIDI instruments and cause anomalies such as stuck notes and delays in playback. If you have this problem, you can try thinning out the MIDI controller data in your Tracks by using Thin Controller Data.CAL. This Program enables you to decrease the amount of data being sent to your MIDI instruments by deleting only a select number of controller Events—enough to reduce the amount of data without adversely affecting the music performance. It works like this:

1. Select the Track or Tracks in the Track View that you want to process. You also can just select a single Clip within a Track, or you can select a specific range of Events within one of the other Views, like the Piano Roll View or the Staff View.

2. Choose Edit > Run CAL to display the File Open dialog box.

3. Choose the Thin Controller Data.CAL file and click Open.

4. The Thin Controller Data.CAL Program asks you for the number of the MIDI controller that you want to process (see Figure 14.7). For example, if you want to remove some of the volume data from a Track, use MIDI Controller number 7. Enter a number from 0 to 127 and click OK.

Figure 14.7
Here, you can enter the Controller number for the Thin Controller Data.CAL Program.

5. The Program then asks you for the thinning factor (see Figure 14.8). For example, if you enter a value of 4, the Program deletes every fourth volume Event it finds in the selected Track or Tracks. Enter a number from 1 to 100 and click OK.

Figure 14.8
Here, you can enter the thinning factor for the Thin Controller Data.CAL Program.

After you answer the last question, Thin Controller Data.CAL processes the selected Track or Tracks and deletes all the MIDI controller Events that correspond to the MIDI Controller number and the thinning factor that you entered. If this procedure doesn't clear up your MIDI playback problems, you can try thinning the data some more, but be careful not to thin it too much; otherwise, your crescendos and decrescendos (or other controller-influenced music passages) will start to sound choppy rather than smooth.

CHAPTER 14

Other Thin.CAL Programs

Also included with Pro Audio are two other controller-thinning CAL Programs. These programs work almost the same way as Thin Controller Data.CAL, but they are each targeted toward one specific type of controller. Thin Channel Aftertouch.CAL thins out Channel Aftertouch MIDI controller data, and Thin Pitch Wheel.CAL thins out Pitch Wheel (or Pitch Bend) MIDI controller data. To run these Programs, you use the same procedure as you do with Thin Controller Data.CAL, but with one exception. The Programs don't ask you to input the number of a MIDI controller, because they are each already targeted toward a specific controller. Other than that, they work in the same manner.

Wipe Automation.CAL Programs

The last two CAL Programs—WipeAllAutomation.CAL and WipeSelectedAutomation.CAL—are somewhat similar to RoughMix.CAL, but instead of simply removing the initial volume and pan settings for each Track in a Project, they remove all the volume and pan settings for each Track in a Project. In other words, RoughMix.CAL removes only the very first volume and pan settings in a Track, whereas these Programs remove any and all volume and pan settings throughout a Track.

Again, using these programs is a good way to dump a mix that isn't sounding so hot and begin again from scratch. WipeAllAutomation.CAL removes all pan and volume settings from every Track in a Project. All you have to do is run the Program, and it takes care of the rest. WipeSelectedAutomation.CAL enables you to first select a Track or Tracks (or even just a part of a Track) in a Project, and then it removes the data from just that selection. To use this Program, make your selection and then run the Program. Nothing more is required.

The CAL View

Unless a CAL Program comes with some written instructions, you won't know what it is designed to do to the data in your Project. This is especially true if you download CAL Programs from the Internet. Many come with documentation, but many don't. Most Programs, however, do come with a brief description (as well as instructions on use) within their source code.

NOTE

Source code (or *Program code*) is the text of the programming language commands used for a particular Program. You create a Program by first writing its source code. A computer can then run the Program by reading the source code and executing the commands in the appropriate manner, thus carrying out the intended task.

To read the source code of a CAL Program, you need to use the CAL View. As an example, take a look at the source code for Major Chord.CAL:

1. Choose File > Open to display the File Open dialog box.
2. Select the Major Chord.CAL file and click Open. Pro Audio then opens Major Chord.CAL and displays its source code in a new CAL View window (see Figure 14.9).

Figure 14.9
You can use the CAL View to examine and edit the source code of a CAL Program.

```
Major Chord.cal

;; Major Chord.cal
;;
;; Treats each note as the root of a major chord, and creates that chord:
;; For each note event, adds two note events with same time, vel, and dur
;; but a major third and a perfect fifth higher.
;;

(do
   (include "need20.cal")  ; Require version 2.0 or higher of CAL

   (forEachEvent
     (if (== Event.Kind NOTE)
        (do
           (insert Event.Time Event.Chan NOTE (+ Note.Key 4) Note.Vel Note.Dur)
           (insert Event.Time Event.Chan NOTE (+ Note.Key 7) Note.Vel Note.Dur)
        )
     )
   )
)
```

CHAPTER 14

As you can see in Figure 14.9, the CAL View enables you to see the source code of Major Chord.CAL and also enables you to read the brief description included there. You can do the same thing with any other CAL Program to find out how that program can be used and what task it's supposed to perform. But that's not all.

By using the CAL View, you also can edit the source code for a CAL Program, as well as create a CAL Program from scratch. This View works in basically the same way as the Notepad program in Windows. You can use the same text-editing techniques, and when you have the CAL View open, you can use Pro Audio's Edit menu for simple undo, cut, copy, and paste text-editing procedures. Three buttons are also available at the top of the CAL View. Using them, you can run, record, and stop a CAL Program. I'll cover these features, as well as creating your own CAL Programs, in Chapter 15, "Advanced CAL Techniques."

15

Advanced CAL Techniques

In Chapter 14, "CAL 101," you learned about the Cakewalk Application Language—what it is, what it does, and how you can run prewritten CAL Programs to tackle some of the editing tasks that the built-in Pro Audio functions can't. I briefly touched on the topic of creating your own CAL Programs. At first glance, you might think that CAL is reserved only for advanced users, but the fact is, even beginners can put it to good use. This chapter continues the CAL discussion and covers the following:

▶ How to create a new CAL Program automatically

▶ Cakewalk Application Language programming basics

▶ Anatomy of a CAL Program

▶ CAL functions reference

Recording a CAL Program

The smart people at Cakewalk knew that not all users were going to want to take the time to learn the Cakewalk Application Language (CAL) just so they could create their own CAL Programs. So, instead of just stating that CAL was appropriate only for advanced users and leaving it at that, they designed a feature that enables anyone to create a CAL Program without the need for any kind of programming knowledge.

If you take a look at the CAL View (see Figure 15.1), you'll notice three buttons along the top of its window. The first button enables you to run the CAL Program that's currently displayed in the CAL View. The other two buttons—Start Record and Stop Record—enable you to create a new CAL Program, based on the actions that you perform within Pro Audio.

CHAPTER 15

Figure 15.1
The three buttons at
the top of the CAL
View enable you to
play, start recording,
and stop recording a
CAL Program.

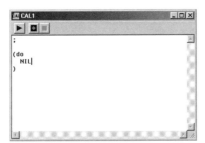

```
;; Major Chord.cal
;;
;; Treats each note as the root of a major chord, and creates that chord:
;; For each note event, adds two note events with same time, vel, and dur
;; but a major third and a perfect fifth higher.
;;

(do
    (include "need20.cal")   ; Require version 2.0 or higher of CAL

    (ForEachEvent
      (if (== Event.Kind NOTE)
          (do
              (insert Event.Time Event.Chan NOTE (+ Note.Key 4) Note.Vel Note.Dur)
              (insert Event.Time Event.Chan NOTE (+ Note.Key 7) Note.Vel Note.Dur)
          )
      )
    )
)
```

In other words, you can create a new CAL Program by performing a series of actions within Pro Audio, such as opening a file, selecting a Track, or changing the velocity of the MIDI notes in the Track, and then saving the file. These same actions can be a possible CAL Program. When you run the program, it takes the exact same steps that you did, but automatically. The following is the basic procedure for recording a new CAL Program:

1. Select File > New to open the New Project File dialog box.

2. From the list of Templates, choose CAL Script (located at the very top of the list). The CAL View opens, showing a blank, new CAL Program ready to be filled by your recorded actions (see Figure 15.2).

Figure 15.2
Before you begin
recording, the CAL
View displays a blank,
new CAL Program
ready to be filled.

```
;
(do
    NIL
)
```

3. Click on the Start Record button to start recording your new CAL Program. As soon as you click on the button, the CAL View window moves to the background, behind any other View windows you might have open in Pro Audio so that you can use the program without the CAL View getting in the way.

4. Perform any actions that you want your new CAL Program to perform later for you automatically. Just as a quick example, try opening a Project file, selecting a Track, using one of the editing commands (such as Scale Velocity), and then saving the file. You might want to use Save As and save the file under a new filename so that you don't overwrite the original file just for this little test.

NOTE

Not all of the features in Pro Audio can be used with CAL. For instance, you can't access any of the MIDI or Audio Effects features. For a full list of all the features that are accessible from CAL, look in the contents of the Pro Audio help file under Reference/CAL Reference/CAL Function Reference.

5. Click on the CAL View window to bring it to the front. If you can't see the CAL View—because it's hidden behind some of the other Views that you have open—use the Window menu to access it.

6. Click on the Stop Record button to stop recording your new CAL Program.

As you can see in Figure 15.3, Pro Audio automatically translates all your actions into CAL programming code.

Figure 15.3
After you finish recording, Pro Audio automatically converts your actions into CAL programming code.

```
CAL2                                               _ □ ×
▶ ■ ■
(do

 ;-- Start of recording --
 (FileOpen "C:\2-Part Invention #13 in A minor.wrk")
 (TrackSelect 1 0)
 (EditVelocityScale40 86 100 0 )
 (FileSaveAs "C:\WINDOWS\Desktop\New Folder\test.wrk")
 ;-- End of recording --

)
```

Don't worry if you can't understand what the code means. You really don't need to know. All you have to do to use this new CAL Program is run it, and it automatically performs the exact steps that you did during the recording process. You also can save the program as a file (for future use) by choosing File > SaveAs, just like you would any other file in Pro Audio. CAL files have a .CAL file extension.

Many of the tasks that you perform manually in Pro Audio can be performed automatically by CAL. The possibilities for utilizing CAL are numerous. I can't illustrate them all, but I can give you a useful example.

CHAPTER 15

Master Presets

One of the most effective uses I've found for CAL is creating what I like to call *Master Presets*. As I mentioned in Chapter 8, "Exploring the Editing Tools," Pro Audio enables you to save the settings for some of its editing functions as Presets. This way, you can easily use the same editing parameters that you created by simply calling them up by name, instead of having to figure out the settings every time you use a function. Presets are a real time-saver, but unfortunately, you can save presets for each of the individual functions only. What if you want to combine a few of the functions to create a certain editing process? For example, say you like to deglitch your MIDI Tracks before you quantize them. To do so, you first need to select the Tracks, use the Deglitch function, and then use the Quantize function to process your Tracks. For each of the editing functions, you have to make the appropriate settings adjustments. If you create a CAL Program to automatically run through the process for you, though, all you need to do is select your Tracks and run the CAL Program.

Deglitch and Quantize Master Preset

To show you what I mean, I've cooked up a sample Master Preset that you can record as a CAL Program and use in your Projects. You need to do the following:

1. Select File > New to open the New Project File dialog box.

2. From the list of Templates, choose CAL Script.

3. Click on the Start Record button in the CAL View to start recording your new CAL Program.

4. Select a MIDI Track in the Track View of your current Project to use as a temporary test Track just for the purpose of creating this CAL Program.

5. Select Edit > Deglitch to open the Deglitch dialog box (see Figure 15.4).

Figure 15.4
The first part of the CAL Program removes any short, unintended notes from the selected MIDI Tracks with the Deglitch editing function.

6. Select the parameter settings that you want to use and click on OK.

7. Select Edit > Quantize to open the Quantize dialog box (see Figure 15.5).

Figure 15.5
The second part of the CAL Program quantizes the notes in the selected MIDI Tracks with the Quantize editing function.

8. Select the parameter settings that you want to use and click on OK.

9. Click on the CAL View window to bring it to the front.

10. Click on the Stop Record button to stop recording your new CAL Program.

11. Select File > Save As to open the Save As dialog box.

12. Type a name for your new CAL Program and click on Save.

Now, when you run this CAL Program, it performs all the editing functions for you automatically with the same exact settings that you used. It's too bad that CAL doesn't support Pro Audio's MIDI or audio Effects functions. I really wish that it did, because then you could create Master Presets to process your audio Tracks, too. That capability would make CAL a hundred times more powerful than it already is. I hope that Cakewalk will add this functionality in the next version. In the meantime, you can still find plenty of uses for CAL. Before you go off on a CAL Program-recording frenzy, though, you have to make one little adjustment to the Deglitch and Quantize Master Preset.

One Final Adjustment

If you select Tracks to be processed while recording a CAL Program (as in the earlier example), CAL incorporates that code into the program. So, the next time you start to use the CAL Program, it will work only with those specific Tracks. To make your recorded CAL Programs work with any selected Tracks, you need to make a few changes to the program code in the CAL View.

Using the Deglitch and Quantize Master Preset example, you can see that the CAL Program code has only a few lines to it (see Figure 15.6). You need to delete the line of code that reads (TrackSelect 1 #)—with # representing the number of the Track you selected while recording the CAL Program. And if you selected more than one Track during recording, the program will have a (TrackSelect 1 #) line of code for each of those Tracks. You need to delete these lines of code as well.

Figure 15.6
The (TrackSelect 1 #) line in the CAL Program code must be deleted.

The new code for the CAL Program needs to contain only the lines representing the editing functions that you used during recording (see Figure 15.7). That way, you can select any Track or Tracks to be processed by the CAL Program when you run it.

Figure 15.7
The CAL Program code should look like this after you edit it.

Be sure to make this adjustment to any CAL Program that you record so that it will work with any selected data. And don't forget to save the program again.

> **TIP**
> Instead of running your CAL Programs by choosing Edit > Run CAL, selecting a program, and clicking on OK, you can just assign a *Key Binding*. That way, you can run your programs with a quick and simple keyboard combination. For more information about Key Bindings, see Chapter 3, "Customizing Pro Audio."

Intro to CAL Programming

Now, recording your own CAL Programs is one thing, but to tap their full power, you need to learn how to create programs from scratch by using the Cakewalk Application Language. The problem is that teaching a course in CAL programming would take up a whole book in and of itself. So instead, I'll just get you started by providing a brief introduction to the language. And the best way to do that is to walk you through the code of one of the CAL Programs that comes included with Pro Audio.

To get started, open the Scale Velocity.CAL Program (see Figure 15.8). The first thing you'll see is a bunch of lines that start with semicolons and contain some text describing the CAL Program. These lines are called *comments*. Whenever you insert a semicolon into the code of a CAL Program, Pro Audio ignores that part of the code when you run the program. This way, you can mark the code with descriptive notes. When you come back to the program at a later date, you will understand what certain parts of the program are supposed to accomplish.

Figure 15.8
The code for the Scale Velocity.CAL Program provides a nice example for an explanation of the Cakewalk Application Language.

```
;; Scale Velocity.cal
;;
;; This is a sample CAL program that implements an editing command to
;; scale note velocities by a certain percentage.
;;
;; Demonstrates:
;;
;;   (forEachEvent)
;;   Getting input from the user
;;   Arithmetic operators
;;   Event kind and parameter variables

(do
  (include "need20.cal")  ; Require version 2.0 or higher of CAL

  (int percent 100)
  (getInt percent "Percentage?" 1 1000)

  (forEachEvent
    (if (== Event.Kind NOTE)
      (do
        (*= Note.Vel percent)
        (/= Note.Vel 100)
      )
    )
  )
)
```

A little further down, you'll notice the first line of the actual code used when the program is run. The line reads (do. All CAL Programs start with this code. The parenthesis designates the start of a function, and the do code designates the start of a group of code. As a matter of fact, a CAL Program is just one big function with a number of other functions within it. You'll notice that for every left parenthesis, you'll have a corresponding right parenthesis. CAL Programs use parentheses to show where a function begins and ends.

Include

The next line in Scale Velocity.CAL reads (include "need20.cal"). This is the Include function. This function enables you to run a CAL Program within a CAL Program. You might want to do so for a number of reasons. For instance, if you're creating a very large program, you might want to break it down into different parts to make it easier to work with. Then you can have one master program that runs all the different parts. You also can combine CAL Programs. For example, you can combine the Thin Channel Aftertouch.CAL, Thin Controller Data.CAL, and Thin Pitch Wheel.CAL Programs that come with Pro Audio by using the Include function in a new CAL Program. Then, when you run the new program, it

CHAPTER 15

will run each of the included programs one right after the other so that you can thin all the types of MIDI controller data from your project in one fell swoop.

In Scale Velocity.CAL, the Include function is used to run the need20.cal Program. This program simply checks the version of CAL and makes sure that it is version 2.0 or higher. Some CAL Programs check the version to avoid an error in case a very old version of CAL is being used. If you're running Pro Audio 9 or 8, you shouldn't have to worry about the version. But if you share your CAL Programs with others, you might want to do this version test within the programs.

Variables

After the Include function, the code for Scale Velocity.CAL shows (int percent 100). This is a Variable function. In CAL Programs, you can define Variables to hold any values that you might need while the program is running. In this instance, the Variable percent is defined as an integer and is given a value of 100. Variables can be used to store both number and text information. After you define a Variable, you can refer to its value later in your code by simply using the Variable name. That's what you see in the next line of code in Scale Velocity.CAL.

User Input

This next line reads (getInt percent "Percentage?" 1 1000). Here, the program asks for input from the user. In English, this line of code translates to "Get an integer between 1 and 1000 from the user by having the user type a value into the displayed dialog box. Then store the value into the Variable named percent." So, basically, when Pro Audio reaches this line of code in the program, it pauses and displays a dialog box (see Figure 15.9). Then it waits for the user to input a value and click on the OK button. It then assigns whatever the inputted value was to the Variable percent. Then it continues running the rest of the program.

Figure 15.9
A CAL Program gets input from the user by displaying dialog boxes.

ForEachEvent

The main part of the Scale Velocity.CAL Program begins with the line of code that reads (forEachEvent. ForEachEvent is known as an *iterating* function. In this type of function, a certain portion of code is run (or cycled through) a specific number of times. In this case, for every Event in the selected Track or Tracks, the code enclosed within the forEachEvent function is cycled through one time. So, in Scale Velocity.CAL, for every Event in the selected Track or Tracks, this block of code is run through once:

```
(if (== Event.Kind NOTE)
  (do
    (*= Note.Vel percent)
    (/= Note.Vel 100)
  )
)
```

What does this code do? Let's talk about it.

Conditions

Within the forEachEvent function in Scale Velocity.CAL, every Event in the selected Track or Tracks is tested by using the if function. This function is known as a *conditional* function. Depending on whether certain conditions are met, the code enclosed within the if function might or might not be run. In Scale Velocity.CAL, every Event is tested to see whether it is a MIDI Note Event. This test is performed with the line of code that reads (== Event.Kind NOTE). In English, this line translates to "Check to see whether the current Event being tested is a MIDI Note Event." If the current Event is a MIDI Note Event, then the next block of code is run. If the current Event is not a MIDI Note Event, then the next block of code is skipped, and the forEachEvent function moves on to the next Event in the selected Track or Tracks until it reaches the last selected Event; then the CAL Program stops running.

Arithmetic

The final part of Scale Velocity.CAL is just some simple arithmetic code. If the current Event is a MIDI Note Event, the Velocity value of the Note is multiplied by the value of the percent Variable, and the resulting value is assigned as the Note Velocity. Then the new Velocity value of the Note is divided by the number 100, and this resulting value is then assigned to be the final value of the Note Velocity. This way, the program scales the velocities of the notes in the selected Track or Tracks.

CHAPTER 15

CAL References

So, are you totally confused yet? If you've had some previous programming experience, you should actually have no trouble picking up the Cakewalk Application Language. If you're familiar with the C or Lisp computer programming languages, CAL is just a stone's throw away in terms of functionality.

Really, the best way to learn about CAL is to study the code of existing CAL Programs. You also can read the reference material included in the Pro Audio Help file. A couple of references cover all the CAL functions and data types, describing what they are and how they work. You can find the references by selecting Help > Help Topics.

If, even after this discussion, you still find yourself lost in all this technical jargon, you can utilize CAL in plenty of ways, either by using prewritten programs or recording your own. As I mentioned before, this part of Pro Audio has a lot of power, and it would be a shame if you let it go to waste. CAL can save you time and even enable you to manipulate your music data in ways you might never have thought of. Don't be afraid to experiment. Just be sure to back up your data in case things get a bit messed up in the process.

TIP

For more information about programming with CAL, check out some of the Web sites I've listed in Appendix D, "Cakewalk Resources on the Web." If you purchased the Deluxe version of Pro Audio, you can check out the included program called CAL Tutor. This product is an instructional aid in learning how to create your own CAL Programs. Unfortunately, CAL Tutor is no longer supported by its publisher, Clockwork Music Software, so you can't download it from the Internet.

16

Taking Your Pro Audio Project to CD

Congratulations! You've made it to the final chapter of the book. Your Project has been recorded, edited, mixed, and now you can share it with the rest of the world. That means creating your very own CD. So, in this chapter, I'll cover the basics of creating a custom audio CD, including the following:

▶ Purchasing a CD recorder (CD-R)

▶ Preparing your Project for CD audio

▶ Using the popular Easy CD Creator software

▶ Taking advantage of advanced Easy CD Creator options

Purchasing a CD Recorder

A CD recorder (or CD-R drive) is similar to a CD-ROM drive except that, in addition to reading CDs, it can write to them, too. Just a short while ago, CD-R drives were available only to a privileged few who could afford them and needed to create their own CDs. These people, however lucky to be early adopters of recordable CD technology, also had to deal with unreliable drives. The creation of unreadable discs was very common.

Today, after several drive generations, prices have come down, and reliability has gone up. In fact, many new computer systems shipping from the likes of Gateway and Dell include CD-R drives as standard components. But despite these incentives, you still might be one of the few computer musicians who hasn't purchased a CD-R drive. Before you run out to the store to spend your hard-earned cash, you should know a little bit about CD-ROM technology and how to get a drive.

A Little Bit About CD-R Drives

You should consider a number of points when purchasing a drive. The first is whether you want a CD-R or CD-RW. CD-R stands for CD-Recordable. These drives were the first ones created. They are essentially write-once drives. After data is written by using these drives, you can't erase or write over the data.

Most drives today are CD-RW, or Read-Write drives. These drives enable you to rewrite to the CD as many as a thousand times before the disc is worn out. The problem with CD-RW drives is that their discs can be read only by multiread CD-ROM drives, which aren't as common as regular CD-ROM drives. You should also know that audio CD players can't handle CD-RW discs; they can play only CD-R discs. But because a CD-RW drive can create both CD-R and CD-RW discs, your purchasing decision is pretty much a given here.

The other major issue to consider is external versus internal. If you're not the type of person who finds it easy to open your computer and install new equipment, then you should get an external drive. Although many external drives require you to install a card in your system, installing a card is easier than installing the entire drive, which requires you to hook up the power and data cables and screw the drive into place. The process isn't really very difficult, but it's not for the novice user either. The easiest drives to install are those that simply connect to the parallel (printer) or USB (universal serial bus) ports on the back of your computer. Be careful when choosing this type of drive, though, because they tend to transfer data a lot more slowly than internal or card-based external drives. If you want the best performance, you should get an internal or card-based drive.

Your next decision is whether you should choose between an IDE/EIDE or SCSI drive. The difference is the interface that connects the drive to your computer. IDE/EIDE is the standard for PCs, and it's a lot cheaper than SCSI. But it's also slower. SCSI is more important for Macintosh machines because they use the SCSI interface exclusively. To attach a SCSI drive on a PC, you have to install a separate SCSI adapter card inside your machine. For IDE/EIDE, all you need to do is plug in and install the drive; no card is required. And to be honest, you don't need the extra speed that SCSI provides. Most IDE/EIDE drives provide excellent performance.

Speed is important, however, when it comes to the speed of the drive itself. Each new generation of recordable drives gets faster and faster, just like the read-only CD-ROM drives have been doing. Right now, it's common to find 2-8x drives. By the way, when you're shopping, be sure to look at the write speed of the drive, not the read speed. CD-R drives write much more slowly than they read. Also, look at a drive's overall throughput when writing. Just because the drive spins the disc really fast doesn't necessarily guarantee that it's as fast as similar drives. Some people avoid buying the fastest drives because newer, faster drives can be a bit unreliable in creating CDs that other drives will be able to read. However, these faster drives can be made to run slower when writing to a disc, so this aspect shouldn't concern you too much.

I recommend that you look into the drives offered by Hewlett-Packard or Ricoh. I'm currently using the CD-Writer Plus 8200i from Hewlett-Packard on my desktop computer and the MP8040SE from Ricoh on my laptop computer. Both products are excellent performers, although they might be a bit outdated by the time you read this book.

Where to Look

The best place currently on the Web to find any computer hardware for purchase is at one of the two major hardware purchasing Web sites: **Computers.com** or **Computershopper.com**. At these sites, you can easily enter some criteria for the type of drive that you want and narrow it to a model and a location within driving distance. For example, on Computershopper.com (see Figure 16.1), you can enter basic speed, interface, and pricing criteria.

Figure 16.1
On **Computershopper.com**, you can specify the type of drive that you want and then search for available makes and price.

CHAPTER 16

On Computers.com (see Figure 16.2), you can enter that criteria as well as sort it by product name and price.

Figure 16.2
On Computers.com, you can sort the drive listings by product name and price.

On average, drives run (at the time of this writing) between $200 and $500, depending on features such as writing speed, external versus internal, and reading speed. You even can find some of the lower-end drives for as little as $150, but it's better to spend a little extra and get a quality drive; otherwise, you might regret your choice later.

Preparing a Project for CD Audio

A Project can't be laid down as audio Tracks on a CD as is. Instead, you have to convert all your MIDI Tracks in a Project to audio Tracks. Then you have to export those audio Tracks to a .WAV file so that your CD recording software can write the file to your CD. To do so, you need to follow a number of steps.

Convert Your MIDI Tracks

The first step is to convert any MIDI Tracks that use your sound card's built-in synthesizer for playback to audio Tracks as follows:

1. Set two new Tracks to record mode and assign the Source for each Track to your sound card's left and right inputs, respectively. For instance, on my system, I would set one Track Source to Left Monster Sound II Record and the other to Right Monster Sound II Record.

2. Mute all the Tracks in your Project except for the two that you just created and the MIDI Tracks that you're going to convert.

3. Open your sound card's mixer controls (see Figure 16.3) by double-clicking on the small speaker icon in the Windows Taskbar.

Figure 16.3
This window shows the sound card mixer controls for the Diamond Multimedia Monster Sound II.

4. Select Options > Properties and click on Recording in the Adjust Volume For section of the resulting Properties dialog box. Then click on the OK button to bring up the recording mixer controls, as shown in Figure 16.4.

Figure 16.4
This window shows the recording mixer controls for the Monster Sound II sound card.

5. Activate the recording source for your sound card's synth by clicking on the appropriate Select option (see Figure 16.5).

Figure 16.5
You need to activate your sound card's synth before you can record its output.

6. Click on the Record button on the toolbar in Pro Audio, and your MIDI Tracks are recorded to a pair of audio Tracks.

Next, you need to convert any MIDI Tracks that use external MIDI instruments for playback to audio Tracks, as shown in the following steps. If you don't have any MIDI Tracks of this kind, you can skip this section.

1. Set two new Tracks to record mode and assign the Source for each Track to your sound card's left and right inputs, respectively. For instance, on my system, I would set one Track Source to Left Monster Sound II Record and the other to Right Monster Sound II Record.

2. Mute all the Tracks in your Project except for the two that you just created and the MIDI Tracks that you're going to convert.

3. Open your sound card's mixer controls by double-clicking on the small speaker icon in the Windows Taskbar.

4. Select Options > Properties and click on Recording in the Adjust Volume For section of the resulting Properties dialog box. Then click on the OK button to bring up the recording mixer controls.

5. Activate the recording source for your sound card's line input(s) by clicking on the appropriate Select option (see Figure 16.6).

Figure 16.6
You need to activate your sound card's line input(s) before you can record any external MIDI instruments.

6. Be sure the audio outputs from your external MIDI instrument are connected to the line input(s) of your sound card. If you have more than one MIDI instrument and you're using a mixing board, connect the stereo output(s) of your mixer to the line input(s) of your sound card.

7. Click on the Rewind button on the toolbar in Pro Audio so that recording will begin at the beginning of the song. Then click on the Record button on the toolbar in Pro Audio, and your MIDI Tracks are recorded to a pair of audio Tracks.

After you're finished, you should have a new pair of audio Tracks representing your sound card's built-in synthesizer and a new pair of audio Tracks representing your external MIDI instruments.

Convert Your Audio Tracks

After all of your MIDI Tracks are converted to audio Tracks, you need to mix and export the audio Tracks down to a .WAV file. Pro Audio provides a very convenient feature expressly for this purpose; it's called Mixdown Audio/Export To File(s). This feature takes any number of original audio Tracks—preserving their volume, pan, and effects settings—and mixes them into a single stereo .WAV file. Here's how to use it:

1. Mute all the MIDI Tracks in your Project and any audio Tracks that you don't want included in the new Track(s).

2. Select Tools > Mixdown Audio > Export To File(s) to open the Mixdown Audio/Export To File(s) dialog box, as shown in Figure 16.7.

Figure 16.7
You use the Mixdown Audio/Export To File(s) dialog box to mix and export your Tracks.

3. From the Look In list, select the folder that you want to save the .WAV file into. Then type a name for the file in the File Name field.

4. Choose the type from the Files Of Type drop-down list. In this case, use the Wave option.

5. Select the Format that you want to use. You can mix your audio Tracks to a single stereo file, two mono files (that, when combined, create a stereo file), or a single mono file.

6. Choose the sound card(s) that you want to use to process your audio Tracks from the Source Bus(es) field.

7. Leave the Each Source To Separate Mix option deactivated.

8. Leave all the Mix Enables options activated to ensure that your new .WAV file will sound exactly the same when played back as the original audio Tracks.

9. Click on the Export button, and Pro Audio mixes all your audio Tracks down to a new .WAV file.

When you're done, you should have a .WAV file that you can use along with your CD recording software to create an audio CD.

Using Easy CD Creator

When it comes to CD recording software, almost 90 percent of the drives on the market include a "lite" version of Easy CD Creator from Adaptec. Also, an upgrade offer is usually included for the full version of the software. Because of its popularity, I'll discuss how to use Easy CD Creator to record your own CDs. If you have some other CD recording software, the process should be similar.

You can use Easy CD Creator in two basic ways: via its step-by-step wizard interface or its more advanced mode. For the most part, the Creator Wizard is very easy to use and takes you through all the choices you need to burn a new CD.

NOTE

Because a laser is used to heat up the blank CD and write the information to it, recording a CD is also referred to as *burning* a CD.

You can follow these basic steps to create an audio CD:

1. Start Easy CD Creator. If the Creator Wizard doesn't open automatically, select File > Wizard to open it manually.

2. When the wizard asks whether you want to create a data or an audio CD, choose Audio CD and click on the Next button.

3. The wizard then enables you to select .WAV files to lay down onto the CD. The dialog box (see Figure 16.8) enables you to move throughout your disk directories and select files. Clicking Add Now puts them in the layout. You should be able to find the .WAV file that you created with Pro Audio in your C:\My Documents\Cakewalk Pro Audio\Audio Files folder if you set up your Pro Audio files as described in Chapter 3, "Customizing Pro Audio."

Figure 16.8
You can easily add files and check remaining room by using the CD Creator Wizard. Choose the .WAV files that you want, and click on the Add Now button.

4.   The dialog box also includes a Play button that enables you to preview files to make sure that you have selected the song you want. Click on the Next button when you're done selecting files.

TIP

You don't have to fill the entire CD at this point. As long as you don't close the CD, you can add to it over time until it is filled.

5.   On the next screen in the wizard (see Figure 16.9), you can create a title and artist listing for the CD. Simply type the name of the CD and the artist or artists in the appropriate text boxes. Then click on the Next button.

Figure 16.9
In this dialog, you can type a title for your CD and add the artist's name.

6. After naming the CD, you must choose to either leave the session open or close the session. You can record more data to the disc if you leave the session open. Closing the session prevents you from adding more data to the disc. If you keep the session open, the CD won't play on a standard audio CD player. Choose Close The Session if you're sure you're not going to add any more songs to the CD; otherwise, keep it open until you're done. Click on the Next button after you've made your choice.

7. The wizard asks whether you want to perform a test before writing to disc. When you're creating a CD, it helps to first have your system do a test. Testing ensures the best quality and betters your chances for a successful burn. Although testing nearly doubles the time required to create a CD, Adaptec recommends testing at least the first few times you use the program. After that, you probably can skip it. Click on the Next button after making your choice.

8. Now you're ready to create your CD. You can choose to go ahead with your order of songs and choices (called a Layout) or to create a CD later, which gives you a chance to edit the Layout (see Figure 16.10). If you choose to create the CD now, click the Finish button, and the CD Creation Status dialog box opens as the drive begins burning the CD.

Figure 16.10
In this dialog box, you can choose whether to burn your CD now or later.

TIP
At any point while using the wizard, you can backtrack to previous choices by clicking on the Back button.

Working with Advanced CD Creator Options

The CD Creator Wizard makes using Easy CD Creator a snap, but you might want to know about some advanced program features.

Previewing Songs, Changing Names, and Rearranging the Order

After you've created a Layout that you like, you can do several things before recording the CD. Click on a song to highlight it, and then right-click on the song to bring up a menu. Choosing Rename from this menu enables you to rename the song. Choosing Properties from the menu opens that file's properties. To preview any song, just double-click on it. To change the order of a song, just drag and drop it anywhere within the list.

Saving and Loading a Layout

Sometimes you might want to save a good Layout to use again at a later date. If you've made a particularly good mix of songs and want to burn it for friends from time to time, it is a good idea to save the final Layout. That way, you don't have to re-create it every time you want to create another copy of the CD.

To save a Layout, select File > Save. You can load previously saved Layouts by choosing File > Open CD Layout.

Recording Your CD

You can use the Creator Wizard for the whole CD recording process (as you learned earlier), but sometimes it's better to just use the wizard to make some initial settings. Then you can take some extra steps to fine-tune your settings:

1. If you haven't told the wizard to immediately burn the CD and instead decide to tweak the Layout before recording, you can click on the Record button on the toolbar or choose Create CD from the File menu. The CD Creation Setup dialog box then opens (see Figure 16.11).

Figure 16.11
In the CD Creation Setup dialog box, you can make final choices before recording your CD.

2. The CD Creation dialog box is composed of three tabs: General, Advanced, and Summary. The General tab shows you the various recordable CD drives attached to your computer (although, like me, you probably have only one). A drop-down list below that shows the available write speeds that the selected drive can handle. You usually don't need to change these settings.

3. Directly below the drop-down lists is an Options area with three choices: Test Only, Test and Create CD, and Create CD. These options enable you to decide whether the burn process will be a test run, a creation only, or a combination test burn and recording. The testing and creating option is usually the best choice. If you want to speed the process along, though, choose Create CD. Remember, however, that a test before the burning will be more reliable.

4. On the Advanced tab, you can choose the status of the recording session when the burn is complete. You have four choices. (Note: More choices are provided here than in the wizard.) The options are divided between Track-At-Once and Disc-At-Once. In the Track-At-Once options, you can choose Leave Session Open, which enables you to add more songs to your CD within the same session. Remember that you have to close the session at some point to listen to the CD on a typical audio CD player.

TIP

If you plan on having your audio CD duplicated professionally, you should have all your songs gathered together and burn them to the CD all at once using the Disc-At-Once option. This option writes and closes a CD in one move, without turning the writing laser on and off between tracks. If you use one of the other options to burn your CD, the writing laser is turned on and off between tracks and multiple sessions to create "links" between them. These "links" will show up as errors when the duplication service tries to create a master copy from your CD-R.

5. Close Session And Leave Disc Open enables you to create multi-session CDs. This option closes the current session but not the overall CD. Using this option, you can record more data to the CD later, but only the data recorded the first time to the disc will be compatible with regular audio CD players.

TIP

By using a multi-session CD, you can store both audio data and computer files on the same disc. Using this type of CD is a cool way to share your Projects with other musicians, especially if you're working on a tune together. In the first session of a CD, you store the tracks as traditional CD audio. You then close that session and store the Project files for those songs on the remaining portion of the disc in data format. Now your partner or partners can hear what you've recorded and access the files to add their own parts to the Project.

6. Click on the OK button to begin the burn after you've chosen Record and set the options. The CD Creation Process dialog box (see Figure 16.12) shows the progress. If you've chosen to test and then write tracks, the entire testing process is looped through first; an identical loop, which actually writes the data, then runs. Click on the Details button to see more information as the CD burn progresses.

Figure 16.12
This dialog box shows the burning process in action with recording details.

TIP

To avoid glitches in the burning process—especially for audio CDs—you should leave your computer alone until the process is complete. If it gets bogged down while burning, you might end up with a ruined CD. Of course, you can just burn another one, but then you'll be wasting both your time and money.

Closing a Session or Disc Separately

Sometimes you need to separately close a session and the CD as a whole, depending on the status that you asked to have after the recording was done. In this case, you need to specifically perform these operations by calling the Disc Information dialog box, as in the following steps:

1. Select Disc > Disc Information to open the Disc Information dialog box (see Figure 16.13). You are greeted with a list of the last current session opened or closed on the disc in your drive.

Figure 16.13
The Disc Information dialog box gives you the status of any CD and its sessions. Using it, you also can close a session or the disc as a whole, so the disc can be played on other CD players.

2. To close a session, select it and choose Close Session.
3. To close a disc, choose Close Disc.

Creating a Jewel Case Printout

After you've burned your CD, you can create a printout to insert into the CD jewel case (for track listings and the like). To activate the automatic Jewel Case Layout mode, click on the Jewel Case Layout tab in the main Easy CD Creator workspace. Using the current Active Track Layout, the program creates a simple Jewel Case Layout that you can print and cut out for your CD (see Figure 16.14).

Figure 16.14
Easy CD Creator automatically creates CD covers for you.

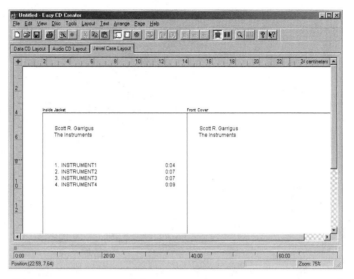

Click on any section of the text to activate it. You can move the text around when it's highlighted. Double-clicking on any object of text enables you to edit it and its font characteristics (see Figure 16.15). If you have a color printer, you can select colors for the text here as well.

Figure 16.15
You can select any piece of text and change its color, size, or font via the Text Edit dialog box.

To change the background color and other options, choose Layout > Options to bring up the Jewel Case Preferences dialog box. Here, you can change the cover colors and overall default fonts for the layout.

TIP

You cannot easily insert graphics into the Jewel Case Layout with the version of Easy CD Creator that ships with most CD drives. You need to use a dedicated graphics program to do so. In your graphics program, copy the picture that you want to use, return to the Easy CD Creator program, and then paste the picture into any area of the Layout.

Appendix A
Sample Project Roadmap: From Recording to Mixdown

Throughout this book, you've learned about everything you need to know to create a Project from start to finish in Pro Audio. This information includes how to set up a Project, record your Tracks, edit your MIDI and audio data, mix your Tracks down to stereo, and burn the final recording to CD. But just to give you a brief overview of the whole process, I've put together this outline of all the steps you need to take to record a song by using Pro Audio.

Set Up Your Project

1. Create a new Project. If you use a Template other than Normal to automatically set the parameters for your Project, you can skip the rest of this section. Otherwise, move on to step 2.

2. Add a Title and other descriptive information to your Project by using the File Info window.

3. Set the types of MIDI data to be recorded in the Global Options dialog box under the MIDI tab.

4. Set the Clock, Metronome, MIDI Input, and MIDI Out parameters in the Project Options dialog box.

5. Set the tempo for the Project by using the Tempo toolbar.

6. Set the Meter and Key for the Project by using the Meter/Key View.

7. Set the bit depth and sampling rate (if you're going to record audio) for the Project on the General tab in the Audio Options dialog box.

For more information, refer to Chapter 4, "Working with Projects."

Record Your Tracks

1. Set up a new Track by typing in a Name and selecting a Source and Port in the Track View.

2. Input initial values for the Volume and Pan parameters if you need them.

3. If the Track is for audio, you can skip this step; otherwise, for a MIDI Track, select values for the Channel, Bank, and Patch parameters.

4. Set the Record Mode by using the Record Options dialog box.

5. Arm the Track and set your input signal level by using the Console View.

6. Click the Record button and start your performance.

7. If you need to add data to only a certain part of the Track, use the Auto Punch Record Mode and set the Punch In and Punch Out Times. You also can use the Loop toolbar to set loop points and have Pro Audio loop a certain section of the song for recording in only that section.

8. Repeat steps 1 through 7 for every Track that you need to complete your song.

9. Save your Project as a Work (.WRK) file if it contains only MIDI data; otherwise, if it contains audio data, save it as a Bundle (.BUN) file.

For more information, refer to Chapter 6, "Recording and Playback."

Edit Your Data

1. Use the Track View to make any arrangement changes to your song. For example, you can move clips from one part of the song to another part. You also can mute any tracks that you don't want to use in the final mix. Also, adjust the Key+, Vel+, and Time+ parameters at this time.

2. If you need to do any precise editing to your MIDI Tracks, use the Piano Roll and Event Views. You use these Views for tasks such as changing the pitch and velocity of different notes or correcting the timing of your performance by using quantizing. You also can use the Staff View for certain tasks if you feel more comfortable using standard music notation. If you want to add any permanent MIDI Effects to your data, do so at this time. Otherwise, you can add Effects in real-time during mixdown.

3. For precise editing of your audio Tracks, use the Audio View. Cut, copy, or paste sections of audio and make adjustments to the volume if you need to. Add any EQ or permanent Effects at this point, too. Otherwise, you can wait to add Effects in real-time during mixdown if your computer system can handle it.

4. Save your Project as a Work (.WRK) file if it contains only MIDI data; otherwise, if it contains audio data, save it as a Bundle (.BUN) file.

For more information, refer to Chapter 7, "Editing Basics," and Chapter 8, "Exploring the Editing Tools."

Mix Down Your Project

1. Open the Console View and set initial values for the volume and panning for each Track in the Project.

2. Set the chorus and reverb settings for the MIDI Tracks.

3. Set the Aux Send settings for the audio Tracks.

4. Add any real-time effects that you want to use for the individual MIDI and/or audio Tracks.

5. Add any real-time effects that you want to use on the Aux Send(s).

6. Add any real-time effects that you want to use on the Mains.

7. Take a Snapshot of the current console setup in case you want to come back to it later.

8. Perform a test run of the mix by playing the song and adjusting the parameters during playback.

9. Record your mix movements by using the Record Automation feature in the Console View. If you find that you need to make two different value changes at once during a mix, just make multiple Record Automation passes.

10. Save your Project as a Work (.WRK) file if it contains only MIDI data; otherwise, if it contains audio data, save it as a Bundle (.BUN) file.

For more information, refer to Chapter 9, "Effects: The Really Cool Stuff," and Chapter 10, "Mixing It Down."

Burn to CD

1. Export your project to a stereo audio WAVE (.WAV) file.

2. Use Easy CD Creator to record your WAVE file to CD.

For more information, refer to Chapter 16, "Taking Your Pro Audio Project to CD."

APPENDIXES

Appendix B
Backing Up Your Project Files

At the end of every recording session, I back up my Project files. It doesn't matter whether I'm running late or whether I'm so tired that I can barely keep my eyes open. I always back up my files. Why? Because not too long ago, I didn't really think much of making backups. I would do it occasionally—just to be safe—but I never thought I'd run into any trouble. Then one day I went to boot up my PC, and *poof*! My hard drive crashed, taking a lot of important files with it, including a Project that I spent weeks working on. Believe me, after that experience, I never took file backups for granted again, and you shouldn't either.

Backing up your files really isn't very difficult, and it doesn't take much extra time. This is especially true if your Project includes only MIDI data. Work (.WRK) files containing only MIDI data are usually very small, and you can make backups of them by simply copying them to a floppy disk, just like you would any other small files. On the other hand, Bundle (.BUN) files—Project files that contain audio data—need to be handled a little differently because of their large size. Most Bundle files do not fit on a floppy disk, but if you have an Iomega Zip disk drive (or similar "super floppy" drive), you might be able to make a quick backup copy that way.

Back Up with Easy CD Creator

If you have a bunch of files to back up, you need a much larger storage format, such as a tape or a CD-recordable drive. In Chapter 16, "Taking Your Pro Audio Project to CD," you learned about using Easy CD Creator to create an audio CD from your Pro Audio Project. Well, in case you didn't know it, you also can use Easy CD Creator along with your CD-R drive to back up data files. The procedure is similar to creating an audio CD, and you can use the Easy CD Creator Wizard to step through the process like this:

1. Start Easy CD Creator. If the Easy CD Creator Wizard doesn't pop open automatically, select File > Wizard.

2. When the wizard asks whether you want to create a data or an audio CD, choose Data CD and click Next.

3. The wizard then lets you select the files you want to copy to CD (see Figure B.1). You can search through any of the file directories on your system, selecting files for backup. To add the files, click the Add Now button.

CAUTION

If you've set up your Pro Audio file folders like I talked about in Chapter 3, "Customizing Pro Audio," you should be able find your Project files in the My Documents/Cakewalk Pro Audio/Project Files folder. If you use video in your Project not only do you have to back up the Work or Bundle file for the Project, but the individual video file, too. Pro Audio does not save video data along with Project data, not even in a Bundle file. For more information about Pro Audio's video features, read Appendix C, "Producing for Multimedia and the Web."

TIP

Instead of selecting individual files for backup, I simply like to select my entire My Documents folder. That way, I can be sure I am backing up all of my important files—not only Pro Audio Project files, but all my other computer files as well. And this way, I don't have to worry about whether or not I'm getting the video files included in my Pro Audio Projects either.

Figure B.1
When you're creating a data CD, you can select any file or files from any of the storage drives connected to your computer system.

4. Sometimes a filename that you select might be incompatible with the way files are stored on a data CD. In this case, the wizard alerts you to the problem after you click the Add Now button. The wizard then suggests a new name for the file and also enables you to change the name if you like.

5. After you finish selecting files, click Next. The wizard then asks whether you want to do a test CD burn before doing the actual burn. It's a good idea to do the test, just so you can be sure the real burning process will go smoothly.

6. The wizard then asks whether you want to burn the CD now or later. You should choose to burn it now because you're backing up your files and you won't be making changes to the file selections.

7. Easy CD Creator then proceeds to test and then burn your files to CD.

Back Up with Windows

If you don't have a CD-recordable drive, or you would rather back up your files to a tape drive or other removable format, you can use the Backup utility that comes with Windows 98. By default, Windows 98 doesn't install the Backup utility during setup, so you might have to install it yourself. To do so, just follow these steps:

1. Click the Start button, and select Programs > Accessories > System Tools. If you see the Backup utility listed there, you're all set. If not, you have to install it from your original Windows CD.

2. To install Backup, open the Windows Control Panel and double-click on the Add/Remove Programs icon to open the Add/Remove Programs Properties dialog box (see Figure B.2).

Figure B.2
You can install the Windows Backup utility by using the Add/Remove Programs Properties dialog box.

3. Select the Windows Setup tab.

4. Select System Tools in the Components list and click the Details button to open the System Tools dialog box (see Figure B.3).

Figure B.3
You can install all the utilities included with Windows via the System Tools dialog box.

5. Find Backup in the Components list and put a check mark next to it.

6. Click the OK buttons to close both dialog boxes.

7. Insert your original Windows CD when Windows asks for it and click OK. The Backup utility is then installed.

When Backup is installed, you can use it to back up all your important files. Just follow these steps:

1. Click the Start button and select Programs > Accessories > System Tools > Backup to run Backup.

2. When the Backup Wizard asks you what you would like to do, choose Create A New Backup Job and click OK.

3. The wizard then asks whether you want to back up everything on your computer or just the files or folders that you select. Because you need to back up just your My Documents folder, choose the Back Up Selected Files, Folders And Drives option and click Next.

4. The wizard then asks you to select the files, folders, or drives that you want to back up (see Figure B.4).

Figure B.4
Here, you can select the files and/or folders that you want to back up.

APPENDIXES

5. Click the + (plus) sign next to your hard drive (C:) to see a list of folders there. Put a check mark next to the My Documents folder and click Next.

6. When you're asked what types of files to back up—all or only new and changed files—choose the All Selected Files option and click Next.

7. The wizard then wants to know where to store your backup files. Your response depends on your storage format, so just select the drive that you want to use.

TIP

You can probably use Backup with your CD-R drive. Most CD-R drives ship with a software program called Adaptec DirectCD. This software enables your computer to "see" your CD-R drive as just another storage device. So, you can copy files to it just like you would to a floppy disk, and Backup works with it, too. Refer to the documentation that came with your CD-R drive to see whether the product includes Adaptec DirectCD.

8. Tell the wizard whether it should compare the original files to the backup files after the backup process is done to make sure that they contain the same data. (I like to keep this option activated to be extra safe.)

9. Choose whether you want your data compressed. If you're short on space, having this feature available is nice, but otherwise, keeping the data uncompressed is a little safer.

10. Give your new backup job a name so that the next time you run Backup, all you need to do is select the job by name and start the process. The program will remember all of your previous option choices.

11. Click Start, and your files are then backed up.

Now, don't you feel better already? You can rest easy knowing that all your hard recording work won't be lost, even if your computer does decide to give up on you one of these days. Believe me, it's not a fun experience.

Appendix C
Producing for Multimedia and the Web

In addition to regular music production, Pro Audio includes a number of features to help you create music for multimedia and the Internet. You can import a video file into a Pro Audio Project and then compose music to it. You also can export video files along with your synchronized music. And you can export your music files to a number of popular Internet audio file formats, including RealAudio, Windows Media Format, and MP3. In essence, these features round out Pro Audio's full set of features, enabling you to use the program for most—if not all—of your music production needs.

Importing Video Files

If you're ever asked to compose music for film, video games, or some other visually based task, Pro Audio's Insert > Video File command will come in very handy. Using this command, you can include an AVI, MPEG, or QuickTime video in your Project and edit the existing audio Track or Tracks or add new ones.

NOTE

AVI, MPEG, and QuickTime are special digital video file formats specifically designed for working with video on computers. Each format uses its own unique compression scheme to achieve video quality that is as good as possible in a file size that is as small as possible. AVI (Audio Video Interleaved) is a Windows-based format, which means that any computer running Windows can play AVI files. QuickTime is a Mac-based format, which means that any Macintosh computer can play QuickTime files. With special player software, a computer running Windows can play QuickTime files, too, which is why the format is supported by Pro Audio. MPEG (Motion Pictures Expert Group) is a more advanced format that usually requires special hardware for playback. Therefore, MPEG video files are usually of much better quality than AVI or QuickTime, and they are also smaller.

To add a video file to your Project, follow these steps:

1.   Select Insert > Video File to open the Video File dialog box
     (see Figure C.1).

Figure C.1
Here, you can select
a video file to add to
your Project.

2.   Choose the type of video file (AVI, MPEG, or QuickTime) that you
     want to add from the Files Of Type drop-down list and select a file.

3.   If the video file contains audio data, you can import that data, too, by
     activating the Import Audio Stream option at the bottom of the box. If
     the audio is in stereo, you can import it as a single stereo audio Track
     or a pair of audio Tracks containing the left and right channels of the
     stereo signal.

4.   Click on Open.

Pro Audio then loads the video file and displays the first video frame
along with the current Now Time (see Figure C.2). If you imported audio
along with the video, the new audio Track or Tracks are inserted into the
Project above the currently selected Track.

Figure C.2
The Video View
displays the video
along with the current
Now Time.

Initially, when you play the Project, the video starts playing back at the beginning, but you can change where the video starts by adjusting the Start Time, as well as the Trim-in Time and Trim-out Time. Using these parameters, you can adjust when within the Project the video will start and end playback. To change these parameters, just follow these steps:

1. Right-click within the Video View and select Video Properties from the pop-up menu to open the Video Properties dialog box.

2. Under the Video Settings tab, input the new values for Start Time, Trim-In Time, and Trim-Out Time. The Start Time uses measures, beats, and frames for its value; and the Trim-in and Trim-out Times use hours, minutes, seconds, and frames just like with SMPTE Time Code.

3. Click on OK.

The video now starts and stops playing back within the Project at the times that you specified. You also can adjust a number of other parameters for the Video View, and you access all of them via the right-click pop-up menu. For instance, if you want to remove the video from your Project, just select the Delete command. If you want to temporarily disable video playback, select the Animate command. You can even change the size of the video display by using the Stretch Options command.

TIP

If you choose Full Screen under the Stretch Options command, the video display covers the entire computer screen, and you cannot access Pro Audio with the mouse (although keyboard commands still work). To get back to the normal display, just press the Esc (Escape) key on your computer keyboard.

Exporting Video Files

After you've imported a video file into your Project and either edited its existing audio or added new audio Tracks to it, you can export the file so that other people can see and hear your work. Follow these steps to export the file:

1. Select Tools > Export Video To AVI to open the Export Video To AVI dialog box (see Figure C.3).

Figure C.3
You can use the Export Video To AVI dialog box to export video files.

2. Type a name for the file in the File Name area. You don't need to select a file type because Pro Audio enables you to save your video to the AVI format only. You can't save to MPEG or QuickTime.

3. Click on Save, and the video file is saved with its original parameter settings. If you want to dabble with the method of compression used in the file, along with other video-related parameters, you can set them in the lower half of the dialog box.

TIP

For more information about multimedia and video-related parameters, you should consult a dedicated book on the subject. I've found *Multimedia: Making It Work* with CD-ROM, Fourth Edition by Tay Vaughn (Osborne Publishing 1998, ISBN 0078825520) to be very informative.

When you save your video file, any audio Tracks in your Project are mixed down and saved along with the video.

Exporting Audio Files

In addition to exporting your audio Tracks as WAVE (.WAV) files for the purpose of burning to CD (as you learned in Chapter 16, "Taking Your Pro Audio Project to CD"), you also can export them as RealAudio, Windows Media Format, and MP3 files for distribution over the Internet.

NOTE

Just as AVI, MPEG, and QuickTime are special digital video file formats, RealAudio, Windows Media, and MP3 are special audio file formats specifically designed for distributing audio over the Internet. Each format uses its own unique compression scheme to achieve the best possible sound quality in the smallest possible file size. All three formats are very popular, and all three support streaming audio as well. This means that you can listen to the audio as you download it rather than having to wait for the whole audio file to be downloaded before you can play it. In terms of quality, the order goes like this: Windows Media, MP3, RealAudio. However, this order depends on who's listening, because everyone has his or her own opinions on the subject. For more information about RealAudio, visit **www.real.com/devzone/**. For more information about Windows Media, visit **www.microsoft.com/windows/windowsmedia/**. For more information about MP3, visit **http://help.mp3.com/help/**.

Exporting to RealAudio

Do the following to mix and save your audio Tracks as a RealAudio file:

1. Select the Track or Tracks that you want to export in the Track View.

2. Select Tools > Mixdown Audio > Export To File(s) to open the Mixdown Audio/Export To File(s) dialog box (see Figure C.4).

Figure C.4
You can use the Mixdown Audio/Export To File(s) dialog box to export to RealAudio.

APPENDIXES

3. From the Look In list, select the folder that you want to save the RealAudio file into. Then type a name for the file in the File Name box.

4. Choose a file type from the File Of Type list. In this case, use the RealAudio option.

5. Select the Format that you want to use. You can mix your audio Tracks to a single stereo file, two mono files (that, when combined, create a stereo file), or a single mono file.

6. Choose the sound card or cards that you want to use to process your audio Tracks from the Source Bus(es) list.

7. Leave all the Mix Enables options activated to ensure that your new RealAudio file will include the same effects and mix automation that you used on the original audio Tracks.

8. Click on Export to open the RealAudio Settings dialog box (see Figure C.5).

Figure C.5
In the RealAudio Settings dialog box, you can adjust specific parameters for the RealAudio file.

9. Under the Settings tab, you can enter Title, Author, and Copyright information for the RealAudio file.

10. Choose from the three Options at the bottom of the dialog: Enable Perfect Play, Enable Mobile Play, and Enable Selective Record. Enable Perfect Play requires the listeners to download the entire RealAudio file before hearing it rather than being able to stream the file. This option ensures uninterrupted playback, but your listeners will also have to wait for the download. Enable Mobile Play gives listeners a choice between downloading and streaming a file. Enable Selective Record enables listeners to save the file to their hard drives for later. If you don't want people to be able to keep a copy of the file, make sure Enable Mobile Play and Enable Selective Record are not activated.

11. Under the Formats tab (see Figure C.6), you can select the modem speeds that you want your RealAudio file to be optimized for. It's really best to just select them all so that your listeners can hear the best quality at their own specific modem speed. For example, someone using a 56Kbps modem will hear a better version of your file than someone listening with a 28Kbps modem. Otherwise, everyone will hear the same low-quality file.

Figure C.6

You can set modem speeds on the Formats tab of the RealAudio Settings dialog box.

12. If you want your file to be compatible with the older 5.0 version of RealAudio, select the Include A RA 5.0 Compatible Stream option. This option makes your file a little bigger, but it's worth the extra size just in case someone using the old RealAudio Player software tries to listen to your file.

13. If you want to optimize the RealAudio file for certain types of content, select the type of music that you've recorded in your Project in the Content Type section. Most of the time, you'll probably use the Stereo Music option.

14. Click on OK, and your audio is saved as a RealAudio file with an .RM extension.

Exporting to Windows Media

To mix and save your audio Tracks as a Windows Media file, just follow these steps:

1. Select the Track or Tracks that you want to export in the Track View.

2. Select Tools > Mixdown Audio > Export To File(s) to open the Mixdown Audio/Export to File(s) dialog box.

3. From the Look In list, select the folder that you want to save the Windows Media file into. Then type a name for the file in the File Name box.

4. Choose the type of file from the File Of Types list. In this case, use the Windows Media option.

5. Select the Format that you want to use. You can mix your audio Tracks to a single stereo file, two mono files (that, when combined, create a stereo file), or a single mono file.

6. Choose the sound card or cards that you want to use to process your audio Tracks from the Source Bus(es) list.

7. Leave all the Mix Enables options activated to ensure that your new RealAudio file will include the same effects and mix automation that you used on the original audio Tracks.

8. Click on Export to open the Microsoft Audio Encode Options dialog box (see Figure C.7).

Figure C.7
In the Microsoft Audio Encode Options dialog box, you can adjust specific parameters for the Windows Media file.

9. Enter Title, Author, Rating, Copyright, and Description information for the Windows Media file.

10. Choose from the three other settings: Stereo, Sample Rate, and Bit Rate. Stereo determines whether the Windows Media file will be in stereo. You learned about sampling rates in Chapter 1, "Understanding MIDI and Digital Audio." Sample Rate enables you to set the sampling rate for the Windows Media file. The higher the rate, the better the file will sound, but the bigger the file size will be. Bit Rate enables you to target the modem speed for the Windows Media file. For example, if you want the file to be able to play over a 28.8Kbps modem, select the 22Kbps bit rate. This bit rate will play

over any modem speed 28.8Kbps and higher. If you want to produce a higher-quality file, select a higher bit rate, but the file won't play on a 28.8Kbps modem. A bit rate of 48Kbps or lower should play on a 56Kbps modem, but you are better off with a 40Kbps or lower setting because the Internet can be slow at times.

11. Click on OK, and your audio is saved as a Windows Media file with a .WMA extension.

Exporting to MP3

To mix and save your audio Tracks as an MP3 file, follow these steps:

1. Select the Track or Tracks that you want to export in the Track View.

2. Select Tools > Mixdown Audio > Export To File(s) to open the Mixdown Audio/Export To File(s) dialog box.

3. From the Look in list, select the folder that you want to save the MP3 file into. Then type a name for the file in the File Name box.

4. Choose the type of file from the File Of Types list. In this case, use the MP3 option.

5. Select the Format that you want to use. You can mix your audio Tracks to a single stereo file, two mono files (that, when combined, create a stereo file), or a single mono file.

6. Choose the sound card or cards that you want to use to process your audio Tracks from the Source Bus(es) list.

7. Leave all the Mix Enables options activated to ensure that your new RealAudio file will include the same effects and mix automation that you used on the original audio Tracks.

8. Click on Export to open the Cakewalk MP3 Encoder dialog box (see Figure C.8).

Figure C.8
In the Cakewalk MP3 Encoder dialog box, you can adjust specific parameters for the MP3 file.

9. Just as with Windows Media, you can select a Sampling Rate, Bit Rate, and Stereo Mode. The only difference is Joint Stereo mode, which enables you to create smaller MP3 files by comparing the left and right audio signals and eliminating any material that is the same in both channels. Using this option usually degrades the audio quality, though, so I advise against choosing it unless you really need smaller MP3 files.

10. Use the Optimize Encoding setting to adjust how long it takes to encode your MP3 file. If you set the slider toward the left, encoding will go faster; to the right, encoding will go slower. But the more time spent on encoding, the better the quality of the file. So, I recommend you just leave the slider set all the way to the right. Encoding a file really doesn't take very long anyway.

11. If you want to include some information about the file, select the Include ID3 Info option. To enter the information, click on Set ID3 Info to open the ID3 Info dialog box. Here, you can enter Title, Artist, Album, Year, Track Number, Comment, and Genre information. Click on OK when you're done.

12. Click on Encode and your audio is saved as an MP3 file with an .MP3 extension.

TIP

If you want to include the music from the MIDI Tracks of your Project in your RealAudio, Windows Media, or MP3 files, read the "Convert Your MIDI Tracks" section of Chapter 16, "Taking Your Pro Audio Project to CD."

Appendix D
Cakewalk Resources on the Web

Although I've made every effort to include as much information as possible about Pro Audio within this book, someone will always have that one question that goes unanswered. And, as I mentioned earlier, some of the topics, such as StudioWare and CAL, could fill up tomes all on their own. But that doesn't mean I'm going to leave you out in the cold with nowhere to turn.

The Internet provides a number of resources that you can use to locate any additional information you might need. I've tried to be sure to list all the quality sites that are available, but I might have missed a few. If you know of a great Cakewalk-related Web site that's not on this list, please drop me a note at **www.garrigus.com**.

Cakewalk Technical Support Homepage

Figure D.1
http://www.cakewalk
.com/Support/

The Cakewalk Technical Support Homepage is the first place you should look for answers. Cakewalk provides a large selection of materials, including answers to the most frequently asked questions (FAQs), product updates, technical documents, and StudioWare panels. You also can find lessons, tips, and tricks, as well as additional helpful publications and resources. And, of course, you can get in touch with Cakewalk's Tech Support people if you need to.

Official Cakewalk Newsgroups

Figure D.2
http://www.cakewalk
.com/Support/
newsgroups.html

The second place you should look for help is the Official Cakewalk Newsgroups. The Cakewalk newsgroups not only provide you with direct access to Cakewalk Technical Support but also to other users. You can find specific topics on digital audio, CAL, MIDI FX, and StudioWare, as well as dedicated groups for general information and beginners.

ProRec Cakewalk Support Resources

Figure D.3
http://www.prorec.com/
prorec/prorecording.nsf/
all?openview&count=
100

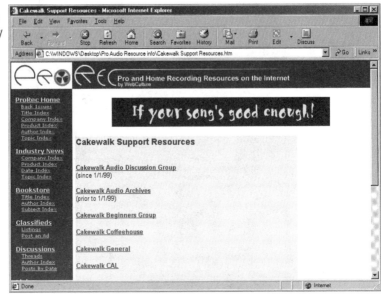

The ProRec (Pro and Home Recording Resources on the Internet) Web site provides a number of discussion areas dedicated to Cakewalk products. Some of these areas include the Cakewalk Audio Discussion Group, Cakewalk Beginners Group, Proaudio General, Cakewalk CAL, and Cakewalk StudioWare. It's a great source of peer-to-peer information. You also should check out the rest of the site for additional audio recording information.

AudioForums.com
Cakewalk Discussion Forum

Figure D.4
http://www.audioforms
.com/

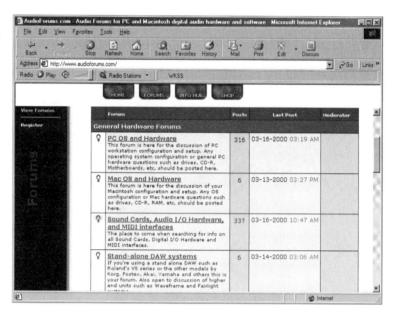

The AudioForums.com Cakewalk Discussion Forum is yet another Web site where you can find discussions about Cakewalk products. You won't find anything overly special, but you can find good information here. This site also includes discussion areas for audio-related topics such as PC Audio Hardware, Mac Audio Hardware, Studio Gear, and more.

Cakewalk Users Guild

Figure D.5
http://www.milan.net/
cakewalk/

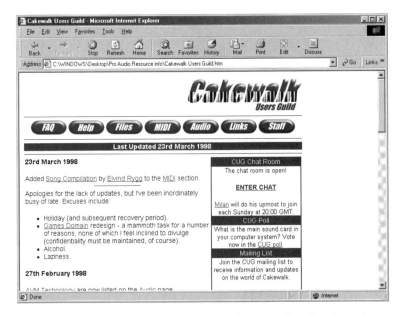

Unfortunately, what could be one of the best unofficial Cakewalk resources on the Web—the Cakewalk Users Guild—hasn't been updated since March 1998. But this site still contains lots of useful information. You can find answers to frequently asked questions (FAQs), file downloads, Projects for download by other users, and so on.

Li'l Chips Cakewalk Area

Figure D.6
http://www.lilchips.com
/cakewalk/index.asp

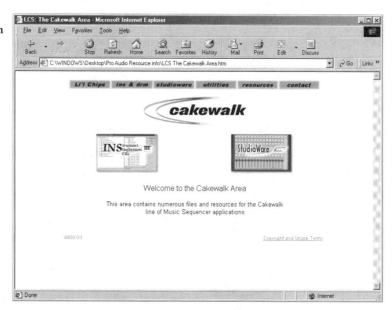

The Li'l Chips Cakewalk Area provides free Instrument Definition files and free StudioWare panels for download. Most of them pertain to Roland MIDI products, but you still can find a nice collection that might be useful to you.

APPENDIXES

The Secret of Cakewalk's CAL Programming

Figure D.7
http://www.cal.pyar
.com/

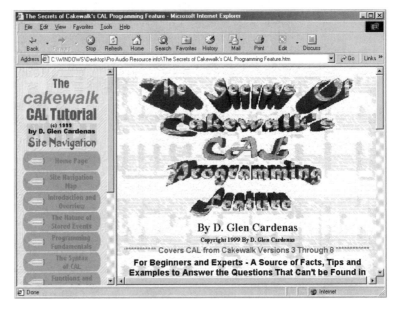

If you want to delve more deeply into the Cakewalk Application
Language (CAL), you should not miss this site. It has a full tutorial that
teaches you how to program by using CAL. Subjects include
Programming Fundamentals, The Syntax of CAL, Techniques and Work-
Arounds, and sample programs for download.

The Ultimate Cakewalk CAL Web Page

Figure D.8
http://www.geocities
.com/SunsetStrip/
Cabaret/5721/cal/

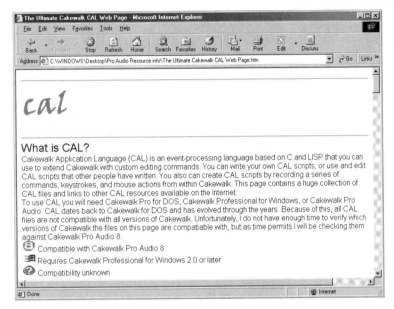

Another nice CAL resource, The Ultimate Cakewalk CAL Web Page is more like a compilation of links to other CAL resources. You can find basic CAL site links, as well as links to information on how to use CAL. The best part of the site, however, is the extensive list of CAL scripts available for download. More than 70 scripts are available, covering a wide variety of useful editing functions.

Synth Zone

Figure D.9
http://www.synthzone
.com/

Although not a dedicated Cakewalk site, the Synth Zone is an excellent MIDI, synthesizer, and electronic music production resource guide. You can find links to a ton of information, such as patches and associated software, for just about any synthesizer product from just about any manufacturer. You also can find links to discussion groups, classifieds ads and auctions, music and audio software downloads, and more.

Harmony Central

Figure D.10
http://www.harmony-
central.com/

Another excellent non-dedicated Cakewalk site, Harmony Central, is one of the best Internet resources for musicians. Updated on a daily basis, the site provides industry news and separate "departments" for Guitar, Bass, Effects, Software, Recording, MIDI, Keyboard and Synths, Drums and Percussion, Computers and Music, and a Bands Page. Sifting through all the information on this site will take awhile, but it's definitely worth the time and effort.

Power Presets

http://www.powerpresets.com/powerpresets/

A new site being developed by yours truly, Power Presets should be open to the public either by the time you read this or shortly thereafter. The site will feature tips, techniques, and function presets for a number of different applications, including Cakewalk Pro Audio. There also will be a free newsletter available, along with a discussion area, and some interesting products for sale.

APPENDIXES

Index

INDEX

INDEX

INDEX

Q

R

T

INDEX

MUSKA&LIPMAN

Order our free catalog by visiting
http://www.muskalipman.com

Order Form

Postal Orders:
Muska & Lipman Publishing
P.O. Box 8225
Cincinnati, Ohio 45208

Online Orders or more information:
http://www.muskalipman.com
Fax Orders:
(513) 924-9333

Title/ISBN	Price/Cost

Cakewalk Power!
1-929685-02-5

Quantity _____

× $29.95

Total Cost _____

MP3 Power! with Winamp
0-9662889-3-9

Quantity _____

× $29.99

Total Cost _____

Title/ISBN	Price/Cost

Online Broadcasting Power!
0-9662889-8-X

Quantity _____

× $29.95

Total Cost _____

Subtotal _____

Sales Tax _____
(please add 6% for books
shipped to Ohio addresses)

Shipping _____
($5.00 for US and Canada
$10.00 other countries)

TOTAL PAYMENT ENCLOSED _____

Ship to:

Company _____

Name _____

Address _____

City _____ State _____ Zip _____ Country _____

E-mail _____

Educational facilities, companies, and organizations interested in multiple copies of these books should contact the publisher for quantity discount information. Training manuals, CD-ROMs, electronic versions, and portions of these books are also available individually or can be tailored for specific needs.

Thank you for your order.